Marketing Management and Trade Policy

Marketing Management and Trade Policy

Edited by

P. Arunachalam

SERIALS PUBLICATIONS
NEW DELHI (INDIA)

First Published - 2010

ISBN: 978-81-8387-351-2

Published by

SERIALS PUBLICATIONS
4830/24, Prahlad Street, Ansari Road
Darya Ganj, New Delhi-110002 (India)
Phone: 23245225 Fax: 91-11-23272135
E-mail: serials@sify.com

CONTENTS

PREFACE

There are so many basic and fundamental dramatic changes which are being taking place in and around the world that have flattened the world economy. The power of these flattening forces lies in their combined ability to promote economic growth, whether in industrialized or developing markets. Growth is driven by the major sectors of an economy that increase overall wealth—the manufacturing and service engines that create jobs, grow personal income levels, generate exports, and increase Gross Domestic Product (Friedman, 2006). Some important changes are:

1. Both Tariff and non-tariff barriers are falling down under the WTO regime after 1995.
2. Due to Globalization business activities are being internationalized. As a result, cross-border investments are actively taking place in the form of Foreign Direct Investment.
3. With trade and overseas investment increase, one nation's economic policies and conditions greatly affect those of the other nations.
4. The triumph of capitalism and the PC-driven information revolution;
5. The rise of the Internet and the dot-com bubble (an investment spree that serendipitously resulted in a glut of cheap fiber-optic capacity);
6. Productivity, workflow and collaboration software;
7. The rise of the intellectual commons;
8. Outsourcing;
9. The growth of China as a manufacturing superpower;
10. Advanced supply-chain technologies;
11. Sophisticated Internet search engines; and
12. The increasing ubiquity of digital devices.

All these changes have been very much affected or paralyzed to a large extent due to the recent global economic recession 2008. There are two meltdowns which have created a panic and fear among the entire human beings. If one talked with an environmentalist he would be very much worried about the meltdown of millions of year's old ice in the Arctic and Antarctica regions due to recent emissions of toxic gases and other environmental degradation done by anthropogenic activities. Polar Ice caps hold most of the water available on the planet frozen, but if this water melts then it will be a disaster for everyone, animals and humans alike. Sea level rise due to melting will spell destruction for everyone living in coastal areas worldwide. If temperatures climbed a few degrees, as most climate scientists now considered likely, the sea level would rise simply because water expands when heated. This is almost the only thing about global change that can be calculated directly from basic physics. The additional effects of glacier melting are highly uncertain. The rough best guess for the total rise in the 21st century was perhaps half a meter. While such a rise will not be a world disaster, by the late 21st century it will bring significant everyday problems, and occasional storm-surge catastrophes, to populous coastal areas from New Orleans to Bangladesh. More likely than not, low-lying areas where tens of millions of people live will be obliterated. Entire island nations are at risk. Then it will get worse. Even if humanity controls greenhouse emissions enough to halt global warming, the heat already in the air will work its way gradually deeper into the oceans, so the tides will continue to creep higher, century after century. So every possible effort must be done and every possible step must be taken to stop global warming and reduce the anthropogenic activities that are effecting our environment.

On the other hand if you talked with social scientists, nowadays, they are very much worried about the ongoing global economic recession started from December 2007. It first started in the Wall Street America, then spread to European countries and to emerging economies like Russia, China, India, Brazil and finally ended with all poor countries. One can find different words for the global economic meltdown with same meaning like global financial crisis, American financial crisis, American economic downturn etc. Why the present crisis is of great importance for us? It is the second longest recession world economic history has seen after the great depression which took place 65 years before in 1929. The Great Depression lasted for 43 months from 1929 to 1933. But its effect was felt up to 1939. During this time the prices of stock fell 40 per cent. 9,000 banks went out of business and 9 million savings accounts were wiped out. About 86,000 businesses failed and wages were decreased by an average of 60 per cent. The unemployment rate went from 9 per cent all the way to 25 per cent. About 15 million became jobless people. About 50 million people died. The International Trade declined to 65 per cent. The economic recession 2008 also brought a lot of miseries to the human kind in the form of asset loss to the level of $50 trillion by the investment banks, employment loss and income loss not only to the developed economies but also to the people developing countries. World economic growth has come down from 3.5 per cent in 2006 to .9 per cent in 2009. India's GDP has come down to 4.3 per cent in 2009. The G -7 Countries alone lost 35 million employment opportunities so far. It has been estimated that America is losing

5 jobs in every minute. In America the unemployment rate increased to 10 per cent in January 2009 itself. World trade has come down from 9.2 per cent in 2006 to 4.4 per cent in 2009. In India nearly 150 million people are working in the export sector. Ten million people already lost their jobs in this sector alone. Gems and Jewellery and textiles are the worst affected areas. About 35 per cent of India's exports are directly targeted to European Union countries and America. So 24 per cent decline also has been recorded in the export sector in India. Service sector is another important sector affected by global economic recession very much. Around 2.25 million people are working in the IT/PBO sector in India. Their jobs are very much under thread now. No fresh recruitment now a day. Students from second tire cities and rural institutions are very much affected. Only 60 per cent of the graduates been assigned jobs so far. Ma Foi Management, a consultant has predicted that 30 per cent reduction in jobs this year. World will be having 220 million unemployed people by the end of 2009. Economists and politicians in many countries have now recognized – and reacted to – the fact that what the *Financial Times* calls the "mother of all financial crises" comes awfully close to the scenario Keynes outlined. Governments from Washington to Tokyo, hoping to slow down the economic decline, want to lower taxes, issue more government contracts and increase public assistance for businesses and the unemployed. The cloak of emergency aid has already been used to conceal a number of new subsidies, including assistance for the US banking industry and the ailing American automotive industry. What India needs now is "heavy investment in schools and Universities and a compact infrastructure investment programmes in rural areas and backward states." The only solution to the global economic crisis is a "global investment boom," and that this is not the time to get bogged down in details, but rather to take a more forceful approach. "Right now, increased government spending is just what the doctor ordered," says this year's winner of the Nobel Prize in Economics, Paul Krugman. Dominique Strauss-Kahn, the director of the International Monetary Fund, seems to agree when he proposes "quick and forceful" multinational spending programs.

Prime Minister Manmohan Singh while talking with G 20 members at Pittsburgh Summit 2009 has stated that it is necessary for India to engage in the management of the world economy because we have a lot at stake, and a lot to contribute.' And conveyed India's interest in seeing the earliest possible return to trend growth and stabilization of the banking and financial sectors in the advanced economies, because this directly affects our exports, capital inflows and investment. 'Having weathered the global meltdown much better than others, a confident India is also expected to seek reform of international financial bodies and forcefully oppose all forms of protectionism that may affect global economic recovery. In this edition eminent professors and researchers have analyzed various core economic, commerce, and management issues which took place during the liberalization period in the globalised India. I am very much indebted to the contributors for sending the papers within the stipulated period. The credit of this work undoubtedly goes to all contributors within and outside India.

DR. P. ARUNACHALAM
Faculty Member,
Head (2004-07),
Department of Applied Economics,
Cochin University of Science and Technology,
Kochi-22 Kerala, India.

International Journal of Marketing and Trade Policy
Vol. 1, No. 1-2, (January-December, 2009) : 1-11

RURAL MARKETING IN INDIAN ECONOMY

J. M. Arul Kamaraj* & J. Arul Suresh**

INTRODUCTION

Market is the ultimate yard-stick with which the sustainability of any economic activity is tested. No enterprise can plead for excuse if it can not pass this test. During the last four decades the rural market in the country has grown highly complex due to a wide range of influencing factors; technological advancement and increase in the managerial competence of the competitors being the two most important in this regard. When markets become complex, they throw out new opportunities as well as challenges.

The real India lives in villages and therefore primarily rural in character. Rural Marketing in Indian Context assumes greater importance as a wind of change is blowing form three angles-firstly, changing rural scene towards development in different spheres owing to success of green revolution, white revolution and grey revolutions and consequent raise in the rural incomes; secondly changes in market conditions resulted from the transformation of sellers' market into buyers' market consequent to new innovations, modern technology, increased production, increased competition and stagnated urban markets; and lastly the changing Government policy towards liberalization and globalisation of the Indian economy.

INDIAN RURAL MARKET

Indian rural market is very vast. Over 750 million consumers (74 per cent) of India's one billion lus population live in 6.27 lakh villages. It is about 12 per cent of world's population. The size of rural market is estimated to be Rs. 3500 billion out of which agricultural products are valued at Rs. 2500 billion i.e. 71.43 per cent. The FMCG's market accounts for 14.29 per cent while market size of agricultural inputs and equipments accounts for 12.86 per cent. Again, market size of durables is estimated to be just 1.43 per cent of total rural market size in India.

* *Lecturer, Department of Social Work, Loyola College, Chennai.*
** *Lecturer, Department of Commerce, Loyola College Chennai.*

Interestingly, therē have been proposals for cumulative investments of over Rs. 720 billion in food and agro-processing industry. It is said that the number of middle income and above households in the rural areas will grow from 80 million to 111 million by 2007. Thus, the absolute size of rural market is expected to be double that of urban India. Moreover, the trend analysis of statistics pertaining to rural marketing of FMCG's shows that there are high rates of growth in rural areas as compared to growth rates of urban areas.

It is said that Indian rural market is 'sleeping giant' since there is vast potential. Rural market environment has changed. So is the rural consumer. The earlier myths are broken into reality while rural consumer is becoming conscious regarding quality, price realization, and enjoying the benefits of services related to product's sales and customer delight. Again, rural market is not confined to marketing of agricultural inputs and agro-products. It is growing to expand and enlarge to encompass marketing of agricultural produce, agro-products, agricultural inputs, non-farm products, FMCG's and durables, services, etc.

Almost all the MNC's and corporates are responding to change environment and trying their best to penetrate and enhance market size through exploiting newly emerged rural markets. Interestingly, the understanding of rural consumers; dynamics of rural business environment; examining problems, challenges and constraints; and exploring and exploiting the potentials is the need of hour. The need for a systematic approach to rural marketing is felt by the academicians, policymakers, marketers and activists of NGO's.

RURAL MARKETING

Rural marketing is a fashionable subject today, though it is far more important for a developing economy like that of India. Different people have different definitions of rural marketing. This happens as the subject has been relatively unattended by serious academic professionals. The opening up of the domestic economy to external competition and the emergence of purchasing power in the rural areas, business and development professional calls for a better understanding of the concept and processes of rural marketing (Singh, 2001, p. viii).

Rural marketing is the process of developing, pricing, promoting, distributing rural specific goods and services leading to exchanges between urban and rural markets which satisfies consumer demand and also achieves organisational objectives (Ramkishen, 2002, p. 10). The term "rural marketing" which was earlier used as an umbrella term to refer to all commercial transactions of rural people, acquired a separate meaning of great significance in 1990s. Since 1980s, India's industrial sector had gained in strength and maturity. It's contribution to GNP increased substantially. A new service sector had emerged signifying the metamorphosis of agricultural society into industrial society. Due to development programmes of the central and state governments, service organisations and socially responsible business groups like Mafatlal, Tatas, Birlas, Goenkas and others, the rural area witnessed an all round socio-economic progress.

Following factors have been identified (by Agadi & Paramashivaiah, 1997) to be responsible for the rural market boom:

- Increase in population, and hence increase in demand. The rural population in 1971 was 43.80 crores, which increased to 52.50 crores in 1981, and 72 crores in 1994;
- A market increase in the rural incomes due to agrarian prosperity;
- Large inflow of investment for rural development programmes from government and other sources;
- Increased contact of rural people with their urban counterparts due to development of transport and a wide communication network;
- Increase in literacy and educational level among rural folks, and the resultant inclination to lead sophisticated lives;
- Inflow of foreign remittances and foreign made goods into rural areas;
- Changes in the land tenure system causing a structural change in the ownership pattern and consequent changes in the buying behaviour (Agadi & Parmashivaiah, 1997, p. 5).

RURAL MARKETING IN INDIA

The concept of Rural Marketing in India Economy has always played an influential role in the lives of people. In India, leaving out a few metropolitan cities, all the districts and industrial townships are connected with rural markets. The rural market in India is not a separate entity in itself and it is highly influenced by the sociological and behavioral factors operating in the country. The rural population in India accounts for around 627 million, which is exactly 74.3 percent of the total population. The rural market in India brings in bigger revenues in the country, as the rural regions comprise of the maximum consumers in this country. The rural market in Indian economy generates almost more than half of the country's income. Rural marketing in Indian economy can be classified under two broad categories. These are:

- The market for consumer goods that comprise of both durable and non-durable goods
- The market for agricultural inputs that include fertilizers, pesticides, seeds, and so on.

The concept of rural marketing in India is often been found to form ambiguity in the minds of people who think rural marketing is all about agricultural marketing. However, rural marketing determines the carrying out of business activities bringing in the flow of goods from urban sectors to the rural regions of the country as well as the marketing of various products manufactured by the non-agricultural workers from rural to urban areas. To be precise, Rural Marketing in India Economy covers two broad sections, namely:

- Selling of agricultural items in the urban areas
- Selling of manufactured products in the rural regions

Some of the important features or characteristics of Rural Marketing in India Economy are being listed below:

- With the initiation of various rural development programmes there have been an upsurge of employment opportunities for the rural poor. One of the biggest cause behind the steady growth of rural market is that it is not exploited and also yet to be explored.
- The rural market in India is vast and scattered and offers a plethora of opportunities in comparison to the urban sector. It covers the maximum population and regions and thereby, the maximum number of consumers.
- The social status of the rural regions is precarious as the income level and literacy is extremely low along with the range of traditional values and superstitious beliefs that have always been a major impediment in the progression of this sector.
- The steps taken by the Government of India to initiate proper irrigation, infrastructural developments, prevention of flood, grants for fertilizers, and various schemes to cut down the poverty line have improved the condition of the rural masses.

INDIAN MARKETERS

Indian Marketers on rural marketing have two understanding (I) The urban metro products and marketing products can be implemented in rural markets with some or no change. (ii) The rural marketing required the separate skills and techniques from its urban counter part. The Marketers have following facilities to make them believe in accepting the truth that rural markets are different in so many terms.

The rural market has the opportunity for.

- Low priced products can be more successful in rural markets because the low purchasing, purchasing powers in rural markets.
- Rural consumers have mostly homogeneous group with similar needs, economic conditions and problems.
- The rural markets can be worked with the different media environment as opposed to press, film, radio and other urban centric media exposure.

RURAL MARKET INDEED IS IMPORTANT

Rural Markets have seen a big boom in terms of opportunities they provide to the corporate sector in India. Rural India had a share of over 55 per cent in total consumption of FMCGs (Fast Moving Consumer Goods), and had a growth of about 14 per cent per annum during the period 1992-93 to 1997-98. This seems to be a fairly good growth by any standard (Brahmankar and Gupta, 2000). The rural market's contribution to the total national market had gone up from 28 per cent in 1985 to 40 per cent in 1990 (Chatterjee, 1992). The size of rural marekt in1992 was of the order of Rs. 40,000 crores, made-up of Rs. 22,000 crores for non-food items and Rs. 18,000 crores for food items (Soritakki, 1992, p. 562). During the period 1992-93 to 1997-98 consumption of FMCGs had grown at a rate of 14 per cent per annum.

According to data furnished by National Council for Applied Economic Research (NCAER) clearly showed a great rural market boom (Business World, 1999). The Chief Economist of NCAER (based on this data) clarified "that rural growth rates have already outpaced urban ones and will continue to do so through the next decade. So, a presence in the rural market, will not remain a choice, but a necessity" (Business World, 1999, p. 27). The companies will have no choice but to go rural if they must survive. Findings of the study conducted by NCAER in 1998-99 showed that, (*i*) Rural markets for group I durables (less than Rs. 1000 in value: items like transistors, pressure cookers, wrist-watches, bicycles, etc.) are bigger than urban markets already; predicted that (*ii*) rural markets for group II durables (Rs. 1001- Rs. 6000 in value:items like B&W TVs, sewing machines, mixers, cassette recorders) will be bigger than urban markets by 2001-02; (*iii*) for group III durables (Rs. 6001 or more in value: like color TVs, refrigerators two-wheelers and washing machines) rural markets will be smaller than urban ones, even in 2006-07; and showed that (*iv*) rural market growth rates are faster than urban ones, even on the larger bases of group I & II (Business World, 1999). The NCAER data also showed that India is now seeing a dramatic shift towards prosperity in rural households.

It predicted that the lowest income class will shrink from more than 60% in1994-95 to 20% in 2006-07. The higher income classes will be more than double. Rural economy has triggered. Ten good rains in a row from 1980-81 to have 1998-99) boosted foodgrain production. Procurement prices have also been rising. This implies growing rural prosperity and demand for goods. The NCAER data clearly showed that Rural FMCG (Fast Moving Consumer Goods) Market will boom (Business World, 1999, p. 28-29).

Some Impressive Facts About Rural Sector

- The number of rural supermarkets (haats) in India 42,000 exceeds the total number of retail chain stores in the US (35,000);
- In 2001-02, LIC sold 55 per cent of it's policies in rural India;
- Of the two million BSNL mobile phone connections, 50 per cent are in rural;
- Of the 20 million who have signed up for Rediffmail, 60 per cent are from small towns. Of the one lakh who have transacted on Rediff online shopping site, 50 per cent are from small towns;

- 24 million Kisan Credit Cards (KCC) issued in rural areas exceeds the 17.7 million credit plus debit cards issued in urban India. A whopping Rs. 52,000 crore has been sanctioned under the KCC scheme;
- The number of middle and higher income families (Having Rs. 70,000 plus annual income) in rural (21.7 million) and urban (24.2 million) is nearly the same;
- Electricity consumption by the agricultural sector has shown a sharp increase from 17.6 per cent of total consumption in 1980-81 to 29.2 per cent in 1999-00. During the same period, industry share has dropped from 58.4 per cent to 34.8 per cent (Kashyap, 2003, p. 6).

CORPORATE INTEREST IN RURAL MARKETS

Television has made inroads into rural homes. Mass-media today has enormous approach and access to rural masses, capable of influencing their habits and lifestyles, and this, creating demand for the (branded) products. Corporate houses then develop new products for rural consumers and attempt their suitable positioning. For example, Hindustan Motors (HM) launched a utility vehicle, the RTV (Rural Transport Vehicle) aimed at rural markets. Titan Industries found their watch brand 'Sonata' getting popular in rural areas, they formulated a new strategy tailored to the requirements of large rural markets (Rai, 2000). The recession and the knowledge that rural customers have not been tapped to their full potential has forced the companies to undertake innovative measures Hyuendai Motors India Limited (HMIL), Coca Cola India, DCM, Shrimram Chemicals Limited, are all doing so (Jacob, 2003).

The companies that are tapping the rural markets, are surprisingly the multinationals like Hindustan Lever Ltd. who have done more to penetrate the rural market than several Indian private sector grants or even the public sector. There are three strong reasons that give multinationals this advantage of tapping rural markets.

- The companies need the resources to understand a large and diverse rural economy. The kind of exploratory study of behaviour that in needed to understand the peculiarities of each segment of the rural market will necessarily be expensive.
- Even if the companies have the resources, they need to believe the expenditure is worthwhile. This belief must co-exist with the recognition that the exercise need not always result in a profit-generating project.
- Companies must not treat the rural market as a dumping ground for lower end products designed for an urban audience. Instead, they must use their technological expertise to create specific products for the rural economy (Pani, 2000).

In meeting these three conditions the multinationals have an edge over several major Indian companies. They have much deeper pockets, have an attitude for greater emphasis on research, are technologically much advanced, and are sensitive to the rural Indian markets.

At a seminar in Chennai on 'rural marketing for competitive advantage in globalised India'..... marketing pundits echoed that a sound network and a thorough understanding of the village psyche are a SINE QUO NON for making in roads into rural market. The pricesensitivity of a consumer in a village in something the marketers should be alive to.

Rural income levels are largely determined by the vagaries of monsoon and, hence, the demand there is not a easy horse to ride on. Apart from increasing the geographical width of their product distribution, the focus of corporates should be on the introduction of brands and develop strategies specific to rural consumers. Britania Industries launched 'Tiger Biscuits' especially for the rural market. It clearly paid dividend. Its share of the glucose biscuits market has increased from 7 per cent to 15 per cent (Kannan, 2001).

Following are the specific reasons as to why corporate houses take enormous interest in rural markets in India.

Untapped Potential: for marketing of branded goods and services for the following two reasons:

- *Large Consumers:* About 12 per cent of world's population, or 126 million household's, lives in rural India. Purchasing power exists. Between 30 and 50 per cent of the consumption of a number of consumer goods comes from rural India (Mishra and Gupta, 1999). As per the projections of National Council for Applied Economic Research (NCAER), the number of middle and high income households in rural India in expected to grow from 80 million to 111 million by 2007....The absolute size of rural India is expected to be double than that of urban India (Kanan, 2001).
- *Largely Untapped Markets:* Penetration levels for many products are low in rural areas (Velayudhan, 2002). Research Organisations like NCAER, ORG-MARG have made substantial studies to show that rural markets are growing at five times the rate of urban markets (Ramakishen Y, 2002, p. 9).

SERVICES MARKETING IN RURAL INDIA

Services have enormous potential to be sold in rural India. This could be seen clearly from the ongoing discussions in this chapter. However, to begin with, let us consider the following facts: In 2001-02, LIC sold 55 per cent of it's policies in rural India (Kashyap, 2003, p. 6). 6.5 crore individuals in rural India are covered by life insurance policies (Jejurikar, 2003, p. 48). Of the two million BSNL mobile phone connections, 50 per cent are in rural (Kashyap, 2003, p. 6). 3.6 HHs have a telephone connection (Jejurikar, 2003, p. 48). Of the 20 million who have signed up for Rediffmail, 60 per cent are from small towns. Of the one lakh who have transacted on Rediff on line shopping site, 50 percent are from small towns (Kashyamp, 2003, p. 6). On travel: five lakh people from rural India have gone abroad; 27 per cent of rural India has taken a holiday within the country (Jejurikar, 2003, p. 48). 24 million Kisan Credit Cards (KCC) issued in rural areas exceeds the 17.7 million credit plus debit cards issued in urban India (Kashyap, 2003, p. 6).

Electricity consumption by the agricultural sector has shown a sharp increase from 17.6 per cent of total consumption in 1980-81 to 29.2 per cent in 1999-2000. During the same period, industry share has dropped from 58.4 per cent to 34.8 per cent (Kashyap, 2003, p. 6). Internet services are still picking up in rural areas. "Several companies are attempting to create virtual 'bazaars' or agri-portals akin to weekly 'mandis'. The most notable virtual 'mandis' are the e-choupal by ITC, India Agriline by EID Parry and Dairy Portal by Amul" (Kashyap, 2003, p. 10). However, the situation is not very rosy in rural India.

- *Tourism and Travel Services:* Having known that the rural people travel and tour to places, even though for undertaking pilgrimage and Haj, would like to be serviced the best way, the professional way. More realisation, of how the rural places (of historical or religious importance) can be promoted and developed as tourists spots, have led the state governments to look at the villages as revenue earners. Tourism Marketing in Madhya Pradesh is an example of how effectively it has been done (Sandeep Kumar, 2002). Hotels, motels have started to be developed in rural areas, partly due to this, and partly due to increase in number of road travelers wanting these facilities on highways. The massive plan of the central government to connect at almost all villages by motorable roads, soon, will further boost the potential. The overall situation is rosy from the point of view of developing tourism and travel services marketing in rural India. Growing number of four wheeler car owners in rural India, will support it.
- *Transportation and Logistics Services:* Transportation in rural areas is largely poor, with the governments not in a position to catch up with the demand Private (passenger, as also freight) transporters are growing in number and quality to encash the opportunity. Other logistic services, such as couriers and other logistic services have enormous opportunities to be marketed. Taking up fresh initiatives for marketing these services in rural areas in a rich area for beginners and is bound to have an advantage in focussing their product and capturing the dominant market share.
- *Financial Services:* Marketing of insurance services, bank marketing, housing and financial intermediation, portfolio management, factoring services, and mutual funds, are all the various areas that have enormous potential of being marketed as rural services products in India.

- *Media Service Marketing:* Post-independence India has seen enormous growth of media such as print, cinema, radio, television networks. "Television became an obsession with the vast majority. Television happens to be the single medium having highest exposure in rural India. This is followed by radio and cinema.
- *Health Services:* In rural India, health services are largely in the control of the governments, whose hospitals, primary health centres, auxiliary mid-wife appointed by the government, are the health service providers. These institutions almost lack the marketing approach. Further, the medical profession, training, and practice, shows lack of managerial and marketing approach, in general.
- *Education and Extension Services:* Marketing of education is a subject with very wide coverage. Formal education begins at the school age and depending upon the choice, vocation, and circumstances of the pursuant, matures into intermediate and higher levels of learning, ramifying into professional and specialized fields. Apparently, benefits sought from higher and professional or vocational courses are more tangible or measurable in terms of entry qualifications to a chosen profession, certification to enable practicing a profession or relative case of access to a suitable form of livelihood (Kaushik, 2002, p. 564). The marketing implications of service characteristics in the context of education is an interesting area for study.

REALITIES BEFORE THE MARKETERS

Seventy percent of India's population lives in 627000 villages in rural areas. 90% of the rural population us concentrated in villages with a population of less than 2000, with agriculture being the main business. This simply shows the great potentiality rural India has to bring the much - needed volume- driven growth. This brings a boon in disguise for the FMCG Company who has already reached the plateau of their business urban India.

As per the National Council for Applied Economic Research (NCAER) study, there are as many 'middle income and above' households in the rural areas as there are in the urban areas. There are almost twice as many' lower middle income' households in rural areas as in the urban areas. At the highest income level there are 2.3 million urban households as against 1.6 million households in rural areas. According to the NCAER projections, the number of middle and high-income households in rural India is expected to grow from 80 million to 111 million by 2007. In urban India, the same is expected to grow from 46 million to 59 million. Thus, the absolute size India is expected to be doubles that of urban India.

The improved agricultural growth is expected to boost rural demand, through not at too sizzling a rate. Moreover, the price drop in personal products, after the recent excise duty reductions, in also expected to drive consumption.

"Better agricultural yields will give farmers more spending power, making the rural markets bullish," says an analyst.

As a result, HLL has planned a rural marketing program that is expected to result in a marked growth in the consumption of the company's products in the rural market. HLL will adopt three-pronged marketing strategy- new price points, sizes and awareness campaigns for its detergents and soaps segment to augment rural growth.

The companies are trying to trigger growth in rural areas. They are identifying the fact that rural people are now in the better position with disposable income. The low rate finance availability has also increased the affordability of purchasing the costly products by the rural people. Marketer should understand the price sensitivity of a consumer in a rural area. The small sachet packs are the examples of price sensitivity.

CONCLUSION

The future lies with those companies who see the poor as their customers.When C K Prahalad addressed to the Indian CEOs in January 2000, he clearly pinpointed on the raw fact that there is vast potential for profits in the rural markets. C.K.Prahalad in his book "The Fortune at the Bottom of the Pyramid" he cites numerous examples of companies that have generated wealth for the poor and profits for themselves by focusing on underserved rural markets. As urban markets become saturated, more businesses are retooling their marketing strategies, and in many case their products, to target rural consumers with tiny incomes but rising aspirations fueled by the media and other forces, giving birth to a new era of rural marketing. Rural marketing involves delivering manufactured or processed inputs or services to rural producers or consumers so as to soak up the huge size of the untapped rural market. In today's congested and difficult markets, both local and global, all FMCG as well as other companies search for new opportunities, consumers and markets. The 800 million potential consumers in rural India presented both an opportunity and a problem, as this market has been characterized by unbalanced growth and infrastructural problems.Thus looking at the opportunities which rural markets offer to the marketers it seems that the future is very promising for those who can understand the dynamics of rural markets and exploit them to their best advantage. A radical change in attitudes of marketers towards the vibrant and burgeoning rural markets is expected in the coming years so that they vividly understand the bottom of the pyramid model and start capitalizing on it.

References

Agadi, R. B. & Paramashivaiah, P. (1997), "Rural Marketing in India", In: Rural Marketing: Thrust and Challenges/Edited by Saimuddin *et. al.*, National Publishing House, Jaipur.

Awadesh Kumar Singh & Satyaprakash Pandey (2005), "Rural Marketing: Indian Perspective", New Age International Publishers, New Delhi.

Brahmankar, S. D. & Gupta, Tarun (2000), "Rural India: Market on Fast Track", *The Economic Times,* July 13, 2000.

Business World (1999), Issues dated 11 October, 1999, pp. 22-32.

Chatterjee, A. (1992), "Gambling on the Rural Roulette", Brand Equity, *The Economic Times,* 8 April.

Dey, N. B. and Adhikari, Kingshuk (1998), "Rural Marketing Challenges and Opportunities", *Yojana,* 42 (5), May 1998, p. 21-22, 41.

Jacob, Anil, G. (2003), "Picking Rural Pockets", *Business Standard-The Strategist,* Tuesday, 22 April.

Jejurikar, Rajesh (2003), "How Mahindra Maxx-ed it!", Praxis - Business Line's *Journal on Management,* Vol. 4 (Issue: 2), July 2003, p. 46-51. Insurance Watch, Dec. 2004.

Jha, Mithileshwar (1998), "Rural Marketing: Some Conceptual Issues", *Economic and Political Weekly,* Vol. XXIII (No. 9), February 27, pp. M-8 to M-16.

Kannan, Shanthi (2001), "Rural Market-A World of Opportunity", *Hindu,*11 October, 2001.

Kashyap, Pradeep (2003), "Revolution in Waiting", Praxis-Business Line's *Journal on Management,* Vol. 4 (Issue: 2), July 2003, pp. 6-11.

Kaushik, Madhulika (2002), "Education Services Marketing", In: Services Marketing/Ravi Shankar, Excel Books, New Delhi, pp. 563-583.

Mishra, Deepak and Gupta, Vinay (1999), "Rethinking The Rural Distribution Strategy", The Strategist-Special Issue on Rural Marketing, *Business Standards,* Tuesday 27, April, 1999, pp. 3.

NCAER (1998), "Indian Market Demographics Report 1998", National Council Applied Economic Research, New Delhi.

Pani, Narender (2000), "The Mirage in Rural Markets", *The Economic Times,* 14 July.

Rai, Asha (2000), "Titan Chimes Rural Times With Sonata's", *The Economic Times,* August 18.

Ramkishen, Y. (2002), "New Perspectives on Rural Marketing: Includes Agricultural Marketing, Jaico,Mumbai.

Sandeep Kumar (2002), "Tourism Marketing", In: Ravi Shanker (2002), Services Marketing: The Indian Perspective", Excel, New Delhi, pp. 129-135.

Singh, Sukhpal (2001), "Rural Marketing Management", Vikas, New Delhi.

Soritakki, C. N. (1992), "Marketing Management in the Indian Background", Kalyani Publishers, Delhi.

www.hill.com

www.indiainfoline.com

INNOVATIONS IN INDIAN SMEs: EFFECTIVE POLICIES FOR SURVIVAL AND PROFITABILITY

A. G. MATANI*

INTRODUCTION

Vitalization of SMEs is a major issue to policy makers. Proper policies can help stimulate R&D and innovation in the SME sector. The Total Factor Productivity (TFP), which is an important indicator for economic growth, is larger for SMEs than for big companies. SMEs are also economically important considering diversity, opportunities they create for start-ups, and the roles they play in employment generation in any industrialized economy.

The globalizations of product and service markets have accelerated small and medium-sized enterprises (SMEs) towards increasing competition for sales, technical know-how and skills. SMEs are generally more flexible, adapt themselves better and are better located to develop and implement new ideas. The flexibility of SMEs, their simple organizational structure, their low risk and their receptivity to changes are the essential features for enabling them to be innovative both within the organization and in the external market. Despite their important role in innovation, SMEs have a number of resource disadvantages. They have limited financial and technical manpower resources, narrow external technical networks, small marketing resources, and lack of management skill. The biggest challenge that Indian entrepreneurs face is set up a 'learning and sharing' Organization. Thus, innovations have to take place at all levels within and outside the firm.

INDUSTRIAL COMPETITIVENESS INDEX

Competitive Industrial Performance (CIP) index combines four main dimensions of industrial competitiveness—industrial capacity, manufactured exports capacity, industrialisation intensity and export quality. Industrialisation intensity is a measure that captures the share of manufacturing in GDP. According to report prepared by the UN Industrial Development Organization

* *Faculty, Department of Mechanical Engineering Government College of Engineering, Amravati (M.S.) India. Email:ashokgm3@yahoo.com, ashokgm333@rediffmail.com*

(UNIDO), Industrial Development Report 2009, from a list of 122 countries Singapore, Ireland and Japan have continued to occupy the top three positions in the CIP. The CIP index for some countries is as stated herewith:

Country	*Current position in 2005*
India	54
China	26
Brazil	38
Russia	81
Pakistan	64
Bangladesh	73

SME SECTOR CONTRIBUTION IN ECONOMY

The following Table highlights the contribution of Small and Medium Enterprises (SMEs) in some of the developed economies.

Country	*Contribution in terms of incremental share in Employment Manufacturing Sector*	*Output*
USA	67%	61%
Japan	80%	72%
France	53%	80%
Korea	74%	61%

In India, the small-scale industries sector contributes almost 40% of the gross industrial value added in the Indian economy. The number of small-scale units has increased from an estimated 0.87 million units in the year 1980-81 to over 3 million in the year 2000. Nearly SSI Sector contributes 45%-50% of the Indian exports. The product groups where the SSI sector dominates in exports are sports goods, readymade garments, woolen garments and knitwear, plastic products, processed food and leather products.

CHOICES FOR SMALL FIRMS TOWARDS COMPETITIVENESS

Competitiveness without innovation is not possible. A small firm has five choices in this regard:

(a) Innovate it,

(b) Acquire or license innovation by others,

(c) Jointly develop innovation with a formal or informal R&D person or institution,

(d) Contract the tasks to professional product developer or

(e) Sponsor a student project.

PHASES OF A SIMPLIFIED INNOVATION PROCESS: CONCEPTION IMPLEMENTATION MARKETING

- Requirement Analysis
- Idea Generation
- Idea Evaluation
- Project Planning
- Development/Construction
- Prototype Dev.
- Pilot Application
- Testing
- Production
- Market Launch and Penetration (national/international)

Innovations have acquired a key-role in the growth and competition strategies of firms today. They are regarded as an essential tool to stimulate growth and enable firms to master the competition brought about by the forces of globalisation. In developed countries they are thought to provide a vital buffer against challenges from low-cost producers from emerging countries.

VARIOUS APPROACHES TO INNOVATIONS

Process Innovations

Process innovations aim to optimize creation of a product/service thereby helping an enterprise to devise operating procedures in a more effective and creative way. Increasing productivity is the optimum aim of process innovation by keeping production costs as low as possible. Process innovations can help improve operational safety and reduce the consumption of raw materials and energy.

Sustaining or Incremental Innovations

Innovation is not just about coming up with new products. It is about coming up with solutions to the problems of customers. An existing product can be improved using any one of eight options:

- Adding a feature,
- Removing a feature,
- Combining two products into one,
- Separating one product into two,
- Substituting components or materials,
- Reducing component size,

- Embedding the product into another or
- Adding complementary functions.

Developing Innovative Products and Services Through a Customer-pull Approach

Customers are most willing to accept those new products it is important to correctly identify the customers' needs. Customer-based knowledge is used to develop innovative products and services through a customer-pull approach as distinct from the job-shop ethos. They must become closer to the customer and ensure they are making innovative use of privileged customer information.

GLOBAL SCENARIO OF INNOVATIONS IN SMES: PRESENT STATUS

Economic and Technological Intelligence Supporting New High-tech Companies in Europe

A Pilot Action of eXcellence on Innovative Start-ups (PAXIS) is to promote regional schemes of support for new high-tech companies, linking existing initiatives, and spreading good practice to other regions. Major responsibilities include identifying existing resources and competencies, to transfer this knowledge, and to exchange and disseminate good practices for promoting innovation throughout the Member States. Economic and Technological Intelligence (ETI) actions provide information on the main technological and market issues via the Internet and through established transnational networks, industrial and professional associations, chambers of commerce and other outlets.

Innovations On-line: Converting Promising Research into Successful New Products and Services

CORDIS-the Community R&D Information Service - is an on-line web-service providing a set of free databases containing news, descriptions of EU research programs and projects, listings of events and publications, key documents, information services designed to assist the process of converting promising research into successful new products and services. Two printed periodicals: - the newsletter *Innovation & Technology Transfer* reports on the work and results of the Innovation and SMEs program, and publications-based magazine *Euroabstracts*, monitors developments in EU research and innovation by means of reviewing recent publications.

Sussex Innovation Centre Helps Technology Start-up Businesses in U.K.

The Sussex Innovation Centre (SInC) in the UK provides support for the creation and growth of technology and knowledge based companies. The Centre provides various facilities for high growth companies working within the IT, Biotech, Media and Engineering sectors. Technology Business incubator (TBI) helps technology start-up businesses with, all the necessary resources and support.

SME Policy in the Netherlands Encouraging Entrepreneurial Environment

The SME policy in the Netherlands specifies "Action for Entrepreneurs" and has a life cycle approach start–growth and consolidation–business transfer. The policies focus on creating an entrepreneurial environment, raising awareness and reducing administrative burdens. "Techno Partner", established in 2004 implements various facilities by providing seed facility, transfer of knowledge into start-ups businesses, support of spin-offs, the creation of a platform for start-ups and a program to stimulate entrepreneurship in the education system.

I-entrepreneurs Club in France Offering Specialist Consultancy Services

A range of specialist consultancy services regarding management coaching, financial, legal, marketing, intellectual property, technology related, etc are available on the park. Five French competitiveness clusters TENERRDIS for renewable energies, IMAGINOVE for digital and media content, PLASTIPOLIS for plastic and composite materials, SPORALTEC for sports and leisure, and TECHTERA for functional and technical textiles are providing access to national and regional business competitions for innovative business projects.

'Collabo Sungakukan' Project of Japan Expanding the Opportunities

Japanese private companies prefer to outsource more R&D to overseas universities as compared to local institutes . Technology License Organizations (TLOs) promotes and commercializes the IPRs of the universities. TLO also provides a wide range of services such as general consultancy, marketing support, planning and administration, to the hiring of temporary staff. A major initiative within the new strategy for collaboration of Industry, universities and government is the 'Collabo SUNGAKUKAN' project. In Edogawa/Sumida, an area of Tokyo with a high concentration of SMEs, Campus Create is playing an important role in a consortium initiated by a bank with 20.000 SME customers. Japan is expanding the opportunities for allocating the government's technology development budget to SMEs through a Small Business Innovation Research system (SBIR).

CONCLUSIONS

The globalizations of product and service markets are accelerating small and medium-sized enterprises towards increasing competition not only for sales, but also for technical know-how and skills. India has a much stronger R&D base but much weaker industrial linkages. Worldwide economic reforms and technological advancements have provided new opportunities to China and India for strong scientific capabilities. If scientific and technological expertise is to be efficiently converted into economic benefits, research programs must be undertaken through innovators. Therefore need of the day is to encourage SMEs towards adopting innovations and R and D projects towards becoming competitive in the present economic slowdown situation.

References

Biemens, W. G. (1992), Managing Innovation with Networks, Routledge, London.

Christian Lendner and Michael Dowling (2007), " The Organizational Structure of University Business Incubators and their Impact on the Success of Start-ups: An International Study " , *International Journal of Entrepreneurship and Innovation Management*, Inderscience Publishers, Vol. 7, pp. 541–555.

Dangayach, G. S., Pathak, S. C. and Sharma, A. D. (2005), Managing Innovation, *Asia Pacific Tech Monitor*, Vol. 22, pp. 30-33.

DSIR Report *Research and Development in Industry: An Overview*, Department of Scientific and Industrial Research, Ministry of Science and Technology, Government of India, New Delhi, 2006.

Dyer, G. (2006), China Overtakes Japan on R&D, *Financial Times*, 3. 12. 2006.

Guo, Y. (2005), Asia's Educational Edge. Current Achievements in Japan, Korea, Taiwan, China, and India, Lexington Books, Lanham.

M. H. Bala Subrahmanya (2005), Technological Innovations in Indian Engineering Industry: Industry and Firm Level Case Studies , *International Journal of Entrepreneurship and Innovation Management*, Inderscience Publishers, Vol. 5, pp. 401–420.

Mehdi Khosrow Pour, Challenges for Information Management in a World Economy: Proceedings of the 4th Information Resources, USA.

Mehdi Khosrow Pour, Innovations Through Information Technology: Proceedings of the 15th Information Resources Management Association International Conference, USA.

Peter M. Frank : Non-profit entrepreneurship: extending the concept of profit opportunities," *International Journal of Entrepreneurship and Innovation Management* Inderscience Publishers, 2006, Vol. 6, pp. 224–240.

Report, Office of the Development Commissioner, (MSME) Ministry of Micro, Small & Medium Enterprises New Delhi, 2009.

Stephen Xingang Xu and Rod B. McNaughton (2006), High-technology Cluster Evolution: A Network Analysis of Canada's Technology Triangle, *International Journal of Entrepreneurship and Innovation Management*, Inderscience Publishers, Vol. 6, pp. 591–608.

Tiwari, R. and Buse, S. : Barriers to innovation in SMEs: can the internationalization of R&D mitigate their effects?" Proceedings *of the First European Conference on Knowledge for Growth: Role and Dynamics of Corporate R&D*, Seville, Spain, 2007 October ,pp. 8-9.

Zairi, M. (1994), "Innovation or Innovativeness, Results of a Benchmarking Study", *TQM Magazine*, Vol. 5, pp. 10-16.

FOREIGN DIRECT INVESTMENT AND ECONOMIC GROWTH IN KARNATAKA

SUMA M. SINGH* & LEELAVATHI**

INTRODUCTION

The era of globalization has seen increased capital movements in the world economy and emerging economies have witnessed the fastest growth in international capital transactions especially in the form of foreign direct investment (FDI).The emergence of the developing economies as preferred destination for foreign direct investment (FDI) has led to many studies which are focusing on the impact of FDI on economic growth and its other implications.

FDI is the process by which residents of one country (home country) acquire ownership of assets for the purpose of controlling the production, distribution and other activities of a firm in another country. (Host country).IMF defines FDI as a category of international investment that reflects the objective of obtaining a 'lasting interest' by the resident entity in one economy in an enterprise in another economy. Lasting interest implies the existence of a long term relationship between the direct investor and the enterprise, and a significant degree of influence by the investor on the management of the enterprise. Generally the direct investor owns at least 10% of the ordinary shares, voting power or equivalent.

Economies have opened up to FDI in a big way as it is believed to act as a catalyst to economic growth by enhancing the capital stock, technology transfer, skill acquisition , increasing competition, export potential, employment generation and stimulating strong linkage effects in the host economies.

FDI AND ECONOMIC GROWTH

International Scenario

The last two decades has been marked by rapid economic growth in many countries and a crucial contributory factor has been FDI. While many

* *Department of Economics, Mount Carmel College (Autonomous), Bangalore, India.*

** *DOS in Economic Studies and Co-operation Mysore University, India.*

economists highlight FDI's positive effects, others blame FDI for "crowding out" domestic investment and lowering certain regularity standards. So the impact of FDI has been a matter of great interest in economic research.

Borensztein (1998) using a cross-country regression framework concluded that FDI is an important vehicle for the transfer of technology, contributing more to growth than domestic investment. Nair-Reichert and D Weinhold (2001) reject the traditional tests that suggest a significant and uniform impact of FDI on growth and using Mixed, Fixed and Random (MFR) panel data estimation test they concluded that casual relationship between investment and economic growth in developing countries to be highly heterogeneous. Graham and Wada (2001) state that FDI has significantly contributed to economic growth in China, which has been a large recipient of FDI in the last 2 decades. Kumar and Prakash (2002) suggest a positive correlation does exist between FDI and growth. However the direction of causality between the 2 is ambiguous, since positive growth also leads to increased FDI.

Arturo Ramos (2001) using evidence and theoretical framework demonstrates that FDI leads to higher rates of human capital formation. The 2 reasons for this are the signaling of future growth processes and a factor of accelerated technological change over time. Mathew J Slaughter (2002) using data from both developed and developing nations finds a positive correlation between skill upgrading and presence of US multinational corporations. Ishak Yussof and Rahmah Ismail (2002) highlight the role of FDI in human capital formation in Malaysia, Thailand, Indonesia and Philippines with FDI acting as decisive source of knowledge, transfer of technology, management skills and international linkages for these countries.

The impact of FDI on employment has been a matter of research interest. Few studies highlight how FDI in labor intensive export sectors has been generating sizeable employment (Tulus Tambunan 2000) Sanjaya Lall (2002) says that no general conclusions can be made about correlation between FDI and domestic employment. However when adequate absorptive capacities are present, FDI was seen to have a positive impact on domestic employment.

Many economies have opened up to FDI as it can push up exports that can contribute to economic growth. B Kaminski and B K Samarzynska (2001) in a study of Poland conclude the Poland's FDI and exports demonstrate an increasingly positive relationship. Rashmi Banga (2002) in a study on effects of FDI on Indian exports finds that FDI has had a significant effect on the export intensity of industries in India. The contribution of FDI to growth according to recent studies is strongly dependent on the circumstances in the recipient countries.

Economies which pursue export promotion policy have attracted higher FDI and FDI impact on growth is positive. (Bhagwati 1973, Balasubramanyam 1996) Liberal trade policies and open economies with high degree of economic freedom and sufficient social capacity are economies which have maximized the benefits of FDI. (Balasubramanyam 1999, B S Robles and M B Calvo Basu, *et al,* Trevino & Upadhaya 2003)

Indian Scenario

The post 1991 period has been extensive research on FDI and its impact on Indian Economy. Earlier studies on growth impact of FDI are quite in contrast to the present euphoria about FDI as a catalyst to attain the magical two-digit growth in GDP. Agarwal (2005) estimates a fixed effects model based on pooled data for five South Asian host nations among which India figures prominently for the period 1965-1996. The co-efficient of FDI to GDP ratios turns out be negative. Pradhan (2002) using a Cobb Douglas Production Function with FDI stocks as an additional input variable concludes that FDI stocks have no significant impact in the period 1968 -1997. Dua and Rasid (1998) using the Granger's Causality test highlighted the negative relation between FDI and IIP (Index of Industrial Product), which was taken as a proxy for GDP.

The study of Gopinath (1997) using the OLS method finds a positive relation between FDI and GDP. Kumar and Pradhan (2002) found FDI-growth relationship to be Granger neutral in the case of India, as the direction of causation was not pronounced. This was corroborated by Sahoo and Mathiyazgagan (2002). Bhat (2004) using Granger Causality and Dickey-Fuller tests state no evidence of causality in either direction. Kamalakanthan and Laurenceson (2005) suspect the FDI cannot be considered to be an important driver of economic growth because its contribution to gross capital formation remained small.

Chakraborthy C and Nunnenkamp P (2006) using the Granger causality tests within a panel co- integration framework found that the growth effects of FDI vary widely across sectors in India. FDI stocks and output are mutually reinforcing in the manufacturing sector and in contract there is no causal relationship in the primary sector. Even in the service sector the causality effect is not very strong.

Another important area of study has been the impact of FDI-induced exports as a possible transmission mechanism for FDI to GDP growth. Sahoo (1999) found that foreign firms have higher export ratios than comparable domestic firms in selected industries in 1990-1994. However many of the studies are in line with ADB's (2004) verdict that FDI accounts for a trivial share in India's exports. Sharma (2000) also corroborates this view by concluding that FDI has had no significant impact on the country's export performance. Paliwar (2001) argues that India has not been able to attract FDI in export-oriented industries. Banga (2003) also agrees that FDI has not played a significant role in exports promotion, but points out that export effects differ between home countries of foreign investors and between traditional and non-traditional exports industries. US FDI has had a positive impact on exports intensity of non-traditional industries whereas Japanese FDI has not had the same effects.

Many opine that economic reforms have not brought about any major change in the character of FDI in India and therefore have not had the desire effect on growth. Balasubramanyam and Mahambare (2003) and Fischer (2002) argue that reforms implemented have failed to eliminate the distinct anti-export bias of India's trade policy. Agarwal and Shahani (2005) also highlight the fact the in India FDI has remained domestic market seeking, which is the worst form of FDI as it displaces local industry.

Asian Development Bank (2004) attributes the weak impact of FDI on growth in India to the apparently limited linkages between Multinational Enterprises and local firms. Kumar (2003) states that linkages with local economy have remained weak even in the software industry where foreign companies are said to operate as "export enclaves". Bhat (2004) opines that lack of local skills may have prevented economic spillovers from foreign to local firms. Studies conducted in early 1990's reveal that almost half of foreign investors did not transfer up to date technology to their Indian subsidiaries or joint venture partners as intellectual property was considered to be too weak in India. Kumar and Agarwal (2000) actually found that Research and Development intensity of foreign firms was lower that of domestic firms.

Since 1991 many studies in India have focused on inter-regional rather then regional inflow of foreign investment. Bhattacharya's (1994) study found descriptive statistical relationship between number of FDI approvals and index of relative development of infrastructure of 8 States during 1993-94. Investor friendliness in terms of numbers of clearances needed was considered to be an important determinant of FDI approvals by Sudhir Kumar. (1994)

Bajpai and Sachs (2000a, 2000b and 2000c) have elaborated on state level reforms and accordingly classified 15 major states into 3 categories- reforms-oriented states, intermediate reformers and lagging reformers. Karnataka, Andhra Pradesh, Tamil Nadu, Gujarat and Maharashtra fall in the first category and these are the states that have also attracted higher FDI.

With respect to Tamil Nadu, Bajpai and Sachs (2000) have identified 3 major determinants for attracting sizeable FDI. They are- availability of relatively better infrastructure, well established industrial culture and fair degree of political stability.

Siddharthan (2005) highlighted the large inflow of approved FDI by states during August 1991 to September 2000 by location i.e. costal areas and national capital region and level of economic development of states i.e. per capita income levels.

Narayana (2006) in his study with respect to Karnataka concluded that there is no consistent trend either increasing or decreasing evident between FDI and economic growth and between FDI and exports during 1993-94 to 2003-04. However there seems to be a positive correlation between FDI inflows and economic growth since 2001-02, and between FDI inflows and total exports before 2001-02.

FDI AND INDIA

India's policy towards FDI can be studied in two crucial phases- the pre 1991 and post 1991 period. The pre-1991 period saw a policy of caution and selectivity being followed with respect to FDI. The Industrial Policy Resolution of 1956 and FERA, 1973 limited the role of FDI in the Indian economy and made India a non attractive destination to FDI. The policy of caution and selectivity of sixties and seventies gave way to partial liberalization in the 1980's, which was mainly extended, to the foreign collaborations.

The 1991 reforms initiated by the Industrial Policy Resolutions 1991 marked a sea change in India's attitude towards FDI. The policy acknowledged FDI's role as an instrument for technological transfer, capital provided and increasing the degree of competition in the economy. Several policy measures were taken to promote FDI- amended of FERA, automatic approval mechanism, single window clearance through FIPB, increased limit for FDI in several sectors, etc.

The post 1991 period has seen a sharp rise in the FDI flows into India. From less than US $2 billion in 1991 when country undertook major reforms to open up the economy it has soared to almost US $39 billions in 2004. (UNCTAD online database). Majority of FDI flows have been into the service sector and in the form of wholly owned subsidiaries. (Nagesh Kumar 1998 & 2000).

India's reforms recognized the superiority of non-debt creating capital inflows like FDI over debt to accelerate our pace of growth. Indeed even now the need to further deregulate FDI restrictions is being discussed by policy makers, as many believe that FDI has a catalytic role to play in India's future growth. "FDI worked wonders in China and can do so in India's too" so believes the former Finance minister P Chidambaram. (Indian Express Nov. 1 2005).

FDI AND KARNATAKA

The reforms of 1991 marked the beginning of intense competition among Indian States to attract FDI. States adopted proactive policies attract FDI as policymakers were convinced the FDI could have a dramatic impact on their economic growth as seen in the provinces of China. The post 1991 period has seen a dramatic increase in the quantum of FDI flow into Indian States. But FDI inflows into India characterized by large regional differences. The states that accounts for more than two thirds of FDI inflows are Maharashtra, Delhi, Tamil Nadu, Karnataka, Andhra Pradesh, Gujarat, Punjab and Haryana. (RBI) These states that received large FDI also happened to be states that received large domestic investments and enjoyed higher per capita income. The politically important northern states do not attract large domestic and foreign investments. So we see an uneven distribution of FDI among states in India.

The state of Karnataka has been a pioneer in industry and has the distinction of building a strong and vibrant industrial base which combined the strengths of large public sector, large and medium privately owned industries and a very wide dispersed small scale sector. Karnataka was one of first states to realize the importance of FDI and took the lead in formulating policies that made the State an attractive destination for FDI .Between the time period 1991 and 2007 the State attracted 6.91% of the total FDI inflow into India. The number of projects approved is 2,704 and the total approved FDI between 1991 and 2007 is Rs.31, 712 crores. Indeed the emergence of Karnataka as the IT hub is also largely attributed to high FDI in that industry. The industrial eminence of the state and the large FDI inflows have been attributed to determinants like investor friendly industrial policies, political stability, manpower availability, good labor relations, its identity as a knowledge and technology capital of the country, concentration of ITES, BT industries and strong presence of research and defense institutions.

GRANGER CAUSALITY

In order to test the impact of FDI on Karnataka's economic growth between 1995 and 2005 we perform a Granger Causality test. Economic growth is measured in terms of State Gross Domestic Product (SGDP). To test the direct causality between FDI and economic growth is the aim of the test.

Tests for Stationarity

Since macroeconomic time series data are usually non stationary and thus conducive to spurious regression we have done the augmented Dickey-Fuller Test.

Null Hypothesis: FDI_APPROVED has a unit root
Exogenous: Constant, Linear Trend
Lag Length: 3 (Automatic based on SIC, MAXLAG=3)

		t-Statistic	*Prob.**
Augmented Dickey-Fuller test statistic		-0.09658	0.9708
Test critical values:	1% level	-6.29206	
	5% level	-4.45043	
	10% level	-3.70153	

Granger's Causality

In econometrics, Granger's Causality is most popular way of defining and testing causality. The hypothesis stem from the definition which says that any event in time period t can only be caused by an event in which has occurred in the past, in some time t-i.

In the present case, we tested for Granger's Causality between FDI and GSDP. The two null hypotheses are as follows:

FDI does not Granger-Cause GSDP

The regression equation is,

$$GSDP_t = c + FDI_{t-3} + \varepsilon$$

P value = 0.43

Hence, based on the p-value, we can reject the hypothesis and say that FDI does Granger Cause GSDP.

GSDP does not Granger-Cause FDI

The regression equation is,

$$FDI_t = c + GSDP_{t-3} + \varepsilon$$

P value = 0.028

Based on the p-value, we are able to reject the null hypothesis and say that GSDP does Granger-cause FDI.

From the above we can conclude that in the case of Karnataka there exists FDI-growth causality. The causality ran both from FDI to growth and growth to FDI.

CONCLUSION

The paper proves that there is evidence of 2 direction causality between FDI and Economic Growth in the state of Karnataka. The analysis was done for data between the time periods 1995 to 2005.It needs to be noted that the amount of data available is very limited, only for ten years on a yearly frequency. Hence the results of the analysis cannot be held as conclusive and can only be treated as indicative. Further work is needed to generalize the result with respect to the state over a longer period. But it does indicate that FDI can overcome the resource constraints for development such as technology, entrepreneurship, organizational ability, market access and fuel growth.

References

Agarwal R. R. and Sahani (2005), Foreign Investment in India- Issues and Implications for Globalisation, In C. Tisdell(ed), "Globalization and World Economic policies- Effects and Policy Responses of Nations and their Groupings", New Delhi 644-658.

Athreye S. and Kapur S. (2001), Private Foreign Direct Investment-Pain or Panacea? *The World Economy*, 24(3)- 399-424.

Asian Development Bank-Asian Development Outlook 2004,"Part 3-FDI in Development Asia" Manila.

Balasubramanyam (1996), Foreign Direct Investment and Growth in EP and IS Countries, *Economic Journal*, 106- 92-105

Balasubramanyam and Mahambare (2003), Foreign Direct Investment in India Transnational Corporations 12(2)- 45-72

Banga R. (2003), The Differential Impact of Japanese and US Foreign Direct Investment on Exports of Indian Manufacturing, Department of Economics, Jesus and Mary College, New Delhi.

Bhat K. S, Tripura Sundari C. U. and K. D. Raj (2004), Causal Nexus between Foreign Direct Investment and Economic Growth in India, *Indian Journal of Economics*, 85(337)-171-185.

Bajpai Nirupam and Sashs Jeffery D. (2000a, 2000b, and 2000c), Reforms in the State-I, II and III, The *Hindu*, January.

Bhattacharya B. (1994), Foreign Direct Investment in India, *Foreign Trade Review*, XXVIII-307-329.

Borensztein F., J. De Gregorio and J. W. Lee (1998), How Does Foreign Direct Investment Affect Economic Growth? *Journal of International Economics*, 45- 115-135.

Basu P., C. Chakraborthy and Reade D. (2003), Liberalization, Foreign Direct Investment and Growth in Developing Countries-A Panel Co-integration Approach, *Economic Enquiry*, 41(3)- 510-516

Chakraborthy C. Nunnenkamp (2006), Economic Reforms, Foreign Direct Investment and its Economic Effects in India, Keil Working Paper No. 1217.

Chowdhury A. and Mavrotas G. (2005), Foreign Direct Investment and Growth-A Causal Relationship, Research Paper No. 2005/25 WIDER United Nations University.

Dua P. and A. I. Rashid (1998), Foreign Direct Investment and Economic Activity in India, *Indian Economic Review*, 33(2)- 153-168.

Basu P., C. Chakraborthy and Reade D. (2003), Liberalization, Foreign Direct Investment and Growth in Developing Countries-A Panel Co-integration Approach, *Economic Enquiry*, 41(3)- 510-516.

Chakraborthy C. Nunnenkamp (2006), Economic Reforms, Foreign Direct Investment and its Economic Effects in India, Keil Working Paper No. 1217.

Kumar Nagesh (2003), Liberlization, Foreign Direct Investment Flows and Economic Development-The Indian Experience in the 1990's, RIS Discussion Papers 65, Research and Information System for Non Aligned and other Developing Countries, New Delhi.

Kumar Nagesh (1998), Liberalization and Changing Patterns of Foreign Direct Investment-Has India's Relative attractiveness as a Host of FDI Improved? *Economic and Political Weekly*, 33(22).

Kumar Nagesh (2000), Economic Reforms and Their Macro Economic Impact, *Economic and Political Weekly*, March 2000.

Kumar N. and A. Agarwal (2000), Liberalization, Outward Orientation and In-house Research Activity of Multinational and Local Firms- A Quantitative Exploration for Indian Manufacturing, RIS Discussion Paper 7, Research and Information System for Non Aligned and other Developing Countries, New Delhi.

Narayan M. R. (2006), Inflow of Foreign Direct Investment into Karnataka-Patterns, Performance, Implications, Foreign Trade Review XLI–2006 Pailwar (2001), Foreign Direct Investment Flows to India and Export Competitiveness, Productivity 42(1)-115-122.

Reserve Bank of India Annual Reports.

Sahoo R. K. (1999), Foreign Direct Investment and Economic Development-A Firm Level Analysis of Manufacturing Sector in Post-Reforms India, *Asian Economic Review*, 41(1): 33-42.

Sahoo and Mathiyazhangam (2002), Economic Growth in India-Does FDI Inflow Matter? Working paper 115, ISEC, Bangalore.

Sanjaya Lall (2002), The Employment Impact of Globalization in Developing Countries, Working Paper 93, Queen Elizabeth House, University of Oxford, Oxford.

Siddharthan N.S (2005), Indian Industrial Policy and Global Competition, Policy Review Seminar, IIMB, August 2005.

A STUDY ON COMPETITIVENESS OF INDIAN SOFTWARE EXPORTS: EXPORT GUIDING FACTORS MODEL

HECTOR J. THAYIL KOCHUKUNNEL* & P. ARUNACHALAM**

INTRODUCTION

For centuries, India has been a dreamland for navigators to reach in. Trade with India had been frenzy for the rulers of different landscapes. The traces of that great interest in trade with India could be seen in many historical and religious texts. For centuries, India has been the epicenter of global trade. However, of late, the profile of India as the economic resource centre has undergone considerable change. It has been started viewing India as an impoverished nation. This image continued to exist till the 1990s. While India was still suffering from abject poverty, epidemic, grave social inequalities, massive unemployment and destructive political upheavals and uncertainties, a latent revolution has been underway in India's technological landscape. India has now been recognized the emerging capital of global software industry. The Indian software industry and export have been projected as one, which could address all of India's chronic development ills.

India, the world's largest democracy and home to over one billion people, is quietly but quickly emerging as a leader in the filed of software engineering. India, one of the poorest countries in the world, better known internationally for its uncompetitive industries, has come a long way with its high growth software industry. India's competitiveness and productivity/effectiveness are not recognized by the nations. However, having recognized its mastery over software production, policy makers started pinning a lot of hope on the capability and potential of this sector in taking India to the front stage of rapid development.

The competitiveness in international trade has, nowadays, acquired a lot of strategic importance. The most powerful nation is not necessarily the nation

* *Research and Development Officer, Neptune Travel Ltd., Holywood Road, Belfast, United Kingdom*

** *Department of Applied Economics, Cochin University of Science and Technology, Kochi, E-mail: arunachalam14@yahoo.co.uk*

with the most potent military backup but a nation with economic muscle. Here comes the strategic importance of international trade. India is more know for its software exports, than the domestic trade. The people from all walks of life are now recognizing the importance of software export and its competitiveness, for facing challenges from other parts of the world by which it can address India's balance of payment deficits, technological backwardness, retarded growth of the economy and unemployment.

RELEVANCE OF THE STUDY

In this study, the researchers attempts to going to the greater depths of India's software industry domain. Software industry in India concentrates its efforts more on exports. India is becoming a major software exporter. This is a country which offers cost-effectiveness, great quality, high reliability, rapid delivery and , above all, state of the art technologies in software development. The profile of the software devel0pment and application by Indian vendors attracted the clients from all parts of the world. It is, in this way, significant to understand the future prospects of this sector.

It is emphasized in many theses that one of India's advantages in software business is its large pool of technically skilled human resources which is available at low cost. However, many developing nations with sufficiently large pool of human resources are striving to make their mark on the map of global software industry. Hence, India may not be able to boast off her competitive advantage in software industry for long. Studying this aspect is important in terms of the sustainability of this industry and export.

Many have pinned their hope in the transformation capability of this sector on the Indian economy. However, much of it depends on how this sector, especially the exports enables itself to innovate and face competition in this highly dynamic society. Hence, the study on export competitiveness deserves merit.

Its export driven model now commands the world's attention for skilled professionals and offer hope to many developing countries, which are struggling to cope with a hyper-competitive post-WTO global economy. How India stands in this kind of a battleground is considered to be crucial.

This is a kind of topic, which attracts the attention of policy makers and the government. The software industry and its earning capacity for foreign exchange have definitely a large bearing on India's economic future. However, studies of serious outlook and a systematic approach are hardly seen before the government in order to take vital policy decisions and measures.

This study was motivated by the need to understand factors that guide the software exports and competitiveness, both positively and negatively. The influence of one factor or another upon the export and export competitiveness is to be understood in great depth, which is necessary to find out the industry's sustainability. It is also important because the strategic loopholes could be identified so that the remedial measures shall be advocated.

A large number of problems or factors, which curtail the prospect of Indian software industry and export, have been spelt through a umber of studies. The devastating capabilities of some of them are much bigger than the others. This study aims to identify such problems.

HISTORY

Technological revolutions, in most circumstances, have far-reaching effects. For some, it may be a life and death problem. However, for most countries, it brings out a number of opportunities. Some of these opportunities are unexpected. One such opportunity was availed when India has recognized that it can derive many advantages in computer and software industry. India's success at software has led to speculation about whether other developing countries can emulate its example, as well as whether this constitutes a completive challenge to software industries in the developed world. In this scenario, it is thoughtful to understand how this nation has been making its voyage in software industry in the context of rough weathers and sever bottlenecks.

India has had a software policy since 1970. Prior to 1984, rigid policy restrictions ensured that there was virtually no software industry. Between 1984 and 1990, the restrictions were eased and Indian firms entered the global market by providing low-cost programming services. After 1990, pro-active promotion of the industry, among with economy-wide policy 00liberalization, led to rapid growth in exports. The nature of exports also changed from providing programming services at client sites, to providing offshore services from India for turnkey projects demanding a wider range of capabilities. (Parthasarathy, 2004).

Before 1984, the policy initiatives were very restrictive in nature. In 1977, the Indian government refused to allow more than 50 per cent ownership by foreigners of any comp0any operating in the nation. IBM refused to sell majority ownership of its Indian operations, and was thus forced to leave India. Later, after 1984, the then Prime Minister Rajive Gandhi changed government polices to encourage an indigenous microcomputer industry (Singhal and Rogers, 2001). Imports were liberalized, ad international standards were followed by Indian computer manufacturers so that their products could compete more effectively in the global market place.

During the initial phase of computer software industry in India, many constraints had to be addressed by itself. These constraints include access to finance and skills, and low level of research and development, access to telecommunications and other infrastructure, access to markets and information about markets, and how demand and high piracy in the domestic market. The firms have had difficulty n various types of capital. Software is moderately capital intensive and very highly technology intensive (Cleetus, 1984). Small firms have been particularly affected by the problems of access to finance since, unlike the largest companies, they do not have access to capital from multinationals or the big sized Indian firms.

Another bottleneck experienced by the firms has been the lack of high skilled manpower. The relative lack of skilled labour is the most serious constraint to the Indian software industry's development (Singhal, 1988, Tandon et al, 1990 and Schware, 1992). Although there has been a shortage of all type of labour, it has been the shortage of the higher-skill levels - programme designers, system analysts, project managers–that has particularly affected this industry.

Software companies, especially exporters, faced a number of telecommunications problems, including the scarcity of actual telecommunications links, delay in obtaining such links, poor transmission quality, and the high cost of installation and use. As a result, overall growth of Indian software exports was stunted and offshore software development viewed by many foreign clients as unacceptable problematic. (Heeks, 1996).

There has been another major problem in the form of market and marketing issues. The ability to monitor and interpret market and technical changes and spot opportunities and shift strategy is vital but beyond the capacity of most individual firms (Sridharan, 1989). This is one of the major reasons behind the low level of software package exports from India,, though lack of market information also makes it difficult for software service companies to locate clients or assess potential partners, and for all companies to keep up with the latest software production technology.

The Department of Electronics (DOE) was the body responsible for policy making for the computer industry. But later on, Computer Policy of 1984 eased the availability of microcomputers and facilitated software exports by encouraging on-site service provision (Parthasarathy, 2004). The 1986 Software Policy encouraged foreign investment in the industry and access to technological development overseas, by allowing easy imports of the latest software and software tools.

While the 1984 and 1986 policies mainly removed hurdles before the industry, positive promotion came in 1990 when the DOE initiated the Software Technology Park (STP) scheme. The Software Technology Parks of India provide data communication facilities using which firms can provide offshore services from India instead of being limited to on-site provision.

In 1988, the industry also formed its own trade body, the National Association of Software and Services Companies (NASSCOM) to promote its interests. When it was formed, NASSCOM had 38 members who accounted for 65 per cent of the industry's revenues. A decade later, it had 464 members, accounting for 95 per cent of Industry's revenues (Parthasarathy, 2004).

The infrastructure in IT took of gradually following the Prime Minister's 1998 IT Task Force and its 108 recommendations, two-thirds of which saw the light of the day. And series of policy changes, and the 2001 Convergence ACT which spoke little of convergence but did replace the 1885 Telegraph Act, with its separate rules for voice and data. And the convergence of the telecom and IT Ministries happened in 2001. All that it needed was for the government to step out of the way (Roy, 2002).

In November 2004, the government announced its Broadband Policy and permitted use of 2.4 GHZin out door locations, (Dataquest, 2005 a)> FROM Rs. 3,455 crore turnover in 1992-93, the Indian IT industry grew to mammoth size of Rs. 1,24,122 crore turnovers in 2004-05. The exports alone grew from a mere Rs. 931 crore in 1992-93 to Rs. 81,096 crore in 2004-05. (Dataquest, 2005, b).

Under this subtitle we have seen the emergence of Software industry in this nation, the major bottlenecks, which had been experienced by this sector, and the major turning points which boosted this industry in becoming a globally competitive software industry in the world today.

STATEMENT OF THE PROBLEM

India is being emulated as an example for the success strategy in software development exports. Many scholars as well as industry experts claim that the sector can answer to many of the problems of chronic ills of India's backwardness. India's software industry is hailed as one of the globally competitive software industries in the world. India has been given number one rank in terms of attractiveness as shown by many attractiveness indices (AT Keamey, 2004).

In this study, the researcher made an attempt to endeavor a comprehensive look at the competitiveness of India's software industry. Indian software ad services industry and exports are bestowed with a number of merits and positive strengths. India is cited as hub of one of the world's largest and most talented human resources-a large number of English speaking skilled labour which, in turn, is a natural advantage which is in consonance with the needs of industries of the developed world. Moreover, of course, a comparatively early preparedness of this country in the filed of hardware a software expertise. Even when this being the case, it is finding it difficult to answer to a number of fundamental questions aroused by the realities of today and concerns about the future.

Is India really worthy of being at the front stage of the global attractiveness of software industry? Are the preparedness, strengths and policy orientations of future really help to sustain with at least the present scale of competitiveness? Could Indian industry outsmart the extent of competition posed by players like Ireland and Israel? Is the level of physical discrepancy in turnover between domestic software sales and exports helping the cause of competitiveness? What are the problems of software industry and exports, which are to be addressed with urgency and a time scale? What is the degree or extent of impact each factors have upon the sect oral performance? This study tries to seek answer to all the above questions.

India and its software sector enjoy plenty of natural advantages. It is also to be categorically specified that it is devoid of many of the strengths the developed world has. In this background the problems is whether India is competitive enough to face challenges from other dominant players as well as contingencies of future. This study discusses how India places itself in the trajectory of global competitiveness of software industry and exports.

OBJECTIVE

To find out the criticality of various problems faced by software industry and export in India.

HYPOTHESES

Based on an extensive and detailed survey of literature and key interactions made with the think-tank in software industry and academics, the following hypotheses was formulated

"The Governing criteria, which guide the software export and its competitiveness, are independent in nature."

METHODOLOGY

Both primary and secondary data have been used in the study. No specific geographical delimitation is made into effect in this study on account of the peculiarity of the topic. Since the export competitiveness is the primary area of interest, the data of both India and international economies have been taken into account. The major sources of secondary data are international reports, websites of National and International Software Export Promotion agencies like National Association of Software and Services companies, research and commercial establishments and reputed journals like Dataquest. When developing models on software success guiding factors, primary data have been resorted to. Both face to face interview and online survey based on a structured questionnaire were employed to collect primary data. In order to fix the sampling size a pilot study has been carried out. No specific study sampling procedure could be employed because of the peculiar nature of the industry and professionals. In order to make sure that all the different sections of the population are duly represented, a large sample size has been taken. Total sample size 1089.

TOOLS USED IN THE STUDY

The data collected through primary and secondary sources were scrutinized and statistical software viz; AMOS (Analysis of Moment Structures) SPSS (Statistical Package for Social Sciences) and E Views (Econometric Views) were used for analysis. The Following tools have been employed for the purpose of analyzing the data and at arriving at inferences.

1. Multi-dimensional Scaling (MDS) is used to identify similarity/ dissimilarity among different factors which guide software export.
2. Structural Equation Model (SEM) has been used to measure the relationship between eleven factors, which guide software export.
3. Canonical Correlation is used to find the extent of correlation between different variables of competitiveness.

Export performance of Indian Software Industry is a case of success story being imitated by many a nation. A detailed examination into the success factors shows some variables which are determining the exports. Different scholars had tried to analyze these factors and some of them had even created suitable models. One such model is the 'Oval Model' Constructed by Carmel. (Camel, 2003). It could be understood that eight major factors were delineated in this model.

Another model has been developed to indicate the export performance of Indian software industry (Heeks and Nicholson, 2002). This model incorporated five success factors. There were some nascent attempts to model the success factors of leading software exporting nations from the beginning of 1990s onwards. An important milestone in this regard was Michael Porter's Model (1990) of competitive advantage of nations that posits four critical factors. An important categorization of nations based on four important criteria could be seen in World Bank report (Garry, 1999). He identified four criteria-cost, English speaking ability, ease of doing business and segment expertise. In a different approach two important factors were identified in a study (Porter *et al*, 2001) viz, socio economic factors and national orientation, the other two factors being technological infrastructure and production capacity. It was named the High Tech Indicators Model by the authors.

HISTORIC MODELS: A CRITICAL APPROACH

Michael Porter's Model (1990) of competition advantages of nations, even though it was a nascent attempt, had tried to find out the crucial factors that lead into success in software exporting. However, it was found out that the approach he adopted in this regard was more general than specific. The model did not delimit its scope to the export spectrum alone. Rather, it had been pulled to give application to a national industry's resolve to achieve global leadership over an extended period of time.

World Bank Report (Garry, 1999) was not a model in itself. However, he has specifically selected some important criteria for categorizing software-exporting nations. An important drawback of this study is that it lacks a systematic approach. Though important factors were highlighted, the whole at one hand and the synergic interaction of these four factors on the other hand were ignored. For example, cost as criteria could be demarcated as the credential for China. But it is to be noted that cost factor alone will not contribute towards a nation's success in its exports-especially in a hi-tech industry like software.

An outstanding feature of the High Tech Indicators Model (Porter *et al*, 2001) is that it has depicted important criteria like socio-economic factors. The study has taken the subject in a macro approach. Both the cultural as well as structural factors could be taken into account in this model. But it is worth mentioning that the approach adopted in the study was abstract rather than concrete.

Perhaps the most comprehensive model, for evaluating national software industries is the Software Export Success Model (Heeks and Nicholson, 2002). This model has already been applied to depict the software exporting success phenomenon of a number of new software exporting nations (Nicholson and Sahay, 2003). The authors developed the model from success factors of India, Ireland and Israel, the success cases of 1990's. The five factors are: demand for software; national software vision and strategy; international linkages and trust; national software industry characteristics; and national software related infrastructure (Heeks and Nicolson, 2002). The model envisages almost all the important factors leading to software export success. As well, the study scripts the need and necessity of the production of high-end services as well as the need for innovative products and packages in order to be a global leader. But it has not spelt in detail how the transition shall be made possible from the exporter of low-end services to an exporter of high-end software products, packages and services. Also, this model cannot aptly be emulated in case of 3rd and 4th tier software exporting nations (Carmel, 2003).

The "Oval Model" constructed by Carmel emphasized on eight important factors, government vision and policy, infrastructure, capital, industry, quality of life, human capital and linkages.

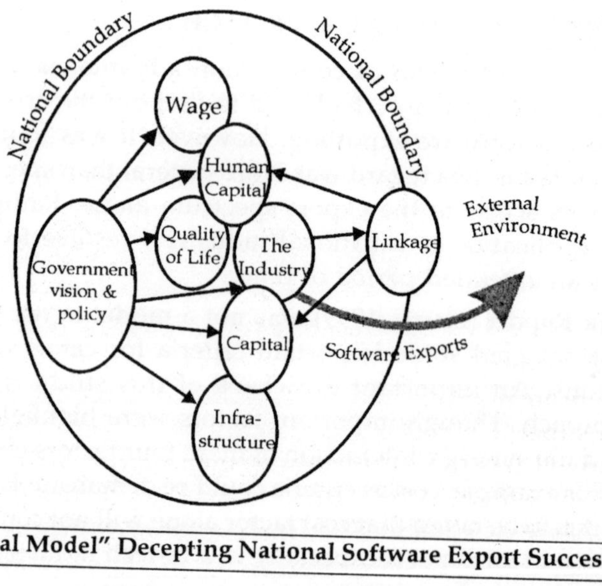

Figure 1: "Oval Model" Decepting National Software Export Success Factor

The study has described all these factors in detail. But the industrial and economic system and its growth and the concerned 'cascading effect' it generates could not be spelt out in any of these studies including the 'Oval Model'. For instance, without the emergence and growth of industries like steel, air traffic, banking etc, there could not have been any need of these software packages and solutions. Notably, the change and growth in one sector of either the national economy or the overseas economy will have its cascading effect on other sectors as well, including the software. This aspect which is one of the most relevant factors influencing software industry and export is almost comprehensively ignored by these studies. This major short coming is reflected in the aforesaid models since it did not incorporate this vital component.

Almost all these works have tried to explore the effect produced by VARIOUS factors on the total export output of software. They could clearly notice many of the relevant aspects of cause. How ever, it is to be specified at none of these studies could specifically measure or quantify the marginal effect of one variable over the other or the combined effect or interactions of different variables and factors upon the whole.

Against this background, this research paper attempts to answer to the following issues.

1. What is the most crucial comparative advantage India has or will have? 2. 2. What are the factors which influence the innovative performance of different software exporting units?
3. What is the effect of one 'actor upon the other?
4. What sort of dynamism is to be effected to achieve the targeted goals?.
5. Has any important factor/ variable not been considered when the study of software export of India or such emerging software exporting nations was undertaken? And,
6. How is it possible to measure each and varied factors which determine/ influence the competitiveness of software export?

DYNAMISM IN THE STRUCTURE OF SOFTWARE EXPORT: MULTIPLE FACTORS

The much popular jargon of India Model of software export success is to a great extent, ironical. There are instances of a few countries like the United States with a high level of IT diffusion with around 400 computers per 1000 people, where IT contributes substantially to its economy (Pohjola, 2002). On the contrary, there are many developing nations where the extent of IT diffusion is minimal and superficial. Such a 'digital divide' or technology gap can best can be summarized by the fact that more than half of humanity has never made a phone call' (Pohjola, 1998). Thus it seems paradoxical that India enjoys enormous comparative advantage in the export of software. The available statistics show that, during the last decade software export from India recorded

Annual Compound Growth Rates of over 60 per cent in rupee terms, at current prices and around 45 per cent in dollar terms. In consequence, the share of software export in the total export earning of the country increased from 1.9 per cent in1994-95 to about 20 per cent in 2002-03 (Parthasarathy and Joseph, 2004). This phenomenal growth India recorded in software export volume and export competitiveness lead to the following governing factors. They are:

(a) Government policy and the resultant economic environment
(b) Infrastructure
(c) Industrial and Economic system, and its growth
(d) Competition
(e) Man power/ Skill
(f) Marketing
(g) Cost
(h) Credibility/ Quality
(i) Management
(j) External Environment, and
(k) Non-economic/Cultural variables

COMPETITION

Economic reforms initiated in India in 1990s had a direct impact on competition. Globalization compelled the Indian firms to compete with their counterparts in other parts of the world and since software industry has more of an international connotation than a domestic one, the opening up of economy had many positive aspects. Increased competition helps these firms to become gradually global. Broad economic reforms are compelling Indian business to respond to increased competition (D'costa, 2000). The act of economic reforms upon other industries had its ripple effects on software industry. For example, Indian banks started increasingly adopting IT for or competitive advantages. The adoption of such competitive practices in other sectors is contributing to diffusion of IT.

Product innovation will assist the Indian industry to diversify domains and markets to preserve and enhance its competitiveness (D'Costa and Sridharan, 2004). A shift from low-value service exports to an innovation driven higher value added trajectory will boost the competitiveness and an increased market capture. A paradigmatic shift in corporate strategy will enable this. This shift is expected to lead to diversification also. The positive impact that it will render Indian firms truly global and competition among the domestic software firms will get marginalized at least in the short run.

Different kinds of 'de-coupling' also harmfully reduces the competitiveness of software industry and its export of emerging software kings especially India. Four forms of de-coupling were identified.

They are:

(a) Between software and hard ware

(b) Between the export and domestic markets.

(c} Between software services and products (D'Costa , 2004)

(d) between the civilian sector and national security sector (Sridharan, 2004).

The synergy which could have been created has not effected on account of these four kinds of decoupling, which happened in India.

There is an argument that the low profile of electronics and hardware sector in India retards the prospects of software. It is already discussed that the decoupling between the software and hardware had its negative impact. Computer hardware industry has not grown significantly in India. It is very clear from the fact that even now, IT diffusion remains low in India. A strong foundation of hardware sector and its bullish sectoral growth would have aid an infrastructural base for software. That would have resulted in a mighty software industry. It can be stated that such fundamentally strong domestic market augurs well for its software export market. But there are stark exceptions in this regard. Mexico and South Africa have a solid software industry with potential for exports, but internal domestic demand has been too strong, inhibiting growth of a national export sector even when other success factors are present (Carmel, 2003). However, what is understood is that with a strong motivation for export which caters to overseas demands, supplemented by developed domestic hardware and software market, software export will get benefited.

The business by the MNC sponsored software development centres established in India is gathering momentum. Whether they are competitors to Indian origin companies are to be carefully studied. However, they are contributing significantly to India's export revenue. During the financial year 2004-05 IBM GSI and HP GDIC had exports to the tune of Rs. 1950 crore and Rs.1056 crore respectively (Dataquest, 2005). Three companies, viz; IBM GSI, Cognizant (IDC operations) and HP GDIC make it to the top 10 software and services exporters and another four firms, viz; Oracle (IDC operations), Accenture (IDC operations), Texas Instruments and Perot Systems TSI make it to the top 20 exporters (Dataquest, 2005). It is certain that competition is encompassing in today's market driven global economy. One or another form of competition will prevail any time and every time. The Indian software houses are to be well prepared to face this competition.

GOVERNMENT POLICY

Government policy is counted as one of the most vital aspects for the emergence and growth of any industry. It is of prime importance in those industries where there is a case of evolution of innovative capability. For instance, in manufacturing, the East Asian governments have successfully fostered high-tech competitive industries through a wide range of fiscal and non-fiscal policy instruments (Dedrik and Kraemer, 1998). Whereas, the protectionists policies followed in India and Brazil hindered the growth of such industries to become innovative and globally competitive. In the Indian context, in the computer hardware sector, restrictive policies compelled several Indian firms to use limited imported know-how. It was termed as 'green-house approach' where in such firms were forced to build their own computer hardware but the growth was hampered (Evans, 1995).

The economic reforms and market liberalization had tremendous impact on different industries including the software industry. Most Indian hardware manufacturers had to abandon the aforesaid line of business (D'Costa, 2004). The kind of fatigue of the government in regulatory intervention had its favorable impact on the software industry. Unlike those sectors which are still heavily relying upon captive market and state protection, the software industry is internationally competitive.

Instead of being a regulator, the state can act as a facilitator. The Information Technology Act which was enacted in June 2000 shall be considered as a promising initiative. The Act provides legal recognition for transactions carried out by means of electronic data interchange and other means of electronic communication. The Act is the first step in the amalgamation of the Internet into India's legal framework (Data quest, 2002).

Infrastructural support like data communication links, tax free export income, duty free imports for the value of exports etc. are tools as well as products of state facilitation.

The free-market guidelines of the New Economic Policy (NEP) eased government controls on importing technology, foreign currency and on raising capital (Singhal and Rogers, 2000). The NEP also invited competition for Indian companies from multinational corporations.

The role of the government is significant in building technopolis since it is seen as an accelerator of innovation as well as software business. The experience of technopolises around the world indicates that collaboration between government, private corporate houses and research centres of Universities is essential. For instance, the Austin technopolis arose because administrators in the Texas state government, at the University of Texas, and in private companies agreed to collaborate in building a technology city (Gibson and Rogers, 1994).

A significant support the entrepreneurs need from their environment is financial, particularly in the early days. In 1999, the Indian government established a $25 million venture capital fund especially to encourage software start-ups. Venture capital investments in Indian high tech companies grew from $20 million in 1996 to $750 million in 2000, and are expected to rise steeply to $10 billion by 2008 (Padmanabhan, 2000). Most start-ups do not have the assets that a traditional investor would consider valuable. The entrepreneurs, therefore, have to rely on their own resources. They have little to offer investors besides their hopes and dreams (Bhide, 2000). But one major drawback which could be noted is that the venture capital is neither availed of to the entrepreneurs nor utilized by them. It is noticed in such a way that personal funds remained a key source of availability of funds for start-ups (Manimala *et al*, 2001).

One of the needs most consistently emphasized by entrepreneurs was a single window that would facilitate on all government-related requirements to enable the entrepreneurs to concentrate comprehensively on their business and also remain within the legal system. A single window facility for an industry, in this case software industry, should be set-up to provide all the relevant information as regards the various legal procedures that are to be complied with and remove all the hiccups. A major complaint which is being heard is the level of corruption in all the departments of government machinery (Ojha and Krishna, 2000). Therefore, it seems very necessary that the government simplify its procedures so that entrepreneurs are easily able to comply with them without being harassed by government agencies for violation that they were unaware of.

A significant number of people have strongly argued against the role of government in the economy (Ojha and Krishna, 2004). Some evidence and literature spell, however, that there is a vital role for the government in guiding the development of an industry (Martinsons,1998; Montealegre,1999). Official machineries/government can attempt in delivering an efficiency - promoting environment by making various resources available, increasing the multitude of opportunities, and most significantly, avoiding policies that create real or perceived obstacles (Chen, Greene and Crick, 1998).

It is reported that, while India did not have the lowest scores on various elements of government policy and programs for new firms evaluated, it ranked below the average of the twenty-nine countries on every element (Manimala *et al*, 2001). Hence it is very clear that the government has a lot to do to encourage entrepreneurship in India.

A relatively decent economic system facilitated and augmented by the government and comfortably better standards of living can help minimize the case of brain-drain from India. It is to be noticed here that the project management expertise which is locally available can set international quality standards for Indian software and save billions of rupees.

The concerns over a system of weak Intellectual Property Rights (IPRs) should be addressed by the government. Proper legal measures are necessary to tackle privacy ills and a constructive mechanism of intellectual property rights has to be in place (John, 2004). Similarly, even though the hiccups of political instability cannot be tackled overnight, the state should embrace a system which facilitates the cause of the industry on a sustainable basis irrespective of political uncertainties and turmoil.

The government also can play a role in creating a brand image for the Indian software industry. Smaller entrepreneurs as well as entrepreneurs need to be benefited from the collective goodwill of the software industry. The co ordination by the government with a motive of facilitation rather than interference will, in any way, help this industry.

INFRASTRUCTURE

The role of infrastructure is unambiguously vital in the point of view of any industry. It shall be described as the backbone of any industry. The role of infrastructure, whether it is physical infrastructure or financial infrastructure, is paramount in a high-tech industry like software.

Infrastructure is one of the most important of support mechanisms entrepreneurs require (Cabral, 1998; Martinsons, 1998; Montealegre, 1999 and Sanchez and Perez, 1998). This may range from Research and Development (R&D) centres to financial infrastructure like a sound system of banking. The scope of infrastructure like a sound system of banking. The scope of infrastructure extends to physical infrastructure such as technology parks to adequate roads, telecommunications facilities, and the like that are essential for doing business. Manimala (Manimala et al, 2001) reports that India had, on average, the lowest scores on adequacy of physical infrastructure among the twenty-nine countries they surveyed.

Industrial infrastructure is a precursor for production, with necessary ingredients of any industrial infrastructure including power, water and transport. Of more specific interest to the software industry is the provision of a telecommunications infrastructure: "the central transport network of the world information economy"(Feketekuty and Aronson, 1984).

In India, this was in a poor state, for much of the 1980s. This was evident in many literatures. "Communications in India are best not described. With perhaps the world's most inefficient telephone system you can safely forget about facsimile, networking, electronic mail or any kind integrated services for quite some time to come" Business India, 1986).

Software firms, particularly, export units faced with a number of structural ills like scarcity or even non-availability of actual telecommunications links, substandard transmission quality and exorbitantly high expenditure of installation and use. Overall growth of Indian software exports was stunted consequently. Foreign clients viewed offshore software development as unacceptable problematic.

However, from the mid - 1980s, the government of India started giving priority to the telecommunication infrastructure. Investments in international links alone was raised from US $ 150m for 1985-1990 to US$ 400m for 1990-95 and overall spending was intended to rise by 15 per cent annually between 1990 and 2000 (Heeks, 2001).

A number of policy initiatives were undertaken by the state machinery in its motive to create and lay down quality infrastructure. A number of software technology parks were established. These were aimed to provide high-speed (64 kbps) satellite links and Satcomm Services, which provided the 'last mile' local connection through microwave and radio links. They reduced the costs of a high-speed link from around US$ 1,80,000 per year to an internationally competitive level of US $ 60,000 making it a feasible option for more companies (Heeks, 2001).

It took off following the Prime Minister's 1998 IT Task Force and its 108 recommendations. Two-thirds of these recommendations finally saw the light of day (Data quest, 2002).

It is quite difficult to narrate the entire story of infrastructure building in India. Still some policy changes demand special attention. The 2001 Convergence Act was such an important milestone. "And a series of policy changes, and the 2001 Convergence Act which spoke little of Convergence, but did replace the cobwebby 1885 Telegraph Act, with its separate rules for voice and data. In addition, there has been the convergence of the telecom and IT ministries in 2001 (Data quest, 2002).

It is a certainty that the tele-communications facilities that are at the doorsteps of industry have improved considerably. However, these infrastructural prerequisites are considered still inadequate. The entrepreneurs want the government to improve these facilities, or to enable private players to provide such facilities.

Service-oriented firms themselves have been successful despite the infrastructure, and not because of it. As of now, infrastructure at the technology parks is more affordable to service-oriented firms and not to entrepreneurs on a very tight budget in the initial phase (Ojha and Krishna, 2004). Making smart gains in infrastructure front would give further fillip in the attempts to create a brand image for Indian software industry.

INDUSTRIAL AND ECONOMIC SYSTEM AND ITS GROWTH

Industrial and Economic System (IES) and its growth might be considered to be the most important determinant for the development of software industry, its expansion and competitiveness. Although this is macro-economic in nature, the attitude of the government and its policies, especially fiscal policies have a great say in this front.

Software industry does not have its existence, independent of the growth and existence of other industries. This is primarily because software industry basically acts only as a supportive mechanism.

Since competition is the buzzword in this era of globalization, software support is gravely in need for firms of different industries to become internationally competitive and to simplify their complex tasks. However, if there would have been no growth and expansion in other industries, software industry alone would not have grown. Therefore, IES and its growth pattern is seen definitely critical, even though it has more of an indirect impact than a direct one.

COMPETITION

The World Economic System at present is characterized by hyper competition mostly among Transnational Corporations (TNCs) from the Triad Nations/ blocks of the USA, E.U. and Japan. A handful of nations, such as South Korea, China, India, Brazil, Taiwan and Singapore, are striving to upgrade or expand heir industrial activities and core competencies. The rest of the developing world either compete vigorously in labor-intense export or are considered 'structurally irrelevant' (Hoogvelt, 2001). Of the $12.4 trillion of global trade, the capitalist countries of the developed world had a share of 65 per cent, while the least development countries, most of which are from Africa, had a mere 0.64 per cent (UNCTAD, 2002).

U.S. Multinational Companies (MNCs) affiliates in five IT industries had global sales of $202 billion, while total U.S. exports of IT goods and services was only $113 billion in 1998 (U.S. Department of Commerce, 2002).

The structural inequality is evident from the size of firms.

Table 1
Size of Firms and the Structure of the World Economy (Average of Top 10)

Top 10 manufacturing MNCs (global) (1999)	$ 134 billion
Top 10 manufacturing MNCs (developing countries) (1999)	$ 24 billion
Top 10 ICT* firms (Global) (2000)	$ 63.4 billion
TOP 10 Software firms MNC's (Global) (2000)	$ 5.9 billion
Top 10 Indian IT firms MNCs(2000)**	$278 billion

Source: UNCTAD (2001) for top manufacturing firms; OECD (2002: 63, 67) for top ICT and software firms; Dataquest (*www.dqindia.com/top1201*) for top Indian IT firms.

Competition at the international level suggests that not all firms can pursue successful activities. Rather, outsourcing, joint ventures, subcontracting, technical collaborations and alliances are institutional arrangements by which firms will try to specialize (Okhi, 2001). Except in case of customized service, Indian software firms have failed to specialize, even though there are genuine attempts to get rejuvenated in other areas of products and packages as well.

Core competence is the buzzword here. Lacking core competence in different aspects of product innovation, upgrading and marketing contributes towards the failure of firms, especially in case of India. However, it has another side as well. With almost muted infrastructure, Indian software exporting firms could create a good brand image of their own, although it is manifested in low-end services. This was the case of India. Core competence and the absence of it divides the industry into two dichotomies. This is where the competition is manifested in second turn. Lacking core competence of a high technological order, most small firms are adjuncts to larger enterprises. For instance, in Internet software development, smaller firms adjust to the standards set by the giant telecommunications companies, while applications software developers are further down the industry hierarchy (Casper and Glimstedt, 2001).

In a transnational perspective, the convergence of MNC attention on core competence helps the firms of developing nations. This means that MNCs farm out non-critical, labour-intensive, low end activities to other suppliers, who are mainly from developing countries. Why MNCs do this? This is found out that these activities are out of synchronization with MNC core competence. (U.S. Department of Commerce, 2002). There is an argument that it offers plenty of opportunities to firms from countries like India. This is right with a short-term perspective in mind. However, over a long duration, this may prove to be a casualty. The software exporting firms from countries like India as well as Business Process Outsourcing contractors will increasingly compete among themselves. This has two negative impacts. (a) The economies of scale will be diminishing from the point of view of service providers like those that Indian IT firms since they are competing among themselves, not with their peers in developed countries, and (b) They will ever remain a low-end service provider.

MANPOWER/ SKILL

The steady supply of qualified software professionals has added to the success of software exporting firms in India. The software industry is characterized by low physical and high human capital intensity (Mowery, 1999). Human capital in software sector encompasses the collective characteristics and abilities of its software professionals: national orientation and traditions, quantity, composition, language skills, and managerial skills.

A sufficiently large pool of skilled manpower is considered to be the most important asset for Indian software industry. Since the present concentration of India's software industry is in the segment of 'services', the role and significance of human capital is crucial.

For any national industry to develop through different stages of maturity there is a need for a balance of entrepreneurial and professional human capital (lyigun and Owen, 1998). Entrepreneurial human capital is the collective capacity of an industry, contributed by the entrepreneurs, to perform unconventional and innovative things that meet the needs and expectations of market (Ojha and Krishna, 2004). They provide an industry with ideas, services and products. Professional human capital refers to the technical capacity of an industry to be involved in a particular technology domain. While entrepreneurs provide some capital and ideas, it is the professional human capital which provides the required know-how and skills.

Entrepreneurial as well as professional human capital have to complement each other for the firms of any industry to succeed in, the role of entrepreneurial human capital is more significant than the professional human capital.

Some studies provide to the importance of cultural capital (Pierre Bourdieu 1977). The author, however, in later years accentuated the importance of economic capital. He categorically declared that the economic capital is more critical than the cultural capital.

In an economy in which economic activity is low, entrepreneurial human capital is critical to initiate economic activity to enable professionals to get gainful employment. The lack of entrepreneurial human capital in the early stages of development is one of the explanations provided for the failure of former East Bloc Economies to develop globally competitive industries despite a highly educated labour force (Ojha and Krishna, 2004). However as economic activity grows, although there will be a growth in the number of entrepreneurs, the ratio of entrepreneurs to professionals normally declines (lyigun and Owen, 1988) and the role of entrepreneurial human capital is less critical.

Much of the success of the software industry in India shall be attributed to the availability of a low cost well qualified workforce that can speak and work in English (Correa, 1996). However, there emerged a number of concerns about the sustainability of Indian software growth. Many reasons are pointed out in this regard. For instance, a substantial part of exports is based on low-end programming (Abraham, Ahlawat and Ahlawat, 1998). The recommendation to the software industry to address many of these concerns is that firms to move up the 'value chain (Abraham, Ahlawat and Ahlawat, 1998; Kumar, 2001). There is significant professional human capital available in India to allow the software industry to move up the value chain. However, there is a dearth of entrepreneurial human capital in India. It prevented India from playing any major role in global industry map, software industry being no exception.

Although India has seen a spurt in the new entrepreneurial ventures, the number of software ventures is still considered to be scarce, in the face of increasing global competition. While software entrepreneurs from India have been successful in Silicon Valley in the US, very few have been returned to India to start firms (Saxenian, 1999). For leading in the next generation software business, the need for human capital-both entrepreneurial and professional is highly required.

As already specified, one major problem faced by Indian software industry is the low-value output. It is felt that programmers are plenty, but the experienced talent in system analysis, networks administration etc. is not found to be encouraging in number. However, the gradual shift from on-site to off-shore development is indicative of greater skill-based activity providing the Indian developers with increased autonomy.

MANAGEMENT

Skills in management are seen as a basic pre-requisite for the success of a business including software industry. The management tasks are critically correlated to not just the marketing activities but extend to a large number of arena like setting up, tunas flow, primary and secondary market activities, innovation, strategy in product/service orientation, diversification, liaison with overseas firms etc.

A core aspect of the management capability is innovation. Innovation is a multifaceted phenomenon covering not only technological innovation but also institutional, organizational, associational, communal, financial and managerial innovations, and their endogenous and exogenous support system. Management capability with a dynamic innovation attitude is vital in different dimensions. It is most important in the sense of creating capability to match technology with specific customer requirements. The task of the management encompasses a whole range of activities like backward integration, core product development, forward integration, after sales service/service-post service etc. The key strategic management tasks are to find and maintain a stable product and/or service niche, find or create new product and/or service niches, and absorb user experience to continue to match technology to user needs and maintain/create stable new product and/or service niches (Sridharan, 2004).

Although management capability is seen as a vital ingredient, different opinions emerged regarding India's potency in this regard. Some studies say that in India, management capability is a weak one. It is argued that many of the existing firms will fail the challenge of moving beyond low--end services (Arora and Arunachalam, 2000). However, they also claim that this should not be a major problem for the industry as a whole because some Indian firms are already looking outside of their boundaries and even outside India to get the managers they need.

It is also pointed out that project management expertise is scarce, in the case of India. It is claimed that it is because the industry is still young in India and large scale projects where project managers who are trained are still relatively rare. This problem is exacerbated by a large number of experienced professionals who emigrate to the U.S.

Management expertise is vital for entrepreneurial ventures to succeed. Management expertise is expected of an entrepreneur. Traditional entrepreneurs were financiers cum managers. However, today's entrepreneur-manager is one who should have awareness as well as experience as regards all the different aspects of a business. This has got special significance in software industry. Prior work experience adds to the management expertise. Lack of experience is a limitation, as indicated by Bhide (2000) and Sanchez and Perez (1998).

Conventional management theories based on studies of large organizations need to be adapted before being applied to entrepreneurial ventures. This implies that while technical knowledge is crucial, managerial knowledge is also essential for the success of a firm, as suggested by Bhide (2000) and Sanchez and Perez (1998).

From the above discussion, it is clear that management task is a multifaceted one. It also has a firm-specific approach. All the different dimensions of the nature of a firm's business, its stated objects, the environment including competition, prospective trends, rapidly changing industry, market and customer behaviour, prospective threats, present and prospective changes in the product line etc. have to be taken into account while devising the management team, management tactics, and management strategy.

MARKETING

Marketing capabilities guide a software firm's growth and development. Not just innovation or quality/credibility helps in a firm's dynamism to development. Marketing expertise is considered to be very important for firm's market penetration. This is particularly important in a world which increasingly embraces globalization. The critical importance of marketing shall be demonstrated through an example. In the early 1980', three operating systems for personal computers existed- CP/M, DOS, and Apple Macintosh. Eventually, Microsoft's DOS became dominant, in part due to its acceptance by IBM, a major manufacturer of personal computers. DOS was not technically the best, but Microsoft became the market leader (Arthur, 1996).

Marketing is crucial in case of a nation like India. This is because majority of its software is export oriented. (John,2004). Marketing limitations always constrain developing software for export. Large-sized firms are always placed safe in this regard on account of their huge potential for liaison building and market capture and the ready availability of funds.

Paucity of funds creates monolithic disaster to firms. Usually high cost is involved in launching a new product in a foreign market. The small software firms who are derelict end up in a complete fiasco in such situations.

Another problem noticed for developing country firms are the lack of proper activism from their foreign partners. In many a circumstance, foreign dealers/ distributors are said to be reluctant in commercializing software from developing country firms.

A weak domestic market is said to be curtailing the prospects of developing software products. There is a wide gap persists between the size of the domestic software market and export market. The domestic market is not a matured and developed market (John, 2004). However, there are other non-technical factors that influence product development (Krishnan and Prabhu, 2004). Most products and applications are off-the--shelf software programs, such as word-processing, financial programs, statistical packages and the like.

The question as to why India is not good at making products has to do with the size of the domestic market (Desai, 2001), which is influenced by the installed base of hardware in the economy and its associated network externalities.

Applications software have a more stable environment with low entry barriers since they are based on standard hardware and operating system platforms (Casper and Glimstedt, 2001). But, at the same time, user Community feed back also directs the application software. There fore Development and expansion of the domestic market will have a favorable impact on software product development. In a global market, collaboration with foreign players is a key for success. Strategic partnership on a macro level helps firms to utilize each others strengths and know-how to improve their scale of innovation, quality standards and market percolation. In India, in recent years, there were signs of overseas collaboration on an increasing scale.

India's software economy is a U.S. driven economy. Most companies focus to expand their business in the U.S. This is evident from the fact that majority of the software export by India firms has been to the U.S. By destination, 68 per cent of software exports went to North America, overwhelmingly to the U.S. 21 per cent to Europe, 2 per cent to Japan, and 10 per cent to the rest of the world (Nasscom, 2003). The relative undue weight age upon Europe and other parts of the world is limiting India's prospects. However, of late, Indian companies have started realizing that to follow a global delivery model; they need to spread across the globe.

The top Indian software companies have realized that to become MNCs in the true sense, they have to be literally spread throughout landscapes. It is being increasingly felt that being present in pockets in the U.S. and U.K. will not fetch the desired targets.

The concept of near shore locations has also entered the outsourcing jargons in the last few years-places in countries close to the actual market being addressed (De, 2005). The near shore centers offer two types of advantages. Primarily, it offers cost advantages over offshore locations in India. The second merit is that the benefits of geographical proximity and cultural similarity often help in business generation.

While Indian software companies have always excelled in onsite and offshore, the onus is now on near shore, primarily by means of establishing development centers and full-fledged business development offices in multiple geographies staffing them with local professionals in the client interfacing team (De, 2005). Thus, in the client interfacing, the staffing of local professionals bears a crucial role. This is a clear hint towards the changing shift in the marketing strategies of Indian software corporate houses.

The novel thinking on the lines of near shore locations is evident from the fact that today a TCS has offices in Budapest or Brasilia or Montevideo

(Uruguay), Wipro in Dubai or Haninge (Sweden) and Kiel (Germany), or an Infosys in Toronto. The U.S.A. still commands the export orientation of Indian software firms. But there is predominantly a European tilt in regard to the establishing near shore location. The researcher feels that this is mainly because Europe is gradually emerging as the market destination for outsourcing.

India predominantly being a software service provider, the marketing expenditure is not analyzed to be a big factor. Selling cost is relevant largely in the case of software products. It has been noted that in the case of software products, large multinational companies dominate the market and spend up to 60-65 per cent of the price component of packages on marketing and distribution (Kumar, 2001). In recent years in India, many Small and Medium Enterprises (SMEs) have come up with a range of products and packages. However, the highly successful packages could be found out to be limited in number.

A relatively high outlay associated with the marketing shall be analyzed to be one of the culprits. However, the share of segment is increasing year on year. As per NASSCOM estimates 50-60 per cent of software industry will be from the SME segment by 2008 (Dataquest,2005). According to Sangeetha Gupta, VP, Nasscom, "70 per cent of NASSCOM's members are SMEs and marketing is their biggest pain point. It is the lack of specialization that is the biggest impediment that SMEs face". (Dataquest, 2005).

When considering the unique nature of Indian market, penetration of technology, increased pace of globalization and faster growth in the economy, the innovation as well as marketing tactics / strategy of the firms need to be re-shaped. New and innovative marketing tools are more relevant in the changing scenario (Mahajan and Wind, 1992). Marketing remains to be a crucial determinant in guiding the volume and orientation of software export of Indian corporate houses.

CREDIBILITY/QUALITY

Credibility and quality are the buzz words of today's industrial world. Competitiveness has become the underlying feature of sustainability today. Quality and the resultant credibility are the sine quo non of an industry's existence and dynamism.

During the last two decades, research on quality management has been showing vibrancy. The evolution of Total Quality Management (TQM) which systemizes management practices, strategy and organizational cut comes to create a quality organization that continuously upgrades and sustains performance, has attracted the attention of top level managers in the manufacturing industry (Samson and Terziovski, 1999). During the last one decade, service industry has also started adopting TQM, having witnessed a dramatic upsurge in the level of competitiveness achieved by TQM organizations in manufacturing. Some studies have been conducted to investigate the relationship between TQM and business performance, and the relationship between quality and productivity (Huff, Fornell and Anderson 1996). Most of these studies were the attempts on quality management in manufacturing and service industries. However, relevant studies on TQM in software industry happened to be very few.

Software industry is growing exponentially all over the world. Present day firms have understood that quality and credibility are the keys to success, competitive advantage and sustainability. Many software development firms from India are obtaining quality certifications such as ISO 9000 or evaluation against the Software Engineers Institute's (SEI), Capability Maturity Model (CMM), to maintain their positions in the global market.

Quality management can be considered to the prime mover for enhanced business performance (CorbettAdam, Adam, Harrison, Rho and Samson, 1998). However, in many cases, top-level executives do not always back TOM unless a correlation between organizational performance and TQM is instituted (Bowles and Hammond, 1991).

Quality has a direct correlation with the success of a firm and the specialization of a country. For instance, Israel has emerged as a source of entrepreneurial firms developing software products in areas such as security and anti-virus technology. This critically explains the scenario that the said country could set quality norms in their specializations viz, security and anti-virus software, and its quality standards are empirically superior to that of other country firms.

The most popular quality certification in India is the ISO 9001 of the International Standards Organization (Radice, 1995). Paulk et al (1993) asserted that many firms hunted for quality certification process developed specifically for software viz; CMM.

CMM model is specifically designed for software and stipulated the standards in different stages of software development that a firm at a given level of maturity must have. ISO certification roughly corresponds to maturity level two in the CMM model (Arora and Arunachalam, 2000).

From a scenario, which speaks that more and more firms are striving to attain quality certifications, it is clear that quality certifications and quality itself are increasingly becoming pertinent for a firm's obtaining of contracts and its business growth strategy. While this being the case there has been contrary resolutions by scholars which note that the correlation between quality and business performance is not as strong as in case of manufacturing industry. Madu, Kuei and Jacob (1996) opined that the correlation between quality management factors and organizational Performance is not strong in service organizations. They argued that unlike a defective product, a substandard quality service cannot be replaced. Some felt that the chief focus of service quality management must be on customers (Schneider and Bowen, 1995).

Issac, Rajendran and Anantharaman (2003) have identified the following as the critical factors of quality management in software development. They are:

(a) Top management commitment and leadership
(b) Organizational Culture (OC)
(c) Customer focus
(d) Process quality management
(e) Quality measures or metrics
(f) Human Resources Management (HRM)
(g) Employee Empowerment
(h) Communication
(i) Continuous Improvement
(j) Benchmarking (BM)
(k) Infrastructure and facilities
(l) Employee Attitude and
(m) Risk management

Issac, Rajedran and Anantharaman (2003) concluded their study with the following observations:

i. Quality has gained acceptance as a key factor that helps organizations to achieve success and competitive edge in the global market.
ii. The quality certified firms have better product attributes and return on quality than the non-certified firms.
iii. There appears to be no difference between non-certified firms and ISO certified firms, where as the CMM highly rated firms are better than non-certified firms and ISO certified firms.
iv. High ratings, such as CMM levels 4 or 5 help software organizations to have superior operational performance relative to ISO 9000 certification.

The researchers of this study feel that the scope of the above said study (Issac, Rajendran and Anantharaman, 2003) is limited since it has ventured only to a limited aspect of searching the differentials in merit scale of two certifications viz. ISO 9000 and CMM. It shall be argued that the elementary students of software industry, even, have well-acknowledged that CMM certifications are much superior to ISO 9000 certification.

In any case, a primary aspect of developing world class products is the establishment of effective quality systems within the product development project and across the organization. Firms like TCS and Infosys have developed specific quality systems for their customized software development projects. However, extending this quality system for their products has been a difficult task (Nambisan, 2001).

The internally developed quality system on the one hand and quality certifications from external agencies on the other hand, serve different purposes. Likewise, it is noted that quality systems for packages are to be different from such a system developed for customized services. Anyhow, quality is the prime parameter for credibility and success of a firm.

COST

Cost is a concept which is vehemently peculiar in case of India's software success. India is known in IT jargons as a country of cost- effectiveness. Managers buying so-called offshore outsourcing services tend to shop for the lowest cost supplier. These costs are driven by the wages of software labor from the junior programmers to the seasoned project managers (Carmel, 2003).

The differences in wage rates are striking and very tempting for IT leaders who are under cost pressures. Along with quality human resources, age differentials are seen to be a comparative advantage which India enjoyed. However, in recent years, wages in India were bid up and India is no longer the lowest cost software nation. Instead, many firms are turning to China, Vietnam, and others where wages may be lower (Carmel, 2003).

Till 2004, the lower cost of labour has been augmented which gave a leverage for India. However, the recent literature shows that the comparative advantage which India enjoyed in low wages is getting mitigated. The vast supply of technology talents in China helps it to keep wage inflation and turnover rates at bay, while higher wage rates have cut into Indian companies' margins. This is termed "race to the bottom" of software exports in services. There is relatively little that nations can do to compete in this cycle in which foreign investment and interest quickly shift to lower wage nations. In the post-war period, industrial manufacturing began shifting to Japan, which then became too expensive, and then it shifted to Korea and Taiwan which then became too expensive, and then it shifted to China, Thailand and elsewhere (Carmel, 2003).

However, it is to be noted here that the qualified software professionals' supply still exceeds its demand and India may still have a call in software services. The pool of IT professionals in India is about 5,22,000 and the total demand is about 4,00,000 (Gartner, 2002). However, India is now counted only one of the destinations where cheap and abundant but inexpensive labour is available.

The Indian software industry faces a number of challenges as the labour cost advantages diminished competition from other countries with supplies of educated and under utilized workers increases (Arora and Arunachalam, 2000). The prime factor behind the current comparative advantage is the relatively low labour cost in India (Mahajan, 2000; Kumar, 2001). But, given the flexible international division of labour, the potential threat of this industry migrating to other countries, in the event of a rise in wage cost cannot be ruled out

(Parthasarathy and Joseph, 2004). Therefore, a dynamism in strategy is needed by embracing innovation based on efficiency thereby replacing the current competition based on labour cost advantage.

While the cost of ICT and software manpower in India is much lower than in developed economies, it is much higher than the prevailing wage rate in other sectors in India. A study notices that the salaries of software personnel have been growing at a rate of 25-30 per cent per annum (Kumar, 2001).

Some totally different aspects of cost are also to be considered. The marginal revenue of Indian software players is lower than that of her counterparts in the developed world. This is partly because a large number of the projects handled by Indian firms are low-end software services.

EXTERNAL FACTORS

External environment influences any system including software. Many external factors guide the growth and development of India's software industry and its export. It is almost difficult to enumerate and elaborate the influence effected by all the different external factors upon the software industry. "Multilateral agreements like GATT/WTO, the pace of industrialization in economies like USA, the periods of boom/depression in the global economy, geographical proximity to certain developed nations, immigration and labour laws of overseas governments etc" shall be counted as some of such factors.

India developed a strong software industry relying on foreign demand in spite of having weak domestic demand for software (Carmel, 2003). This is an important pointer to the fact of a great emphasis the external changes have upon the software business of India.

Important determinants like US visa policy guide the fortunes of Indian players. US policy guidelines on H1B visa is important. The H1B visa (or simply called H1 Visa) is a non-immigrant employment based visa for workers coming to the USA to perform a "specialty-occupation". Starting in the 1990s and continuing to 2001, the tremendous demand for good quality and relatively inexpensive Indian workforce saw body shoppers processing H1B visas with practiced ease (Dataquest, 2005).

Since the Indian software export is heavily U.S. concentric, there is a dire need for Indian players to seek other markets like Europe. Increased concentration on markets other than the U.S. could be noticed these days (Dataquest, 2005).

CULTURAL/NON-ECONOMIC FACTORS

The factors affecting the export system of Indian software are not always necessarily economic in nature. The cultural variables are said to be having a considerable impact upon the emergence as well as the growth of different geographies are different.

"India is not a very assertive culture; Indians tend to go along with what other people say, especially with authority figures" (Nicholson and Sahay 2001).

The cultural lag (Ogburn, 1964) which is created on account of the rapid growth in ICT industry in India and comparatively lower rate of simultaneous growth in non-material culture creates problems in embracing the new technologies. The consumer is a part of the society here. When cultural lag is created, considerable unhealthy environment is also created in societal outlook.

Many studies have been conducted on cultural and political issues in the information systems areas (Giddens, 1990, 1991). The work culture of Indian software professionals is said to be one of "role of discipline" (Nichoilson and Sahay, 2001). The role of non-economic forces could be analyzed - by many scholars. Some important facets of it can be seen in the works of Labor (1996), Wastell (1996), Baskerville, Travis and Truex ˉ992).

The traditional cultural setup directs the logical reasoning of human brain. For example, Nicholson and Sahay (2001) suggest that the 'traditional skilling' help Indians to be mathematically adept and disciplined in their thinking. It is to be argued that the role of non-economic and cultural factors are significant in the growth of an industry like software since this industry is one of the most dynamic industries of the world. Shore and Venkatachalam (1995) discuss the influence of national cultural factors on the approaches to parts of the systems development life style.

Work culture in a scenario of disciplined software development environment is so crucial that it guides both the quality as well as the time frame within which the contract has to be executed and transferred back to the client organization. Hierarchical structuring is so ingrained in India that it is often easier to work in a superior-subordinate role than as equals on contractual terms (Sinha, 1988).

Cultural assimilation and cross-cultural fertilization are also the issues where the norms of the society and the expectations and ethos of people keep changing. The openness to the idea of computerization on a large scale in the economy, for example, may be the result of influence of foreign media. Western mass media bring images, symbols, products and entertainment into developing nations (Hall, 1991; Marin, 1995). The role of cultural or non-economic variables is conspicuous. However, the researcher is constrained here to discuss arid elaborate each and every non-economic variable which are supposed to have a bearing on software development, innovation and software industry, since it is a Herculean task on account of time and space constraints.

Structural Equation Model (SEM)

In the earlier section there had been discussed the application of univariate analysis and its various utilities across a spectrum of factors which correlate with the software industry and export. Although it had been useful for a systematic analysis from the point of view of a confirmatory research analysis, it is perplexed with number of anomalies. It has failed to take into account nonlinearities, correlated independents, measurement error, correlated error terms, multiple latent independents each measured by multiple indicators, and one or more latent dependents also each with multiple indicators. On the other hand, SEM may be used as a more powerful alternative to multiple regression, path analysis, factor analysis, time series analysis and analysis of covariance. That is, these procedures may be seen as special cases of SEM, or to put it another way, SEM is an extension of the general linear model (GLM) of which multiple regression is a part.

SEM includes more flexible assumptions (particularly allowing interpretation even in the face of multicollinearity, use of confirmatory factor analysis to reduce measurement error by including multiple indicators per latent variable. The attraction of SEM's graphical modeling interface, the desirability of testing models overall rather than coefficients individually, the ability to test models with multiple dependents, the ability to model mediating variables, the ability to model error terms, the ability to test coefficients across multiple between-subjects groups, and ability to handle difficult data.

The SEM implies a structure for the covariance between the observed variables, which provides the alternative name covariance structure modeling (Hox and Bechger, 1995). However, the model can be extended to include means of observed variables or factors in the model , which makes covariance structure modeling a less accurate name. Structural equation model is often visualized by a diagram. The statistical model is usually represented in a set of matrix equations. SEM is usually viewed as a confirmatory rather than exploratory procedure, using any one of the following three approaches.

Strictly Confirmatory Approach

A model is tested using SEM goodness-of-fit tests to determine if the pattern of variances and covariances in the data is consistent with a structural (path) model specified by the researcher.

Alternative Models Approach

One may test two or more causal models to determine which has the best fit. There are many goodness-of-fit measures, reflecting different considerations, and usually three or four are reported by the researchers. Although desirable in principle, this approach runs into the real world problem that in most specific research topics areas, the researcher does not find in the literature two well-developed alternative models to test.

Model Development Approach

In practice, much SEM research combines confirmatory and exploratory purposes: a model is tested using SEM procedures, found to be deficient, and an alternative model is then tested based on changes suggested by SEM modification indexes. This is the most common approach found in the literature. The problem with the models confirmed in this manner are post-hoc ones which may not be stable. Researchers may attempt to overcome this problem by using a cross-validation strategy under which the model is developed using a calibration data sample and then confirmed using an independent validation sample.

Mathematically, SEM shall be represented in the following set of equations:

$$\eta = B\eta + (\xi + \zeta\,(mX_1))$$

$$Y = Ay\eta + \varepsilon$$

$$X = Ax\xi + \delta$$

With

$$E(\xi) = 0 \qquad \text{cov}(\zeta) = \psi$$

$$E(\varepsilon) = 0 \qquad \text{cov}(\varepsilon) = \theta\varepsilon$$

$$E(\delta) = 0 \qquad \text{cov}(\delta) = \theta\varepsilon$$

Here ξ, ε are mutually uncorrelated

Cov $(\xi) = \theta$;ξ is uncorrelated with ζ;ε is uncorrelated with η : δ is uncorrelated with ζ; B has zeros on the diagonal; and I-B is nonsingular. In addition to the above assumptions, we take E $(\zeta) = 0$ and E $(\eta) = 0$.

The qualities ζ, η in the first model are the cause-and-effect variables, respectively, and, ordinarily, are not directly observed. They are some times called latent variables. A good discussion on SEM shall be seen in the work of Jorskog and Sorbom (1989). The quantities Y and X are variables that are linearly related to η and ζ through the coefficient matrices Ay and Ax, and these variables can be measured. Their observed values constitute the data.

The structural equation modeling process centres around two steps: (1) validating the measurement model and (2) fitting the structural model. The former is accomplished primarily through path analysis with latent variables. One starts by specifying a model on the basis of theory. Each variable in the model is conceptualized as a latent one, measured by multiple indicators.

Estimation and Model Fit

In SEM, it is usually assumed that the sample data follow a multivariate normal distribution, so that means and covariance matrix contains all the information (Hox and Bechger, 1995). The method most widely used for estimation is Maximum Likelihood (MLE) estimation, which assumes multivariate normal data.

For a given set of data, researcher can suggest a large number of models. The most suitable model can be chosen by applying goodness-of-fit measures. Jaccard and Wan (1996) recommend at least 3 fit tests. Following are some of the important fit tests.

1. *Model Chi Square:* Model Chi-square, also called discrepancy, is the most common fit test. The Chi-square value should be significant if there is a good model fit, while a significant chi-square indicates lack of satisfactory model fit.
2. *Satorra-Bentler Scaled Chi-Square:* This is an adjustment to Chi-square which penalizes Chi-square for the amount of Kurtosis in the data.
3. *Goodness-of-Fit Index* (GFI): It is the per cent of observed covariances explained by the covariances implied by the model. GFI deals with error in reproducing the variance-covariance matrix. GFI should be greater than or equivalent to 0.90 to accept the model.
4. *Adjusted Goodness-of-Fit Index,* AGFI: AGFI is a variant of GFI which uses mean squares instead of total sums of squares. AGFI should be at least 0.90
5. *Root Mean Square Residuals, or RMS Residuals, or RMSR or RMR:* The closer the RMR to 0 for a model being tested, the better the model fit.
6. *Centrality Index, C1:* CI is a function of model Chi-square, degrees of freedom in the model, and sample size. By convention, CI should be 0.90 or higher to accept the model.
7. *Relative Non-Centrality Index, RNI:* It penalizes for sample size as well as model complexity. It should be greater than 0.90 for good fit.
8. *Comparative Fit Index, CFI:* CFI compares the existing model fit with a null model which assumes the latent variables in the model are uncorrelated.
9. *Incremental Fit Index, IFI:* It is also known as DELTA 2. By convention, IFI should be equal to or greater than 0.90 to accept the model.
10. *Parsimony Ratio (PRATIO):* It is the ratio of the degrees of freedom in the model to degrees of freedom in the null model.
11. *Root Mean Square Error of Approximation, RMSEA:* It is also known as RMS or RMSE or discrepancy per degree of freedom. By convention, there is good model fit if RMSEA is less than or equal to 0.05.
12. AIC: It is the Akaike Information Criterion. AIC is a goodness-of-fit measure which adjust model Chi-square to penalize for model complexity.
13. *BIC:* It is the Bayesian Information Criterion. It is also known as Akaike's Bayesian Information Criterion (ABIC) and the Schwarz Bayesian Criterion (SBC). BIC penalizes for sample size as well as model complexity.

A large number other goodness of fit measures are also available. But since explaining all these are practically impossible, the researchers have taken into account only those which are considered to be the most important.

The researchers designed Structural Equation Model (SEM) based on the data obtained from interview method and online survey. The model is drawn using the Analysis of Moment Structures (AMOS 4.0). The model is shown in Figure 2.

For the above model, it is very important to identify how adequately the model reflected the worth and range of data. Here, the Comparative Fit Index is 0.980 which confirms that the model is highly suitable. Also, Incremental Fit Index in the model is 0.980 and Parsimony ratio is 0.910. This shows that the model's acceptability is at the confirmatory level.

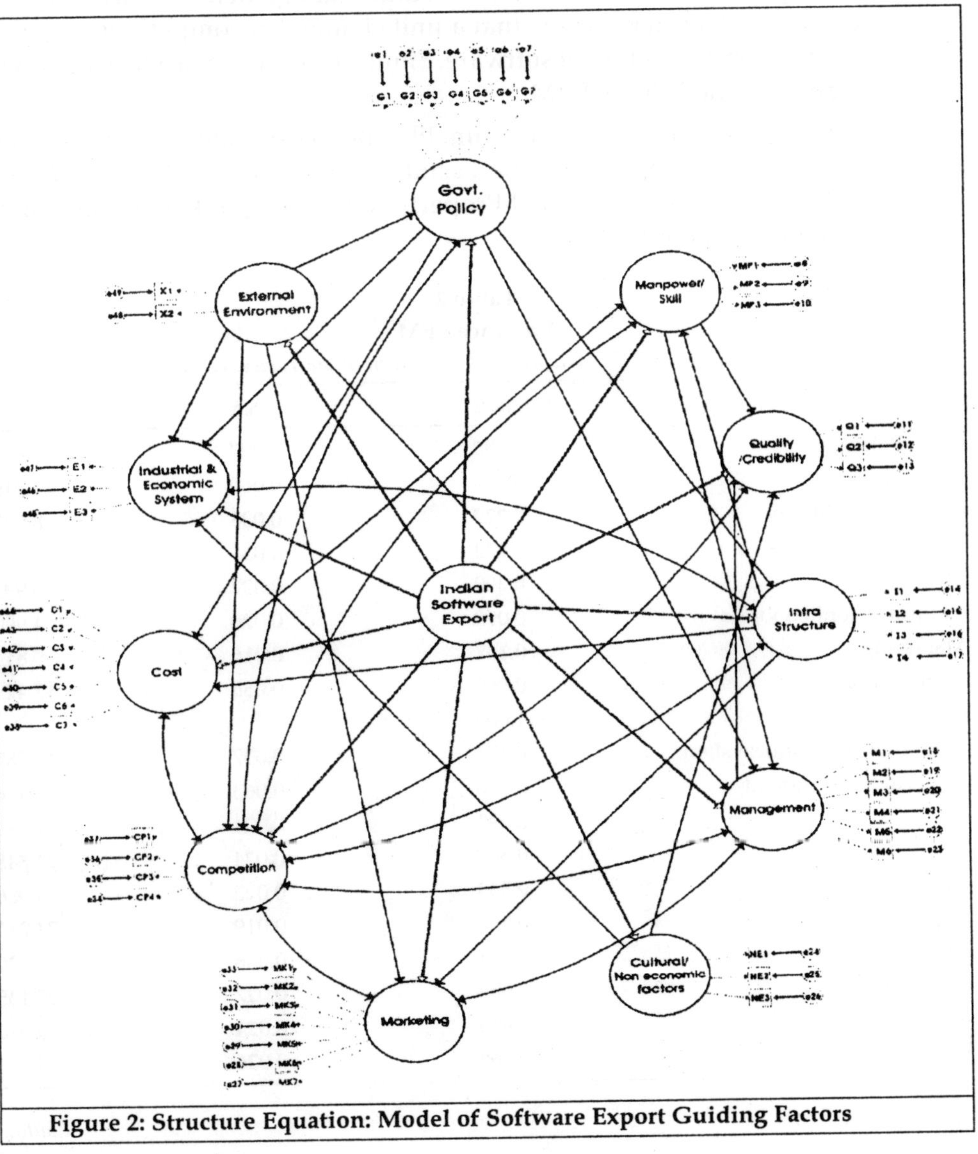

Figure 2: Structure Equation: Model of Software Export Guiding Factors

Root mean square error of approximation (RMSEA) is 0.0490 in the model which claims that the totality of error terms is limited and within the prescribed level. The root mean square error of Approximation (RMSEA) is 0.0490 in the model which claims that the totality of error terms is limited and within the prescribed level.

It is also inferred from Table 1 that Cost, Competition, Manpower, Government Policy and External Environment are having greater impact upon the software export of the country.

From Table 2 it is understood that Competition & Marketing, Government Policy & Competition, Competition & Cost and Management & Marketing are highly correlated. This also means that a unit changes in competition impacts 30 percent effect on marketing of software. Similarly, other covariance relations shall also be explained in the SEM.

The Table 3 discusses the maximum likelihood estimates of all the eleven factors. For instance, Single Window Facility (G7) has a significance of four times the significance of Intellectual Property Rights (G4). Likewise, the other estimates shall also be interpreted.

Table 2
Variance SEM

The out put obtained from the SEM using AMOS is given in the Tables, 2.1, 2.2, 2.3 and 2.4

	Estimate	*S.E*	*C.R*
Govt. Policy	0.592	0.097	6.087
Manpower	0.710	0.062	11.416
Quality/Credibility	0.222	0.028	8.061
In fracture	0.272	0.038	7.174
Management	0.299	0.027	10.993
Cultural/NonEconomic	0.099	0.020	4.990
Marketing	0.157	0.016	9.817
Competition	0.965	0.055	17.429
Cost	1.000		
Industrial/Economicsystem	0.372	0.037	7.287
External Environment	0.610	0.063	8.416
e1	0.593	0.024	24.489
e2	0.600	0.024	24.848
e3	0.543	0.022	24.986
e4	0.465	0.019	24.712
e5	0.664	0.026	25.120
e6	0.680	0.027	25.135
e7	0.613	0.024	25.022
e8	0.668	0.026	25.283

Contd...

	Estimate	*S.E*	*C.R*
e9	0.640	0.025	25.111
e10	0.663	0.026	25.197
e11	0.713	0.028	25.312
e12	0.736	0.029	25.468
e13	0.846	0.033	25.481
e14	0. 770	0.030	25.489
e15	0.799	0.031	25.680
e16	0.716	0.028	25.565
e17	0.703	0.028	25.551
e18	0.708	0.028	25.671
e19	0.842	0.033	25.610
e20	0.938	0.036	25.774
e21	0.642	0.025	25.625
e22	0.661	0.026	25.478
e23	0.691	0.027	25.578
e24	0.975	0.038	25.909
e25	1.314	0.051	26.017
e26	0.417	0.017	24.798
e27	0.426	0.019	22.845
e28	0.398	0.017	23.850
e29	0.957	0.034	21.914
e30	0.395	0.017	23.182
e31	0.715	0.030	23.840
e32	0.858	0.044	23.924
e33	0.278	0.013	20.884
e34	0.584	0.024	23.878
e35	0.664	0.027	24.190
e36	0.411	0.016	25.044
e37	0.388	0.018	21.193
e38	0.398	0.018	21.802
e39	1.104	0.047	23.384
e40	0.744	0.057	13.144
e41	0.819	0.054	15.267
e42	0.813	0.033	17.360
e43	0.958	0.044	21.924
e44	0.673	0.039	17.360
e45	0.844	0.033	25.486
e46	1.258	0.050	25.265
e47	0.760	0.049	15.448
e48	0.985	0.045	21.676
e49	0.844	0.092	9.129

Table 3
Covariance–SEM

	Estimate	*S.E*	*C.R*
Govt. Policy ↔ competition	0.183	0.033	5.490
Manpower ↔ competition	0.068	0.017	4.124
Quality ↔ competition	0.038	0.017	2.253
Infrastructure ↔ Competition	0.095	0.009	2.571
Infrastructure–Industrial Environment	0.019	5.185	0.099
Management ↔ Competition	0.046	0.012	3.782
Management ↔ Marketing	0.119	0.028	4.232
competition ↔ Marketing	0.300	0.026	11.556
Competition ↔ cost	0.162	0.22	7.323

Table 4
Maximum Likelihood Estimates-SEM

Regression Weight	*Estimate*	*S.E*	*C.R*
G1 ← Govt. Policy	1.000		
G 2 ← Govt. Policy	1.098	0.164	6.706
G 3 ← Gov. Policy	0.784	0.051	15.378
G 4 ← Govt. Policy	1.155	0.059	19.549
G 5 ← Govt. Policy	0.441	0.046	9.583
G 6 ← Govt. Policy	0.670	0.072	9.358
G 7 ← Govt. Policy	1.563	0.114	13.742
MP1 ← Man Power	1.000		
MP2 ← Man Power	1.557	0.128	12.193
MP3 ← Man Power	1.103	0.057	19.191
Q1 ← Quality	1.000		
Q2 ← Quality	1.155	0.059	19.549
Q31 ← Quality	0.616	0.043	14.371
I1 ← infrastructure	1.000		
I2 ← infrastructure	0.999	0.060	16.525
I3 ← infrastructure	1.259	0.137	9.210
M1 ← Management	1.000		
M2 ← Management	1.430	0.152	9.394
M3 ← Management	1.307	0.140	9.305
M4 ← Management	1.391	0.149	9.320
M5 ← Management	1.656	0.100	16.523
M6 ← Management	1.379	0.080	17.186
M7 ← Management	1.089	0.089	12.225
NE1 ← Cultural /Non economic	1.000		
NE2 ← Cultural /Non economic	1.234	0.075	16.511
NE3 ← Cultural /Non economic	1.505	0.086	17.449
MK1 ← Marketing	1.806	0.123	14.701
MK2 ← Marketing	0.647	0.035	14.537
MK3 ← Marketing	0.636	0.031	20.664

Contd...

Regression Weight	Estimate	S.E	C.R
MK4 ← Marketing	0.701	0.028	26.314
MK5 ← Marketing	0.728	0.028	26372
MK6 ← Marketing	0.655	0.026	24.773
MK7 ← Marketing	0.710	0.031	22.842
CP1 ← Competition	1.000		
CP2 ← Competition	0.667	0.028	24.224
CP3 ← Competition	0.719	0.028	25.612
CP4 ← Competition	0.720	0.028	25.495
C1 ← Cost	1.000		
C2 ← Cost	0.781	0.030	26.295
C3 ← Cost	0.822	0..031	26.339
C4 ← Cost	0.772	0.029	26.472
C5 ← Cost	0.823	0.030	27.882
C6 ← Cost	0.836	0.029	18.794
C7 ← Cost	0.850	0.029	29.411
E1 ← Industrial Ecosystem	1.000		
E2 ← Industrial Ecosystem	0.758	0.030	24.949
E3 ← Industrial Ecosystem	0.704	0.029	24.100
X1 ← External Environment	1.000		
X2 ← External Environment	0.807	0.029	28.121

Table 5
Summary of Models SEM

Model	NPAR	CMIN	DF	P	CMIN/DF
Default Model	188	5842.832	1351	0.0000	4.325
Saturated Model			1539	0.0000	0
Independence Model	54	223448.185	1485	0.0000	150.470

	DELTA 1	RHO 1	DELTA 2	RHO 2	
Model	NFI	RFI	IFI	TLI	CFI
Default Model	0.74	0.971	0.980	0.978	0.980
Saturated Model	1.000	1.000		1.000	
Independence Model	0.000	0.000	0.000	0.000	0.000

Model	PRATIO	PNFI	PCFI
Default Model	0.910	0.886	0.891
Saturated Model	0.000	0.000	0.000
Independence Model	1.000	0.000	0.000

Model	NCP	LIO 90	HI 90
Default Model	4491.832	4258.766	4731.968
Saturated Model	0.000	0.000	0.000
Independence Model	21963.639	159.517	158.457

Contd...

Model	*FMIN*	*FO*	*LO90*
Default Model	4.200	3.229	3.062
Saturated Model	0.000	0.000	0.000
Independence Model	160.639	159.571	158.457
Model	*RMSEA*	*LO 90*	*HI 90*
Default model	0.049	0.048	0.050
Independence model	0.328	0.327	0.329
Model	*AIC*	*BCC*	*BIC*
Default Model	621.000	8.832	623.000
Saturated Model	307.00	8.000	320.000
Independence Model	223556.185	22.000	356.000
Model	*ECVI*	*LO 90*	*HI 90*
Default Model	4.471	4.303	4.643
Saturated Model	2.213	2.213	2.213
Independence Model	160.716	159.602	161.835
		HOELTER	*HOELTER*
Model		0.05	0.01
Default Model		343	352
Independence Model		10	11

CONCLUSION

The designing of SEM of Software Export Guiding factors has got both theoretical as well practical advantages. The crucial point of significance of this study and model is its ability of quantifying each and very weightage of all the different variables and factors influencing software export and its competitiveness. Also, since the objectivity criteria are maintained, the model conveys a value free approach. The policy makers including government machinery would be at advantage while using this model for future policy decisions, since the relative importance and criticality of all the factors and its variable are detailed in the model.

References

Abraham,T., S. Ahlawat, S. Ahlawat (1998), "The India Option: Perception of Indian Software Solutions." *International Journal of Technology Management*, 15 (6/7): 605-621.

Arora, A. and V. S. Arunachalam (2000), "The Globalization of Software: The Case of the Indian Software Industry: A Report Submitted to the Sloan Foundation." *http;/ www.Scip.stanford.edu/scip/avsgt/how 1197.pf*

Arthur, B. W. (1996), "Increasing Returns and the New world of Business." *Harward Business Review,* 74(4): 100-109.

Avnimelech, G., M. Teubal (2004), "The Indian Software Industry from an Israeli Perspective; a Systems Evolutionary and Policy View. In: India in the Global Software Industry: Innovation, Firm Strategies and Development D'Costa, A.P and E.Sridhran (eds) Palgrave Macmillan, Hamsphire.

A.T. Kearney (2004), 'At Kearney's Offshore Location Attractiveness Index." *www.atkearny.com*

Baskerville, R., J. Travis, D. Truex (1992), "Systems Without Method: the Impact of New Technologies Information Systems Development Projects." In K.E.

Bhide, A.V. (2000), "The Origin and Evolution of New Business;" Oxford University Press, New York.

Bowles, J., J. Hammond (1991), "Beyond Quality: New Standards of Total Performance that can Change the Future of Corporate America, Berkley Books, New York.

Cabral, R. (1998), "From University-Industry Interfaces to the making of a Science Part: Florianopolis, Southern Brazil." *International Journal of Technology Management,* 16 (8): 778-799.

Camel, E. (2003), "The New Software Exporting Nations; Success Factors." *The Electronic Journal on Information Systems in Developing Countries,* 13(4): 1-12.

Camel, E. & P. Tija (2005), "Off Shoring Information Technology: Sourcing and Outsourcing to a Global Work Force, Cambridge. University Press, London.

Casper, S., H. Glimstedt (2001), "Economic Organization, Innovation Systems, and the Internet." *Oxford Review of Economic Policy,* 17 (2): 265-281.

Chakraborthy, C., D. Dutta (2002), "Indian Software Industry: Growth Patterns, Constraints and Government Initiatives" *http:/rspas.anu.edu.au/papers/asarc/chakraborty.pdf*

Chen, C. C., P. G. Greenee, A. Crick (1988), "Does Entrepreneurial Self-Efficacy Distinguish Entrepreneurs from Managers?" *Journal of Business Venturing,* 13: 295-316.

Corbett, L. M., E. E.Adam, J. J. Harrisons, T. S. Lee, B. H. Rho, D. Samson (1998), " A Study on Quality Management Practices and Performance in Asia and South Pacific." *International Journal of Production Research,* 36(9): 2597-2607.

Cleetus, K. J. (1984), "Is Software an Industry in India?" Data Quest: May, 37-39.

D'Costa, A. (2000), "Capitalist Maturity and Corporate Responses of Economic Liberalization in India: the Steel, Auto, and Software Sectors." Contemporary South Asia, 9 (2): 141-163.

D'Costa, A. P. (2004), "The Indian Software Industry in the Global Division of labor. In: India in the Global Software Industry; Innovation, Firm Strategies and Development. D'Costa, A.p. And E. Sridharan (eds) Palgrave Macmillan, Hampshire.

De, R. (2005), "Globetrotting." Dataquest, XXIII (12): 54-60.

De R. (2005), "IT: An Opportunity for India and Canada."*www.atkearney.com.*

Dedrik, J., K. L. Kraemer (1998), "Asian's Computer Challenge: Threat or Opportunity for the United States and the World? Oxford University Press, New York.

Desai, A. V. (2001), "The Peril and the Promise: Broader Implications of the Indian Presence in Information Technologies." Workshop on lthe Indian Software Industry in a Global Context, India Institute of Management, Ahmedabad, India.

Dataquest Various issues.

Durkheim, E. (1933), "The Division of Labor in Society, Translated by George Simpson, The Free Press, New York.

Evans, P. (1995), "Embedded Autonomy: States and Industrial Transformation, Princeton University Press, Princeton."

Eindor,P. E. S., M. Orgad (1992)," The Effect of National Culture on IS; Implications for International Information Systems." *Journal of Global Information Magement,* (1):33-44

Feketekuty, G., J. D. Aronson (1994), "Management Decision." U. S. National Competitiveness, Council, 32(2), pp. 49.

Garry, G. C. (1999), "Offshore Programmers: The Wave of the Future? Performance Computing 17(5): 14-19.

Gartner (2002), "Comparison: Indian and Chinese Software Services Markets." Gartner Research, M-16-1762 May 2002.

Gibson, D. V. Rogers, E. M. (1994), R & D Collaboration on Trial: The Microelectronics and Computer Technology Consortia, Harvard Business School Press Boston, M.A.

Giddens, A. (1990), "Consequences of Modernity, Oxford; Blackwell.

Gideens, A. (1991), "Modernity and Self Identity, Cambridge; Polity.

Gupta.,U. & V. Raval (1999), "Critical Success Factors for Anchoring Offshore Projects." *Information Strategy,* 15 (2): 21-27.

Hall, S. (1991), "The Local and the Global: Globalization and Ethnicity," In a K. King (ed): Culture, Globalization and the World System, Macmillan, London: 19-40.

Hatcher, L. (1994), "A Step-by-step Approach to Using the SAS System for Factor Analysis and Structural Equation Modeling. Cary, NC: SAS Institute.

Heeks, R. (1996), "India's Software Industry; State Policy, Liberalization and Industrial Development, Sage Publications, New Delhi.

Heeks, R. & B. Nicholson (2002), "Software Export Success Factors and Strategies in Developing and Transitional Economies" University of Manchester, Institute for Development Policy and Management. Paper No. 2002:12

Hoogvelt, A. (2001), "Globalization and the Post Colonial World: The New Political Economy of Development, John Hopkins University Press, Baltimore, M.D.

Hox, J. J., T. M. Bechger (1995), "An Introduction to Structural Equation Modeling." *Family Science Review,* 11, 354-373.

Huff, L. C. F., E. Anderson (1996), "Quality and Productivity: Contradictory and Complementary: *Quality Management Journal,* 4: 22-39.

Issac, G., C. Rajendran, R. N. Ananthraman (2003), "Do Quality Certifications Improve the Software Industry's Operational Performance?"

Jaccard, J., C. K. Wan (1996), LISERL Approaches to Interaction Effects in Multiple Regression. Thousand Oaks, C.A: Sage Publications.

John, T. H. (2004)," Low Profile Domestic Software Market- A study of India's Case." *Science and Society,* 2(2): 57-64

Jorskong, K. G., D. Sorbom (1998), "LISREL 7: A Guide to the Programme and Applications. Chicago: SPSS.

Kern, T., & L. Silva (1998)," Mapping the Areas of Potential Conflict in the Management of Information Technology Outsourcing". In: W. R. J. Baets Proceedings of the 6th European Conference on Information Systems." Granada, Spain, 612-627.

Kumar, N. (2001), "Indian Software Industry Development: International and National Perspective." *Economic and Political Weekly,* 36 (44): 4278-4290.

Lacity, M. & R. Hirschheim (1993)," Information Systems Outsourcing: Myths, Metaphors an Realities, Chichester: Wiley.

Madu, C. N., C. H. Kuei, R. A. Jacop (1996), "An Empirical Assessment of the Influence of Quality Dimensions in Organizational Performance," *International Journal of Production Research,* 34(7): 1943-1962.

Mahajan, V., J. Wind (1992), "New Product Models: Practice, Shortcomings and Desired Improvements," *Journal of Product Innovatin Management*, 128-139.

Manimala, M. J., S. Prakhya, M. Y. Gopal, J. Shelds (2001), " Global Entrepreneurship Monitor: India Report (2001) Bangalore; Raghavan Centre for Entrepreneurial Learning, Indian Institute of Management)

Martinsons, M. G. (1998)," Hong Kong Government Policy and Information Technology Innovation: the Invisible Hand, the Helping Hand, and the Hand-Over to China." IEEEE Transitions of Engineering Management, 45(4): 366-380.

Mehta, D. (1999), "Indian Software; The Emerging Software Superpower." *Forbes Global Business and Finance*, January 11.

Millar, J. (1999), "Software Tele Trade in Bangalore: The Case Study for Sustainability" *http:www.intech.unu.edu/progam/proj9899/telework.htm.*

Montealegre, R. (1999), "A Temporal Model of Institutional Interventions for Information Technology Adoption in Less-Developed Countries." *Journal of Management Information Systems*, 16(1): 207-232.

Nambisan, S. (2001), "Why Services Business are Not Product Business? Sloan Management Review (Summer): 72-80

NASSCOM 2003.

Nicholson, B., S. Sahay (2003), "Building Iran's Software Industry: An Assessment of Plans and Prospects." *Electronic Journal on Information Systems in Developing Countries*, 13(6): 1-19

Ojha, A. K. & S. Krishna (2004)," Originative Innovation and Entrepreneurship in the Software Industry in India. In: India in the Global Software Industry: Innovation, Firm Strategies and Development D'costa, A.P. and E. Sridharan (Eds) Palgrave Macmillan, Hampshire.

Ogburn, W. F. (1964), "On Culture and Social Change Otis Dudley Duncan (ed), Phoenix Books, University of Chicago Press, Chicago.

Okhi, H. (2001), "International Division of Labur in East Asia's IT Industry." In M. Kagami, and M. Tsuji, The IT Revolution and Developing Countries: Late-comer Advantage? , Tokyo: Institute of Developing Economies, Japan External Trade Organization, 63-91.

Parthasarathy, B. (2004), "Globalizing Information Technology: The Domestic Policy Context for India's Software Production and Exports; iteration: an Interdisciplinary Journal of Software History:, The Charles Babbage Institute for the History of Information Technology, MN, USA.

Parthsarathy, A., K. J. Joseph (2004), "Innovation under Export Orientation. In India in the Global Software Industry; Innovation, Firm Strategies and Development D' Costa, A.P. an E. Sridhran (eds.), Pal grave Macmillan , Hampshire.

Paulk, M. C., B. Curtis: M. B. Chrissis, C. V. Weber (1993), "Capability Maturity Model for Software." Version 1.1 (CMU/SEI-93-TR-24, ADA 263403) Pittsburgh, PA: Software Engineering Institute, Carnegie Mellon University.

Pohjola, M. (1998), "Information Technology and Economic Development: An Introduction to the Research Issues. Working paper No. 153, UNU/WIDER.

Porter, A. K., J. D. Roessner; X. Jin, N. C. Newman (2001), "Changes in National Technological Competitiveness, 1990, 1993, 1996, 1999, Technology Analysis and Strategic Management", 13 (4):477-495.

Samson, D., M. Terziovski (1999), "The Relationship between Total Quality Management Practices and Operational Performance." *Journal of Operations Management*, (17): 393-409.

Sanchez, A. M., O. U. Perex (1998), "Entrepreneurship Networks and High Technology Firms: The Case of Aragon.." *Technovation,* 18(5): 335-345.

Saxenian, A. (2004), "The Silicon Valley Connecting: Transnational Netwroks and Regional Development in Taiwan, China and India. In: India in the Global Software Industry: Innovation, Firms Strategies and Development D'Costa, A. P. and E. Sridharan (Eds) Pl grave Macmillan, Hampshire.

Schneider, B., D. E. Bowen (1995), "The Service Organization: Human Resources Management is Crucial." *Organizational Dynamics,* (21): 39-52.

Roy, P. K. (2002), Beyond Tomorrow: Foundation and Empire." *Dataquest,* XX: 26-28.

Singhal, A. & Rogers E. M. (2001), India's Communication Revolution: From Bullock Carts to Cyber Marts, Sage Publications, New Delhi.

Schware, R. (1992), "Software Industry Entry Strategies for Developing Countries". World Development, 20 (2): 143-164.

Sinha, D. (1998), "Basic Indian Values and Dispositions in the Context of National Development." In D.Sinha and H.Kao (ed), Social Values and Development Asian Perspectives, Sage, New Delhi, 31-55.

Singhal, V. K. (1998), "Computer Manpower for India" CSI Communications, 8(88): 15-20.

Sridharan, E. (1989), "World Trends and India's Software Products." Dataquest.

Sridharan, E. (2004), "Evolving Towards Innovation? The Recent Evolution and Future Trajectory of the Indian Software Industry. In D'Costa *et al.*

Tandon, A. e.a. (1990), "Indian IT: High Tech Spree, and Still a Seller's Market" Data Quest November, 56-63.

Varma,Y. (2005), "Industry Overview: Indian IT Key Events." *Dataquest,* XXXII(13): 28

Wastell, D. (1996), "The Fetish of Technique; Methodology as a Social Defense." *Information Systems Journal,* 6: 25-40.

FOREIGN EXCHANGE

MADHULIKA SINHA*

INTRODUCTION

International trade and investment would be impossible without the mechanism for buying and selling foreign currencies. The foreign exchange market is a necessary constituent to international transactions.

Foreign Exchange in the Indian Context

According to Foreign Exchange Regulation Act (FERA), 1973, foreign exchange means foreign currency and it includes all deposits, credits and balances payable in any foreign currency and any drafts, traveller's cheques expressed or drawn in Indian currency but payable in any foreign currency. The market in which national monetary units are exchanged for the foreign monetary units is known as the foreign exchange market. This market facilitates the transfer of purchasing power denominated in one currency to another.

GLOBAL FOREIGN EXCHANGE MARKET

It is one of the oldest, biggest, most extensive, most active and fastest growing markets in the world. It is an informal, electronically linked network of big banks, foreign exchange brokers and dealers. It is dispersed throughout the big and small financial centres in the world, the leading ones in New York, London, Zurich, Paris, Tokyo, Milan and Frankfurt. The trading in these markets is done 24 hours a day through telephones, display monitors, fax machines and satellite communications network.

STRUCTURE OF FOREIGN EXCHANGE MARKET (FEM)

It has two parts:

(a) *Wholesale Market:* This market is an inter-bank market in which major banks trade in currencies held in different currency dominated bank accounts, i.e., they transfer bank deposit from seller's to buyer's

* *Faculty, MSB, Pune.*

accounts. In this market, only the head offices and regional offices of the major commercial banks are the players.

(b) *Retail Market:* In this market, the exchange of bank notes, bank drafts, currency, ordinary and traveller's cheques between private customers, tourists and banks takes place.

EXCHANGE RATES

The exchange rate (ER) is the price of one country's currency in terms of another country's currency. ER is determined by the government and Central Bank (CB) which use certain methods for fixing it. The demand and supply of currency is adjusted to ensure that the ER stays at or near the rate fixed by them.

The main factors which influence the ER are:

(a) growth in GDP,

(b) Inflation

(c) Interest rates

(d) Foreign Debt

(e) Terms of trade

(f) Rates of profit

(g) Money supply

(h) Risk

RECENT DEVELOPMENTS IN FOREIGN EXCHANGE MARKET

The three major participants in FEM are:

(a) Central Banks,

(b) Commercial Banks, and

(c) Corporations.

Merchant Transactions: The large commercial banks make the market by trading with each other, they provide FEM with continuity. Banks buy/sell foreign exchange from/to exporters, importers and other customers.

Inter-bank transaction: In this, one bank buys/sells foreign exchange from/to another bank.

Overseas transaction: In this, the bank buys/sells foreign exchange in the overseas market.

In India, FEM is a four-tier structure comprising:

(a) Reserve Bank of India (RBI) at the apex,

(b) Authorised dealers licensed by the RBI,

(c) Customers such as exporters, importers, corporate, etc.

(d) Foreign exchange money changers who bring buyers and sellers together.

Foreign Exchange Management Strategy

(a) Short-term debt management,

(b) Earning adequate foreign exchange

(c) Creating market based exchange regime

(d) Encouragement of equity rather than debt in the capital inflows,

(e) Liberalisation of import of gold,

(f) Checking rupee appreciation and encouraging orderly depreciation of rupee,

(g) Regular purchase of dollars from the market by the RBI to ensure that the value of dollar did not fall against the rupee.

ROLE OF RBI

The RBI very often intervenes in the foreign exchange market to stabilize the value of rupee against foreign currencies. Intervention is the sale and purchase of foreign currencies in the foreign exchange market. The RBI's intervention in the foreign exchange market could be either passive (it engages off-market deals) or active (it purchases and sells dollars). It may also change domestic interest rates.

FOREIGN EXCHANGE RESERVES (FERs)

It has increased substantially in the recent years and they are now among one of the largest in the world. The volume of a country's FER is an indicator of its health and high levels of FERs is considered a good sign of economy of a country.

The high level of FERs in India reflects the achievement of reforms, India's ability to maintain the country's monetary stability and meet financial obligations, India's ability to import more goods, to absorb the uncertainties in the world economy, her ability to cope up with crisis. High level of FERs means greater availability of liquidity and finer terms on debt.

The adverse impact of very high level of FERs is that their maintenance or holding is costly. High FERs have increased the interest burden of the economy, because a large part of them are in the form of NRI deposits.

WHY WE NEED FOREIGN EXCHANGE?

Almost every nation has its own national currency or monetary unit—its dollar, its franc, its rupee—used for making and receiving payments within its own borders. But foreign currencies are usually needed for payments across national borders. Thus, in any nation whose residents conduct business abroad or engage in financial transactions with people in other countries, there must be a mechanism for providing access to foreign currencies, so that payments can be made in a form acceptable to foreigners. In other words, there is need for "foreign exchange" transactions—exchanges of one currency for another.

WHAT FOREIGN EXCHANGE MEANS?

"Foreign exchange" refers to money denominated in the currency of another nation or group of nations. Any person who exchanges money denominated in his own nation's currency for money denominated in another nation's currency acquires foreign exchange. That holds true whether the amount of the transaction is equal to a few dollars or to billions of dollars; whether the person involved is a tourist cashing a traveler's check in a restaurant abroad or an investor exchanging hundreds of millions of dollars for the acquisition of a foreign company; and whether the form of money being acquired is foreign currency notes, foreign currency denominated bank deposits, or other short-term claims denominated in foreign currency. A foreign exchange transaction is still a shift of funds, or short-term financial claims, from one country and currency to another. Thus, within the United States, any money denominated in any currency other than the U.S. dollar is "foreign exchange." Foreign exchange can be cash, funds available on credit cards and debit cards, traveler's checks, bank deposits, or other short-term claims. It is still "foreign exchange" if it is a short-term negotiable financial claim denominated in a currency other than the U.S. dollar. Foreign exchange transactions almost always take the form of an exchange of bank deposits of different national currency denominations. If one bank agrees to sell dollars for Deutsche marks to another bank, there will be an exchange between the two parties of a dollar bank deposit for a DEM bank deposit.

STRUCTURE OF FOREIGN EXCHANGE MARKET

The foreign exchange market is by far the largest and most liquid market in the world. The estimated worldwide turnover is several times the level of turnover in the U.S. Government securities market, the world's second largest market. The breadth, depth, and liquidity of the market are truly impressive. Individual trades of $200 million to $500 million are common. Quoted prices change as often as 20 times a minute. It has been estimated that the world's most active exchange rates can change up to 18,000 times during a single day. Large trades can be made, yet studies indicate that prices tend to move in relatively small increments, a sign of a smoothly functioning liquid market. While turnover of around $1½ trillion per day is a good indication of the level of activity and liquidity in the global foreign exchange market, it is not necessarily a useful measure of other forces in the world economy. Almost two-thirds of the total represents transactions among the reporting dealers themselves – with only one-third accounted for by their transactions with financial and non-financial customers. The result is that the amount of trading with customers of a large dealer institution active in the interbank market often accounts for a very small share of that institution's total foreign exchange activity.

Among the various financial centers around the world, a large amount of foreign exchange trading takes place in the United Kingdom, even though their currency, the pound is less widely traded in the market. The large volume of trading activity in the United Kingdom reflects London's strong position as an international financial center where a large number of financial institutions are located.

IT IS A TWENTY FOUR HOUR MARKET

The twenty-four hour market means that exchange rates and market conditions can change at any time in response to developments that can take place at any time. It also means that traders and other market participants must be alert to the possibility that a sharp move in an exchange rate can occur during an off hour, elsewhere in the world. The large dealing institutions have adapted to these conditions, and have introduced various arrangements for monitoring markets and trading on a twenty-four hour basis.

However, foreign exchange activity does not flow evenly. During the course of a day, there is a cycle characterized by periods of very heavy activity and other periods of relatively light activity. Most of the trading takes place when the largest number of potential counterparties is available or accessible on a global basis. Market liquidity is of great importance to participants. Sellers want to sell when they have access to the maximum number of potential buyers, and buyers want to buy when they have access to the maximum number of potential sellers. Business is heavy when both the U.S. markets and the major European markets are open—that is, when it is morning in New York and afternoon in London. In the New York market, nearly two-thirds of the day's activity typically takes place in the morning hours. Activity normally becomes very slow in New York in the mid- to late afternoon, after European markets have closed and before the Tokyo, Hong Kong, and Singapore markets have opened.

MARKET IS COMPOSED OF INTERNATIONAL NETWORK OF DEALERS

The market consists of a limited number of major dealer institutions that are particularly active in foreign exchange, trading with customers and often with each other. Most are commercial banks and investment banks. These dealer institutions are geographically dispersed, located in various financial centers around the world. Wherever located, these institutions are linked to, and in close communication with, each other through electronic means, telephones, computers, etc.

Foreign exchange trading takes place among dealers and other market professionals in a number of individual financial centers—New York, Chicago, Los Angeles, London, Tokyo, Singapore, Frankfurt, Paris, Zurich, Milan, and many others. But no matter in which financial center a trade occurs, the same currencies, or rather, bank deposits denominated in the same currencies, are being bought and sold. A foreign exchange dealer buying dollars in one of those markets actually is buying a dollar-denominated deposit in a bank located in the United States, or a claim of a bank abroad on a dollar deposit in a bank located in the United States. This holds true regardless of the location of the financial center at which the dollar deposit is purchased. Similarly, a dealer buying

Deutsche marks, no matter where the purchase is made, actually is buying a mark deposit in a bank in Germany or a claim on a mark deposit in a bank in Germany. And so on for other currencies. Each nation's market has its own infrastructure. For foreign exchange market operations, each country enforces its own laws, banking regulations, accounting rules, and tax code, and it operates its own payment and settlement systems. Thus, even in a global foreign exchange market with currencies traded on the same terms simultaneously in many financial centers, there are different national financial systems and infrastructures through which transactions are executed, and within which currencies are held. With access to all of the foreign exchange markets generally open to participants from all countries, and with vast amounts of market information transmitted simultaneously and almost instantly to dealers throughout the world, there is an enormous amount of cross-border foreign exchange trading among dealers as well as between dealers and their customers. At any moment, the exchange rates of major currencies tend to be virtually identical in all of the financial centers where there is active trading.

DOLLAR IS THE MOST WIDELY TRADED CURRENCY

The dollar is by far the most widely traded currency. The widespread use of the dollar reflects its substantial international role as: "investment" currency in many capital markets, "reserve" currency held by many central banks, "transaction" currency in many international commodity markets, "invoice" currency in many contracts, and "intervention" currency employed by monetary authorities in market operations to influence their own exchange rates. In addition, the widespread trading of the dollar reflects its use as a "vehicle" currency in foreign exchange transactions, a use that is reinforced by, its international role in trade and finance. For most pairs of currencies, the market practice is to trade each of the two currencies against a common third currency as a vehicle, rather than to trade the two currencies directly against each other. The vehicle currency used most often is the dollar.

Most Traded Currencies

Rank	*Currency*	*(Symbol)*
1	United States dollar	USD ($)
2	Euro	EUR (€)
3	Japanese yen	JPY (¥)
4	Pound sterling	GBP (£)
5	Swiss franc	CHF (Fr)
6	Australian dollar	AUD ($)
7	Canadian dollar	CAD ($)
8-9	Swedish krona	SEK (kr)
8-9	Hong Kong dollar	HKD ($)
10	Norwegian krone	NOK (kr)
11	New Zealand dollar	NZD ($)
12	Mexican peso	MXN ($)
13	Singapore dollar	SGD ($)
14	South Korean won	KRW (₩)

Top 10 Currency Traders[1]

Rank	*Name*
1	Deutsche Bank
2	UBS AG
3	Barclays Capital
4	Citi
5	Royal Bank of Scotland
6	JP Morgan
7	HSBC
8	Lehman Brothers
9	Goldman Sachs
10	Morgan Stanley

Source: [1]Euromoney FX survey FX Poll 2008: The Euromoney FX survey is a global poll of foreign exchange service providers.

References

1. Managing Global Financial and Foreign Exchange Rate Risk by Ghassem Homaifar.
2. The Foreign Exchange Market–Theory and Econometric Evidence by Baillie, Mc Mahon.

MEASUREMENT OF SERVICE QUALITY MEASUREMENT IN ICICI INSURANCE SECTOR

V. Sampath* & K. Rajamani**

INTRODUCTION

Initial efforts in defining and measuring service quality emerged from the product quality and customer satisfaction literature, particularly the disconfirmation paradigm employed in the physical goods literature (Cardozoo 1965; Churchill and Surprenant 1982; Howard and Sheth 1969; Oliver 1977; Olshavsky and Miller 1972; Olson and Dover 1976). Disconfirmation paradigm maintains that satisfaction is related to the size and direction of the disconfirmation experience, where disconfirmation is related to the person's initial expectations. This framework provides grounding for the vast majority of satisfaction studies and encompasses four constructs: expectations, performance, disconfirmation, and satisfaction. Disconfirmation arises from discrepancies between prior expectations and perceived actual performance. There are three possibilities of disconfirmation: zero disconfirmation, when there is no difference between expectation and performance; positive disconfirmation, when performance exceeds expectation and negative disconfirmation, when performance falls short of expectations.

On the basis of exploratory study that constituted executive interviews and focus group interviews, Parasuraman, Ziethaml and Berry (1985) suggested ten key categories into which consumer's evaluation of service quality fell, regardless of the type of service. These categories were labelled as service quality dimensions by them. Parasuraman et al.(1988) later conceptualised a five dimensional model of service quality in which these ten dimensions were refined into five global dimensions: reliability, responsiveness, empathy, assurance and tangibility.

Reliability refers to delivering on promises, responsiveness means being willing to help the customer, assurance refers to inspiring trust and confidence in customers by the employees of the service provider, empathy means treating

* Professor & Reader in Commerce, Yadava College, Madurai.

** Lecturer/MBA, Velammal College of Engineering, Chennai, E-mail: rajamaniravi@yahoo.com

customers individually while tangibles represent the physical aspects of service. Their SERVUQL measurement model (Parsuraman et al. 1988) is based on this five dimensional model of service quality. It computes gap between the expected level of service and the actual performance of the service, based on the disconfirmation paradigm.

RESEARCH OBJECTIVES

- To design a conceptual model linkage between RATER dimensions and satisfaction (SAT) of ICICI.
- To determine the service gap between the service quality dimensions of ICICI Life Insurance Co Ltd in Virudhunagar taluk.
- To suggest the way to improve service quality of the ICICI Life Insurance Co Ltd.

HYPOTHESIS DEVELOPMENT

H_1: There is no significance difference between over all service quality and Education Qualification of internal customer.

H_2: There is no relationship between the Perception & Expectation mean of RATER dimensions

H_3: There is no relationship between the Perception mean & Gap Scores of RATER dimensions

H_4: There is no relationship between the Expectation mean & Gap Scores of RATER dimensions.

RESEARCH METHODOLOGY

The primary data was collected from Chennai city of Tamil Nadu by personally administering the questionnaire. The data was collected in the month of April to June 2008. The population consider for the research is Non probability technique and meanwhile multiple stage sampling procedure was used. In the first stage, data was collected on convenience and judgment sampling techniques. In the second stage, techniques of area sampling and systematic sampling on one hand and mall intercept type on the other hand were used. The final sample consisted of 200 from usable questionnaires. For analyzing the primary data, we used softwares AMOS 7.1 & SPSS 15 Version. The statistical tools used to interpret data are as follows SEM (Structural Equation Model), Path analysis, Reliability analysis, Factor analysis, Correlation, Chi-Square Test, ANOVA, Cross tabulation, Percentage method. Depth interviews were conducted with the Internal Customers (Agents) of the target population to elicit items for outcome quality. The respondents were asked about their perceptions of quality of services, which they had received from their service provider. They were asked about their expectations from these services. The items that measured the same construct as

SERVQUAL items were discarded. The remaining items were collected separately and sorted into different outcome quality dimensions. On the basis of comments of some service quality academicians, the number of items was further reduced and refined.

MEASUREMENT OF EXTERNAL SERVICE QUALITY

SERVQUAL scale developed by Parasuraman, Ziethaml and Berry measures service quality along five dimensions of reliability, responsiveness, assurance, empathy and tangibles with 22 items. The scale measures perception of service performance, the minimum expectation level of service quality and the desired level of service quality. The perception of service quality is computed by the gap scores of perceptions and expectations. The scale has been attacked for its gap scores and the five dimensional structure. The gap scores have been defended for their diagnostic value - to find out the service quality components that need improvement (Jain and Gupta 2004, Parasuraman, Zeithaml and Berry 1994a, 1994b). Perception only measures fail to highlight any deficiency in service quality vis-a-vis the desired expectations. Only through a comparison of the perceptions with expectations, a firm can reach at a conclusion as to which service quality dimension it should focus upon for further improvement. Two columns SERVQUAL scale (Zeithaml et al., 1996) supplemented with self-generated outcome quality items is used to capture different dimensions of service quality. The scale contains 22 pairs of Likert-type items.

PRE-TEST QUESTIONNAIRE

The pilot study was carried out among the thirty customers (Internal Customers: Agents) was surveyed for pre-testing the questionnaire. The final questionnaire was arrived at after making the necessary corrections. SERVQUAL questionnaire was (22 items) tested by using Reliability Analysis by using SPSS 15 Version. The Cronpha Alpha value is calculated for the Perception & Expectation of Questionnaire which is listed below.

Reliability Analysis-SCALE (ALPHA)

Perception

Reliability Coefficients: N of Cases = 172.0 N of Items = 22 Alpha = .9053

Expectation

Reliability Coefficients: N of Cases = 172.0 N of Items = 22 Alpha = .8812

Inference: The SERVQUAL Questionnaire (Contained 22 items) was tested by Reliability Analysis by using SPSS 15, Cronpha Alpha value is 0.9053 & 0.8812. As per reliably norms, the Cronpha Alpha value should be effective when it is greater than 0.7.

STRUCTURAL EQUATION MODEL (SEM)

Structural Equation Modeling (SEM) is a statistical technique for testing and estimating causal relationships using a combination of statistical data and qualitative causal assumptions. This view of SEM was articulated by the geneticist Sewall Wright (1921), the economists Trygve Haavelmo (1943) and Herbert Simon (1953), and formally defined by Judea Pearl (2000) using a calculus of counterfactuals. SEM encourages confirmatory rather than exploratory modeling; thus, it is suited to theory testing rather than theory development. It usually starts with a hypothesis, represents it as a model, operationalises the constructs of interest with a measurement instrument, and tests the model. The causal assumptions embedded in the model often have falsifiable implications which can be tested against the data. With an accepted theory or otherwise confirmed model, SEM can also be used inductively by specifying the model and using data to estimate the values of free parameters. Often the initial hypothesis requires adjustment in light of model evidence, but SEM is rarely used purely for exploration. Among its strengths is the ability to model constructs as latent variables (variables which are not measured directly, but are estimated in the model from measured variables which are assumed to 'tap into' the latent variables). This allows the modeler to explicitly capture the unreliability of measurement in the model, which in theory allows the structural relations between latent variables to be accurately estimated. In SEM, the qualitative causal assumptions are represented by the missing variables in each equation, as well as vanishing covariance among some error terms.

PROPOSED CONCEPTUAL MODEL

SEM was articulated by the geneticist Sewall Wright (1921), the economists Trygve Haavelmo (1943) and Herbert Simon (1953), and formally defined by Judea Pearl (2000) using a calculus of counterfactuals. SEM encourages confirmatory rather than exploratory modeling, thus it is suited to theory testing rather than theory development. It usually starts with a hypothesis, represents it as a model, operationalises the constructs of interest with a measurement instrument, and tests the model. This model is designed with the mediating dimension tangible which is compared with the RATER dimensions on SAT. Goldberger (1973) outlined three situations in which multiple regression falls short of structural equations:

- When the observed variables contain measurement errors and the interesting relationship is among the true variables,
- When there is interdependence or simultaneous causation among the observed response variables, and
- When important explanatory variables have not been included in the analysis.

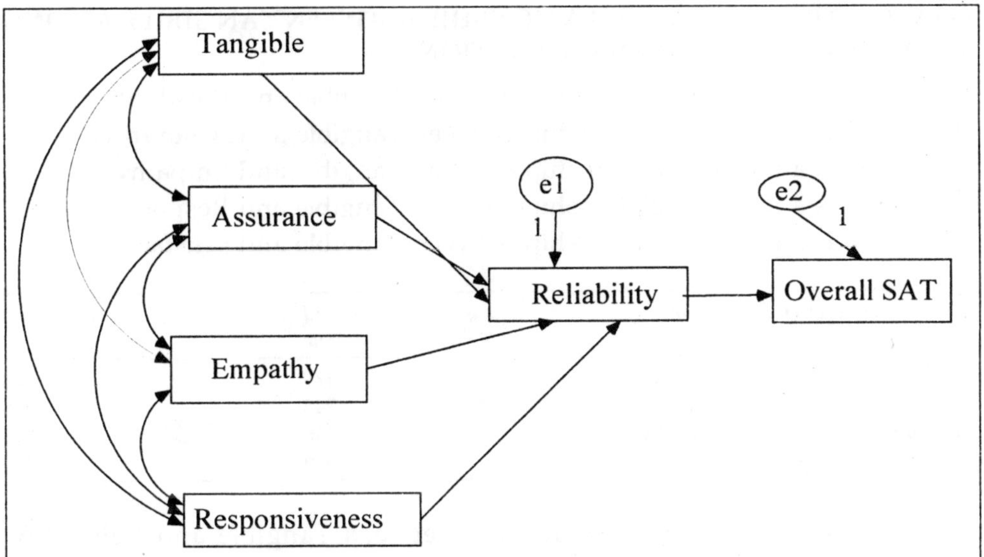

Mediating Dimension "Reliability" with in RATER Dimensions on SAT

Testing of Conceptual Model

The hypothesis is framed to find out the positive or negative relationship within the factors and the overall satisfaction towards ICICI service. RMSEA value will infer, whether the model indicates a close fit or not.

Evaluating Fittness of the Model

Model	*CMIN*	*DF*	*CMIN/DF*	*IFI*	*CFI*
Default model	3.829	4	.957	1.000	1.000
Saturated model	.000	0	.000	1.000	1.000
Independence model	700.741	15	46.716	.000	.000

To asses the model fit, in view of the fact that chi-square and CMIN/DF are satisfied. The comparative fit indexes, incremental fit index, were used to asses model fit. The CFI, IFI were higher than 0.9 this index indicates a good fit.

Root Mean Square Error Approximation

Model	*RMSEA*	*LO 90*	*HI 90*	*PCLOSE*
Default model	.000	.000	.086	.733
Independence model	.391	.367	.416	.000

The conceptual framework was examined using AMOS 7.0. The Pearson's correlation results were used as the input to run the model fit test. The overall fit of the conceptual framework is adequate with RMSEA .000 and not exceeding 0.1 and it indicates a close fit.

CORRELATION FOR THE RELATIONSHIP BETWEEN TANGIBILE AMONG RATER DIMENSIONS ON SATISFACTION

H_1 = There is a positive relationship between Tangible and Reliability.
H_2 = There is a positive relationship between Tangible and Assurance.
H_3 = There is a positive relationship between Tangible and Empathy.
H_4 = There is a positive relationship between Tangible and Responsiveness.
H_5 = There is a positive relationship between Tangible and satisfaction.

Relationship between Dimensions			*Standardized Estimate*	*Hypothesis .supported*
Reliability	←	Tangible	.479	Yes
Reliability	←	Assurance	.243	Yes
Reliability	←	Empathy	.046	Yes
Reliability	←	Responsiveness	-.069	No

- There is a positive relationship between Tangible and Reliability, Reliability and Assurance, Reliability and Empathy.
- There is a negative relationship between Reliability and Responsiveness.

Inter Relationship between Reliability Among "ATER" Dimensions on Satisfaction (SAT)

Relationship between Dimensions			*Standardized Estimate*
Reliability	←	Tangible	.491
Reliability	←	Assurance	.270
Reliability	←	Empathy	.065
Reliability	←	Responsiveness	-.083
Satisfaction	←	Reliability	.020

- The estimate value indicate the influence of the entered variables, that is reliability has the greatest influence on tangible (beta = .491), followed by assurance (beta = .270), followed by empathy (beta = .203) .The direction of influence for all the three is positive.
- Responsiveness has negative influence on tangible (beta = -.083), followed by satisfaction (beta = -.020). The direction of influence is negative.

Inter Relationship between RATER Dimensions

Relationship between RATER Dimensions			*Standardized Estimate*	*Hypothesis supported*
Tangible	↔	Assurance	.306	Yes
Tangible	↔	Empathy	.335	Yes
Tangible	↔	Responsiveness	.108	Yes
Assurance	↔	Responsiveness	.574	Yes
Empathy	↔	Responsiveness	.721	Yes
Assurance	↔	Empathy	.840	Yes

H_1 = There is a positive relationship between Tangible and assurance.

H_2 = There is a positive relationship between Tangible and empathy.

H_3 = There is a positive relationship between Tangible and responsiveness.

H_4 = There is a positive relationship between assurance and responsiveness.

H_5 = There is a positive relationship between empathy and responsiveness.

H_6 = There is a positive relationship between assurance and empathy.

BAYESIAN CURVE FOR THE RELATIONSHIP BETWEEN RATER DIMENSIONS ON SATISFACTION

Bayesian estimation uses prior information about model parameters to calculate posterior distribution. Bayesian estimation is often preferred for small samples. Bayesian methods are interactive and the displayed proposition simply mean of the normal distribution of many estimates. These estimates are displayed as a curve and a histogram.

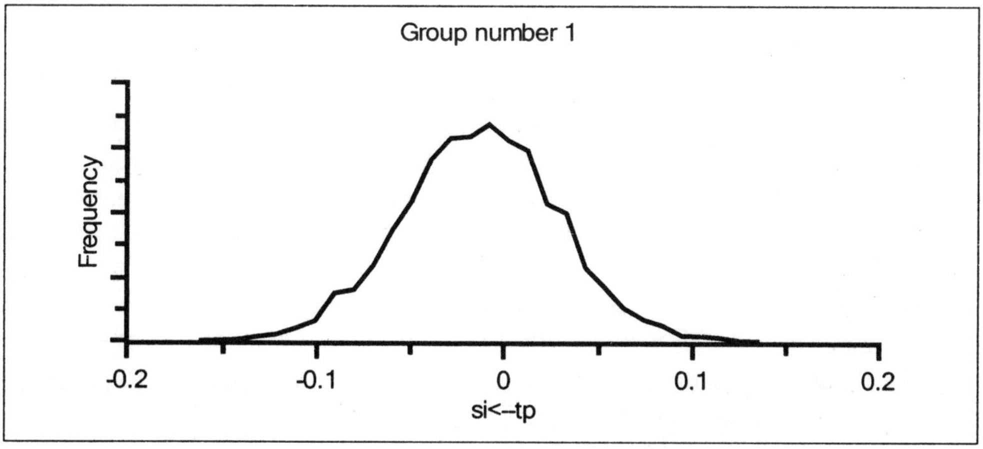

From the Bayesian curve it is inferred that the skew ness was obtained in IInd iteration (42). Bayesian is done for the small sample size and it is found to be a reliable one. The above graph shows that the primary data which was collected lies with in the normal distribution i.e, having reliability data.

REASON FOR PREFERRING ICICI

From the Table, it was inferred that 38 %of the respondents are preferring ICICI business for increase the income, 20% of the respondents are preferring ICICI business to spend the time, 17% of the respondents are preferring ICICI business due to the family situation, 25% of the respondents are preferring ICICI business to rendering service.

Reasons	*Percentage of respondents*
Increase income	38
To spend time	20
Family situation	17
To rendering service	25

HYPOTHESIS TESTING

H_0-There is no significance difference between over all service quality and Education Qualification of internal customer.

H_1- There is significance difference between over all service quality and Education qualification of internal customer.

Over All Service Quality

	Sum of Squares	*df*	*Mean Square*	*F*	*Sig.*
Between Groups	1.080	3	.360	.469	.704
Within Groups	128.967	168	.768		
Total	130.047	171			

Level of Significance = 5% Degree of freedom v1 = 3, v2 = 168 Tabulated value = 5.32. Calculated value = .469. Here tabulated value is greater than calculated value So Null hypothesis was accepted. So there is no significance difference between over all service quality and education qualification of Internal Customers.

H_0: There is Negative relationship between the Perception & Expectation mean of RATER dimensions.

H_1: There is a Positive relationship between the Perception & Expectation mean of RATER dimensions.

		Average Perception Mean of RATER	*Average expectation Mean of RATER*
Average Perception Mean of RATER	Pearson Correlation	1.000	-.319
Average expectation Mean of RATER		-.319	1.000
	Sig. (2-tailed)	.080	

There is a Negative correlation between the perception and Expectation among the RATER dimensions. Because the expectation of the Internal Customer is higher than the perception of the service rendered by ICICI. Hence H_0 is accepted There is Positive relationship between the Perception & Expectation mean of RATER dimensions.

H_0: There is Positive relationship between the Perception mean & Gap Scores of RATER dimensions.

H_1: There is a Negative relationship between the Perception mean & Gap Scores of RATER Dimensions.

		Average Perception Mean of RATER	*Average GAP SCORE of RATER*
Average Perception Mean of RATER	Pearson Correlation	1.000	.751
Average GAP SCORE of RATER		.751	1.000
	Sig. (2-tailed)	.000	

** Correlation is significant at the 0.01 level (2-tailed).

H_0 is accepted. There is a HIGH Positive correlation between Perception and GAP score among the RATER dimensions.

H_0: There is Positive relationship between the Expectation mean & Gap Scores of RATER dimensions.

H_1: There is a Negative relationship between the Expectation mean & Gap Scores of RATER dimensions.

		Average expectation Mean of RATER	*Average GAP SCORE of RATER*
Average expectation Mean of RATER	Pearson Correlation	1.000	-.865
Average GAP SCORE of RATER		-.865	1.000
	Sig. (2-tailed)	.000	

** Correlation is significant at the 0.01 level (2-tailed).

Hence H_0 is rejected. There is a HIGH Negative correlation between the Expectation and GAP score among the RATER dimensions.

GAP ANALYSIS OF RATER DIMENSIONS

The above table, the Service Gap between the RATER dimensions were determined by using the formula Perception–Expectation (P-E). The Gap score was listed below. The Major Gap was determined in the Assurance, Empathy & Tangible Dimensions.

Dimension	*Gap Score (P-E)*
Reliability	-1.27
Assurance	-1.69
Tangible	-1.45
Empathy	-1.48
Responsiveness	-1.36

CONDUCTING FACTOR ANALYSIS

Aim

The Main objective of the Factor Analysis is to reduce the Number of Factors (Items) & to determine the major factor influence among the Internal Customers of ICICI in Chennai city. The explorative factor analysis was done by using the software SPSS, Principal Component Method was applied. From the component matrix we extracted 8 factors from the 22 Items of the SERVQUAL questionnaire.

The factors are selected by using the Factor Loading (giving weight age of the factors).

Extraction Method: Principal Component Analysis

1. Convenience of the service (.816)
2. Way of staff treat the customer (.722)
3. Opening hours of operation (.579)
4. Staff giving customer best intent at heart (.456)
5. Speed & Efficiency of Transaction (.548)
6. Staff Never busy in customer responsive (.473)
7. Politeness and friendly Staff (.460)
8. Company understanding needs of customer (.422)

FINDINGS

From the Analysis

- Among the RATER dimensions, Reliability is the mediating dimension for influencing the customer satisfaction. The conceptual model was successfully evaluated by using AMOS.7.1, RMSEA value is 0.00 which is less than 0.05 and then the proposed model is perfect fit.
- Among the customers, fifty seven percentage lies with in the Age limit 30 to 40.
- From the factor analysis 8 factors were extracted from the 31 Items of the SERVQUAL questionnaire. The factors are selected by using the Factor Loading (giving weight age of the factors)Convenience of the service (.816), Way of staff treat the customer (.722), Opening hours of operation (.579), Staff giving customer best intent at heart (.456), Speed & Efficiency of Transaction (.548), Staff Never busy in customer responsive (.473), Politeness and friendly Staff (.460) and Company understanding needs of customer (.422).
- Majority of the Internal Customers (46%) are having the educational qualification of 12th standard.

- Thirty Eight Percentage of the customers of part time are getting the income Rs. 2000 to 5000 from their business with ICICI.
- Fifty two percentage of the part time customers are interested to convert their part time job into full time and their reason is the business dealing with ICICI is comfortable for them.
- Majority of the full time customers are getting income Rs 2000 to 5000 from their business with ICICI.
- There is a Negative correlation between the perception and Expectation among the RATER dimensions. Because the expectation of the Internal Customer is higher than the perception of the service rendered by ICICI.
- By Gap analysis the major service gap was determined in the Assurance, Empathy & Tangible Dimensions of ICICI customers.
- 38%of the respondents are preferring ICICI business for increase the income, 20% of the respondents are preferring ICICI business to spend the time, 17% of the respondents are preferring ICICI business due to the family situation, 25% of the respondents are preferring ICICI business to rendering service.

CONCLUSION

The study investigated service quality dimensions in Insurance Sector services in Indian service environment. The results provide an insight into the perceptions of service quality in ICICI Internal customers, particularly on functional quality components and the outcome quality dimension. However, caution should be used to generalise the results. A moderate sample has been used in the study. The scale was refined with repeated factor analyses on the collected data; and subsequent analyses were performed on the same data. The refined scale can be pretested and used afresh in future studies. Moderate level of variance explained in overall service quality by functional quality and outcome quality dimensions shows that operationalistion of these service quality dimensions requires improvement. The study was limited to only one insurance service industry and needs to be replicated in other service industries to find out the importance of industry specific outcome quality dimensions. The items generated for the outcome service quality have been industry specific.

Reference

Babukus, E and Boller, G. W. (1991), Empirical Assessment of SERVQUAL Scale. *Journal of Business Research*, 24: 253-268.

Babukus, E. and Mangold, W. G. (1989), Adapting the SERVQUAL Scale to Health Care Environment: An Empirical Assessment. In Bloom, P. (Ed.), *Enhancing Knowledge Development in Marketing*, 195. Chicago: American Marketing Association.

Bitner, M. J. (1992), Servicecapes: The Impact of Physical Surroundings on Customers and Employees. *Journal of Marketing*, 56(April).

Bitner, M. J., Booms, B. H. and Mohr, L. A. (1994), Critical Service Encounters: The Employee's View. *Journal of Marketing*, 56 (April): 57-71.

Bowers, M. and Swan, J. E. (1992), *Generic Versus Service Specific Dimensions of Service Quality: Does SERVQUAL Cover Hospital Health Care?* Unpublished Manuscript, Birmingham, AL.

Brensinger, R. and Lambert, D. M. (1990), Can the SERVQUAL Scale be Generalised to Business-to-business Services? In Bearden, W., Deshpande R.,, Madden, T. J., Varadarajan, P. R., Parasuraman, A., Folkes, V. S., Stewart, D. W., and Wlikie, W. L. (Eds.), *Knowledge Development in Marketing, AMA Educators' Proceedings*, 289. Chicago: American Marketing Association.

Cardozo, R. (1965), An Experimental Study of Customer Effort, Expectation and Satisfaction. *Journal of Marketing Research*, 2 (August): 244-49.

Carman, J. M. (1990), Consumer Perceptions of Service Quality: An Assessment of the SERVQUAL Dimensions. *Journal of Retailing, 66* (Spring): 33-35.

Churchill, G. A., Surprenant, C. (1982), An Investigation into Determinants of Customer Satisfaction. *Journal of Marketing Research, 19* (November): 491-504.

Dhabolkar, P. A., Thorpe, D. I., and Rentz, J. O. (1996), A Measure of Service Quality for Retail Stores: Scale Development and Validation. *Journal of the Academy of Marketing Science, 24*(1): 3-16.

Finn, D. W. and Lamb, C. W. (1991), An Evaluation of the SERVQUAL Scales in a Retailing Setting. In Homan, R. and Solomon, M. R. (Eds.), *Advances in Consumer Research*, 483-490. Provo, UT: Association for Consumer Research.

Gronroos, C. (1982), *Strategic Management and Marketing in the Service Sector*. Swedish School of Economics and Business Administration, Helsingrors.

Gronroos, C. (1984), A Service Quality Model and Its Market Implications. *European Journal of Marketing*, 18: 36-44.

Guiry, M., Hutchinson, W. and Weitz, B. A. (1992), *Consumers' Evaluation of Retail Store Service Quality and its Influence on Store Choice*. Working paper, University of Florida.

Howard, J. A., Sheth, J. N. (1969), *The Theory of Buyer Behaviour*. New York: John Wiley & Sons.

GLOBAL ECONOMIC AND FINANCIAL CRISIS, ECONOMIC TURMOIL

K. V. RAMACHANDRAN*

INTRODUCTION

The Global Economic Crisis is now, underway, and will be the leading news and business story in the world for many years to come. In addition, just as the world economic crisis of the 1930's was known as "The Great Depression" or "Global Glut", the evolving world economic meltdown is already being referred to as "Global Economic Crisis" or "Global Gloom". The present global economic crisis is the most important financial and economic phenomenon since the Great Depression.

The world financial system is now undergoing a global economic crisis of staggering proportions. The root cause of the economic and financial crisis was the United State's mortgage market selling sub-prime mortgages to large number of consumers with inadequate incomes. These mortgages were bundled into securitized paper investments and sold by Wall Street to major financial institutions across the globe.

When the mortgages became non-performing these securitized assets were transformed into toxic acid infecting the entire world- wide financial system. The ensuing global economic and financial crisis has destroyed trust in banks and borrowers in all the major economies of the world. Depositors are withdrawing their money from uninsured and even insured accounts. Coinciding with this massive run of the world's banks, these financial institutions are no longer lending capital to each other, reflected in the rising LIBOR, Short term inter-bank loan rates.

Capital is fleeing, and the global credit crunch ensuing has frozen the arteries of a global economy based on easy, cheap credit. As corporations are being denied normal flows of credit, a massive global crisis is transforming the financial meltdown on Wall Street into an economic disaster on Main Street. This evolving global and financial crisis and credit crunch will afflict developed and developing economies leading to massive unemployment, demand destruction and price deflation among many pivotal asset classes.

* *Reader, Department of Economics, University of Calicut, Dr. John Matthai Centre, Thrissur.*

The attempts by the Federal Reserve Bank and Treasury Department in the United States to inject liquidity into the credit market, along with intervention by Central banks in many other developed economies, is proving ineffective in responding to the global economic crisis. A growing number of economists are speculating that the global economic crisis will lead to a world-wide recession of such intensity; it may rival the Great Depression of the 1930's in its calamitous economic devastation.

GLOBAL ECONOMIC CRISIS SPREADING THROUGHOUT INTERNATIONAL COMMUNITY

What started as a financial disaster in the United States has become a truly global economic crisis. Banks and other financial institutions throughout the world purchased toxic financial instruments engineered on Wall Street in the USA and the world's nations have all now been impacted by the credit crunch.

What began as financial crisis has now impacted the real economy globally. The United Kingdom, Germany, France and other European countries have poured trillions of dollars in tax payer money into stopping the rot of the world's financial system.

The United States has initiated its own costly rescue on Wall Street. However, the global economic crisis is raging out of control and cannot be stopped. China has begun to lay off factory workers. Japan and Singapore have economies that are in recession. Iceland is bankrupt. The stock market in Russia has been decimated. India also is suffering lot by this crisis.

Commodity prices are undergoing radical deflation. As the consumer economy in the United States continues to erode, the repercussions will continue to spread globally. Highly respected economists including Nouriel Roubini and Nassim Taleb have issued warnings based on their analyses that with respect to the global economic crisis, the worst is yet to come.

Uganda also hit by global economic crisis. The Ugandan government warned that the country faces a drop in funding from overseas because of the global financial crisis. The Finance Minister EzraSuruma told parliament that while Uganda was not "directly exposed" to risk, the economic downturn could lead to a reduction of money coming into the country from outside investments, tourism, remittances from abroad and aid flows from donor countries,- reported the Daily Monitor. Soroti MP Alice said: "Suruma is holding an economic bomb which is about to explode". Unfortunately, he doesn't seem to be serious in offering solutions before it is too late. We need to prepare, the dollar crisis is just the beginning and we can't afford to sit back when the bomb is about to explode.

His comments followed those of the governor of the Central bank, Emmanuel Tumusiime Mutebile, who warned that the global crisis would slow Uganda's growth. Uganda expect the recession in Europe and the US to reduce on our exports. This will lead to fewer earnings from exports; earnings from tourism are also going to be affected. Mutebile reportedly said, "Tentatively, I can say that instead of the 8% growth rate, it will be in the range of 5% or 6%.

Vladimir Putin, the Russian Prime Minister blames America for world economic crisis. He said that the irresponsibility of America's financial system was to blame for the global economic crisis in what marks the latest episode has been one of the biggest victims of this summer's global banking crisis. Since May, the RTS, the Moscow's main index of shares, has lost 50% of its value and in September the Kremlin was forced to pump $60 billion into its financial system as credit markets froze. Mr. Putin said "Everything happening now in the economic and financial sphere began in the United States. This is not the irresponsibility of specific individuals but the irresponsibility of the system that claims leadership".

Mr. Putin also urged ministers to create a "modern credit finance system" that depends more on Russia's own resources and has "a strong immunity to global financial Viruses". Mr. Putin also gave warning that the country's substantial cash pile built up during the past two years of soaring oil prices would not be a fat enough cushion to protect the Russian economy from the global financial crisis. His comments came as capital markets across the world waited for the US congress to vote on a new bail out scheme for Wall Street: It is hoped that the rescue scheme will draw to a close a period of unprecedented uncertainty about the future of America's financial institutions.

Henry Paulson, the US Treasury Secretary, has already given warning that failure to force through a rescue program would trigger a financial meltdown in America, the world's largest economy. However, while Moscow blamed America for the global banking crisis, some analysts have pointed out that this summer's invasion of Georgia by Russia exacerbated anxieties across international capital markets. They have argued that investors pulling their money out of Russia added to instability in the financial world. The Russian economy has also been hit by the slide in commodity prices. Before the vote in Washington, the Russian stock market closed down almost 2%.

France also moves into the recession. The French Premier, Francois Fillon warned that the world was "on the edge of the abyss", as his country moved into an official recession. Fillon's comments, blaming an "irresponsible" financial system, came as the Dutch government seized control of banc assurer Fortis's Netherland's operations in € 16.8bn (£ 13.06bn) deal greed with the Belgian and Luxembourg authorities.

The shock decision came just days after the three governments injected € 11.2bn into Fortis, Belgium's biggest bank, to keep it afloat. He said that the president, Nicola's Sarkozy, would propose that Europe make its banking systems secure, unfreeze credit and co-ordinate it's economic and monetary strategy. The European has mounted rescue operations for several banks. But Gordon Brown, Germany's Angela Merkel, Italy's Silvio Berlusconi and Sarkozy are expected, at most, to agree to set aside national reserves to help ailing banks.

Official data said the French economy will probably contract by 0.1% in both the third and fourth quarters of 2008, following a 0.3% contraction between April and June. But the government said the economy would still register 0.9% growth for the year.

Things being so, it is evident that there certainly clear parallels between the present crisis and events of eight decades ago(Great Depression).In both cases, the economic collapse came after a period of political dominance by the Republican party. The 1920s saw three successive Republican politicians elected to the White House; Warren G Harding, Calvin Coolidge and Herbert Hoover. These administrators shared a fervent commitment to Laissez faire capitalism, encouraging growth through tax cuts, low interest rates and minimum business regulation. Coolidge encapsulated Republican faith in the free market economy in the aphoristic observation: "the business of America is business".

The financial agility increased as a result of the funds flow into the derivatives market. The transactions in the derivatives market in 2007 was about 40 times the value of goods produced in the world. The danger in the derivatives market is that the paper becomes a commodity. The risk borne by others and there is a tendency to undervalue the risk. Speculators tend to become euphoric in the boom period and this helps the market to go up further. The Wall Street crisis is not new. Economies had faced similar crash in the 1930s. The crisis would repeat periodically and governments have to be cautious.

The IMF Chief Dominique Strauss-Khan warned that the financial system risked collapse. Intensifying solvency concerns about a number of the largest US based and European financial institutions have pushed the global financial system to the brink of systematic meltdown.

The UK banks are less safe than those in Third world confidence in British banks, once considered among the safest in the world, has plummeted so low as a result of the global economic crisis that they are now less safe than their more modest Third world counterparts, according to a survey by the World Economic Forum [WEF].

The survey covering 134 countries, suggests it might be safer to put money in a bank in Gaborone, capital of Botswana, than a High Street Bank in London. It places Britain below Botswana in terms of confidence in its banking system. Other countries whose banking system is rated safer than Britain's include Namibia, Brazil, Chile, Senegal and Peru. All are far ahead in rankings than Britain which has dropped from among the top five to 44th position.

Take the case of unemployment, in America, the total number of unemployed people amounts to 12 lakhs, by the crisis. It is a quantum jump from the previous level of unemployment. The rate of growth of unemployment is 6.5%. The total number of people who lost their job in companies is around 240,000. The number of people who applied for unemployment allowance is

481,000. This is the clear evidence of the hit over the America's domestic economy by the crisis.

With the financial turmoil ravaging world economies, Indian Stocks listed on the US bourses saw their value erode by nearly $12 billion and the country's leading private sector lender, ICICI Bank lost about $3 billion. IT bellwether Infosys and another private sector lender HDFC Bank too saw their market capitalization tumble by over $2 billion during this time.

The world markets, including Asia and Europe have seen one of their worst trading, with Japan's benchmark Nikkei 225 touching a 20-year low, while the Indian markets are continuing to trade in the negative territory. In India, the Sensex dropped, touching level below 10,000. Among the 16 stocks listed as American Depository Receipts (ADRs) in NASDAQ and New York Stock Exchange, ICICI Bank's market capitalization plunged by $2.89 billion, while that of Infosys and HDFC Bank tumbled by $2.32 billion and $2.25 billion respectively. IT firm WIPRO saw its value fall by $2.24 billion.

The financial crisis would pull down the GDP growth rate, credit crunch would have an impact on the economy and there would definitely be a slowdown in the expansion of the major sectors of the economy.

Punjab, the granary of India ranks below countries like Honduras and Vietnam in terms of hunger levels while Mạdhya Pradesh has the most severe level of hunger in the country followed by Jharkhand and Bihar, says a report prepared by US based International Food Policy Research Institute (IFPRI).

When Indian states are compared to countries in the 2008 Global Hunger Index, Madhya Pradesh ranks between Ethiopia and Chad. Punjab- the best performing state, is below Gabon, Honduras and Vietnam, says the Country Report released by G.K. Chadha, Member of Prime Minister's Economic Advisory Council. India is home to the world's largest food insecure population with more than 200 million people who are hungry; the Indian States Hunger Index (ISHI) said.

THE GREAT DEPRESSION OF 1930S & THE FINANCIAL CRISIS 2006–07-BY VISION LACKING

Demonstrations by unemployed and homeless people shook many cities during the 1930s. In 1930, Hoover introduced higher tariffs to protect American manufacturers from foreign competition. The Smoot Hawley Act led to a protectionist war between the US and other countries. American exports fell sharply, crippling businesses, which lay off workers in ever higher numbers. The President became so unpopular that the shanty towns erected by homeless people became known as "Hoovervilles" and an empty pocket turned inside out a "Hoover flag".

The public perception that Hoover had failed either to avert or remedy the economic crisis led to his resounding defeat to Democratic challenger Franklin

Roosevelt in the presidential election of 1932. Roosevelt won a landslide victory with 22.8 million votes to Hoover's 15.7 million. How the US government acts now is very important, but while Mr. Bush is unlikely to repeat Hoover's mistakes so far he has lacked the vision of Roosevelt.

One of the most striking contrasts between the past and present crisis concerns presidential rhetoric. The only thing we have to fear "proclaimed Roosevelt in his inaugural address of January 1932, is fear itself". The Great Depression had a profound psychological as well as material impact on Americans, shattering their individual and collective self – confidence. In times of unprecedented trouble, Roosevelt sought to restore public optimism through his regular radio broadcasts, the " fireside chats" in which he presented himself as not only a politician but a personnel friend to ordinary Americans. In sharp contrast, the address that Mr. Bush delivered to rally support for the bailout plan exploited public fears & tears. With the $700 billion bailout plan, can the US government do enough to restore confidence and assuage the trauma? The bursting of the speculative bubble in the US housing market has destroyed billions of dollars in investor wealth across the world, crippled the banking system, expunged close to a million jobs... and India has not been spared either. With banks failing by the day, definitely, these are uncertain times for the financial services industry while many people who have lost their jobs are faced with permanent shrinkage of their lifestyle; others in the industry are going through the trauma of not knowing if and when their turn would come. Who is to blame?

WHAT ACTUALLY HAPPENED IN WALL STREET?

A global financial cobweb started getting built around the American dream of purchasing a home and it rested on the assumption that "home prices will keep rising". As demand for the CDOs started growing across the global investment community, the investment bankers (like Lehman) who were meant to sell these instruments also started investing a significant portion of their own capital in these. Gradually, the markets for CDOs and credit default swaps started expanding with traders and investors buying and selling these as if they were shares of a company, happily for setting the underlying people behind these products, who took the home loans in the first place and on whose capacity to repay the loans, the safety of these products depended.

As Wall Street firms like Lehman were churning more and more loans in to CDOs and selling them or investing their own money, there was a pressure on the banks to issue more loans so that they can be sold to the Wall Street firms in return for a commission. Slowly, banks started lowering the credit quality (qualification criteria) for availing a home loan and aggressively used agents to source new loans. This slippery slope went to such an extent that in 2005, almost anyone in the US could buy a home worth $ 100,000 (45lakhs

INR) or more without income proof, without credit history, sometimes even without a proper job. These loans were called NINA–No Income No Assets.

The US housing market went in to a classic speculative bubble. Home loans were easy to get, so more and more people were buying houses. The increased demand for houses caused the price to increase. The rising prices created even more demand, as people started to look at homes as investments–investments that never went down in value.

In late 2006, mortgage lenders noticed something that they'd almost never seen before. People would choose a house, sign all the mortgage papers, and then default on their very first repayment. Although no one could really hear it, that was probably the moment when one of the biggest speculative bubbles in American history popped. Another factor that led to the burst of the housing bubble was the rise in interest rates from 2004–2006. Many people had taken variable rate home loans that started getting reset to higher rates, which in turn meant higher EMIs that had not planned for.

The problem was that once property values starting going down, it set off a reverse chain reaction, the opposite of what had been happening in the bubble. As more people defaulted, more houses came on the market, with no buyers, prices went even further down.

In early 2007, as prices began their plunge, alarm bells started going off across mortgage backed securities' desks all over Wall Street. The investors are not getting their interest payments that were due. Wall Street firms stopped buying home loans from the local banks. This had a devastating effect on particularly the small banks and finance companies, which had borrowed money from larger banks to issue more home loans thinking they could sell these loans to Wall Street firms like Lehman and make money.

Everyone got into a mad scramble to seize and sell the homes in order to get back at least some of the money. But there were just not enough buyers. The global financial cobweb built around mortgages is on the brink of collapse. Firms, large and small, some young, some as old as a 100 years have crumbled as a result of suing each other over the dwindling asset values.

The "invited" advent of the current financial crisis has exposed the fragility of the system. Wall Street is blaming the entire episode on people who could not repay their home loans. But, the reality seems to point towards the stupidity of people who lent all these money, financial institutions that built fancy derivative packages and in effect facilitated billions in trading and investments in these fragile low quality loans. The US government is planning to grant 700 billion dollars to the Wall Street firms to compensate the financial speculators for the money that they have lost. Isn't this like rewarding greed and stupidity? The head of a leading investment bank has stated "this is necessary to sustain financial ingenuity".

AMERICA'S HUGE NATIONAL DEBT GRIM OVER IT'S ECONOMY

The US national debt clock runs out of digits. Such is the surge in America's debt that even technology is finding it difficult to measure its level as a clock earmarked for keeping a tab on the country's national debt has run out of digits.

The operator of the National Debt Clock, installed at Times Square in New York, has now dropped the dollar sign in the total figure to accommodate a ten trillion dollar figure. A replacement for the clock with two additional digits that would be able to account for up to a quadrillion (million billion) dollars of debt is expected only by the next year.

The existing clock can accommodate up to 9, 999,999,999,999 (just one dollar short of $10 trillion) of debt with a dollar sign $ preceding it, but the clock has started showing the figure without the dollar sign after the debt level recently reached the 10 trillion dollar level.

At the last check, the clock showed the United State's total national debt at about 10,250,000,000,000 dollars ($ 10.25 trillion). With an estimated population of about 305 million, this results into an average debt of close to $ 34, ooo for every US citizen. The clock is said to have been first installed in 1989 when the national debt stood at about $ 2.7 trillion.

The financial rescue package totaling over a trillion dollar, including the latest $ 700- billion plan, and the government's expected move to buy shares in some banks, are expected to further inflate the country's debt levels.

WORLD ECONOMY AFFECTED BY THE CRISIS – HOW & HOW MUCH?

In India, the industrial growth has slowed substantially. The new generation banks like ICICI & HDFC are also adversely affected. Even in the nationalized banks the issuance of various loans slumped. The IT & IT based companies collapsed which created several jobless persons. The leading business giants like TATA, BIRLA and AMBANY cut short the employment in their companies. Still, these "jobless workers" are groping in the darkness to sustain.

There is serious concern about the likely impact on the economy of the heavy foreign exchange outflows in the wake of sustained selling by FIIs on the bourses and withdrawal of funds by others. Panicky selling since the beginning of April 2009 has led to a fall of over 33 per cent in the BSE index. This came on top of a 25 per cent decline up to April from the peak level touched in January. Thus the gains made over a long period have been nearly wiped out in less than ten months.

Equity values came down and many established companies are unable to complete their rights issues even after fixing offer prices below related market quotations at the time of announcement. Subsequently market rates went down below issue prices and shareholders are considering purchases from the cheaper open market or deferring fresh investments. This situation naturally has upset the plans of corporate to raise resources in various forms for their ambitious projects involving heavy outlays.

In Sweden, Volvo is cutting thousands of jobs. In Japan, a credit squeeze seems to be forcing small companies into bankruptcy. In Korea, people don't buy consumer electronics. The exporters are suddenly struggling. China's exports fell for the first time in three years, by 5.7 per cent in the first half of the year, with falling demand from the US and Europe. More than 7000 workers were laid off when one of the country's largest toy manufacturers, Smart Union, closed its factory in Don Guan. In 2008 alone, 3631 toy exporters went out of business–that is half of all enterprises in the toy industry. In Germany, companies are hoarding cash because credit markets are tight. Consumers have pulled back. Even creditworthy companies cannot get money in Europe. And across Asia, export growth has slowed to a crawl or started declining in real terms. The United States, once the engine of the global economy, is ailing and in no position to inspire confidence. Americans are seen as both the root of the problem, and powerless to solve it.

However, the global financial crisis will raise world unemployment to 210 million people by the end of next year, its highest rate in the past decade, the UN Labor Agency has said. Across the world, there have been severe disruptions in money markets, sharp declines in stock markets and extreme risk aversion in financial markets. Governments, central banks and financial regulators are responding to the crisis with radical, unconventional and aggressive measures to restore confidence and stabilize the markets.

WORLD FINANCIAL CRISIS AND INDIAN MARKET

With the financial turmoil ravaging world economies, Indian stocks listed on the US bourses saw their value erode by nearly &12 billion in the first week o f October 2008 and the country's leading private sector lender ICICI Bank lost about $3billion. The IT bellwether Infosys and another private sector lender HDFC Bank too saw their market capitalization tumble by over $2billion during this time. The world markets, including Asia and Europe, have seen one of their worst trading during October2008, with Japan's benchmark Nikkei 225 touching a 20 year low, while the Indian markets are continuing to trade in the negative territory. Among the 16 stocks listed as American Depository Receipts (ADRs) in NASDAQ and Newyork Stock Exchange, ICICI Bank's market capitalization plunged by $2.89 billion, while that of Infosys and HDFC Bank tumbled by $2.32 billion and $2.25 billion, respectively. IT firm Wipro saw its value fall by $2.24 billion.

The Bombay Stock Exchange (BSE) benchmark Sensex closed below the psychologically important 10,000- level for the first time in two years as institutional investors continued their selling spree amid strong signs of recession in the US becoming a reality. After opening sharply higher, the 30–share barometer on the BSE shed606.14 points or 5.73 per cent to close the day at 9975.35, a level last seen on June 19, 2006. The 50 share Nifty of the National Stock Exchange (NSE) also fell by 194.95 points, or 5.96 per cent, to 3074.35. The US stocks were down: Dow Jones Industrial Average (DJIA) was down by 109.20 points at887.06, NASDAQ by 14.77 points at 1702.94 and S&P 500 was down by 11.54 points at 936.89. Meanwhile, the rupee fell to a six year low against the US dollar. It weakened by 0.8 per cent (October 2008) to 48.88 a dollar. This is the lowest since June 2002 and the rupee's 10 week losing streak is the longest since December 2005.

The former commerce secretary S. N. Menon has said that the global financial crisis will definitely impact different sectors of the national economy and the effect on the crisis will have to be factored in when making any protection about the economy as a whole. Menon cautioned that unless export growth rate was sustained, there would be pressure on the balance of payments front and felt that India must now look for FDI from countries, such as Taiwan, Singapore, Japan and Korea, particularly in the manufacturing sector and that too in the electronics Industry. Special Economic Zones, he said, could play a major role here. The country must also focus on labor intensive sectors such as textiles and gems and jewelers in which the country already had several advantages.

No one can forecast at this stage about the duration of impact of the US crisis on the Indian economy. There was a huge balance of payments deficit on India. The current account deficit was higher at $10.72 billion in April-June 2008 against $6.3 billion a year ago. The increase in current account deficit was mainly on account of a large trade gap of $31.57 billion against $20.70 billion according to RBI while net invisibles improved to BCCI was $30.38 billion in the same quarter against $21.50 billion comparably.

In 2007–08 addition to foreign reserves was as much as $108.03 billion in spite of a rise in current account deficit to $17.40 billion from $9.76 billion. The increase in the previous year was $45.77 billion. Since the reserves declined by $6.84 billion from the end of June to $291.82 billion during the week ended September 26 and the trade deficit is likely to rise to $58 billion in April–September, the current account deficit in the second quarter may exceed the $10.72 billion recorded in April–June.

The heavy FII selling and withdrawal by others have been responsible for the sharp deterioration in the external value of the rupee to 48.50 to a dollar after touching a low of 49.30 on October 10 against 40.02 in April and 39.33 on October 30, 2007. The rupee has thus declined by as much as 19 per cent in less than a year. But the drop has been pronounced than against the British Pound and the Euro. The Japanese Yen, on the other hand, has appreciated sharply against the US dollar as well as the rupee.

The sale of dollars by the RBI to arrest sharp depreciation of the Indian currency could have been more aggressive from the beginning. Its purchases of the greenback were as much as $78.2 billion in 2007–08 and $26.8 billion 2006-07. The purchases of dollars continued in April–May to the extent of $4.5 billion but in June there were net sales of $5.2billion. Thus in April–June net sales were only $756 million.

THE GLOBAL MELTDOWN AND REALTY SECTOR

The reality in realty sector during 2008–09 was not a correction in land prices but a recession. The global economic crisis that started with sub - prime woes in the US in August 2007 has now engulfed European banks and there is the fear that it will spread to Asian countries. So, the property developers were in panic and them reluctant to invest in real estate sector. As a result, the recession not only reduced the investment on realty sector but also reduced the demand from the side of buyers. The slow down in the real estate sector is evident from various factors, such as the poor transactions between banks and real estate developers. Home loan disbursement declined in the range of 25 per cent to 40 per cent and inquiries for housing loans by 25 per cent. Besides, banks have become choosy in funding projects, including commercial buildings and apartments. Builders say the bookings have sharply declined from those the previous year. Cancellations also have increased. Home aspirants have started to rethink real estate as an investment option. The enthusiasm seen a year ago has suddenly vanished.

In India, Foreign Direct Investment (FDI) has been considerable in various sectors with the boom in the real estate business for the past few years. This has come down significantly as it is evident from the Foreign Institutional Investors (FIIs) pulling their money out of the stock markets.

RELIEF AND RESCUE MEASURES BY INDIA TO ARREST GLOBAL MELTDOWN

The US financial crisis has had its reverberations on both developed and developing world. It is not possible to insulate Indian economy completely from what is happening in the financial systems of the world. Effectively speaking, however, the Indian banks and financial institutions have not experienced the kinds of losses and write- downs that even venerable banks and financial institutions in the western world have faced. By and large, India has been spared the panic that followed the collapse of banking institutions, such as Fortis in Europe, and Merrill Lynch, Lehman Brothers and Washington Mutual in the US.

The major comforting feature is the downward in crude oil prices to around $78 from the peak of $147 a barrel. It has been stated that the average price for 2007-08 was around $79. Hence the OPEC countries were thinking about the cutting down the production of crude oil to avoid further sharp decline in prices.

However, in rupee terms, oil as well as other imports will be costlier and it may not be possible to derive full advantage out of the drop in prices of crude, metals and other products. It is now clear that hectic speculation in the world commodity markets was mainly responsible for the boom in the gold last year along with base metalś and other commodities.

Both the Central Government and Central Bank have suddenly responded with rescue measures to fight against the symptoms of financial crisis infected by global meltdown started in America. The Union Finance Minister P. Chidambaram has indicated a substantial injection of funds in to the banking system, probably exceeding Rs. 25, ooo crore.

The RBI announced measures to infuse Rs. 20, 000 crore through the short term lending route for the Mutual Funds to meet their liquidity needs and redemption pressure. As a first step, the RBI cut the Cash Reserve Ratio (CRR) by 150 basis points to provide Rs. 60,000 crore to the banking system. RBI has decided to conduct a special 14-day repo at a 9 per cent per annum for a notified amount of Rs. 20,000 crore with a view to enabling bank to meet the liquidity requirements of Mutual Funds. This repo will be in addition to the repo/reverse repo auctions conducted under Liquidity Adjustment Facility (LAF) and Second Liquidity Adjustment Facility (SLAF) which has been held as usual.

In a major move to pump in liquidity in to the system the RBI announced a slew of measures, including reducing the CRR by 100 basis points, which released additional Rs. 40,000 crore. Again, the RBI reduced the CRR (a portion of deposits the banks have to set aside as reserve) by 150 basis points with effective October 11, 2008, which already released an amount of Rs. 60,000 crore in to the system. With the least cut in CRR to 6.5 per cent, the Central Bank injected a total of Rs. 100,000 crore in to the financial markets with effect from current reporting fortnight that began on October11. Further, the RBI decided to provide Rs. 25,000 crore to banks as the first installment under the Agricultural Debt Waiver and Debt Relief Scheme of the Government of India. It also raised the interest rates ceiling on Non Resident Indian (NRI) deposits to attract foreign currency funds to the country.

Further, banks have allowed borrowing funds from their overseas branches and correspondent banks up to a limit of 50 per cent of their unimpaired Tier I capital as the close of the previous quarter or $10 million, whichever is higher, as against the existing limit of 25 per cent.

CONCLUSION

India is recovering from the hit by the global crisis. The sectors like Tourism, Export (especially sea food products), Textile and Information Technology are much adversely affected by the crisis. But the severity of the problem cannot be overthrown by the Government all on a sudden. It may take time. Anyhow, the implication of the current financial crisis has been muted in the Indian economy when compared to other countries because of the timely intervention by the Central Government and RBI.

As a part of policy drives the following things are also to be followed to recover from the crisis (viewed by Prof. Chadha, Prof. Prabhath Patnaik & S. Menon).

(i) The nation should ensure that prices are protected so as to minimize the sufferings emerging out of recession.

(ii) Expansionary policies are required to counter the imported recession.

(iii) Capital control/financial engineering are essential to insulate the country from the impact of global recession.

(iv) Protect the peasantry from fall in prices of agricultural commodities and take appropriate trade policy measures to prevent the import of unemployment in the country.

(v) High GDP growth is not sufficient. Inclusive growth is necessary.

(vi) Strengthening the public distribution system.

(vii) Liberalizing the financial regulatory measures.

(viii) Much focus on labor intensive sectors.

(ix) Special attention to IT Sector.

(x) Ensure equitable distribution of wealth & resources.

References

Global Economic Crisis – By Sapphire Website Designers.

Liz Ford (2008), "Uganda Hit by Global Economic Crisis", Africa News Round up, October 24.

Suzy Jagger in New York , Katy, Moscow, Samuel, Brisbane and Jon Exeter, UK "Vladimir Putin Blames America for World Economic Crisis"

David Gow in Brussels, "World Economic Crisis: France Moves in to Recession" – Article history, October 3, 2008.

Clive Webb (2008), Reader in American History at the University of Sussex, England - " Does the US face Great Depression II?, October 04, 2008.

P. A. Seshan (2008), "Concern Over Impact of U. S. Crisis", *Hindu* News Paper, October 13.

"The Global Meltdown and the Realty Sector", *Hindu,* News Paper, October18, 2008.

Shyam, P. (2008), Financial Consultant, "When the Bubble Burst", *Hindu* News Paper, October 5.

IMPORT SUBSTITUTING PROTECTIVE TRADE AND EXPORT PROMOTING LIBERAL TRADE: A REVIEW

P. Abdul Kareem*

INTRODUCTION

The last six decades have witnessed remarkable economic development in the developing countries which has been achieved largely through the implementation of development programmes. Industrialization is the main such development programme in these developing counties. Development strategies for industrialization can be broadly divided into two: Import substitution and Export promotion. While import substitution strategy follows a closed protective trade strategy, export promotion strategy is based on liberal open trade strategy. The developing countries generally followed the protective trade strategy in the early stages of their development experience. Subsequently the stress was on export promoting free trade experiments. Thus, import substitution and protective trade was clearly the development strategy to develop the economies of developing countries in the earlier decades of 1950's, 1960's and 1970's. But later especially since 1980 there was a shift towards export-led growth. Moreover, in the recent periods, the liberal trade strategy has convincingly resulted in higher economic growth in developing economies. However, the related issues of complementarity and competitiveness of these protective and liberal trade strategies have not been systematically discussed. Therefore, a detailed discussion of the difference between these import substituting closed trade strategy and export promoting open trade strategy is useful. Moreover, this discussion will throw more light on the current discussion on trade and growth in the context of developing countries. Most of the developing countries have now liberalised the foreign trade regimes. The tariff rates have been cut very significantly, exports have been promoted with deliberate measures such as setting up of special economic zones, etc. The trade sector is now performing very heavily in countries like India. In India while exports increased from Rs. 32,558 Crores in 1991 to 2,91,582 Crores in 2004, imports increased from Rs. 43,193 crores in 1991 to Rs. 3,53,976 crores in 2004. In 2006, the degree of openness measured as export + import/GDP is around

* *Senior Lecturer, Department of Economics, University of Calicut, Kerala, India.*

53% in India. Against this context, we in this paper make an attempt to critically review the literature on the related issues of the complimentarity and competitiveness of these two strategies of industrialization, namely, Import substitution (IS) and Export promotion (EP). This paper is divided into seven sections. The first section gives introduction. The second section reviews import substitution. In the third section we review difficulties of IS strategy and the fourth section reviews studies related to India's IS. Export promotion is reviewed in Section Five. Studies of export function are given in Section six. Section seven gives studies on India's EP.

IMPORT SUBSTITUTING PROTECTIVE TRADE STRATEGY

According to Mithra (1974) IS and EP are not necessarily fully competitive but complementary. In general, Mithra argues that the less developed countries do offer some scope for promotion of both exports and import substitution activities. To Edward Chen (1987) both IS and EP strategies are not mutually exclusive. He perceives two stages of IS and two stages of EP. In the first stage of "easy" IS, non-durable consumer goods are produced and in the second stage of "difficult" IS intermediate goods and capital goods are produced. Export orientation, according to Chen, can also be divided into first stage of exporting manufactures that are more labour intensive and second stage of exporting products more capital and technology intensive. Thus, for industrialization in developing countries, four possible stage of development exists IS1, IS2, EP1 and EP2.

Bruton H.J. (1981) believes that IS was mainly aimed to change the structure of dependence as the existing structure makes the economy undesirably dependant on matters outside its own control. In this context Burton (1981) suggest that since the second stage of IS is difficult the first stage should be extended to a maximum extent by the way of providing protection on a wide range of consumer goods as possible. David Felix (1964) calls this as "premature widening of the protective structure", ie, an expansion into a large number of relative small scale activities rather than a concentration on a few. But, according to Winston (1967), the impressive performance of consumer goods sector leaves much negative impact on the saving capacity in the economy. In recent times, much analytical effort has gone into devising measures to evaluate the economic efficiency in the allocation of resources under the IS policies. Two prominent concepts-Effective Rates of Protection (ERP) and Domestic Resource Cost (DRC) have played a key role in such efforts (H.G. Johnson, 1960). Empirical estimates by Balassa and Guisingar suggests that an excessively high rate of effective protection to IS industries and consequent movement of resources away from agriculture and other primary sectors. The main use of ERP has been in measuring the real contribution of an activity to national product by comparing the discrepancy between value added at domestic prices and world prices, when there are tariffs on final goods and intermediate goods. Soligo and Stern

(1970), for instance estimates that, in twenty three out of forty eight manufacturing industries in Pakistan the value added at world prices is negative. King (1940) provides further examples of negative value added in Mexico automobile industry. However, King also points out that negative value added does not necessarily means that country wastes resources or is worse off. Citing the example of Mexican motor assembly, King underlines the generally favourable external economies generated as a result. There is also the question of the treatment of the sunk cost. Guisinger (1968) estimates that the elimination of the sunk cost from the "real" resources costs in Ethiopian industries would render all but two socially profitable.

According to Bruno (1965), difference in DRC among different activities represent non optional allocation of resources. Bhagawati and Krueger (1963) believe that allowing a higher marginal of saving than of earning foreign exchange is not justifiable. Leela's (1984) estimate of DRC for the Indian Nitorgenous fertilizer industry indicate that feed stocks is relatively efficient.

THE DIFFICULTIES OF IMPORT SUBSTITUTING PROTECTION

Paradoxically enough, the growth of IS has been paralleled by doubts over its continuing viability to support economic growth in countries which have already attained a high degree industrialization. Further growth of IS requires extension of the process into more difficult areas of intermediate and capital goods. IS in consumer goods alone in the absence of significant growth, could not continue to lower the economy's average import coefficient. A few countries, notably Brazil and India, were able to grow faster than the capacity to import by haltingly extending IS to intermediate and capital goods, but these are largely exception. Felix (1964) also draws attention to a persistent import bias in the change in final demand which tends to diminish the effectiveness of IS. In this connection, Diaz-Alezandro (1965) has argued that the continued frustration of foreign exchange saving of the kind noted by Felix requires some very drastic assumptions about rising capital-output ratios and import-intensity of production processes, for which there is little justification. Diaz-Alenjandro's analysis is undoubtedly directed to a long-run viability of IS, where savings in imports from completed import-substituting products offset the rise in capital-intensity of future investments (Griffin and Enos (1970)). Power (1971) has noted that the unbalanced growth of import substituting consumer goods industries may also have diverted resources away from investment. The discussion by Albert Hirschman (1968) projects one of the major weakness of IS. Sketching a naive and a semi naïve exhaustion model, Hirschman contends that the first step of IS opens up new opportunities for the establishment of domestic manufactures through both income and backward linkage effects. The industrial sector is particularly prone to the phenomenon of negative value added at world prices, as indeed shown by the limited evidence from Pakistan by Lewis and Guisinger (1968). On the negative side, these same pressures may lead to building of capacity haphazardly, frequently without regard to social opportunity cost of resources, as well as create domestic monopoly positions. Bhagawati and Krueger (1963) are of the view that such sheltered monopoly positions in import substituting industries are the prime cases of low productivity. The classical example of this proliferation and a consequent disregard to economics of scale is documented by Johnson (1967) for the automobile industry in Chile. Further, a comparison of Argentina to US. Prices presented by Felix (1968) suggests a "heedless fragmentation of firms within industries where demand would be inadequate at most barely adequate, to support one or two large firms at minimum efficient scale". On the other hand, Reppy (1972) in an extensive empirical investigation of the Columbian experience concludes that "for a wide range of manufactured products diseconomies of scale are the significant in the range of output represented by the Columbian markets". The study of tariffs and protection led Harry G. Johnson (1964) to believe that the economic policy of import substitution almost inevitably creates the political problem of foreign "Control" of the economy. Another criticism leveled against IS that it has not proved itself capable of generating substantial increases in manufacturing employment (Maria de Conceicao Tavares (1978)). According to Werner Baer (1972), "Something of a controversy has been developing between the "structural" critics and the "market" critics of IS. Another major lacuna of IS policies, according to Bhagawati and Krueger (1973), has been their indiscriminate nature in influencing the growth of firms. In addition too these criticisms leveled against IS there persist serious doubts among those who worked on the area of research as to the gradual extension of IS process to intermediate and capital goods sectors (Kareem 1989). The main remedy to escape from these shortcomings of IS was suggested by the "outward looking" strategies to whom export will bring economic prosperity to the nation through the foreign trade multiplier.

STUDIES ON INDIA'S IMPORT SUBSTITUTING PROTECTION

While reading the literature on IS in India what the impression one gets is that our country obviously lacked a coherent policy of IS. What all the little achievement we have attained in replacing the imports and activating the productive elements at home, it was not often a result of carefully planned programme based on consideration of priorities, scale economies, comparative advantage, balance of payment strategies etc, but a hurried response to the quick profit making opportunities presented in a protected market by policy of import restriction or IS. This is probably aided by official anxiety to show rapid rise in production. Below we present the review of the works at hand on the process and progress of IS policy followed in India.

Weisskoff (1967) presents a detailed empirical application of an inter-industry programming model to Indian economy, designed primarily to analyse the structure of imports and the scope for IS in Indian Industry. The inter-linked aspects of IS in the framework of an input-output model has also been well discussed by Panchamukhi (1967). In another paper Panchamukhi (1969) examines the relationship between import dependence and production efficiency index on the basis of cross section data for the three import-using sectors, namely paper and production sector, the non-ferrous metals and alloys sector, and the machinery manufacturing sector for the period 1957-63. However, Ramana's (1968) study throws some light on the evil effects of deficit financing on the Indian Economy during 1951-1965. Bhagawati and Srinivasan (1975) largely examine India's foreign trade regime in its interaction with domestic policies and objectives so as to assess its efficiency and outcome of the liberalization efforts represented by the June 1966 devaluation and the accompanying policy measure. The study by Vidhya Pitre (1979) attempts to assess the extent of import substitution that has taken place in the machinery and transport equipment sector during the period 1960-70. V.V. Desai's (1969) cogent argument that India lacks a clear focus on IS policy was based on his finding that the neglect of comparative advantage paves way for high cost structure in the industry and also for the misallocation of resources between various firms involved in the industry. The criticism of the inefficiency in the IS process in India has been received much attention in Nambiar's (1977) study. The failure story of India's IS strategy has been further established in a micro level study of automobiles and ancillary industry by Anne Krueger (1975). Kareem (1989) has estimated the degree and magnitude of IS that has taken place in the Indian Engineering Industry during 1970-87 and also estimated the merit of IS to industry development.

From the above discussion it appears that India's experience in relation to IS has not been one of encouraging. The prevalence of high cost structure and the structural bottlenecks operating in the economy have discouraged smooth transition of IS process from the initial phases to other advanced stages of economic performance as visualized in various analytical and empirical works. Therefore, the enthusiasm of IS lasted only upto 1960's. The availability of advanced human skills and the large resources in the country have compelled us to think about alternative strategies of industrialization so as to attain the economic growth and development of the country.

EXPORT PROMOTING LIBERAL TRADE STRATEGY

The proponents of exports as a catalyst of economic growth base their argument on the creation of a favourable industrial climate originating from the increased foreign demand. The existing literature on the role of exports in industrialization of developing countries is predominantly based on national macro aggregates. For example, Raymond Lubitz (1973) examines two hypotheses in this connection. Firstly, export growth is said to stimulate industries with important economies of scale, that is manufacturing industries. Secondly, export growth, by creating a strong balance of payments is said to encourage investment, and thereby raises the rate of technical progress and productivity growth, setting up a second virtuous circle. The study by Metawally and Tamaschke (1980) of the role of oil exports in stimulating industrial activity in the Middle East, suggests that gross fixed capital formation is extremely sensitive to growth in oil exports in all countries considered with the exception of Kuwait and Libya. Based on the sample of 73 developing countries Rostam. M.Kavoussi (1984) argues that important cause of the association between export and better economic performance is the favorable impact of exports on total factor productivity. In the estimation of this equation Rostam has used annual growth rate of G.N.P. investment, labour force, and exports between 1960 and 1978. The factor intensities do not explain much of the variance of the net export ratios but do explain a substantial part of the variance of the home market. This is the result of the regression analysis carried out by Lennart Ohlsson (1980) in his study of engineering trade specialization in Sweden. Reviewing the evolution of Brazilian cotton manufacturing before 1914, Flavio Rableo Versiani (1980) suggests that export-led income growth provided an expanding market for the new activity, after the turn of 19th century. The tremendous growth success attained by NICs during the 1970's, and 1980's also further strengthen the export-oriented industrialization strategy. The first five NICs such as South Korea, Taiwan, Hong Kong, Singapore and Brazil achieved annual growth rates of GDP (at constant prices) of between eight and eleven per cent over the period 1965-78, and their yearly increases in manufactured exports lay between 20 and 40 per cent (UNCTAD, 1982). Manufacturing employment in that period increased by between 4% and 8% yearly, leading in some regions of those countries (and in some years) to labour shortage and real wage increases (Kaplinsky, 1984).. Balassa (1981) explains that reliance on market forces and integration into the world economy yielded results superior to protection and dissociation from the world economy.

STUDIES OF EXPORT FUNCTION

The various studies attempting to explain the export performance of individual countries take quantifiable factors on both supply and demand sides. The variables taken differ across studies. Pomfret estimated export functions for Israel which is the form.

$$Xt = f(Rt, Ut, Pt, Wt)$$

Where Rt is effective exchange rate, Ut is capacity utilization in terms of deviations from the exponential growth rate, Pt is industrial production and Wt is world trade in manufactured goods. A trend term is also included which raised the statistics into the zone where it no longer indicates significant serial correlation. Tyler's study for Brazil takes the following factors into export function:

$$Xt = f(Rt, Tt, Bt, Pt, E, Wt)$$

Where Rt is real exchange rate, Pt is tax incentive given to exporters Bt is recession boom effect, Pt is industrial production, E is effect of Latin American Free Trade Area and Wt is world trade. Time trend is also included to take care of "Strong growth trend in industrial exports". In another paper Sajid Anwar (1985) has well analysed the export performance of Pakistan by considering both supply and demand sides. The estimated two-equation models which is estimated for primary and manufactured goods exports for the period, 1960-80.

STUDIES ON INDIA'S EXPORT PROMOTION AND LIBERAL TRADE

There have been various studies dealing with India's exports and the enormous demand and supply bottlenecks operating upon its smooth performance. The statistical estimation of the contribution of exports to the growth of GNP by Tripathy (1985) shows that one crore of export is capable of generating additional income worth Rs. 14 crores. Judging by the criteria of incremental export- output ratio (IEOR) Banerji (1975) finds that many of India's manufacturing industries, especially consumer and investment goods industries, have exhibited a growing degree of openness over time. While Tiwaris's (1986) study highlights that the increasing pressures of internal demand, lack of comparative advantage and price responsibilities hamper the export performance. However, these studies face one or another serious limitations. Firstly, most of these studies having largely carried out at an aggregated level. A meaningful and deep insight into the problems calls for the examination of industries and markets at a more disaggregate level. Secondly, the difference in the determinats of export performance across various studies led to conflicting results of the contribution and importance of each variable. A significant feature of India's export has been their declining share in world export. In the planning era export trend could be broadly divided into two phases : (a) Period of stagnation (1950-60) and (b) Period of expression (1960 onwards). The study of Singh (1964) is an attempt to separate the relative influence of the external factors (those emanating from abroad) and internal factors (those operating within India) i.e., demand and supply factors. Bhagawati and Desai (1970) also attribute stagnation in India's expots to domestic policies. Kelkar and Sharma (1976) hold that India's falling share in the world market could be due to declining share of export in domestic production in India. For Ragnekar (1970) the decline in the share of traditional export is to the absorpition of a rising proportion of output in the domestic economy, and they seem to have best lost their comparative advantage. Kareem (2001) has estimated the various determinants of Inda's machinery exports and fond that world income positively result in high export performance.

The above review of studies in regard to Indian export promotion broadly suggests that in the presence of stagnant or slowly growing world demand for India's export of traditional goods coupled with the supply bottelenecks, achievements of export growth targeted in Indian plans would depend mostly on non-traditional exports, particularly manufacturing exports. The diversification of manufacturing exports towards new non-traditional markets is important. Because traditional export market witnessed lower growth rates. Also, the export basket of manufactured commodities have witnessed changes in the composition (Kareem 2004). In the changed environment of liberal trade policy also the role of export is important (Singer etal 1992). Higher the growth of exports, higher is the economic growth. Also, the export sector in India is growing at a very high rate for the recent periods (Tseng and Cowen 2005). Hence, one can argue that in India the high export growth is leading to better economic development. In other words, in India there is export-led growth (Singer *et al* 2002).

References

Ahamed, Jaleel (1976), "Import Substitution and Growth of Export: An Econometric Test", *Revue Economique*, Vol. 27, No. 2.

Ahamed, Jaleel (1976), "Domestic Demand and Ability to Export in Developing Economies: Some Preliminary Results", *World Development*, Vol. 4, No. 8.

Ahamed, Jaleel (1978), *Import Substitution, Trade and Development*, Johnson Associate Press, Connectiut.

Anwar, Sajid (1985), "Export Functions for Pakistan: A Simultaneous Approch", *Pakistan Journal of Applied Economics*, Vol. IV, No. 1, Summer, pp. 29-34.

Baer, Werner and Isacc Kerstenezky (1964), "Import Substitution and Industrialisation in Brazil", *American Economic Review*, Vol. LIV, No. 3, p. 424.

Baer W. and A. Maneschil (1971), "Import Substitution, Stagnation and Structural Change: An Interpretation of the Brazilian Case", *Journal of Developing Areas*, Vol. 5, No. 2.

Baer, Werner and Mechael Herve (1966), "Employment and Industrialaisation in Developing Countries", *Quarterly Journal of Economics*, Vol. IXXX, No. 1, pp. 88-107.

Balassa B. (1981), *The Newly Industrializing Countries in the World Economy*, Pergamon Press, Oxford.

Benerji, Ranadev (1975), *Export of Manufactures from India: An Appraisal of Emerging Pattern*. J. C. B. Mohr (Paul Siebeck), Tubingen.

Bhagwati, J. N., and Desai P. (1970), *India-planning for Industrialaisation and Trade Policies Since 1951*, OECD, Paris.

Bhagwati, J, and A. O. Krueger (1973), "Exchange Control, Liberalaization and Economic Development", *American Economic Review-Papers and Proceedings*, Vol. 63, No. 2, p. 420.

Bhagwati, J. N. and T. N. and T. N. Srinivasan (1975), *Foregn Trade Regimes and Economic Development:India*, Columbia University Press, New York and London.

Bruton, H. J. (1981), "The Import-substitution Strategy of Economic Development: A Survey", in Lan Livingsten (ed), *Development Economics and Policy Readings*, George Allen and Unwin, London, pp. 167-172.

Chen, K. Y., Edward (1987), *National Economic Policies for Industrial Development–Complementarity and Incompatibility among Countries in Asian Pacific Region*, Seventh Biennial General Meeting on Commonalities and Complementarities in the Asia and the Pacific Region, Vigyan Bhavan, New Delhi, pp. 2-7.

Cohen, B. (1963), "A Comment on S. J. Patel's Analysis of Indian Exports", *Indian Economic Journal*, July-September, pp. 37-46.

Daniel, M. Schydlowsky (1967), "From Import Subtitution to Export Promotion for Semi-Grown-up Industreis: A Policy Proposal", *The Journal of Development Studies*, Vol. 3, No. 4, pp. 405-413.

Desai, V. V. (1969), "IS and Growth of Consumer Industries", *EPW*, March, 15, pp. 499-504.

Diaz-Alejandro, C. F. (1965), "On the Import Intensity of the Import Substitution", *Kyklos*, Vol. 18., No. 3.

Felix, D. (1968), "The Dilemma of Import Substitution–Argentina", In G.F. Papnek, *Development Policy–Theory and Practice*, Harward Unversity Press, Massachuesttes, Cambrdge.

Felix, David (1964), "Monetarists, Structuralists, and Import Substituting Indistrialisation: A Critical Appraisal", in W. Baer and I. Kerstenezky (eds), *Inflation and Growth in Latin America*, Homewood, Illnois.

Findlay, R. (1973), *International Trade and Development, Theory*, Columbia University, New York.

Griffin, K. B. and J. L. Enos (1970), *Planning Development*, Addison-Wesley Publishing Co., London.

Henry, G. G. (1970), "Domestic Demand Pressure and Short-Run Export Fluctuations", Yale *Economic Essays*, Spring, pp. 43-81.

Hirschman, Albert (1968), "The Political Economy of Import Substituting Industralization in Latin America", *Quarterly Journal of Economics*, Vol. 82, No. 1, February, pp. 1-32.

Isher Judge Ahluwalia (1984), *Industrial Stagnation since Mid-Sixties*, Oxford University Press, Delli.

Johnson, G. Harry (1960), "The Cost of Protection and The Scientific Tariff", *The Journal of Political Economy*, Vol. LXVIII, No. 4., pp. 327-332.

Johnson, G. Harry (1964), "Tariffs and Economic Development: Some Theoretical Issues", *The Journal of Development Studies*, Vol. 1, No. 1, pp. 131.

Johnson, L. L. (1967), "Problem of Import Substitution : The Chilean Automobile Industry", *Economic Development and Cultural Changes*, Vol. 15, No. 2, Part 1, January.

Kaplinsky, Rephall (ed) (1984), *Third World Industrialaization in the 1980's : Open Economies in a Closing World*. Frank Class and Co. Ltd., p. 9.

Kareem, P. Abdul (1989), "The Second Stage of Import Substitution : A Case of India", *Indian Economic Journal*, Vol. 36, No. 3.

Kareem, P. Abdul (1989),"Import Substitution in Indian Engineering Industry", *Artha Vijnana*, Vol. 31, No. 4.

Kareem, P. Abdul (2001), "Determinants of India's Machinery Exports, 1970 -87 ", *Indian Economic Journal*, Vol. 48, No. 2.

Kareem, P. Abdul (2004), "Trend, Composition and Direction of India's Machinery Exports, 1970-87", *International Journal of Applied Economics and Econometrics*, Vol. 12, No. 4.

Kavoussi, M. Rostam, (1984), "Export Expansion and Economic Growth: Further Empirical Evidence", *Journal of Development Economics*, Vol. 14, Nos. 1-2. Jan-Feb., pp. 241-250.

Kelkar, V. L. and Sharma O. P. (1976), "Trends and Determinats of India's Export Performance 1961-74", *Foreign Trade Review*, October-December, pp. 283-311.

Khan, A. R. (1970), "Import Substitution, Export Expansion and Consumption Liberalization, A Preliminary Report", in *Nurul Islam*, pp. 121-139.

King, T. (1970), *Mexico Industrialisation and Trade Policies since 1940*. Oxford University Press, London.

Krueger, A. O. (1975), *The Benefits and Cost of Import Substitution in India: A Micro-Economic Study*, University of Minnesota Press.

Leela, Pillalamarri (1984), *Import Substitution and Economic Efficiency*, Himalaya Publishing House, Bombay.

Lewis, S. R. and Guisinger S. E. (1968), "Measuring Protection in a Developing Country: The Case of Pakistan", *Journal of Political Economy*, Vol. 76, No. 6 December.

Lubitz, Raymaond (1973), "Export-led Growth in Industrial Economices". *Kyklos*, Vol. XXVI, pp. 307-321.

Macarious (1964), "Protectionism and Industrialisation in Latin America", *Economic Bullettin for Latin America*, United Nations, Vol. 9.

Metawally, M. M. and H. U. Thamaschke (1980), "Oil Export and Economic Growth in the Middle East", *Kykols*, Vol. 33, Fasc. 3, pp. 499-522.

Mithra, P.K. (1974), "Import Substitution and Export Promotion as Means to Industrialization", *Economia Internazoinale*, Vol. XXVII, No. 3-4, August-November, pp. 524-537.

Nambiar, R. G. (1977), "Is, Domestic Resources Cost and Key Sectors in the Indian Economy", *Economic and Political Weekly*, June 11, pp. 954-962.

Ohlsson, A. Lennart (1980), *Engineering Trade Specialization of Sweden and other Industrial Countries*, North Holland Publishing Company, New York.

Panchamukhi, V. R. (1969), "Import Dependence and Export Production Efficiency", *EPW* Annul Number, pp. 77-78.

Panchamukhi, V. R. (1967), "Planning for Import Substitution: Some Methological and Emperical Results", *Artha Vijnana*, Vol. 9, No. 1, March, pp. 466-501.

Pitre, Vidya (1979), "Import Subtitution in Mechinery and Transport Eqipment Sector, 1960-70", *Economic and Political Weekly*, July 21, pp. 1212-1216.

Pomfret, R. W. T. (1975), "Manufactured Export Expansion in a Semi Developed Economy: The Israeli Case", *Economia Internazionale*, August-November, pp. 464-477.

Power, J. G. (1971), "Import Substitution as an Industrialaization Srategy", *Philippine Economic Journal*, Vol. 6, No. 1, spring.

Rangnekar, K. B. (1970), "Is the Indian Export Structure Change", in J. C. Sandesara (Ed)., *Problems of Indian Economic Development*, Bombay University, Bombay.

Ramana, D. V. (1968), "Deficit Financing and Import Substitution in India, 1951-1965", *Institute for Economic Development and Planning*, Monograph No. 8, Bangtok, Thailand.

Reppy, J. V. (1972), "Small Market Constraints on Import Substituting Industrialaization", *(Ph.D Thesis*, Cornell University, p. 119).

Singer, H. W. (*et al*) (1993), *Trade Liberalisation in the 1990's*, Indus Publishing Company, New Delhi.

Singer, H. W. (*et al*) (2002), *Export–led Versus Balanced Growth in the 1990's*, B.R. Publishing Corparation, Delhi.

Singh, Manmohan (1964), *India's Export Trends and the Prospects for Self-sustained Growth*, Clarendon Press, Oxford.

Soligo R. and Joseph J. Stern (1970), *Tariff Protection, Import Substitution and Investment Efficiency* in Nurul Islam (ed), Studies on Commercial Policy and Economic Growth. *The Pakistan Institute of Development Economics*, Karachi, pp. 243–267.

Tavares, M. C. (1964), "The Growth and Decline of Import Substitution of Bazil", *ECLA, Economic Bulletin for Latin America*, Vol. IX, No.1, United Nations, New York.

Tavares, Maria deconceicao (1978), "The Growth and Decline of Import Substitution in Brazil", *Economic Papers*, Vol. 30, No. 1, March.

Tiwari, R. S. (1986), *India's Export Performance: Factors Influencing Export and Policy Directions*, Deep and Deep Publications, New Delhi.

Tripathy, B. N. (1985), *Export and Economic Growth*, Mittal Publications, Delhi.

Tseng, Wanda and David Cowen (Eds.) (2005), *India's and China's Recent Experience with Reform and Growth*, IMF, Palgrave Macmillan, NewYork.

Tyler, W. G. (1973), "Manufactured Export Promotion in a Semi-Industrialised Economy: The Brazilian Case", *The Journal of Development Studies*, October, pp. 3-15.

Tyler, W. G. (1974), "Lalour Absorption with Import Substituting Industrialization: An Examination of Elasticities of Substitution in the Brazilian Manufacturing Sector", *Oxford Economic Papers*, Vol. No. 1, March, pp. 93-103.

UNCTAD (1982), *Hand Book of International Trade and Development Statistics*, 1981, Supplimentary, TD/STAT/10, Geneva.

Versiani, Flavi Roberlo (1980), "Industrial Investment in an Export Economy: The Brazilian Experience before 1914", *Journal of Development Economics*, Vol. 7, No. 3, September, pp. 307-329.

Wasow, Bernard (1978), "Development Growth in a Capital-Importing Economy: The Case of Puerto Rico", *Oxford Economic papers*, Vol. 30, No. 1, March.

Weiskoff, E. Thomas (1967), "A Programing Model for Import Substitution in India", *Sankhya*, Series B., Vol. 29, Parts 3 and 4, December, pp. 257-306.

Winston, G. C. (1967), "Consumer Goods and Capital Goods Supply Constistency in Developing Planning", *Pakistan Development Review*, Autumn.

CHANGING PHILOSOPHY OF MARKETING MANAGEMENT

MATHEW EMMANUEL*

INTRODUCTION

The role of marketing in economic development is well reflected in the words of Malcolm P. McNair, who described marketing as "the creation and delivery of standard of living". The 'Modern Guru' of Management, Peter F. Drucker believes firmly that marketing occupies a critical role in respect of the development of under-developed areas: indeed marketing is the most important multiplier of such development. Marketing puts the machinery of production and consumption in gear. It converts the economy consumption oriented. Marketing is practiced today in all modern nations, regardless of their political philosophy. Today the former socialist economies are undertaking a major effort to convert to market-driven economies. Market economy is a private enterprise economy governed by consumer sovereignty, a price system and the forces of supply and demand. In the case of developed economies like the USA, Japan, UK, Germany etc., the innovations in marketing act as a catalyst for further development. In such countries the volume of production with all its up-to-date technology is generally more than the demand. These have contributed considerable dynamism in evolving marketing techniques and new marketing strategies. The gradual development in the field of know-how pay avenues for the show-how. Noted economic historian W. W. Rostow has tried to prove that marketing throws its positive imprint on the national economy. In developing economies, marketing is still in its infancy. Marketing in these countries is probably the most neglected area. Industrialisation and organisation go hand in hand with application of modern refinements in the field of marketing. An effective marketing system alone can bring the fruits of production to the people. India provides the best example in this connection. Marketing is a multiplier of managers and entrepreneurs and an effective engine of development.

It mobilise latent economic resources and thus is the creator of small business. Indeed, economic growth in the less developed nations of the world

* *Reader in Economics, St. Xavier's College, Vaikom, Kerala.*

depends greatly on their ability to design effective marketing systems to produce global customers for their raw materials and industrial output. Production may be the door to economic growth of the developing countries, but marketing is the key that turns the lock. It is now strongly held that the process of economic growth is one of increasing the size of the market.

Non-profit organisations are now recognised the importance of marketing functions. This is a result of broadening the concept of marketing to include any entity that engages in exchanges of "something-of-value". Libraries, colleges and universities, houses of worship, civic organisations, charitable organisations, and community centres are just a few examples of Non-profit marketing. The 'Four *Ps* in Marketing' (product, price, place, and promotion) with the help of marketing research can be used to plan programmes aimed at influencing acceptability of social ideas.

In the context of the above background we would now introduce to a more general role of marketing.

1. The first and foremost role is that it stimulates potential aggregate demand and thus enlarges the size of the market.
2. Another important role which marketing plays is that it helps in the discovery of entrepreneurial talent.
3. It helps to achieve, maintain and raise standard of living of the society.
4. Still another important contribution which marketing makes is that it helps in sustaining and improving the existing levels of employment.
5. Effective marketing system enables to maintain price level stable by equating demand and supply.
6. Export trade and tourism promotion calls for a comprehensive marketing strategy designed to provide a well-knit package of services.
7. Economic integration is made possible through proper distribution of products.
8. Marketing has also been used to promote tourism in various countries.

PART–II

Marketing activities should be carried out under some philosophy. Historical accounts of trade practices have led some to conclude that marketing has always existed. As long as there have been people, some form of exchange has existed. Over 6000 years of recorded history document that the roots of both Western and Eastern civilisation included some form of trade. Barter system may be regarded as the initial beginning of the concept and approach of marketing in the evolution process. Under the Barter system of marketing the goods are exchanged against goods without the medium of money.

The marketing concept or philosophy has undergone a thorough and gradual change since the great Industrial Revolution that took place during the latter half of the 18th and first half of the 19th centuries. According to Kotler and Keller there are five alternative philosophies which could give the marketing management.

THE PRODUCTION CONCEPT

The production concept is one of the oldest concepts guiding sellers. Production orientation is a business philosophy that emphasises the manufacture and delivery of products. According to Kotler and Armstrong, production concept holds that consumers will favour products that are available and highly affordable. Production is considered to be an ultimate aim. Whatever is produced is fed into the market. In such a situation consumers readily accepts the product that is made available. The Industrial Revolution of the eighteenth century was the beginning of the production era, which lasted until the late 1920s. The production era had seller's markets in many industries in which the demand for products exceeds the supply.

The production concept is still a useful philosophy in two types of situations. The first is where the demand for a product exceeds supply, as in many third world countries. Here the consumers are more interested in obtaining the product than in its fine points. The second situation is where the product's cost is high and has to be brought down through increased productivity to expand the market. For many years, Texas Instruments (US) followed a philosophy of increased production and lower costs in order to bring down prices.

THE PRODUCT CONCEPT

The product concept holds that a consumer will favour those products that offer the most quality, performance or innovative features. Managers in product-oriented organisations focus their energy on making superior products and improving them over time. Till 1930s, there prevailed a strong feeling that whenever a firm has a good product, it results in automatic consumer response. This product oriented marketing philosophy was built on "good wine needs no bush".

The product concept leads to the kind of marketing myopia. Prof. Theodore Levitt introduced the term marketing myopia-an undue concentration on the product rather than on the needs of the consumers. The producers are much immersed in their product and they enter into a "love affair with the product" forgetting other factors that contribute to consumers' satisfaction. In marketing myopia, Levitt argued that the central preoccupation of corporations should be with satisfying customers rather than simply producing goods.

THE SELLING CONCEPT

The selling concept holds that consumers and businesses, if left alone, will ordinarily not buy enough of the organisation's products.

Sales orientation is a business philosophy that focuses marketing activities on selling available products. The organisation must therefore undertake an aggressive selling and promotion effort. The essence of sales orientation philosophy is "goods are not bought but sold". This philosophy has been prevailing since 1940. Most of the companies in our country are practicing the selling concept. It is more prevalent in selling insurance policies, encyclopedias and other unsought goods. In non-profit areas, selling concept is also practiced by fund-raisers, political parties etc.

THE MARKETING CONCEPT

Marketing concept accepts the consumer as the 'king'. According to Kotler and Keller the marketing concept holds that the key to achieving its organisational goals consists of the company being more effective than competitors in creating, delivering and communicating customer value to its chosen target markets. In the marketing-orientation stage companies identify what consumers want and tailor all of the activities of the firm to satisfy those needs as efficiently and effectively as possible. Its central tenets crystallized in the mid-1950s. Only the Marketing concept is capable of keeping the organisation free from 'marketing myopia'.

Instead of a product-centered "make and sell" philosophy, the marketing concept is a customer centered "sense and respond" philosophy. It views marketing not as "hunting", but to find the right products for your customers. The marketing concept starts with a well-defined market, focuses on customer needs, and integrates all the marketing activities that affect customers. In turn, it yields profits by creating lasting relationships with the right customers based on customer value and satisfaction. Modern marketing starts and ends with the customer. The producers of the 19th century had little care for the consumers. The marketer aims to develop the market; the market becomes seller's market. But this situation has changed. We have a gradual shift from caveat emptor (buyer beware) to caveat vendor (seller beware). Consumer becomes the pivot of all business decisions. To satisfy the customer, his/her needs are to be known. Marketing research starts at this stage. Marketing starts and ends with the consumer with information flowing from the consumer to the producer and goods flowing back to the consumer from the producer. Forty five years ago Peter Drucker, the most influential business writer of the 20th century, observed that companies exist not to make a profit, but to create and satisfy customers. . Marketing, thus, is the creation and delivery of standard of living. Marketing orientation requires an organization wide commitment to researching and responding to customer needs. A marketing orientation involves being responsive to ever-changing customer needs and wants. The market or customer—orientation philosophy can be illustrated as under:

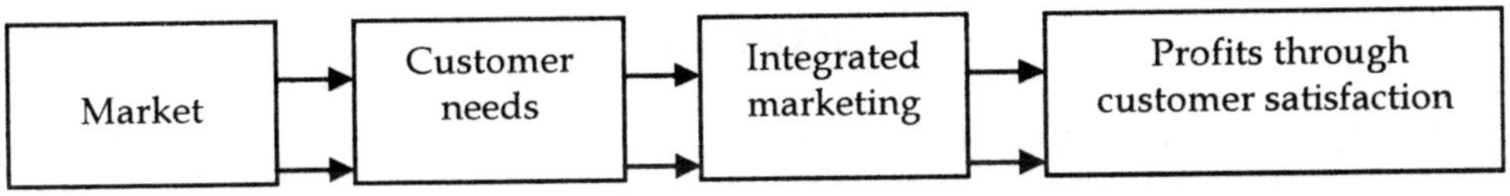

To implement the marketing concept, a marketing oriented organization must accept some general conditions and recognize and deal with several problems. Management must first establish information to create satisfying products. Again, to satisfy customers' objectives as well as its own, a company must also coordinate all its activities. Examples of implementation of the marketing concept include relationship building, mass customization, heightened sensitivity to quality, value creation, and the societal marketing concept. *Mass customization* is developing, producing, and delivering affordable products with enough variety and uniqueness that nearly every potential customer can have exactly what he or she wants.

BENEFITS OF MARKETING CONCEPT

Contemporary marketing management is founded on the marketing concept and a large number of companies in business sector, both national and international are increasingly adopting marketing approach. Indian companies like Nirma, SAIL, Godrej, Reliance, ACC, Tata, Hindustan Lever, DCM, Birla etc are adopting the marketing approach and pledging better products, better value, better living. Besides, a large number of non-profit and service organisations are also using the marketing approach. Schools, colleges, universities, hospitals, theatre companies are offering their services through advertisements. The following are the important uses of marketing concept.

1. Long term success is assured to an enterprise if it recognises that needs of the market are paramount or supreme.
2. Customer needs, wants and desires receive top consideration in all business activities.
3. Greater attention is paid to the product planning and development so that merchandising can become more effective.
4. Interests of the enterprise and society can be harmonised as profit through service is emphasised.
5. It ensures effective utilisation of physical and human resources. Under a market minded firm, management has the responsibility to create value-satisfying goods and services that consumers will want to buy.
6. Demand side of the equation of exchange is honoured more and supply is adjusted to changing demand.

PART–III

HOLISTIC MARKETING CONCEPT

The holistic approach for business firms is required for developing the organization and promoting the marketing of the goods and services thereof. Peterson and Waterman had prescribed the concepts of 7 Ss comprising systems, structure, strategy, style, staff, skills, and shared values for effective organizational development. Holistic marketing concept is based on the development, design, and implementation of marketing programmes, and activities that recognizes their breadth and interdependencies. Holistic marketing recognizes that "everything matters" with marketing- and that a broad, integrated perspective is often necessary. Four components of holistic marketing are relationship marketing, integrated marketing, internal marketing, and social responsibility marketing. It is an approach to marketing that attempt to recognize and reconcile the scope and complexities of marketing activities. Four components of holistic marketing are relationship marketing, integrated marketing, internal marketing, and social responsibility marketing.

RELATIONSHIP MARKETING

Relationship marketing has the aim of building mutually satisfying long-term relationships with key parties- customers, suppliers, distributors, and other marketing partners -in order to earn and retain their business. It brings strong economic, technical and social ties among the parties. Relationship marketing involves cultivating the right kind of relationships with the right constituent groups. Marketing must not only do customer relationship management (CRM), but also partner relationship management (PRM) as well. Customer Relationship Management is establishing multidimensional connections with a customer such that the organization is seen as a partner. Under Partner Relationship Management activities the firm undertakes to build mutually satisfying long-term relations with key partners such as suppliers, distributors, ad agencies and marketing research suppliers.

INTEGRATED MARKETING

The holistic approach of the company to satisfying the customer should have the vision, mission, and strategy, creativity, knowledge, and shared values. Many companies agree with Peter F. Drucker that "the purpose of the company is to create a customer" but fail to take the necessary organisational steps to implement the marketing concept. When all the company's departments work together to the customer's interest the result is integrated marketing. Integrated marketing takes place on two levels. First, the various marketing functions—salespeople, advertising, product management, marketing research and so on—must work together. Second, marketing must be well coordinated with the other company departments. To foster teamwork among all departments, the company carries out internal marketing and external marketing.

INTERNAL MARKETING

Holistic marketing incorporates internal marketing, ensuring that everyone in the organization embraces appropriate marketing principles, especially senior management. Internal marketing is the task of hiring, training, and motivating able employees who want to serve customers well. External marketing is marketing directed at people outside the company.

SOCIETAL MARKETING CONCEPT/SOCIAL RESPONSIBILITY MARKETING

Holistic marketing incorporates social responsibility marketing and understanding broader concerns and the ethical environmental, legal, and social context of marketing activities and programmes. The cause and effects of marketing clearly extend beyond the company and the consumer to society as a whole. Social responsibility also requires that marketers carefully consider the role that they are playing and could play in terms of social welfare.

Marketing is a social process involving the activities necessary to enable individuals and organizations to obtain what they need and want through exchanges with others and to develop ongoing exchange relationships. Social or societal marketing concept has been the brain child of Philip Kotler and his team. It is broadened marketing concept. Since 1980, management is called up on to bring about balance of three factors: 1. Consumer wants 2. Public interest and 3. Profitability. The societal marketing concept is a principle of enlightened marketing that holds that company make good marketing decisions by considering consumers' wants, the company's requirements, consumers' long run interests, and society's long run interests. Societal marketing concept is a management philosophy that considers the welfare of society as well as the interests of the firm and its customers. Firms adopting the social marketing concept make marketing decisions in an ethical and socially responsible manner. Social marketing is the design, implementation and control of programmes calculated to influence the acceptability of social ideas. It is also called humanistic marketing and ecological marketing. We witness a change in the emphasis from materialism to humanism in our society. According to Prof. Amartya Sen, markets can be powerful institutions with far reaching consequences and the role of market mechanism in socialist systems must be seen as an instrumental question. It means that the firm is to produce not only what is needed by the consumers but that is good for the society. It has been charged with its social responsibility. The following figure shows three considerations underlying the societal marketing.

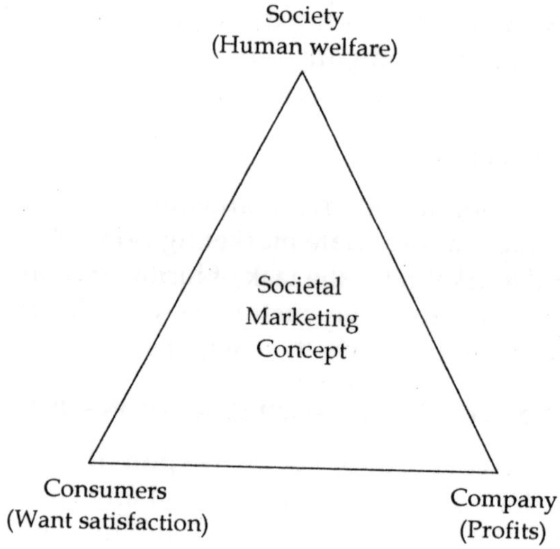

The societal marketing concept constitutes an adequate business philosophy in an age of environmental problems, resource shortages, inflation, rapid population growth and neglected social services. Now many companies are beginning to think of society's interests when making their marketing decisions. Amul, a near monopoly in India's dairy industry, was meant to meet welfare objectives. Corporate ethics has become a hot topic in almost every business area, from the corporate board room to the business school classroom.

References

Philip Kotler, Kevin Lane Keller, *et. al* (2009), Marketing Management, 13th edn, Pearson Education, Delhi

J. C. Gandhi (2001), Marketing: A Managerial Introduction, Tata McGraw-Hill Publishing Co., Delhi

S. A. Sherlekar (2006), Marketing Management, 13th edn, Himalayala Publishing House, Mumbai

Philip Kotler & Gary Armstrong (2008), Principles of Marketing, Prentice-Hall of India, Delhi

William J. Stanton *et. al* (2004), Marketing, 14th edn, Tata McGraw-Hill Publishing Co., Delhi.

William M. Pride and O. C. Ferrell (2005), Marketing: Concepts and Strategies, 12th edn, Biztantra, Delhi. American Marketing Association, December 2006, Accessed at *www.marketingpower.com/mg-dictionary-view*

V. S. Ramaswamy & S. Namakumari (2009), Marketing Management, 4th edn, Macmillan Publishers India Ltd.

William D. Perreault Jr. & Jerome McCarthy (2005), Basic Marketing: A Global-Managerial Approach, Tata McGraw-Hill Publishing Co., Delhi.

AN ATTEMPT TO HIT TWO BIRDS WITH A STONE–HOW SMART A CHOICE?[1]

AVANI BANSAL*

PART–I

EMERGENCE OF 'SUSTAINABLE DEVELOPMENT'–A MERE EYEWASH?

Bureaucratic socialism collapsed because it did not allow prices to tell the economic truth. Market economy may ruin the environment and ultimately itself if prices are not allowed to tell the ecological truth.
– Ernst U. Von Weizsacker[2]

BEFORE SUSTAINABLE DEVELOPMENT: EMERGENCE OF 'FREE TRADE' AND 'ENVIRONMENT PROTECTION' AS CONCEPTS ON GLOBAL SCALE :

Trade and Environment are two themes that has dominated the thought of mankind for generations. They seem to be as old as humanity itself.[3] When first two human beings would have exchanged something, that would have been the beginning of 'trade' and when they would have halted to appreciate the beauty of a nature around them or watch a tree growing with surprise, that would have been the emergence of first thoughts towards 'environment protection'.[4]

From then to today, things have a changed a great deal and so has humanity. However the purpose of this paper will be served if we trace the emergence of these two concepts on the world forum. From Adam Smith, who is considered to be the originator of the concept of 'free trade' based on 'principle of comparative advantage' to the WTO mechanism, all barriers to trade have only come to weaken and so has the number of its critics. On the other hand, though there were some bilateral and multilateral treatise on preserving birds[5] and fur seals [6] in the beginning of the 20th century, International Environmental Law has had only recently captured the imagination of the thinkers around the globe.[7] It is surprising that environment protection was not an issue on the UN agenda when it was established over 50 years ago and so the UN was not given a specific mandate to address issues concerning the environment though it had carved out a role for itself by widely interpreting its preamble and articles

* *Hidayatullah National Law University, Raipur.*

such as 1(4), and 3 of the Charter to the UN.[8] However the Stockholm Conference in 1972[9], marks the birth of International Environmental Law from where world community has never looked back in this sphere of 'environment protection.' But so far so good, the question arises as to why was a need felt for bringing these two concepts together?

BIRTH OF 'SUSTAINABLE DEVELOPMENT': PROVIDING A LINK BETWEEN ENVIRONMENT AND DEVELOPMENT ISSUES

The Maltese proposal at the UN General Assembly 1967 contended that "there is a common heritage of mankind" which requires legal protection. In the words of M. Schroder Sustainable Development is a principle, action and instrument "to secure conditions" for the survival of future generations of Mankind.[10]

Stockholm Declaration on Human Environment gave impetus on: Control of pollution and conservation of natural resources and socio economic development which is the key element of environment protection.[11]

The Montreal Protocol, 1987 aimed at the elimination of ozone depleting substances. The term "Sustainable Development" with reference to environment was rolled into circulation in the World Commission on Environment and Development (Brundtland Commission) in 1987.[12] However this term 'Sustainable Development' was defined by Rio Declaration, in 1992, in the following words–"an action to secure the conditions for survival of future generation."[13] The purpose of the 1992 UN Conference on Environment and Development (UNCED or Rio) was to revisit the environmental issues raised at the 1972 Stockholm Conference and provide a better linkage of environmental and developmental issues. One commentator observed that UNCED "may mark the eruption of vastly complex issues of environmental management and sustainability into every nook and cranny of international economic relations."[14] The establishment of the Commission on Sustainable Development and ten years later, the convening of the World Summit on Sustainable Development in Johannesburg, South Africa, attest to the validity of the observation, atleast theoritically.[15] UNCED did reach its goal, at least in part, be establishing "irrevocably the connection between environmental protection and economic growth."[16]

SYNTHESIS OF FREE TRADE AND ENVIRONMENT PROTECTION: HOW AND WHY?

The synthesis emerged from adoption of Agenda 21[17] by the world community, which calls for making trade and environment mutually supportive. It states:

> *"An open, multilateral trading system makes possible a more efficient allocation and use of resources and thereby contributes to an increase in production and incomes and to lessening demands on the environment. It thus provides additional resources needed for economic growth and development and improved environmental protection. A sound environment, on the other hand, provides the ecological and other resources needed to sustain growth and*

underpin a continuing expansion of trade. An open, multilateral trading system, supported by the adoption of sound environment policies, would have a positive impact on the environment and contribute to sustainable development."[18]

Agenda 21 cautions that trade restrictions should address the "root causes of environmental degradation so as not to result in unjustified restrictions on trade,"[19] and be implemented with care. Agenda 21 also calls on GATT/WTO to "develop more precision, where necessary, and clarify the relationship between GATT provisions and some of the multilateral measures adopted in the environment area,"[20] and to "ensure that environmental policies provide the appropriate legal and institutional framework t respond to needs for the protection of the environment that may result from changes in production and trade specialization."[21] Following the Rio Summit, UNEP has been collaborating with WTO and the United Nations Conference on Trade and Development (UNCTAD)[22] on trade and environment issues, with a view to ensuring that trade and environment policies become mutually supportive.[23]

Thus the question arises as to why was this need to synthesize these two branches felt in the first place especially when champions of the growth and liberalization of international trade and those equally passionate about the environment have traditionally carved separate paths, finding little in common.[24] For proponents of liberalizing international trade, focus on the environment meant a potential adverse impact on world trade. Environmentalists on the other hand, generally perceived the liberalization, growth, and integration of world trade as a threat to the environment.[25]

The hypothesis that underlies this synthesis is that increased trade leads to greater wealth, thus allowing a state to undertake environmentally protective measures and resulting in a win-win situation.[26] A second argument advanced in favour of this synthesis is that trade restrictions will facilitate implementation of environmental agreements[27] and also that trade agreements involve many countries working together for a common interest, which in turn provide a convenient for a in which to discuss other common interests as well, such as the environment. A third argument is that liberalized trade fosters "common standards for environment protection," which all states must meet.[28]

HAS THIS SYNTHESIS SERVED ITS PURPOSE?

The experience with international environment agreements invoking trade measures has been largely that they are of doubtful impact although the impact on environmental trade is not too insignificant. The fact is that some of the soft provisions of hard laws, and some of the soft laws themselves , tend to lay foundations for more coherent and effective international environmental laws.[29] But the question still arises as to how long will we take in building on this foundation or will we ever have a body of international environmental laws that will be effective in answering the relevant questions? After analyzing the reasons that were advanced for the synthesis of trade and environment, it is imperative to analyze how well has this synthesis achieved what it had sought to achieve–a balance between the two.

Right from the beginning, this argument in favour of the synthesis has not been without criticism. The perspective of the environmentalists simply stated is this–"Trade means more goods produced and thus in many cases more environmental damage. The wealth created by trade will not necessarily result in environmental improvements."[30] Thus there is, to begin with, opposition to the very idea of synthesis. Then there is a question of 'implementation' of this idea of 'sustainable development'.

Firstly, although Agenda 21, contains the detailed agreement of over 170 countries to pursue the goal of sustainable development, it is largely hortatory and recommendatory in nature and does not purport to bind UNCED participants to particular actions.[31] Over after more than 10 years after the adoption of this noble document, the gap between rhetoric and reality in promoting sustainable development has only widened.[32]

Secondly, Committee on Trade and Environment (CTE)[33], even after more than a decade of its existence has failed to come up with any substantial recommendations. Directed by the Marrakesh decision to report to the first WTO Ministerial Conference in Singapore 1996, the report of the Committee summarizes the result of the two years of deliberation as follows: ' Work in the WTO on contributing to build a constructive policy relationship between trade environment and sustainable development needs to continue'.[34]

Thirdly, the Commission on Sustainable Development (CSD) which was created to monitor the implementation of Agenda 21 and to integrate the roles of different actors in the linking of environment and development has not achieved its goal.[35] While its scope and jurisdiction are broad, the tremendous responsibilities assigned to the CSD far exceed the modest resources it has for implementing them. Furthermore it was not given any power or authority with which to discipline member states who failed to comply with Agenda 21. As a result of these two issues, the CSD has little influence over the governing bodies of international organizations such as the World Bank Groups and the World Trade Organisations. Furthermore, the submission of country reports to the CSD is done on a voluntary basis, and the decision about what material to include them is entirely discretionary. Not surprisingly, these reports tend to be long on self-congratulation and short on substantive analysis of remaining challenges.[36]

Fourthly, there is a fear that trade rules will lead to multinational companies (MNCs) seeking out countries with weak regulatory standards for products and production processes, often in developing countries, in order to lower their compliance costs leading to more production in areas with lower standards. This might also trigger 'race to bottom' in lowering standards and harmonisation of laws around these low standards.[37] Therefore the synthesis of the two is important to protect the environment.

Fifthly, there is a fear that the laws of developed countries which create higher standards domestically or try to promote environmental goals abroad will be challenged as disguised protection that violates trade rule, and thus environmental protection will be undermined in this way as well. The US-Gasoline case is an example of the former, the Tuna/Dolphin and Shrimp/Turtle case are examples of the latter.[38]

It can thus be seen that inspite of the noble intents, nothing concrete has been done to convert them into reality. No systematic study has been undertaken to see the extent to which the eight conventions which use trade measures to protect environment such as BASEL, CITES, Montreal Protocol etc. have been successful in realizing their goal.

PART–II

IS THERE A NEED FOR AN ALTERNATIVE? LET'S SET OUR PRIORITIES RIGHT

After tracing the history behind the concept of 'sustainable development' and analyzing the ground reality, a question of paramount importance is how the WTO/GATT system will accommodate MEAs that employ trade restrictions, especially in the wake of the most favoured principle and the national treatment principle.[39] No WTO/GATT dispute resolution panel yet has directly addressed the conformity of any MEA trade restrictions with GATT rules and the validity of some MEA trade restrictions is atleast doubtful, in particular those involving process and production methods, discrimination between parties and non-parties and extra-territorial application.[40] Thus Article XX (b) and (g) of the GATT will have to be interpreted on a case-to-case[41] basis for balancing trade and environment[42]. It will not be difficult for anyone to guess, that when such a question will be left for WTO dispute settlement body to decide upon, which way will the balance tilt.[43] This skepticism has all reasons to hold ground and there is absolutely no reason why this skepticism should not be given rest by clearly setting our priorities and finding an answer to this question, rather than letting it hang in doldrums.

The need for a relook on this forged synthesis also arises from the fact that the Environmental Kuznets curve which posits the idea that during the process of economic development, the quality of the environment initially deteriorates as pollution emissions increase and then after some time the environment improves again as the economy achieves higher levels of income and development, has not proved itself over these decades. USA, a developed country is facing and contributing to environmental degradation just as any developing or underdeveloped country is. Some studies have also indicated that though some pollutants seem to become less of a problem with any economic growth; others simply get worse with economic growth without any apparent limit; and some that look like they obey the EKC may stop doing so and follow an unpleasant N-curve pattern instead.[44]

Thus to continue with this synthesis on two thesis viz. (1) free trade will promote economic development and (2) economic development will lead to environment protection seems to me nothing but a mere eye wash created by the developed countries who continue to pocket the benefits of economic development at the cost of the developing and underdeveloped countries.

PART–III

WHAT IS THE ALTERNATIVE? THE WAY AHEAD

This might sound as just another attempt to undo all those attempts so far that tried to create a balance between the competing interests–free trade and environment protection. It might also sound like an attempt to negate all the arguments in favour of free trade and its benefits and thus challenge the wisdom behind free capitalistic world economy. If it does, it would have served its purpose.

The alternative that I wish to propose to this 'synthesis model' is very simple. It is to settle this debate of priorities between free trade and environmental protection in favour of the latter. To take it one step further, it is to give priority to environment protection over and above everything else. It is to understand the urgency required to save our planet earth, to save it for this generation. I am no scientist, no environmentalist, who is armed with all the statistics that reminds us of the grim situation that our world is facing today in the wake of imminent environmental hazards, for this has already been done. I am only a citizen who knows that she like everyone else has only been overly optimistic, having convinced herself, that all the problems that are being talked about will not lead in my extinction, which reduces all my fears, because then it is not my problem! But like everybody else, I also sense the fast approaching danger or calamity, call it by any name. And thus I do not think that it needs an International conference to understand this simple thing. However it definitely does need an International conference to propagate this simple idea. The details can always be chalked down, structures built, mechanism discussed. But it is the approach that to my mind is important. And the proposed model calls for a leap towards an ecocentric approach in all that the international community do, saying goodbye to the anthropocentic approach that has dominated our minds for too long.

PART–IV

DO I SEE FROWNED FACES AND RAISED EYEBROWS? POSSIBLE ARGUMENTS IN DISSENT

Amongst many possible arguments against the proposed model, I have deliberated on the two most important of them–

There is a possibility that even those who agree with the proposed model may not be sure if this will not be misused by the nations. For example, Seymour

J. Rubin states–'There can hardly be a quarrel with the proposition that, in many cases, the requirements of environmental policy take precedence over the desiderata of world trade. Nonetheless, a measure that speaks to environmental protection may well be aimed principally at trade restriction... Other measures may have indeed environmental or other legitimate societal goals as their justification, but may have restrictive trade effects beyond those required by the environmental objective.'[45] This to my mind brings out the essence of the major possible opposition to the proposed model. He further suggests way to deal with this problem. Though this problem is a genuine one, solutions are available in the model itself. If we have convinced ourselves of the importance that we have accorded to environment protection, then we should not declare a policy of a nation aimed at environment protection to be illegal merely because it also restricts trade. Secondly, for those policies that are aimed at trade restriction, but also serve the goal of environment protection, also should be allowed as it fits in the model. However, in the third category of the cases, where the environment protection is only minimal with huge losses in trade to the country against whom the ban is issued, there should be a fair appraisal of the facts. However it should be done not by WTO, but rather by an independent body. It might be said that this is nothing but again balancing of competing interests, however to my mind, in this model, we haven't treated both free trade and environment protection as being on equal pedestal, rather we have tilted the balance clearly in favour of the latter, with some exception regarding the third category.

A second possible argument is that those countries who do not adopt this model may give rise to the problem of 'Pollution havens' ie the country might attract more investment by lowering its standards as opposed to those countries who are adhering to strict and hard environmental laws.[46] This would give the advantage of 'external free riding' to those who do not follow the model, thereby further bringing down the incentive of those who do. The solution to this problem lies in making the model universally applicable though a body of agreements aimed at creating a jurisprudence of hard environmental laws. However in order to punish the non-compliant states, it is not the trade restrictions that need to be adhered to, as several other option exist in International law which can be implemented by the UN.

PART–V

IS THE PROBLEM SO SIMPLE? CONCLUSION

Yes the problem is really that simple. What we need today is not the synthesis of free trade and environment protection rather a symbiosis[47] between man and his environment. Dr. Paul Sears of Yale University has written:

> *Any species survives by virtue of its niche, the opportunity afforded by its environment. But in occupying this niche it also assumes a role in relation to its surroundings. For further survival it is necessary that its role atleast be not a disruptive one. Thus, one generally*

finds in nature that each component of a highly organized community serves a constructive, or at any rate, a stabilizing role. The habitat furnishes the niche, and if any species breaks up the habitat, the niche goes with it. .....That is, to persist they (ecological communities) must be able to utilize radiant energy not merely to perform work, but to maintain the working system I reasonable good order. This requires the presence of organisms adjusted to the habitat and to each other, so organized as to make the fullest use of the influent radiation and to conserve for use and re-use the materials which the system requires. The degree to which a living community meets these conditions is therefore a test of its efficiency and stability.[48]

We have often heard statements like these but still we refuse to believe and understand this simple truth. 'Environmental spiritualism' can be the only answer, the panacea of all our ills.[49] Therefore if our natural resources are to be preserved, and mother earth has to live, we need to fix our priorities, give up hypocrisy, and should not exhaust all our energy in developing concepts that we don't want should work. Even if we do want them to work, then we should make all attempts to do so. But after our experiences for all these decades, I think there is a need for a change–a change in our attitude–lets us stop hitting two birds with a stone. One at a time. And that one a long as it is in our hands should be preserved.

Notes

1. Submitted by Avani Bansal (IV year), Hidayatullah National Law University, Raipur, C.G.
2. *See* P. K. Rao (2000), *Sustainable Development- Economics and Policy*, Blackwell Publishers, p. 261.
3. *See* Richard M. Auty and Katrina Brown (1997), *An Overview of Approaches to Sustainable Development in Approaches to Sustainable Development*, ed. Richard Mu. Auty and Katrina Brown, Printer, London and Washington, pp. 3-20.
4. *See generally* J. Ashok A. (1998), Desai, *Environmental Jurisprudence*, Vikas Publishing House Pvt. Ltd..
5. International Convention for the Protection of Birds Useful to Agriculture (Paris, March 19, 1902), 30 Martens (2d) 686; 102 B.F.S.P. 969.
6. Treaty for the Preservation and Protection of the Fur Seals (Washington D.C., February 7, 1911), 104 B.F.S.P. 175; Convention for the Preservation and Protection of Fur Seals in the North Pacific, 5 Martens (3rd) 720.
7. *See Birth and Evolution of International Environmental Law* in Alexander Kiss and Dinah Shelton, *International Environmental Law*, Transnational Publishers Inc, 1991, pp. 33-55.
8. *See* Shawkat Alam (2006), *The United Nations' Approach to Trade, the Environment and Sustainable Development*, ILSA Journal of International and Comparative Law, Vol. 12, No. 3, p. 609.
9. *See* Stockholm Declaration on the Human Environment adopted by the United Nations Conference on the Human Environment, June 16, 1972, Section I of the Report of the United Nations Conference on the Environment, U.N. Doc. A/CONF.48/14 and Corr. 1 (1972), reprinted in 11 I.L.M. 1416.
10. Meinhard Sehroder (1995), Law and State, Vol. 51, 1995, pp. 101-113.

11. For details *see* Stockholm Declaration, 1972.

12. *See* Towards Sustainable Development, in Our World Future-World Commission on Environment and Development, Oxford University Press, New York, Rep.1987, pp. 43-66.

13. *See* for detail "The Earth Summit's " Rio Declaration.

14. *See* K. Von Moltke (1993), *The Last Round: The General Agreement on Tariffs and Trade in Light of the Earth Summit*, 23 Envt. L., pp. 519- 520.

15. *See generally Principles of Sustainable Development*, ed. F. Douglas Muschett, St. Lucie Press, Florida, 1997.

16. *See* D. Esty, *Beyond Rio: Trade and Environment*, 23 Envt. L., 1993, pp. 3-87; P. H. Sand, UNCED and the Development of International Environmental Law. C795 ALI-ABA 747 (1993). *See generally Sustainability, the Environment and Urbanization, ed. Cedric Pugh,* Earthscan Publications Ltd., London.

17. Agenda 21, Report of the United Nations Conference on Environment and Development, Vol.1, Annex II, at 9, U.N. Doc. A/CONF.151/26/ Rev. 1 (1993).

18. *Id.* Para 2.19.

19. *Id.* Para 2.20.

20. *Id.* Para 2.22(2)

21. Id. Para 2.22 (8).

22. For Criticism of UNCTAD *see* P.T.Bauer, *A Critique of UNCTAD* in *Dissent on Development-Studies and Debates in Development Economics*, Weidenfeld and Nicolson, 1971, pp. 234-271.

23. UNEP, Report of the Governing Council, 21 Sess (5-9 Feb 2001), 56 GAOR Supp.25. decision 21/14, U.N. Doc., A/56/25 (2001).

24. *See* Ved P. Nanda and George (Rock) Pring, *International Environmental Law and Policy for the 21st century*, Transnationla Publishers, Inc., Ardsley, New York, p. 393.

25. *See generally* T. J. Schoenbaum ((1993)), *Free International Trade and Protection of the Environment: Irreconcilable Conflict?* 86 AM. J.Int'l L. 700 (1992); G.Feketykuty. *the Link Between Trade and Environment Policy*, 2 Minn. J. Global Trade 171.

26. *See* United Nations Environment Programme (UNEP) and International Institute for Sustainable Development (IISD), Environment and Trade–A Handbook, at 4 (2000) (the trade perspective: "Trade can actually be good for the environment, since it creates wealth that can be used for environment improvement, and the efficiency gains from trade can mean fewer resources used and less waste produced."; S.Charnovitz, *The Environment v. Trade Rules: Defogging the Debate*, 23 ENVTL.L. 475 (1993). *See also* John Young, *Sustainable Development and Green Politics in The Environment-Global Problems and Local Solutions*, ed. James E.Hickey Jr., and Linda A. Longmire, Greenwood Press, London, pp.25-33, wherein he states " Like most of the current advocates of sustainable development, Hawke argues that since environmental reform is going to be expensive we need, if anything, faster growth rates in order to pay for it.This is rather like telling a fat man that if he wants to get thin, he will need to eat more, so that he has the energy to take some exercise so that he can lose some weight" at 27-28.

27. *See* Stuart Bell and Donald McGillivray, *Environmental Law*, edn 5th, Universal Law Publishing Co. Pvt. Ltd., Indian rep.2001, wherein the author states that–" A potent mechanism for making international agreements effective is the prospect of trade restrictions being imposed against non-compliant states, and some treaties make provision for such restrictions." At 105.

28. *See* Charnovitz, supra note 27 at 576.
29. *See* P K Rao, *International Environmental Law and Economics*, Blackwell publishers, 2002, at 270.
30. United Nations Environment Programme (UNEP) and International Institute for Sustainable Development (IISD), Environment and Trade–A Handbook (2000) at 4.
31. *See* Jacob D.Werksman, *Greening Bretton Woods*, The EarthScan Reader in Sustainable Development, *et al* John Kirby, 1995, pp. 274, 281.
32. *See Supra note* 8 at 626.
33. Establsihed by the Ministerial Decision of the GATT contracting parties on 14 April 1994. *See* Trade and Environment, GATT Ministerial Decision of 14 April 1994, 33 ILM (1994), p. 1267.
34. WTO Doc. Wt/CTE/1 (1996) p. 47.
35. United Nations Conference on Environment and Development, Rio De Janerio, Brazil, June 3-4, 1992, Resolutions Adopted by the Conference, U.N.Doc A/CONF.151/26/ Rev.1 (June 14, 1992), Ch.38. Para 11.
36. *See International Environmental Law and Policy, et al* David Hunter, 1998, p. 402.
37. *See* Simon Lester and Bryan Mercurio with Arvel Davies and Kura Leither, *World Trade Law- Text, Materials and Commentary*, Hart Publishing, 2008, p. 822.
38. *Ibid* at 824.
39. *See* Patricia Birnie and Alan Boyle, *International Law and the Environment*, edn 2nd , Oxford Univresity Press, 2002, p. 699-705.
40. *Ibid* at 705.
41. *See* Ved P Nanda and George (Rock) Pring, *International Environmental Law and Policy for the 21st century*, Transnational Publishers Inc, New York, for a discussion on all the case decided by the WTO on this question.
42. *See* Sabrina Shaw and Risa Schwartz, *Trade and Environment in the WTO- State of Play* , Journal of World Trade, VOl.36, No.1, (2002), p. 129, where the authors state – " ..Owing to the lack of recommendations from the CTE to date on various trade and environment issues, compounded by the delay in launching a new round of tradenegotiatios, it has been argued that the relationship between trade and environment in the WTO is, in effect, being created through disputes."
43. *See* Ravindra Pratap, *Trade and Environment: Trends in International Dispute Settlement*, Indian Journal of International Law, Vol. 42, No. 4 (2002), pp. 451-488.
44. *See* J.barkley Rosser, Jr., *Institutional Evolution and the Environmental Kuznets curve in Economic Development, Climate Change and the Environment*, edt. Ajit SInha and Siddhartha Mitra, Routledge, 2006, p. 39.
45. *See* Seymour J.Rubin, *A Predominantly Commercial Perspective in Environment and Trade– The Relation of International Trade and Environmental Policy*, ed. Seymour J. Rubin and Thomas R. Graham, pp. 3-4.
46. For more on Pollution havens, *see Supra* 39 pp. 721-725.
47. *See generally* S Bhatt, *Environment Protection and International Law*, Radiant Publishers, 1985, p.111 where he states that "Professor Falk, who like Arnold Toynbee has also advocated spiritual control of technology to safeguard our global environments ." *See also* B.D. Nagchudhari, *The Global Environment Movement- A New Hope for Mankind*, Sterling Publishers Pvt. Ltd., 1987, pp.5-12.

48. Paul B., Sears, *The Process of Environmental Change by Man*, in *Man's Role in Changing the face of Earth*, ed. W.L.Thomas Jr., Universty of Chicago Press, Chicago, 1956. *See also* David L Wheeler, *The Human Habitat-Contemporary Readings*, Van Nostrand Reinhold Company, 1971, pp. 255-272.

49. *See* J.V.R.Krishna Iyer, *Towards a Natural World- The rights of nature, animals, citizens and other essays*, Hope India, 2004, p. 11 where the author describes environmental spiritualism as–"Spiritually speaking, the quintessence of the environmental movement, in its widest sweep, is that everything belongs to the Supreme Self and performs its Karma with a functional nexus. In practical terms, there is a purpose for everything in Nature too sacred to be destroyed."

REBRANDING AND ITS IMPACT IN CONSUMER PREFERENCE–A STUDY

T. Samson Joe Dhinakaran*

INTRODUCTION

In this dynamic world nothing is permanent except change. We witness changes in all aspects of modern world. It is said that necessity is the mother of invention. In the often-day, there were a lot of unsophisticated way and means of communication like birds, messenger, postal mail, etc. Today, in the era of communication novel means of communication came into existence. Postal mail has been replaced to certain extent by e-mail and landline is being replaced by hand phones called cell phones. It is reported by relevant authorizes that after the invention and introduction of cell phones the rate of surrounding landline is at a decreasing rate and the number of users of cell phones is increasing even day by day. Usage of cell phones is not restricted to urban talk and educated youth.

OPERATIONAL DEFINITIONS

Brand Name

A word or combination of words used to identify a product and differentiate it from other products.

REBRANDING

Rebranding is as much about changing corporate iconography as it is about changing the way of communication with the customers. This is especially true today due to the media and advertising consumption changes that have occurred with the advent of the internet and other new media technologies. These changes are impossible to ignore.

OBJECTIVES OF THE STUDY

Present study is made on the basis of following objectives

* *Lecturer in Commerce, (Self-financing wing), St. Johns College, Palayamkottai, Tirunelveli, E-mail :samson_dhina@yahoo.com*

- to study the growth of the company after Rebranding,
- to know the effectiveness of the Sales Promotional Activities,
- to find out the awareness made by the Company,
- to know about the offers provided to the Customers and
- to Study the customer attitude towards Vodafone and to Other Brands.

METHODOLOGY

The present study is an empirical research based on survey method. Primary data were collected directly from the customer and retailer by using a well framed questionnaire. The relevant secondary data have been collected from the Journals, and Internet. The Collected data were coded, calculated and analyzed with the help of statistical tools like Measures of central tendencies, Ranking, Chi-square test, Anova table, Percentiles, Tabulation were used. The researcher has made the convenient random sampling of 200 Customers and 60 Retailers in his report.

LIMITATION OF THE STUDY

The present study is limited to the area of Tirunelveli Corporation. Only Rebranding and its effects on consumer are taken into account. Since, there is no previous study in this topic; the researcher could not do any intensive study.

COMPANY PROFILE

The Vodafone Group Foundation was set up as a registered Charity and acts as an umbrella organization to make social investments that help the people of the world lead fuller lives. The Vodafone Group Foundation received recognition as registered charity number 1089625 from the Charity Commission for England and Wales on 4th December 2001. The Vodafone Group foundation is driven by one of the four passions of Vodafone Group–Passion of the world around the company. The Vodafone Group Foundation is at the Centre of a network of global and local social investment programmes. Globally, Companies Foundation make social Investments by funding projects which support disaster relief and preparedness or fund in sport and music projects which benefit some of the most disadvantaged young people and their communities. Locally, the company's social investment is delivered by a unique foot print of 24 Vodafone foundations and social investment programmes.

INDIAN OPERATION

In India, Hutch became Vodafone, now; the pink colour logo of Hutch is replaced by Vodafone Corporate red coloured one. In 2005–2006, the Orange brand in Mumbai was phased out to introduce Hutch. The company also changed the colours of its logo from orange to pink last year. After acquiring 67 per cent of stake (around Rs. 250 crores) in Hutchison Essar from Hong

Kong-based Hutchison Whampoa, Vodafone Essar is expecting to Hutch over 35 million customers across 400000 shops and thousands of own employees along with employees of its business associates.

AREA PROFILE

Tirunelveli District was formed in 1790 by the East India Company, later came under the direct control of the British Crown Queen Victtoria. The name Tirunelveli has been composed from the three Tamil words i.e. 'Thiru-Nel-Veli' meaning Sacred Paddy Hedge. Tirunelveli District having geographical area of 6823 sq.kms, in the Southeastern portion of Tamil Nadu is triangular in shape. It lies between 8°.05' and 9°.30' of the Northern latitude and 77°.05' and 78°.25'of Eastern longitude. The district is located in the southern part of Tamil Nadu and surrounded by Virudhunagar District on the north, Western Ghats on the west, Kanniyakumari District on the south, Tuticorin District on the East. The lifeline of the district river Tamiraparani feeds the district and quenches the thirst of Tuticorin district too.

GROWTH RATE OF CELL PHONE COMPANIES AS ON "OCT. TO NOV. 07"

After rebranded of hutch as Vodafone the increase level of the new customers are shown.

Company	*Total Customers*	*New Customers*	*Market Share%*	*Growth Rate %*
Airtel	5.30 Crore	21 Lakhs	31.90	4.03
Vodafone	3.86 Crore	14 Lakhs	23.30	3.70
BSNL	3.20 Crore	9 Lakhs	19.30	2.90
IDEA	2.02 Crore	8 Lakhs	12.20	4.10
Aircel	90 Lakhs	5 Lakhs	5.40	5.90
SPICE	37 Lakhs	1 Lakh	2.20	2.60
MDLN	29 Lakhs	60 thousand	1.70	2.30

Source: *Economics Times* dated 12.12.07.

From the above table, it is clear to see the growth rate of the cell phone companies. On which the Vodafone gets the second place among the rebranded company. Vodafone company within the short period of time increased the customers after rebranding.

RANKING

The factors which helps consumers satisfaction while selecting the Vodafone connection are listed below.

- Continuous Connectivity
- Provide Good Service
- Call Rate

- Connection with Handset
- Replacement Warranty

The Weighted arithmetic mean is computed for each reason. The Computed Weighted Arithmetic mean for the above reasons for factors satisfied the customers to select the Vodafone Connection are listed.

Option	*Rank* 5	4	3	2	1	*Total*
Satisfactory factors						
Continuous Connectivity	12	59	49	14	66	200
Provide Good Service	28	62	59	37	14	200
Call Rate	131	24	32	7	6	200
Connection with Handset	20	32	37	65	46	200
Replacement Warranty	9	23	23	77	68	200
Total	200	200	200	200	200	

Reason	*Weighted Reasons for Satisfactory factors* *Rank*
Call Rate	1
Provide good service	2
Continuous Connectivity	3
Connection with Handset	4
Replacement Warranty	5

The table displays that the weighted arithmetic mean for various reasons. The most weighted reasons for the factors satisfies the customer by Vodafone are, Price (4.34) next to price, good services provided by Vodafone Company (3.27), Continuous Connectivity comes third place (2.69) followed by connection with Handset (2.58) and Replacement Warranty (2.14) respectively.

The Customer prefers Vodafone for many reasons. The needs of the customer vary from person to person. The Customer select Vodafone Company to fulfill the Cost compared to other Mobile connection.

RANKING

RANKING – H. Test or Kruskal-Wallis

A	*RANK*	*B*	*RANK*	*C*	*RANK*	*D*	*RANK*	*E*	*RANK*	*F*	*RANK*
5	35	27	32	28	31	13	33	36	29	0	36
90	19	56	28	60	26	30	30	56	28	74	24
102	16	84	21	68	25	80	22	78	23	108	15
150	8	135	11	99	18	196	6	85	20	147	9
176	7	136	10	100	19	648	1	116	14	222	5
225	4	260	2	120	13	8	34	132	12	250	3
$N_1 = 6 : R_1 89$		$N_2 6 : R_2 104$		$N_3 6 : R_3 132$		$N_4 6 : R_4 126$		$N_5 6 : R_5 126$		$N_6 6 : R_6 92$	

OFFERS SATISFIED BY VODAFONE TO CUSTOMER

$$H = \frac{12}{n(n+1)} * \sum_{i=1}^{k} \frac{R_i^2}{n_i} - 3(n-1)$$

= 0.009 (12729.51) – 111

=114.57 – 111

Calculated Value = 3.57

N = 6-1 = 5

Table Value 5% level = 11.07

Hypothesis is *Accepted* because the Calculated value is *less* than the Table Value

AGE AND PERIOD OF USING HUTCH/ VODAFONE

The researcher used Anova table to find out any significant difference between the respondents age and period of using Vodafone.

Null Hypothesis: There is no significant difference between the respondents Age and Period of using Hutch/Vodafone.

	Age					
Option	*15-25*	*25-35*	*35-45*	*45-55*	*55 & above*	*Total*
How long Using						
Less than 1 year	23	-	-	-	-	23
1-2 year	35	-	-	-	-	35
3-4 year	8	52	-	-	-	60
4 & above	-	-	41	30	11	82
Total	66	52	41	30	11	200

Correction Factor CF = T^2/n

= $200^2/(5*4)$

= 2000

Sum of Square Between Column = $\Sigma x^2/n$ – (CF)

= 440.5

Sum of Square Between Row = $\Sigma y^2/n$ – (CF)

= 415.6

Sum of Individual = (Sum of Square) - (CF)

= 7224-2000

= 5224

ANOVA Table

Option	*Sum of Squares*	*Degree of freedom*	*Mean Square*	*F Ratio*	*F Test @ 5%*
Sum of Squares between Column	440.5	4	110.13	0.30	3.26
Sum of Squares between Row	415.6	3	138.53	0.38	3.49
Residual	4368.4	12	364.03		
Total	5224	19			

Degrees of freedom in this case

$$= (r - 1)(c - 1)$$
$$= (5 - 1)(4 - 1)$$
$$= 12$$

Hence the Researcher Accepted the Hypothesis because the calculated value is Less than the table value. So, there is no significant difference between the respondents Age and Period of using Hutch/Vodafone.

DISTRIBUTION OF THE RESPONDENTS ON THE BASIS OF WAY OF KNOWING VODAFONE

The way of knowing Vodafone by the respondents was evident by the Table

Source of knowledge	*Number of respondents*	*Per centage*
Friends	78	39
Relatives	31	15.5
Advertisement	78	39
Through Outlets	13	6.5
Total	200	100

Source: Primary data.

The above table shows that respondents have come to know about Vodafone equally through friends and advertisements is 39 percentage, 15.5 percentage of respondents come to know about Vodafone through relatives and 6.5 percentage through outlets.

BUYING PURPOSE OF THE RESPONDENTS

Null Hypothesis: There is no significant relationship between the purpose of purchasing Vodafone mobile phone and users gender.

Chi-square Test

Gender	*Business*	*House use*	*Friend-ship*	*Love relationship*	*Social relation*	*Total*
Male	20	46	42	9	3	120
Female	8	25	38	8	1	80
Total	28	71	80	17	4	200

O	E	O – E	$(O-E)^2$	$(O-E)^2/E$
20	16.8	3.2	10.24	.61
8	11.2	-3.2	10.24	.91
46	42.6	3.4	11.56	.27
25	28.4	-3.4	11.56	.41
42	48	6	36	.75
38	32	6	36	1.13
9	10.2	-1.2	1.44	.14
8	6.8	1.2	1.44	.21
3	2.4	-.6	.36	.15
1	1.6	-.6	.36	.23
				4.81

Degrees of freedom in this case

$$= (r - 1)(c - 1)$$
$$= (5 - 1)(2 - 1)$$
$$= 4$$

Tabulated Value = 9.48

Calculated Value = 4.81

Hence the Researcher Accepted the Hypothesis because the calculated value is Less than the table value. So, there is no significant relationship between the purpose of purchasing Vodafone mobile phone and users gender

FINDINGS

After analyzing the data which were collected from the respondents the following findings are derived.

- The number of users using Vodafone has doubled after the transition.
- The main source of exposing this transition is through advertisements.
- Most of the users like Life Card.
- Most of the users of Vodafone are satisfied with the trouble free performance of the instruments and so most of its user feels that it is good.
- As a result none of the users of Vodafone would like to replace it in the future.

CONCLUSION

This study revealed the existing realities about cell phone usage as prevalent among people in Tirunelveli. From the above findings the researcher could come to the conclusion that the process of transition from Hutch to Vodafone is outstanding, that in a few years the Sale of Vodafone is increased and that its popularity among the people is also be quite good. The researcher believes that cell phone usage has become a habit of the people, rebranding has positive impact on both customer loyalty and revenue. With the positive note the researcher conclude his study with real satisfaction.

DYNAMICS OF DEBT ACCUMULATION IN INDIA DURING POST-LIBERALISATION PERIOD

R. BALASUBBIRAMANI*

INTRODUCTION

India's fiscal situation has been at the very centre of the process as well as literature on reforms. The inability to bring the fiscal deficit under control after more than decade of reforms is perceived to be one of the latter's failures. This concern has especially grown since 1998-99 with the reversal in the trend of the earlier years of reforms of a declining debt to GDP ratio. As a result, the perception has gained ground that the debt to GDP ratio could soon become unsustainable, that is, government will not be able to service the debt, leading eventually to fiscal collapse.

Rangarajan and Srivastava (2003) made an attempt to analyse the dynamics of debt accumulation in India over the period 1951-52 to 2001-02 with reference to the impact of primary deficit, growth and interest rate. Our analysis starts from 1992-2006, and takes into consideration the impact of fiscal deficit along with growth and interest rates. Further the period of analysis has been extended upto 2006-07 and the entire period from 1992-93 to 2006-07 has been divided into post liberalisation periods.

In the accumulation of debt, two factors are identified as contributing to the debt-GDP ratio. One is the cumulated primary deficits and the other, the cumulated effect of the difference between growth rate and interest rate. This paper looks at the relative contribution of cumulated primary deficits and the cumulated effect of the excess of growth rate over interest rate on the accumulation of outstanding liabilities of the government of India over the post (1992-93 to 2006-07) liberalisation periods.

Many economists ponder over the problem of sustainability of debt. The following three recent papers reinforce the problem of India's debt situation.

Rangarajan and Srivastava (2003) after examining the trends in debt-GDP ratio since 1951-52 conclude, "The cushion provided by the excess of growth

* *Faculty of Economics, Department of Management, Sree Amman Arts And Science College, Chittode, Erode, Tamilnadu, India, E-mail:econbalu@yahoo.com*

over interest rate may not continue for long. For three years, viz 2000-01 to 2002-03, the interest rate exceeded the growth rate. This, together with the continuing primary deficits, though at a reduced level, led to acceleration in the debt-GDP ratio in recent years....... where corrections in the primary balance profile of the central government have become imperative." In other words, they opined that growth by itself cannot be expected to bring down the problem under control.

In a similar vein, Pinto and Zahir (2004) contended that a programme of robust fiscal reform is needed to combat unsustainable public debt dynamics. Ram Mohan *et al.,* (2005) revisited the proposition that India's debt problem is unsustainable, in the light of the recently changed outlook for growth and interest rates and concluded that if recent government behaviour were to continue, the economy would need to grow at 6.1 per cent in the coming years for the centre's debt to be sustainable."

This paper re-examines the question of fiscal sustainability in the light of present outlook for growth and interest rates. We confine ourselves to the fiscal position of the centre and do not address the wider problem of the combined debt of the centre and the states. Starting off with the present level of central debt, we ask what order of fiscal adjustment would be required in order to reach a tolerable level of debt in a reasonable time frame. Our projections suggest that the general consensus on the fiscal situation at the centre may be unduly alarmistic, conditioned as it is by growth and interest rate assumptions of a decade ago. Neither the potential for acceleration in the growth rate nor for a reduction in the overall interest rate on debt appears to have been adequately taken into account in most projections.

FINANCING DEFICITS BY ALTERNATIVE CHANNELS

It has received attention relates to the relative merits of financing fiscal deficits by domestic borrowing, external borrowing, or borrowing from the central bank. In theory, financing by external debt would lead to pressure on the exchange rate. Financing domestic debt by monetisation would put pressure on inflation and that by domestic borrowing, on interest rates. For example, Moorthy *et al.,* (2000), while examining the issue of bond-financing versus monetisation, in the context of debt stabilisation, conclude that the emphasis on market borrowing rather than borrowing from the RBI as part of the economic reforms in India in the 1990s has proved to be beneficial. In Rangarajan *et al.,* (1989), the inter-temporal budget constraint was used to study the dynamic interlink ages between government deficits and alternative modes of financing these. In particular, given the set of revenue and expenditure parameters, relevant for the late 1980s, it was shown that the bond financing scenario led to an explosive growth in the debt-GDP ratio, and the monetary financing scenario led to an unacceptably high inflation rate within a short span of time.

TOLERABLE LEVEL OF CENTRAL PUBLIC DEBT FOR INDIA

What would be tolerable level of central debt in India? While there is no theoretical basis for determining an absolute tolerable level (Reinhart *et al.*, 2003) we may be guided by norms available elsewhere.

The debt level that European Union States are committed to under the Maastricht treaty is 60 per cent of GDP. The Eleventh Finance Commission (EFC 2000) argued infavour of a total debt GDP ratio of 55 per cent. Ram Mohan, Ravindra Dholakia and Navendu Karan advocated 50 per cent from the present level of 56.8 per cent and suggested a growth rate of 6.1 per cent would suffice for this purpose.

Rangarajan and Srivastava (2005) suggested stabilisation of fiscal deficit at 6 per cent of GDP and the debt-GDP ratio at 56 per cent. Thus it is evident that the tolerable level is determined by stable debt/GDP ratio (D/Y).

CONTROLLING DEBT AND FISCAL DEFICIT: RULES AND TARGETS

Borrowing by the government often appears to be a softer option than increasing taxes or reducing expenditures. That is why, as established by international experience also, it is important to provide exogenous limits on borrowing by governments, whether central or sub-national. Such limits can be exercised through fiscal responsibility legislations, or other institutional arrangements like the Australian Loan Council and the Maastricht Treaty for member countries of the European Economic Community. The Maastricht Treaty on Economic and Monetary Union, for example, has two convergence conditions for members of the European Monetary Union country's overall budget deficit for each fiscal year must be equal to or below 3 per cent of the GDP and a country's stock of public debt must be equal to or less than 60 per cent of the GDP. The 3 per cent limit is not meant to be exceeded in 'normal' economic downturns.

DATA ISSUES

The study covers the period 1992-93 to 2006-07. This study is based on the secondary data collected from Hand Book of Statistics on Indian Economy 2006-07 Published by Reserve Bank of India and details available in Rangarajan and Srivastava's study (2003).

DECOMPOSITION MODEL

The standard specification of the equation describing debt dynamics with discrete time periods as given by Rangarajan and Srivatsava (2003) is

$$b_t = p_t + b_t-1\ [(1+i_t)/(1+g_t)] \qquad (1)$$

Where

b_t = debt-GDP ratio in period t

p_t = ratio of primary-deficit to GDP in period t

g_t = growth rate of GDP in period t
i_t = effective nominal interest in period t

Writing $z_t = b_t - b_t - 1$, equation (1) can also be written as

$$Z_t = p_t - b_{t-1}\left[\frac{(g_t - i_t)}{(1+g_t)}\right] \tag{2}$$

The increment in debt can be cumulated over any relevant period t = 1 to T. Thus

$$\sum_{t=1}^{T} z_t = \sum_{t=1}^{T} p_t - \sum_{t=1}^{T} b_{t-1}\left[(g_t - i_i)/(1+g_t)\right] \tag{3}$$

Equation 3 helps in decomposing the change in the debt-GDP ratio between any two benchmark years $\left[\sum_{t-1}^{T} zt = (b_T - b_o)\right]$ into the contribution of cumulated primary deficit relative to GDP and that of the cumulated effect of the weighted excess of growth over the interest rate. In the Indian case Σp_t has been much larger than Σz_t for long stretches of time, and the role of the growth/interest rate differential has been to absorb the impact of the cumulated primary deficits from getting translated into accretion to the debt-GDP ratio. It is, therefore, useful to write equation (3) as

$$\sum_{t=1}^{T} p_t = \sum_{t=1}^{T} z_t - \sum_{t=1}^{T} b_{t-1}\left[(g_t - i_t)/(1+g_t)\right] \tag{4}$$

Of the cumulated primary deficit relative to GDP, that part which was absorbed by the differential of growth rate and interest rate is given by,

$$\sum_{t=1}^{T} b_{t-1}\left[(g_t - i_t)/(1+g_t)\right] / \sum_{t=1}^{T} p_t \tag{5}$$

Correspondingly, the share of the cumulated primary deficit which results in the accretion to the debt-GDP ratio is given by

$$\sum_{t=1}^{T} z_t / \sum_{t=1}^{T} p_t$$

It might be useful to further decompose the term containing the effect of growth-interest rate differential between the effect of GDP growth and effective interest rate differential. Writing g and i for GDP growth and effective interest rates, then using formula is that g_t-i_t.

CENTRAL GOVERNMENT DEBT AND DERIVED FISCAL AND PRIMARY DEFICITS IN INDIA DURING POST-LIBERALISATION (1992- 93 TO 2006-07) PERIOD

Table 1 shows the central government debt and derived fiscal and primary deficits during Post- Liberalisation Period. The annual rate of growth of debt was 18.9 per cent in 1993-94, and declined 12.7 per cent in 2006-07 with mild fluctuations in the intermitant years. It is evident that all variables, especially the variables which influence the debt build up were on the increasing mode in a liberalised regime.

Table 1

Central Government Debt and Derived Fiscal and Primary Deficits in India During Post-Liberalisation (1992-93 to 2006-07) Period

(Rupees Crore)

Year	*Total Central Debt*	*Derived Fiscal Deficit*	*Interest Payments*	*Derived Primary Deficit*	*Rate of Growth of Debt (per cent)*
1992-93	401923	47261	31075	16186	13.3
1993-94	477968	76045	36741	39304	18.9
1994-95	538610	60642	44060	16582	12.7
1995-96	606233	67623	50045	17578	12.6
1996-97	675676	69443	59478	9965	11.5
1997-98	778294	102618	65637	36981	15.2
1998-99	891806	113512	77882	35630	14.6
1999-00	1021029	129223	90249	38974	14.5
2000-01	1168541	147512	99314	48198	14.4
2001-02	1366408	197867	107460	90407	16.9
2002-03	1559201	192793	117804	74989	14.1
2003-04	1736678	177477	124088	53389	11.4
2004-05	1994422	257744	126934	130810	14.8
2005-06	2195387	200965	130032	70933	10.1
2006-07	2473562	278175	139823	138352	12.7

Source: C. Rangarajan and D. K. Srivatsva (2003).
Hand Book of Statistics on the Indian Economy, RBI Bulletin 2006-07.

DEBT RELATIVE TO GDP AND GROWTH AND INTEREST RATE IN INDIA DURING POST-LIBERALISATION (1992-93 TO 2006-07) PERIOD

Table 2 indicates that the debt-GDP ratio in the initial year of the liberalised regime was 53.71 per cent and it settled at 61.48 per cent in 2006-07, thus gaining 8 percentage points during the period under review. It is to be noted that the increase was gradual without much volatility. The GDP growth moved up form 5.48 per cent in 1992-93 to 9.354 per cent in 2006-07 gaining about 5 percentage points and gross fiscal deficit GDP ratio up by around 6 percentage points. Effective interest which was 8.762 per cent in the beginning rose to 10.12 per cent in 1999-2000 and declined to 6.36 per cent in 2006-07 leading to negative differences between real growth rate and interest rate thus pushing down the debt-GDP ratio marginally. However gross fiscal deficit-GDP ratio has gone out of control *vis-à-vis* 3 per cent fixed by Eleventh Finance Commission and 6 per cent advocated by KTF, Rangarajan and Srivastava (2005).

Table 2
Debt Relative to GDP and Growth and Interest Rate in India during Post-Liberalisation (1992- 93 to 2006-07) period

(Rupees Crore)

Year	*GDPmp (1999-2000=100)*	*GDP Growth Rate*	*Debt GDP Ratio*	*Derived Fiscal Deficit to GDP-Ratio*	*Effective Interest Rate*	*Real Growth Rate/Real Interest Rate (Per cent)*
1992-93	1272457	5.480	53.71	3.71	8.762	-3.282
1993-94	1333123	4.768	55.63	5.70	9.141	-4.374
1994-95	1421831	6.654	53.18	4.27	9.218	-2.564
1995-96	1529453	7.569	51.03	4.42	9.292	-1.722
1996-97	1645037	7.557	49.38	4.22	9.811	-2.254
1997-98	1711735	4.054	51.12	5.99	9.714	-5.660
1998-99	1817752	6.194	51.22	6.24	10.007	-3.813
1999-00	1952035	7.387	52.31	6.62	10.120	-2.732
2000-01	2030867	4.038	55.58	7.26	9.727	-5.688
2001-02	2136635	5.208	59.9	9.26	9.196	-3.988
2002-03	2216260	3.727	63.43	8.70	8.621	-4.895
2003-04	2402247	8.392	62.8	7.39	7.958	0.433
2004-05	2602235	8.325	63.79	9.90	7.309	1.016
2005-06	2842478	9.232	63.36	7.07	6.520	2.712
2006-07	3108360	9.354	61.48	8.95	6.369	2.985

Source: Hand Book of Statistics on the Indian Economy, RBI Bulletin 2006-07.
Note: GDPmp–Gross Domestic Product–Market Price.

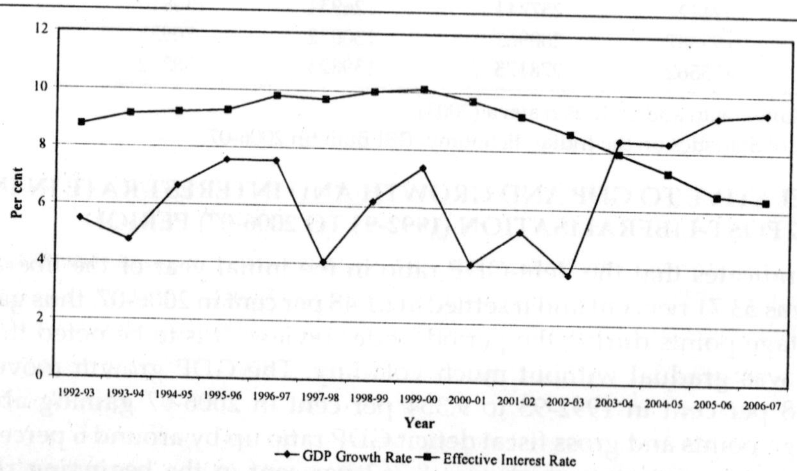

Figure 1: Debt Relative to GDP and Growth and Interest Rate in India during Post-Liberalisation Period

DECOMPOSITION OF PRIMARY DEFICIT AND DEBT RELATIVE TO GDP IN INDIA DURING POST- LIBERALISATION (1992-93 TO 2006-07) PERIOD

The primary deficit to GDP ratio is less volatile and more autonomous than the (g-i) differential. Table 3 shows that the maximum build up of primary deficit was in the years 2001-02, 2004-05 and 2006-07. Similarly changes in debt-GDP ratio were also high during 2000-01 to 2002-03.

However, throughout this period, build up of the debt-GDP ratio could be contained because of the excess of growth rate over interest rate. The primary deficit to GDP ratio since 1993-94 remained below 2.5 per cent of GDP and the change in the debt-GDP ratio was modest till 1999-2000, because the growth rate during this period exceeded the interest rate.

Table 3
Decomposition of Primary Deficit and Debt Relative to GDP in India during Post- Liberalisation (1992-93 to 2006-07) Period

Year	*Primary Deficit to GDP-Ratio (Per cent)*	*Change in Debt-GDP Ratio (Per cent Points)*	*$W(g\text{-}i)[W=b_{t-1}/(1+g_t)]$(Per cent Points)*
1992-93	1.272	-0.590	1.862
1993-94	2.948	1.920	1.028
1994-95	1.166	-2.450	3.616
1995-96	1.149	-2.150	3.299
1996-97	0.606	-1.650	2.256
1997-98	2.160	1.740	0.420
1998-99	1.960	0.100	1.860
1999-00	1.997	1.090	0.907
2000-01	2.373	3.270	-0.897
2001-02	4.231	4.320	-0.089
2002-03	3.384	3.530	-0.146
2003-04	2.222	-0.630	2.852
2004-05	5.027	0.990	4.037
2005-06	2.495	-0.430	2.925
2006-07	4.451	-1.880	6.331

Source: Hand Book of Statistics on the Indian Economy, RBI Bulletin 2006-07.

CUMULATED CHANGES IN DEBT, PRIMARY DEFICIT AND FACTOR REFLECTING EXCESS OF GROWTH OVER INTEREST RATE IN INDIA DURING POST-LIBERALISATION (1992-93 TO 2006-07) PERIOD

Table 4 presents the above details for post-liberalisation period. The debt–GDP ratio which was 24.870 in 1992-93 gradually increased to 32.640 in 2006-07 recording a moderate increase of about 8 percentage points.And the primary deficit-GDP ratio which was 25.627 in 1992-93, increased to 61.797 in 2006-07 gaining 36 percentage pointes during the period under review. Since sign of (g-i) was reversed (from negative) to positive, it stared absorbing the impact of

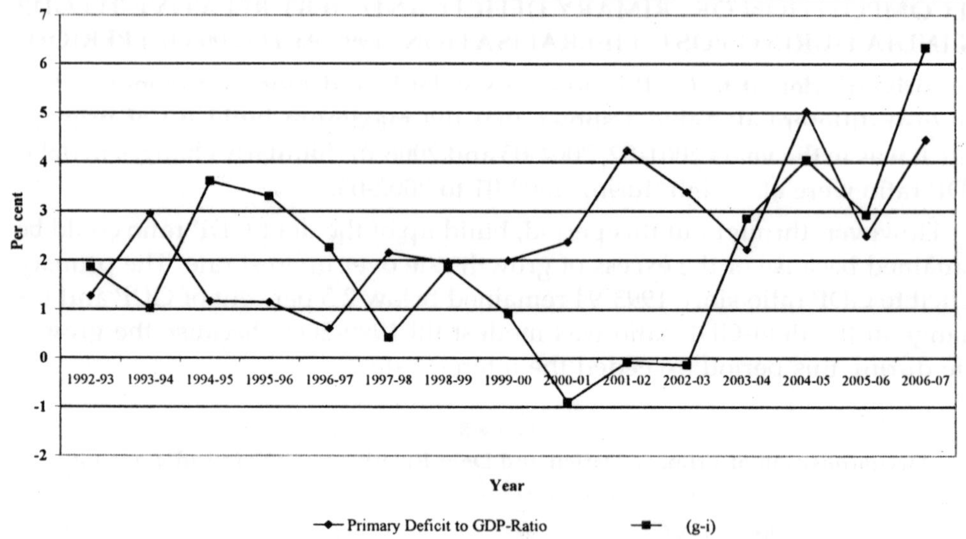

Figure 2: Decomposition of Primary Deficit and Debt Relative to GDP-Ratio during Post-Liberalisation Period

Table 4

Cumulated Changes in Debt, Primary Deficit and Factor Reflecting Excess of Growth over Interest Rate in India during Post-Liberalisation (1992-93 to 2006-07) Period

Year	*Change in Debt-GDP-Ratio Cum b (Per cent Points)*	*Primary Deficits to GDP-Ratio Cum p (Per cent Points)*	*Factor Reflecting Excess of Growth Over Interest Rate Cum w (g-i) (Per cent Points)*
1992-93	24.870	25.627	0.757
1993-94	26.790	28.575	1.785
1994-95	24.340	29.742	5.402
1995-96	22.190	30.891	8.701
1996-97	20.540	31.497	10.957
1997-98	22.280	33.657	11.377
1998-99	22.380	35.617	13.237
1999-00	23.470	37.614	14.144
2000-01	26.740	39.987	13.247
2001-02	31.060	44.218	13.158
2002-03	34.590	47.602	13.012
2003-04	33.960	49.824	15.864
2004-05	34.950	54.851	19.901
2005-06	34.520	57.347	22.827
2006-07	32.640	61.797	29.157

Source: Hand Book of Statistics on the Indian Economy, RBI Bulletin 2006-07.

cumulated primary deficit thus reducing the quantum of debt -GDP ratio considerably during post-liberalisation period. Another note worthy feature during the post-liberalisation period was (g–i) differential turning out to be positive in the initial year itself and as the period progressed the value has increased substantially absorbing higher quantum of primary deficit.

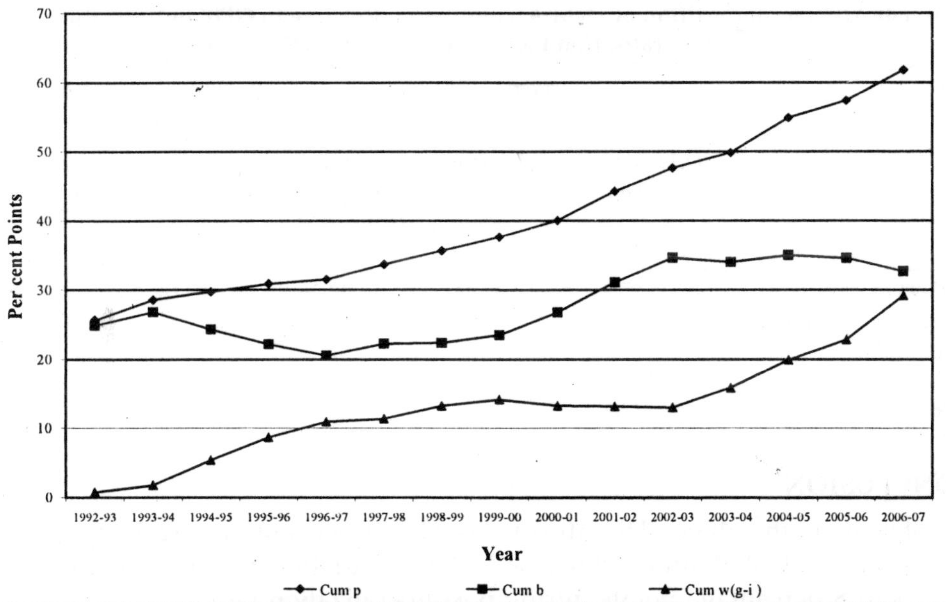

Figure 3: Cumulated Changes in Debt, Primary Deficit and Factor Reflecting Excess of Growth over Interest Rate during Post- Liberalisation Period

DECADEWISE DECOMPOSITION OF DEBT ACCUMULATION RELATIVE TO GDP IN INDIA DURING POST-LIBERALISATION PERIOD

In the post-liberalisation period, the pressure put by the cumulated primary deficit was relatively larger (37.44 percentage points). However, 80.82 per cent of this was absorbed by the differential of growth over interest rate, resulting in only a small increase of 7.18 percentage points in the debt-GDP ratio. That means, the excess of growth rate over interest rate helped to mitigate the situation. In the case of the OECD countries, while both factors contributed to rise in the debt-GDP ratio, the growth-interest differential had become more important in recent years.

Using a similar decomposition for the OECD countries, in a recent contribution, Shigehara (1995) observes that "for the two decades 1974 to 1994, the ratio of net debt to GDP for the OECD area as a whole rose by about 23 percentage points, of which about 18 percentage points can be accounted for by cumulated primary deficits and 5 percentage points can be attributed to the differential between interest rates and growth rates. However since 1980 when the debt dynamics became unfavorable for the OECD area, the debt-GDP ratio has risen by about 18 percentage points of which only 8 percentage points can be attributed to primary deficits and 10 percentage points are accounted for by the effect of the interest rate/growth rate differential".

Table 5

Decadewise Decomposition of Debt Accumulation Relative to GDP in India during Post-Liberalisation Period (Base - 1999-2000 = 100)

	Cumulated Changes in			*Impact of Cumulated Primary Deficit*	
	Debt-GDP Ratio	*Primary Deficit-GDP Ratio*	*Growth and Interest Rate Differential*	*Increase in Debt-GDP Ratio*	*Absorption by Growth/ Interest Differential*
1992-93 to 2006-07	7.18	37.44	30.26	19.18	80.82
Memo: Debt-GDP Ratio at the end of-					
1992-93	53.71				
2006-07	61.48				

CONCLUSION

- Starting with a debt-GDP ratio of about 53.71 per cent in 1992-93, by 2006-07, the debt GDP ratio had reached a level of 61.48 per cent, an increase of about 8 percentage points during post-liberalization period.
- Accumulation of debt relative to GDP during 1992-2006 has been due to cumulated primary deficit caused with the factor of excess of interest rate over growth rate.
- The debt dynamics changed dramatically during post-liberalization period with (g-i) differential turning out to be positive and mitigating the impact of primary deficit in the debt accumulation in a significant way.
- All variables especially interest payments and derived primary deficit which influence the debt build up were on the increasing mode during post liberalization periods.
- Inter-year variability in the debt accumulation process was largely due to growth rate volatility.
- Factor reflecting excess of growth over interest rate cumulated w (g-i) was negative with high magnitude in all the years during 1992-93 to 2006-07.
- Higher negative differential (g-i) led to low absorption of primary deficit (29.89 per cent) and higher build up of debt (70.11 per cent).
- Since, the sign of (g-i) government reversed from negative to positive, it started absorbing the impact of cumulated primary deficit (80.82 per cent)

thus reducing the quantum of debt-GDP ratio (19.18 per cent) in a liberalised regime.

- Another note worthy feature during the post liberalisation period was (g-i) differential turned out to be positive in the initial year itself and as the period progressed the value has increased substantially absorbing higher quantum of primary deficit (80.82 per cent).

References

Moorthy, Vivek, B. Singh and S. C. Dhal (2000), "Bond Financing and Debt Stability: The Oretical Issues and Empirical Analysis for India," Development Research Group Study, 19, Reserve Bank of India, Mumbai June.

Ram Mohan T. T., Ravindra H. Dholakia and Navendu Karan (2005), "Is India's Central Debt Sustainable? Revisiting an Old Debate," *Economic and Political Weekly,* Vol. XL, No. 10, pp. 951-959.

Rangarajan C. and Srivastava, D. K. (2003), "Dynamics of Debt Accumulation in India: Impact of Primary Deficit, Growth and Interest Rate," *Economic and Political Weekly,* Vol. XXXVII, No. 46, pp. 4851-4858.

Rangarajan C. and Srivastava, D. K. (2005), "Fiscal Deficits and Government Debt Implications for Growth and Stabilisation," *Economic and Political Weekly,* Vol. XL, No. 27, pp. 2919-2934.

Rangarajan, C., Anupam Basu and Narendra Jadhav (1989), 'Dynamics of Interaction between Government Deficit and Domestic Debt in India', RBI Occasional Papers, September, also included in Amaresh Bagchi and Nicholas Stern (eds), Tax Policy and Planning in Developing Countries, Oxford University Press, Delhi.

Reinhart, Carmen M., Kenneth S. Rogoff, Miguel A. Savastano (2003), 'Debt Intolerance', Brookings Papers on Economic Activity, Issue 1.

Sanjeev K. Sobhee (2000), "Modelling the Sustainability of Public Debt: The Case of Mauritius," *Indian Journal of Economics,* October Vol. 81, pp. 491-502.

Shigehara, K. (1995), 'Commentary: Long-Term Tendencies in Budget Deficits and Debt' in Budget Deficits and Debt: Issues and Options, Proceedings of a Symposium, (August 31-September 2), Federal Reserve Bank of Kansas City, US.

World Bank (2003), India: Sustaining Reform, Reducing Poverty, Report No 25797-IN.

GROWTH AND STRUCTURE OF GROSS FISCAL DEFICIT IN INDIA

R. BALASUBBIRAMANI*

INTRODUCTION

Fiscal deficits are like obesity. You can see your weight rising on the scale and your clothing size increasing, but there is no sense of urgency in dealing with the problem. (Martin Feldstein 2004). High levels of fiscal deficit relative to GDP tend not only to cause sharp increases in the debt-GDP ratio, but also adversely affect savings and investment, and consequently growth. The usability of fiscal policy as a tool of countercyclical intervention is also compromised when the fiscal deficit is high and structural in nature. This paper examines the growth and structure of gross fiscal deficits in India, its impact on growth that arises from its impact on savings and investment, which may occur directly or through its effects on interest rates and inflation. It also looks at relevant considerations for determining the levels of debt and deficit relative to GDP at which these should be stabilized in India, given the current configuration of key determinants like the revenue to GDP ratio and public and private saving rates, consistent with the objective of achieving higher growth.

THEORETICAL PERSPECTIVES

There is no agreement among economists either on analytical grounds or on the basis of empirical results whether financing government expenditure by incurring a fiscal deficit is good, bad or neutral in terms of its real effects, particularly on investment and growth. Among the mainstream analytical perspectives, the Neoclassical view considers fiscal deficits detrimental to investment and growth, while in the Keynesian paradigm, it constitutes a key policy prescriptive. Theorists persuaded by Ricardian equivalence assert that fiscal deficits do not really matter except for smoothening the adjustment to expenditure or revenue shocks. While the Neoclassical and Ricardian schools focus on the long run, the Keynesian view emphasises the short-run effects.

* *Faculty of Economics, Department of Management, Sree Amman Arts And Science College, Chittode, Erode, Tamilnadu, India, E-mail:econbalu@yahoo.com*

THE NEOCLASSICAL VIEW

The component of revenue deficit in fiscal deficits implies a reduction in government saving or an increase in government dissaving. In the Neoclassical perspective (Bernheim 1989), this will have a detrimental effect on growth if the reduction in government saving is not fully offset by a rise in private saving, thereby resulting in a fall in the overall saving rate. This, apart from putting pressure on the interest rate, will adversely affect growth. The Neoclassical economists assume that markets clear so that full employment of resources is attained. In this paradigm, fiscal deficits raise lifetime consumption by shifting taxes to the future generations.

If economic resources are fully employed, increased consumption necessarily implies decreased savings in a closed economy. In an open economy, real interest rates and investment may remain unaffected, but the fall in national saving is financed by higher external borrowing accompanied by an appreciation of the domestic currency and fall in exports. In both cases, net national saving falls and consumption rises accompanied by some combination of fall in investment and exports. The Neoclassical paradigm assumes that the consumption of each individual is determined as the solution to an inter-temporal optimisation problem where both borrowing and lending are permitted at the market rate of interest. It also assumes that individuals have finite lifespans where each consumer belongs to a specific generation and the lifespans of successive generations overlap.

KEYNESIAN VIEW OF FISCAL DEFICITS

The Keynesian view (Eisner 1989), in the context of the existence of some unemployed resources, envisages that an increase in autonomous government expenditure, whether investment or consumption, financed by borrowing would cause output to expand through a multiplier process. The traditional Keynesian framework does not distinguish between alternative uses of the fiscal deficit as between government consumption or investment expenditure, nor does it distinguish between alternative sources of financing the fiscal deficit through monetisation or external or internal borrowing. In fact, there is no explicit budget constraint in the analysis. Subsequent elaborations of the Keynesian paradigm envisage that the multiplier-based expansion of output leads to a rise in the demand for money, and if money supply is fixed and deficit is bond financed, interest rates would rise partially offsetting the multiplier effect. However, the Keynesians argue that increased aggregate demand enhances the profitability of private investment and leads to higher investment at any given rate of interest. The effect of a rise in interest rate may thus be more than neutralised by the increased profitability of investment. Keynesians argue that deficits may stimulate savings and investment even if the interest rate rises, primarily because of the employment of hitherto unutilised resources. However, at full employment, deficits would lead to crowding out even in the Keynesian paradigm. In the standard Keynesian analysis, if everyone thinks that a budget deficit makes them wealthier, it would raise output and employment, and thereby actually make people wealthier. Unlike the loanable funds theory, the Keynesian paradigm rules out any direct effect on the interest rate of borrowing by the government.

RICARDIAN EQUIVALENCE PERSPECTIVE

In the perspective of Ricardian equivalence (Barro 1989), fiscal deficits are viewed as neutral in terms of their impact on growth. The financing of budgets by deficits amounts only to the postponement of taxes. The deficit in any current period is exactly equal to the present value of future taxation that is required to pay off the increment to debt resulting from the deficit. In other words, government spending must be paid for, whether now or later, and the present value of spending must be equal to the present value of tax and non-tax revenues. Fiscal deficits are a useful device for smoothening the impact of revenue shocks or for meeting the requirements of lumpy expenditures, the financing of which through taxes may be spread over a period of time. However, such fiscal deficits do not have an impact on aggregate demand if household spending decisions are based on the present value of their incomes that takes into account the present value of their future tax liabilities. Alternatively, a decrease in current government saving that is implied by the fiscal deficit may be accompanied by an offsetting increase in private saving, leaving the national saving and therefore, investment unchanged. Then, there is no impact on the real interest rate. Ricardian equivalence requires the assumption that individuals in the economy are foresighted, they have discount rates that are equal to governments' discount rates on spending and they have extremely long time horizons for evaluating the present value of future taxes. In particular, such a time horizon may well extend beyond their own lives in which case they save with a view to making altruistic transfers to take care of the tax liabilities of their future generations.

FISCAL DEFICIT ISSUES IN THE INDIAN CONTEXT

The issue of the fiscal deficit assumed importance in India since the middle 1980s when the fiscal deficit to GDP ratio rose to levels above 7 per cent. In 1990-91 it was about 8 per cent, and after some improvement, it started declining and reached 3.76 per cent of GDP in 2006-07. In the context of fiscal deficits in India, several distinct sets of issues have been examined from time to time. Some of the important issues that have been listed:

(i) Whether fiscal deficits of the central governments are sustainable.

(ii) Whether the Central governments is solvent, given its debt and deficit levels.

(iii) Whether the presence of high levels of structural fiscal deficits has constrained the usability of fiscal policy as a tool of stabilisation in respect of output as well as prices.

(iv) Whether there is need to formulate rules and targets to stabilize debt and deficits, and how these targets should be derived and

(v) Whether fiscal deficits have crowded out private investment by putting pressure on interest rates, thereby adversely affecting growth.

These issues are interdependent as the impact of fiscal deficits on growth affects its sustainability. Although the major focus of this study is on the implications of fiscal deficits for growth and stabilization, some of the extant literature on the above issues is briefly reviewed here under different heads.

GROWTH MODEL

Growth rates are usually computed to time series data on variables to answer the question whether deceleration or acceleration has taken place over a given period.

The growth rate is the change in the variable, in question. Suppose, we have time series data on the stock of gross fiscal deficit, then the rate of change in Y per unit of time is $dY/dt = Y_{t-1} - Y_t$. It takes only discrete values if 't' value varies continuously. As we are dealing with a time series, we can show that there is growth or stagnancy or decay in Y at 't' with the help of (dY_t/d_t). It gives only absolute change in Y per unit of time.

The proportional change in Y per unit of time gives us the growth rate (G_t), which is equal to $((dY_t / d_t) / (Y_t))$ or $((Y_{t+1} - Y_t) / (Y_t))$. Therefore, the following equation, as adopted by World Bank, is used to compute the growth rates in this paper.

$$\text{Log-lin Equation: } \text{Log } Y_t = a + b_t + u_t$$

This equation is semi-log or exponential or log-lin equation. Growth is given by this equation i.e $G_t = b$. It implies that there is a growth and the growth rate is constant over the study period if $b>0$. There is retardation or decay in growth if $b < 0$. The 'b' value is actually the growth rate per unit of time. The percentage compound growth rate over the study period can be obtained by using the relation–[(antilog of b-1) x 100)]. The log–linear equation, like the linear equation, also assumes that the rate of growth of the variable would be constant over a period of time.

GROWTH AND STRUCTURE OF GROSS FISCAL DEFICIT IN INDIA DURING POST-LIBERALISATION (1992-93 TO 2006-07) PERIOD

In the current economic scenario, fiscal transparency has acquired prime importance for achieving macroeconomic stability and economic growth. Fiscal transparency makes the public aware of the structure and the functions of the government, fiscal policy intentions and projections. There is a need for pursuing sustainable fiscal policies by optimum utilization of resources. In this regard, there is an ongoing debate on the problems related to fiscal deficit in the last one decade. There was a rapid growth in fiscal deficit in India, which is evident in the growth of government expenditure. The most important factor that is alarming with regard to the escalating fiscal deficit is the mammoth expenses incurred on the revenue expenditure or non-plan expenditure side.

Table 1.presents the growth and structure of Gross Fiscal Deficit in_India during postliberalization period. The aggregate expenditure increased from Rs.1, 16, 262cr in 1992-93 to 5, 55,991cr in 2006-07 recording a growth rate of 11.46 per cent and the receipts increased from Rs. 76,089cr in 1992-93 to Rs. 4,07,305cr in 2006-07 thus recording a rate of growth of 12.66 per cent leaving a fiscal deficit of Rs. 1,48,686cr in 2006-07. The steep increase in aggregate expenditure is due overwhelming increase in revenue expenditure, which includes subsidies, interest payments, grants to state and Union territories, defence expenditure and other expenditures. The fiscal deficit as a proportion of GDP was 5.3 per cent in 1992-93 and this ratio has increased to 7.01 per cent in 1993-94 but gradually declined to 3.76 per cent in 2006-07 with a considerable cut in the monetized deficit, primary deficit and some restraint in the revenue deficit.

The Major Highlights are

- The proportion of Tax Revenue to Total Revenue was above 70 per cent in most of the years and reached 81 per cent in 2006-07 indicating heavy dependency on Tax collections.
- The proportion of Revenue Expenditure to Total Expenditure was on the increase during the entire period under review and reached almost 90 per cent in many years.
- Correspondingly, there was a considerable reduction in the proportion of Capital Expenditure and it went down to just 10 per cent in the terminal year of the analysis.
- Even though GFD has grown at 9.14 per cent, the GFD-GDP ratio was on the decline in all years and reached the minimum of 3.76 per cent in 2006-07 converging towards the bench mark rate of 3 per cent stipulated in the Fiscal Responsibility and Budget Management Act. (FRBM Act).
- It is expected that the huge fiscal deficit will have grave implications on money supply, inflation and investment.
- Since fiscal deficit adds to government debt, debt servicing will further increase revenue expenditure in the form of interest burden.
- Heavy debt servicing results in 'crowding out' of necessary public expenditure on health, education, social and economic welfare.

Table 1
Growth and Structure of Gross Fiscal Deficit in India during Post-Liberalisation (1992- 93 to 2006 - 07) Period

Year	*Total Receipts*	*Net Tax Revenue*	*Non-tax Revenue*	*Disinvest-ment*	*Total Expendi-ture*	*Revenue Expendi-ture*	*Capital Expendi-ture*	*GFD*
1992-93	76089	54044	20084	1961	116262	92702	23560	40173
	(100)	(71.03)*	(26.40)*	(2.57)*	(100)	(79.74)**	(20.26)**	(5.37)@
1993-94	75405	53449	22004	-48	135662	108169	27493	60257
	(100)	(70.88)*	(29.18)*	(-0.06)*	(100)	(79.73)**	(20.27s)**	(7.01)@
1994-95	96691	67454	24159	5078	154394	122112	32282	57703
	(100)	(69.76)*	(24.99)*	(5.25)*	(100)	(79.09)**	(20.91)**	(5.70)@
1995-96	111527	81939	29226	362	171770	139861	31909	60243
	(100)	(73.47)*	(26.21)*	(0.32)*	(100)	(81.42)**	(18.58)**	(5.07)@
1996-97	126734	93701	32653	380	193468	153933	39535	66733
	(100)	(73.94)*	(25.76)*	(0.30)*	(100)	(79.57)**	(20.43)**	(4.88)@
1997-98	134798	95672	38214	912	223735	180335	43400	88937
	(100)	(70.97)*	(28.35)*	(0.68)*	(100)	(80.60)**	(19.40)**	(5.84)@
1998-99	155359	104652	44833	5874	268707	216461	52246	113348
	(100)	(67.36)*	(28.86)*	(3.78)*	(100)	(80.56)**	(19.44)**	(6.51)@
1999-00	183206	128271	53211	1724	287922	249078	38844	104716
	(100)	(70.02)*	(29.04)*	(0.94)*	(100)	(86.51)**	(13.49)**	(5.35)@
2000-01	194730	136658	55947	2125	313546	277839	35707	118816
	(100)	(70.18)*	(28.73)*	(1.09)*	(100)	(88.61)**	(11.39)**	(5.64)@
2001-02	204952	133532	67774	3646	345907	301468	44439	140955
	(100)	(65.15)*	(33.07)*	(1.78)*	(100)	(87.15)**	(12.85)**	(6.18)@
2002-03	233985	158544	72290	3151	379057	338713	40344	145072
	(100)	(67.75)*	(30.90)*	(1.35)*	(100)	(89.36)**	(10.64)**	(5.92)@
2003-04	280766	186982	76831	16953	404038	362074	41964	123272
	(100)	(66.60)*	(27.36)*	(6.04)*	(100)	(89.61)**	(10.39)**	(4.47)@
2004-05	310437	224798	81215	4424	435639	384351	51288	125202
	(100)	(72.41)*	(26.16)*	(1.43)*	(100)	(88.23)**	(11.77)**	(4.01)@
2005-06	350830	274139	74335	2356	497005	440295	56710	146175
	(100)	(78.14)*	(21.19)*	(0.67)*	(100)	(88.59)**	(11.41)**	(4.14)@
2006-07	407305	327205	76260	3840	555991	488192	67799	148686
	(100)	(80.34)*	(18.72)*	(0.94)*	(100)	(87.81)**	(12.19)**	(3.76)@
CGR	12.66	13.01	11.44	12.01	11.46	12.60	5.46	9.14

Source: Hand Book of Statistics on the Indian Economy, RBI Bulletin 2006-07
Note: *percentage of Total Receipts;
**percentage of Total Expenditure;
@ percentage of GDP-ratio
GFD: Gross Fiscal Deficit CGR: Compound Growth Rate

COMPONENTS OF NET TAX REVENUE IN INDIA DURING POST-LIBERALISATION (1992- 93 TO 2006-07) PERIOD

Tax reforms were initiated in 1991 as a part of the structural reform process, following the economic crisis of 1991. In keeping with the best practice approaches, the Tax Reforms Committee (TRC) adopted an approach of combining economic principles with conventional wisdom in recommending comprehensive tax system reforms (Bird 1989). There are three parts of reports, the government accepted the recommendations of the TRC and has implemented them in phases. Although it did not entirely follow the recommendations and is yet to implement many of the measures to strengthen the administration and enforcement machinery, most of the recommendations have been implemented. It must also be noted that the pace and content of reforms have not been exactly true to TRC recommendations.

Table 2 presents components of net tax revenue during 1992-93 to 2006-07. As a result of rationalization of Tax structure by the government based on the recommendation of the Tax Reforms Committee (TRC), the composition of Net Tax Revenue during post liberalisation presents a different picture. Direct Tax has grown at a higher rate of 19.17 per cent vis-à-vis 9.95 per cent recorded by the Indirect Tax. The ratio of Direct Tax to Indirect Tax which was 20:80 in 1992-93 changed dramatically to almost 50:50 towards the close of 2006-07. In direct Tax, the rate of growth of Income Tax was highly impressive at 30.75 per cent and Corporate Tax (16.54 per cent), where as in Indirect Tax the growth rate of excise was 14.56 per cent and Customs (3.82 per cent).

In fact, the tax reforms in India began in June 1991. Subsequently, the Tax Reforms Committee (TRC) headed by Chelliah made several proposals for tax reforms (Government of India, 1992, 1993). Highlights of the proposals put forward by the TRC were reduction of the rates of all the major taxes, viz., income tax, corporate tax, excises and customs duties, widening of their base by removing or curtailing exemptions and concessions, drastic simplification of the laws and procedures, replacement of the existing taxes on domestic production and trade by a value added tax and through revamping and modernization of the administration. The Committee also suggested that the system should become more income elastic. Several of recommendations of TRC have been implemented in India since 1991.

India's tax structure is quite comprehensive. Now almost every conceivable direct and indirect tax is levied in this country. In terms of the ratios of tax proceeds to national income, India is one of the highly taxed country. And if today the government feels that its resources are inadequate and it has no alternative but to have resource to government debt and deficit financing, it is mainly due to its colossal unproductive expenditure and complete indifference to the canon of economy.

Because of these efforts, the Tax Revenue scenario has changed completely during the post-liberalisation period as evidence by the details in Table.2 proving the effectiveness of structural reform policies of the government of India.

Table 2
Components of Net Tax Revenue in India during Post-Liberalisation (1992–93 to 2006-07) Period

(Rupees Crore)

Year	*Net Tax Revenue (I+II)*	*Direct-Tax (I)*	*Income-Tax*	*Corporate-Tax*	*Indirect-Tax (II)*	*Excise Duties*	*Customs Duties*
1992-93	54044	12075	1831	8899	41969	16367	23776
	(100)	(22.34)*	(15.16)**	(73.70)**	(77.66)*	(39.00) @	(56.65) @
1993-94	53449	12522	1355	10060	40927	17224	22193
	(100)	(23.43)*	(10.82)**	(80.34)**	(76.57)*	(42.08) @	(54.23) @
1994-95	67454	18409	3468	13822	49045	21064	26789
	(100)	(27.29)*	(18.84)**	(75.08)**	(72.71)*	(42.95) @	(54.62) @
1995-96	81939	22287	4318	16487	59652	22176	35757
	(100)	(27.20)*	(19.37)**	(73.98)**	(72.80)*	(37.18) @	(59.94) @
1996-97	93701	25374	4715	18567	68326	23463	42851
	(100)	(27.08)*	(18.58)**	(73.17)**	(72.92)*	(34.34) @	(62.72) @
1997-98	95672	27172	3589	20016	68500	25516	40193
	(100)	(28.40)*	(13.21)**	(73.66)**	(71.60)*	(37.25) @	(58.68) @
1998-99	104652	32120	5760	24529	72532	28581	40668
	(100)	(30.69)*	(17.93)**	(76.37)**	(69.31)*	(39.40) @	(56.07) @
1999-00	128271	41435	9131	30692	86836	34944	48419
	(100)	(32.30)*	(22.04)**	(74.07)**	(67.70)*	(40.24) @	(55.76) @
2000-01	136658	49651	23766	25177	87007	49758	34163
	(100)	(36.33)*	(47.87)**	(50.71)**	(63.67)*	(57.19) @	(39.26) @
2001-02	133532	47704	22106	25133	85828	54469	28340
	(100)	(35.72)*	(46.34)**	(52.69)**	(64.28)*	(63.46) @	(33.02) @
2002-03	158544	61612	27779	33893	96932	62388	31898
	(100)	(38.86)*	(45.09)**	(55.01)**	(61.14)*	(64.36) @	(32.91) @
2003-04	186982	76590	30765	45706	110392	70245	34586
	(100)	(40.96)*	(40.17)**	(59.68)**	(59.04)*	(63.63) @	(31.33) @
2004-05	224798	95935	34867	60289	128863	77241	41811
	(100)	(42.68)*	(36.34)**	(62.84)**	(57.32)*	(59.94) @	(32.45) @
2005-06	274139	125550	47848	77483	148589	87416	45793
	(100)	(45.80)*	(38.11)**	(61.71)**	-54.2	(58.83) @	(30.82) @
2006-07	327205	155253	55810	99221	171952	93667	54691
	(100)	(47.45)*	(35.95)**	(63.91)**	-52.55	(54.47) @	(31.81) @
CGR	13.01	19.17	30.75	16.54	9.95	14.56	3.82

Source: Hand Book of Statistics on the Indian Economy, RBI Bulletin 2006-07

Note: * per centage of Net-tax Revenue;
** percentage of Direct Tax
@ percentage of Indirect Tax;
CGR: Compound Growth Rate

COMPONENTS OF NON-TAX REVENUE IN INDIA DURING POST-LIBERALISATION (1992-93 TO 2006-07) PERIOD

Table 3 presents the components of non-tax revenue during.1992-93 to 2006 – 07. The scenario changed dramatically during post liberalisation period. The proportion of interest receipts which was 62 per cent in 1992-93 has declined to just 25 per cent in 2006-07 with an impressive contribution of 'other receipts (75 per cent)'. The spectacular growth in 'other receipts' could be due to significant turnaround in the operational efficiency of government undertakings such as Railways, etc. besides rationalization of interest rates for government loan's.

Table 3

Components of Non Tax Revenue in India during Post-Liberalisation (1992-93 to 2006- 07) Period

(Rupees Crore)

Year	*Non-Tax Revenue*	*Interest Receipts*	*Other Receipts*
1992-93	20084	12487	7597
	(100)	(62.17)	(37.83)
1993-94	22004	15078	6926
	(100)	(68.52)	(31.48)
1994-95	24159	15797	8362
	(100)	(65.39)	(34.61)
1995-96	29226	18419	10807
	(100)	(63.02)	(36.98)
1996-97	32653	22106	10547
	(100)	(67.70)	(32.30)
1997-98	38214	25323	12891
	(100)	(66.27)	(33.73)
1998-99	44833	30076	14757
	(100)	(67.08)	(32.92)
1999-00	53211	33895	19316
	(100)	(63.70)	(36.30)
2000-01	55947	32811	23136
	(100)	(58.65)	(41.35)
2001-02	67774	35538	32236
	(100)	(52.44)	(47.56)
2002-03	72290	37622	34668
	(100)	(52.04)	(47.96)
2003-04	76896	38538	38358
	(100)	(50.12)	(49.88)
2004-05	81215	32364	48851
	(100)	(39.85)	(60.15)
2005-06	74335	21245	53090
	(100)	(28.58)	(71.42)
2006-07	76260	19263	56997
	(100)	(25.26)	(74.74)
CGR	11.44	5.12	17.89

Source: Hand Book of Statistics on the Indian Economy, RBI Bulletin 2006-07

Note: Figures in parentheses are percentage of Non-Tax Revenue.

CGR: Compound Growth Rate

COMPONENTS OF REVENUE EXPENDITURE IN INDIA DURING POST-LIBERALISATION (1992-93 TO 2006-07) PERIOD

Table 4 presents components of revenue expenditure during 1992-93 to 2006-07. The revenue expenditure in a liberalised regime has grown at the rate of 12.60 per cent and the growth rates of its components were also almost similar with slight variations. 'Other expenditure' has grown at the rate of 13.89 per cent and subsidies 13.04 per cent. The rate of growth of interest payments was 11.43 per cent and defence expenditure was around 11 per cent. A near uniformity was maintained in the inter- component growth rates and it is not clear whether it was a deliberate attempt or mere coincidence. As regards the composition, defence expenditure and subsidies maintained a stable proportion of around 11 to 13 per cent and 10 to 12 per cent respectively during the entire period under review. Interest payments recorded a slight reduction of 5 per cent and 10 per cent increase in 'other expenditure'.

The interest payment burden kept on increasing even in the post liberalisation period despite a softer interest rate regime reflecting impact of sizeable outstanding liabilities contracted at high interest rates during the early part of the decade and also a return to rising deficits. In respect of Centre, interest payments were more than half of the revenue receipts in the late post liberalisation period and early years of the current decade. It may be noted that the combined interest payments to revenue receipts ratio is lower than that of the Centre reflecting the intergovernmental interest payments (which are netted out while calculating the combined interest payments).

With the dismantling of administered price mechanism, petroleum subsidies were introduced in the union budget in 2002-03.Among the various components, the most critical one is the food subsidy which nearly recorded a ten-fold increase during the period 1990-91 to 2003-04 on account of carrying costs of piling excessive quantity of food stocks. This has reflected the government's policy of encouraging food procurement through assured minimum support prices even while there was no commensurate off-take. The food subsidies could be an effective instrument to address the problems of economically deprived sections of the society; however, the proper targeting of such expenditure is a major concern. While data on state government subsidies are not available, the trend observed from other indicators like subsidy support to the State Electricity Boards (SEBs) shows that they also displayed similar movement. It led to misallocation of resources and also reflected inadequate revenue generating capacity through poor recovery of services costs, particularly in the non-merit goods sector.

Table 4
Components of Revenue Expenditure in India during Post-Liberalisation (1992-93 to 2006-07) Period

(Rupees Crore)

Year	*Revenue Expenditure*	*Defence Expenditure*	*Interest Payments*	*Subsidies*	*Other Expenditures*
1992-93	92702	12109	31075	10824	38694
	(100)	(13.06)	(33.52)	(11.68)	(41.74)
1993-94	108169	14978	36741	11605	44845
	(100)	(13.85)	(33.96)	(10.73)	(41.46)
1994-95	122112	16426	44060	11854	49772
	(100)	(13.45)	(36.08)	(9.71)	(40.76)
1995-96	139861	18841	50045	12666	58309
	(100)	(13.47)	(35.78)	(9.06)	(41.69)
1996-97	153933	20997	59478	15499	57959
	(100)	(13.64)	(38.64)	(10.07)	(37.65)
1997-98	180335	26174	65637	18540	69984
	(100)	(14.51)	(36.40)	(10.28)	(38.81)
1998-99	216461	29861	77882	23593	85125
	(100)	(13.80)	(35.97)	(10.90)	(39.33)
1999-00	249078	35216	90249	24487	99126
	(100)	(14.14)	(36.23)	(9.83)	(39.80)
2000-01	277839	37238	99314	26838	114449
	(100)	(13.40)	(35.75)	(9.66)	(41.19)
2001-02	301468	38059	107460	31210	124739
	(100)	(12.62)	(35.65)	(10.35)	(41.38)
2002-03	338713	40709	117804	43533	136667
	(100)	(12.02)	(34.78)	(12.85)	(40.35)
2003-04	362074	43203	124088	44323	150460
	(100)	(11.93)	(34.27)	(12.24)	(41.56)
2004-05	384351	43862	126934	43653	169902
	(100)	(11.41)	(33.03)	(11.36)	(44.20)
2005-06	440295	48625	130032	46874	214764
	(100)	(11.04)	(29.53)	(10.65)	(48.78)
2006-07	488192	51542	139823	46213	250614
	(100)	(10.56)	(28.63)	(9.47)	(51.34)
CGR	12.60	10.67	11.43	13.04	13.89

Source: Hand Book of Statistics on the Indian Economy, RBI Bulletin 2006-07.
Note: Figures in parentheses are percentage of Revenue Expenditure.
CGR: Compound Growth Rate.

COMPONENTS OF CAPITAL EXPENDITURE IN INDIA DURING POST-LIBERALISATION (1992- 93 TO 2006-07) PERIOD

Table 5 presents the components of capital expenditure and their growth rates in a liberalised regime. The rate of growth of capital expenditure during the period under review was 5.46 per cent down by 8 per cent compared to previous period. However, the proportion of loans and advance was drastically reduced from 64 per cent in 1998-99 to 1.27 per cent which augurs well for the capital outlay. In other words, starting from 1999-2000, the proportion of capital outlay to the total capital expenditure has increased and reached 98.73 per cent in 2006-07.

Table 5
Components of Capital Expenditure in India during Post-Liberalisation (1992-93 to 2006-07) Period

(Rupees Crore)

Year	*Capital Expenditure*	*Loans and Advances*	*Capital Outlay*
1992-93	23560	9941	13619
	(100)	(42.19)	(57.81)
1993-94	27493	14263	13230
	(100)	(51.88)	(48.12)
1994-95	32282	17391	14891
	(100)	(53.87)	(46.13)
1995-96	31909	17810	14099
	(100)	(55.81)	(44.19)
1996-97	39535	25339	14196
	(100)	(64.09)	(35.91)
1997-98	43400	25874	17526
	(100)	(59.62)	(40.38)
1998-99	52246	33405	18841
	(100)	(63.94)	(36.06)
1999-00	38844	14807	24037
	(100)	(38.12)	(61.88)
2000-01	35707	10962	24745
	(100)	(30.70)	(69.30)
2001-02	44439	17881	26558
	(100)	(40.24)	(59.76)
2002-03	40344	11243	29101
	(100)	(27.87)	(72.13)
2003-04	41964	7814	34150
	(100)	(18.62)	(81.38)
2004-05	51288	11838	39450
	(100)	(23.08)	(76.92)
2005-06	56710	14410	42300
	(100)	(25.41)	(74.59)
2006-07	67799	861	66938
	(100)	(1.27)	(98.73)
CGR	5.46	-9.05	11.22

Source: Hand Book of Statistics on the Indian Economy, RBI Bulletin 2006-07
Note: Figures in parentheses are percentage of Capital Expenditure
CGR: Compound Growth Rate

FINANCING OF GROSS FISCAL DEFICIT IN INDIA DURING POST-LIBERALISATION (1992-93 TO 2006-07) PERIOD

Till the 1990s, the government securities market had been a captive market. With fixed lower yields on government securities unrelated to market conditions, scheduled commercial banks were the major or sole investors in these securities who were obliged to subscribe to these securities to fulfil their statutory requirements. However, with progressive alignment of yield on government securities to market rates and introduction of a number of other institutional and structural reforms since the early 1990s, including auction system for government dated securities, system of primary dealers, delivery versus payment, etc. gilt market got widened and deepened considerably and this resulted in movement from investment by the captive investors to wider market participation.

The wider market participation in government securities market has been significant, as it was no longer required to pre-empt bank deposits through high SLR to finance the fiscal deficit. Moreover, as market willingly absorbed higher amounts of government securities, the level of monetization could also be reduced considerably.

The mode of financing changed dramatically during post liberalisation period where in the RBI credit turned negative in 1996-97 and the entire GFD was met by debt financing, other borrowings and only a small proportion of total requirement is met through the net RBI credit to the government and external assistance. Infact, the other borrowings mainly consist of small savings, state provident fund, special deposits and reserve funds constitute around 63.25 per cent in 1997-98. Since 1998-99 market borrowing dominated the mode of financing and reached the peak level of 76.52 per cent in 2006-07. Similarly, external assistance in financing of fiscal gap declined sharply to 6 per cent in 2006-07 from nearly 13 per cent in 1992-93. More importantly, the contribution of RBI credit, which financed about 33 per cent of fiscal gap in the year 1992-93, turned negative with RBI reducing its holding of government securities in 2006-07. The shift in financing pattern in the 1990s essentially reflects the change in stance of monetary and fiscal policy, which led to considerable development of government securities market during the adjustment period.

These developments, which resulted in financing of fiscal gap at market related rates as compared to concessional financing in the post-liberalisation period, seem to have important implications for the interest rate and also for the level of fiscal deficit.

As government is now required to compete for funds along with other borrowings in the market, theory would suggest that rising GFD is likely to put upward pressure on the interest rates. Further, the higher cost of government market borrowings as a consequence may reflect in increased revenue expenditure and in fact alleged to be, one of the major factors contributing to the rising fiscal deficit in the recent years.

Table 6
Financing of Gross Fiscal Deficit in India during Post-Liberalisation (1992-93 to 2006-07) Period

(Rupees Crore)

Year	*GFD*	*External Finance*	*Market Borrowings*	*Other Borrowings*	*Draw Down of Cash Balances*
1992-93	40173	5319	3676	18866	12312
	(100)	(13.24)	(9.15)	(46.96)	(30.65)
1993-94	60257	5074	28928	15295	10960
	(100)	(8.42)	(48.01)	(25.38)	(18.19)
1994-95	57703	3582	20326	32834	961
	(100)	(6.21)	(35.23)	(56.90)	(1.66)
1995-96	60243	318	34001	16117	9807
	(100)	(0.53)	(56.44)	(26.75)	(16.28)
1996-97	66733	2987	19093	31469	13184
	(100)	(4.48)	(28.61)	(47.15)	(19.76)
1997-98	88937	1091	32499	56257	-910
	(100)	(1.23)	(36.54)	(63.25)	(-1.02)
1998-99	113348	1920	68988	42650	-209
	(100)	(1.69)	(60.86)	(37.63)	(-0.18)
1999-00	104716	1180	62076	40596	864
	(100)	(1.13)	(59.28)	(38.76)	(0.83)
2000-01	118816	7505	73431	39077	-1197
	(100)	(6.32)	(61.80)	(32.89)	(-1.01)
2001-02	140955	5601	90812	46038	-1496
	(100)	(3.97)	(64.43)	(32.66)	(-1.06)
2002-03	145072	-11934	104126	50997	1883
	(100)	(-8.23)	(71.77)	(35.15)	(1.30)
2003-04	123272	-13488	88870	51833	-3942
	(100)	(-10.94)	(72.09)	(42.05)	(-3.20)
2004-05	125202	14753	50939	67640	-8130
	(100)	(11.78)	(40.69)	(54.02)	(-6.49)
2005-06	146175	7514	101082	22541	15037
	(100)	(5.14)	(69.15)	(15.42)	(10.28)
2006-07	148686	8324	113778	26584	0
	(100)	(5.60)	(76.52)	(17.88)	(0.0)
CGR	9.14	-29.04	18.35	5.11	-54.72

Source: Hand Book of Statistics on the Indian Economy, RBI Bulletin 2006-07
Note: Figures in parentheses are percentage of Gross Fiscal Deficit.
CGR: Compound Growth Rate GFD: Gross Fiscal Deficit

CONCLUSION

- The proportion of Tax Revenue to Total Revenue was above 70 per cent in most of the years and reached 81 per cent in 2006-07 indicating heavy dependency on Tax collections during post-liberalisation period.

- The proportion of Revenue Expenditure to Total Expenditure was on the increase during the entire period under review and reached almost 90 per cent in many years.
- Correspondingly, there was a considerable reduction in the proportion of Capital Expenditure and it went down to just 10 per cent in the terminal year of the analysis.
- Even though GFD has grown at 9.14 per cent, the GFD-GDP ratio was declining in all years and the reached the minimum of 3.76 per cent in 2006-07.
- Direct Tax has grown at a higher rate of 19.17 per cent vis-à-vis 9.95 per cent recorded by the Indirect Tax. The ratio of Direct Tax to Indirect Tax which was 20:80 in 1992-93 changed dramatically to almost 50:50 towards the close of 2006-07.
- In direct Tax, the rate of growth of Income Tax was highly impressive at 30.75 per cent and Corporate Tax (16.54 per cent), where as in Indirect Tax the growth rate of excise was 14.56 per cent and Customs (3.82 per cent).
- The scenario changed dramatically during post liberalisation period. The proportion of interest receipts which was 62 per cent in 1992-93 has declined to just 25 per cent in 2006-07 with an impressive contribution of 'other receipts (75 per cent)'.
- The interest payment burden kept on increasing even in the post liberalisation period despite a softer interest rate regime reflecting impact of sizeable outstanding liabilities contracted at high interest rates during the early part of the decade and also a return to rising deficits.
- The proportion of loans and advance was drastically reduced from 64 per cent in 1998-99 to 1.27 per cent which augurs well for the capital outlay. In other words, starting from 1999-00, the proportion of capital outlay to the total capital expenditure has increased and reached 98.73 per cent in 2006-07.
- Since the over all proportion of market borrowings plus other borrowings were 65 per cent it could exert heavy pressure on interest payments and debt servicing besides raising debt GDP ratio.
- The contribution of RBI credit, which financed about 33 per cent of fiscal gap in the year 1992-93, turned negative with RBI reducing its holding of government securities in 2006-07.
- The shift in financing pattern in the 1990s essentially reflects the change in stance of monetary and fiscal policy, which led to considerable development of government securities market during the adjustment period.

References

Amarjit Singh Sidhu (2003), "Direct Tax Reforms in India: post-Liberalisation Scenario," in Tax Reforms in India, (ed), P.T. Chaudhari, Shree Niwas Publications, Jaipur (India).

Annadurai C. (1999), "India's External Debt: A Study of Growth, Composition, Determinants and Debt Servicing: 1970-1996", Unpublished Ph.D., Thesis, Bharathiar University, Coimbatore, Tamilnadu, India.

Arvind Panagariya (2004), "Growth and Reforms during 1980s and 1990s," *Economic and Political Weekly*, Vol. XXXIX, No. 25, pp. 2581-2594.

Barro, Robert J. (1989), 'The Ricardian Approach to Budget Deficit', *Journal of Economic Perspectives*, Vol. 3, No. 2, pp. 37-54.

Bernheim, Douglas B. (1989), 'A Neoclassical Perspective on Budget Deficits', *Journal of Economic Perspectives*, Vol. 3, No. 2, pp. 55-72.

Bird, R. M. (1989), "Administrative Dimension of Tax Reform in Ddeveloping Countries", in Malcolm Gillis, ed. Tax Reform in Developing Countries (London, Duke University Press).

Bird, R. M. (1993), "Tax Reform in India", *Economic and Political Weekly*, Vol. XXVIII, 11 pp. 2721-2726.

Eisner, Robert (1989), 'Budget Deficits: Rhetoric and Reality', *Journal of Economic Perspectives*, Vol. 3, No. 2, Spring, pp. 73-93.

Govinda Rao M. (2000), "Tax Reform in India: Achievements and Challenges," *Asia-Pacific Development Journal*, Vol. 7, No. 2, pp. 59-74.

Lekha S. Chakraborty (2002), "Fiscal Deficit and Rate of Interest an Econometric Analysis of the Deregulated Financial Regime," *Economic and Political Weekly*, Vol. XXXVII, No. 19, pp. 1831-1838.

Martin Feldstein (2004), Address to Reserve Bank of India, January 12, 2004.

Paramjeet Kaur (2007), "Growth Acceleration in India", *Economic and Political Weekly*, Vol. XLII, No. 15, pp. 1380-1386.

Rangarajan C. and Srivastava, D. K. (2005), "Fiscal Deficits and Government Debt Implications for Growth and Stabilisation," *Economic and Political Weekly*, Vol. XL, No. 27, pp. 2919-2934.

RETAIL MARKET IN INDIA–AN OVERVIEW

C. ANBALAGAN*

INTRODUCTION

Retailing encompasses the business activities involved in selling goods and services to consumers for their personal, family, or household use. It includes every sale to the final consumer- ranging from cars to apparel to meals at restaurants to theater tickets. Retailing is the last stage in the distribution process. Retailing today is at an interesting crossroads. On the one hand, retail sales are at their highest point in history. Wal-Mart is now the leading company in the terms of sales-ahead of Exxon Mobile, General Motors, and other manufacturing giants. New technologies are improving retail productivity. There are lots of opportunities to start a new retail business-or work for an existing one-and to become a franchisee. Global retailing possibilities abound. On the other hand, retailers face numerous challenges. Many consumers are bored with shopping or do not have much time for it. Some locals have too many stores, and retailers often spur one another in to frequent price cutting. Customer service expectations are high at a time when more retailers offer self-service and automated systems. At the same time, many retailers remain unsure what to do with the web; they are still grappling with the emphasis to place on image enhancement, customer information and feedback, and sales transactions.

RELATIONSHIPS AMONG RETAILERS AND THEIR SUPPLIERS

Relationships among retailers and suppliers can be complex. Because retailers are part of a distribution channel, manufacturers and wholesalers must be concerned about the caliber of displays, customer service, store hours, and retailer's reliability as business partners. Retailers are also major customers of goods and services for resale, store, fixtures, computers, management consulting, and insurance.

There are some issues over which retailers and suppliers have different priorities. Channel relations tend to be smoothest with exclusive distribution,

* *Professor of Management (MBA), Audyogik Shikshan Mandal's, Institute of Business Management & Research, University of Pune, Chinchwad, Pune (Maha.), E-mail: dr.chinlakshanbu@gmail.com*

whereby suppliers make agreements with one or a few retailers that designate the latter as the only ones in specified geographic areas to carry certain brands or products. Channel relations tend to be most volatile with intensive distribution, whereby suppliers sell through as many retailers as possible. With selective distribution, suppliers sell through a moderate number of retailers. This combines aspects of exclusive and intensive distribution.

THE SPECIAL CHARACTERISTICS OF RETAILING

The Average Amount of a Sales Transaction for Retailers is Much Less than for Manufacturers

The average sales transaction per shopping trip is well under $ 100 for department stores, specialty stores, and supermarkets. This low amount creates a need to tightly control the costs associated with each transaction, to maximize the number of customers drawn to the retailer, which may place more emphasis on ads and special promotions; and to increase impulse sales by more aggressive selling. However, cost control can be tough.

FINAL CONSUMERS MAKE MANY UNPLANNED OR IMPULSE PURCHASES

Surveys show that a large percentage of consumers do not look at ads before shopping, do not prepare shopping lists and make fully unplanned purchases This behavior indicates the value of in-store displays, attractive store layouts, and well-organized stores, catalogs, and web sites. Candy, cosmetics, snak foods, magazines, and other items are sold as impulse goods when placed in visible, high-traffic areas in a store, catalog, r web sites. Because so many purchases are unplanned, the retailer's ability to forecast, budget, order merchandise, and have sufficient personnel on the selling floor is more difficult.

RETAIL CUSTOMERS USUALLY VISIT A STORE, EVEN THOUGH MAIL, PHONE, AND WEB SALES HAVE INCREASED

Despite the inroads made by non-store retailers, most retail transactions are still conducted in store- and will continue to be in the future. Many people like to shop in person; want to touch, smell, and/ or Tryon products; like to browse for unplanned purchases; feel more comfortable taking a purchases home with them than waiting for a delivery; and desire privacy while at home. This store-based shopping orientation has implications for retailers; they must work to attract shoppers to their stores and consider such factors as store location, transportation, and store hours, proximity of competitors, product selection, parking, and ads.

ORGANIZED RETAIL-LOSING ITS PATH

Organized retailers remain unsure as to which format works best and, given their loss levels, cannot even invest in the kind of supply chains they need to be competitive. Each square foot of retail needs Rs. 2,000 of capital; organized retail makes a profit of just Rs 300! So who's going to fund it? With more than $300 billion of retail sales annually, an economy growing at seven per cent, 500 million people below the age of 24 who don't have any guilt about consumption, I'm a big fan of organized Indian retail. But in the near future, organized retail's story is a poor one. Superimposing a new channel in a non-differentiated business is always a long haul—even after being in the market for more than 15 years, some of India's largest consumer companies like ITC, HUL, Nestle and the Tatas have got less than three per cent of the branded staples market. The same applies to all the attempts to digitalize the cable industry.

NEW FDI POLICY WILL BENEFIT RETAIL SECTOR

Retail, telecom, media and a host of sectors in which foreign direct investment (FDI) is restricted stand to gain from changes in FDI policy that the Cabinet Committee on Economic Affairs (CCEA) cleared today linking approvals to the concept of control for the first time. The new norms were proposed by the Department of Industrial Policy and Promotion (DIPP) and discussed by a Group of Ministers on February 3. "The objective of these new guidelines is to make FDI norms simple and transparent according to DIPP," Home Minister P Chidambaram told reporters today when he announced the new measures. The new measures will be implemented with prospective effect. Government sources said two Press Notes—policy documents governing FDI norms—of the 2009 series will be released in the next 10 days.

BIG RETAIL PLAYERS SEEK REDUCTION IN RENT

This could be the flip side to the slowdown story which modern retailers are welcoming with open arms. At a time when growth has slowed down, large retailers like the Future group, Reliance Retail and Aditya Birla Retail are in the midst of furiously renegotiating rentals to bring down costs. A correction in the real estate industry has been long overdue, and taking advantage of the situation, modern retailers have called a war on costs to tide over the slowdown. Most of the modern retailers either purchased or rented properties at the peak of the real estate market. This has seriously dented their ability to make profits from the retail business, especially at the time of an economic slowdown.

Said a Reliance Retail spokesperson: "We are actively renegotiating rentals across formats and hope that, on an average, this would bring down costs by about 20%-30%." According to Pranay Vakil, chairman of of real estate services company Knight Frank: "The headroom for reducing rentals could be anywhere between 10-35%. In exceptional cases, it could even go up to 40%. The exact amount would depend on the location." Aditya Birla Retail, which is expected to more than double its turnover from Rs 500 crore last year to Rs 1,200 crore this financial year, is quite clear that if a real estate owner does not bring down the rentals of a certain store, it would not hesitate to relocate. 2009 is expected to be a year of consolidation for Indian retail sector. As a result of adoption of best practices and restructuring of business models by the retailers, organized retail is expected to realign itself to the market conditions and create new areas of growth in 2009. Given the market malady being faced by developers and retailers alike, it is possible that partnership models of growth through mechanisms such as revenue sharing would become more prominent. More deals are going to get renegotiated as priced drop in over-priced locations. The process of rationalization should reach its peak by March, 2009. In 2009, it is anticipated that the supply pipeline may witness further stalling most players' expansion plans for 2009 will slow down considerably. However, Projects that are planned well (incorporating approaches like proper zoning, optimal tenant mix strategies), implemented with high quality standards and incorporating appropriate mall management practices are anticipated to be successful. In 2009, premier brands will look at Tier II cities, but certainly not Tier III. Luxury brands will stick to metros.

SPANISH INVESTMENT IN INDIA INCREASES

The Spanish investments in India rose five-fold to $158 million in the past year. Over 10 leading companies entered the country during the period, according to senior Spain government officials. "Many Spanish companies are present in sectors like infrastructure, insurance, auto components and ports and more are keen to enter the market as India's economy is quite promising," Javier Sanz, chief executive officer of 'Invest in Spain' told ET. 'Invest in Spain' is a government agency for promotion and attraction of foreign investments in Spain.

Spanish firms such as Navantia (naval construction) Dragados (container terminal), Grupo Roca (parryware), Gropo Antolin (auto components) Mapfre (insurance) Televent (urban infrastructure), Isolux (infrastructure) Cobra (infrastructure) and Indolink (consultancy) set shop in the country in the past one year. "Spanish investment in India was $158 million during the first three quarters of calendar year 2008. This had increased by 500% from the previous year," Mr Sanz said. 'Invest in Spain' recently met 14 well-known Indian entrepreneurs to explore business opportunities.

DEVELOPERS UNABLE TO FULFILL RETAIL SPACE TARGET

DLF, Parsvnath and other real estate developers have lagged behind by 54 per cent in their target to open retail space even as retailers' vacancy climbed to 16 per cent in 2008, according to a study. Cash-strapped real estate developers failed to deliver 11 million sq ft of retail space in 2008, according to a study released by Cushman & Wakefield. Out of the proposed 74 malls in key eight cities at the beginning of 2008, only 34 were delivered through the year, the study showed. Developers in the National Capital Region (NCR) lagged the most with a supply of 4.7 million sq ft compared with the earlier target of 7.1 million sq ft. Developers may continue to restrict their supply, or go slow on retail space by a similar amount in 2009 across key major cities, the study showed.

"For any developer, the vacancy level should not cross over 5 per cent. The vacancy level of 16 per cent suggests that most of the malls across India are finding it difficult to manage their operational cost," said Rajneesh Mahajan, director of retail services at Cushman & Wakefield. The reason for the shortfall was the mismatch between the potential and actual occupancy. The Indian organised retail sector grew at 25 per cent in 2007. Anticipating the growth of retail sector at above 35 per cent in the coming years, developers had announced big retail projects. However, owing to economic slowdown, the growth of the retail sector has come down to 15 per cent in 2008, resulting in developers deferring their projects for 12-24 months. "From the projected supply of 20.8 million sq ft space in the first quarter of 2008, we will see a spill over of about ten million sq ft development in 2009-10. Lack of funds leading to construction delays and cautious expansion by retailers have resulted in slow absorption of retail space in malls," said Mahajan.

LIFESTYLE RETAILERS ON A ROLE DESPITE ECONOMIC SLOWDOWN

In the face of the economic slowdown, lifestyle brands are putting up a brave front. While consumer buying may not be as big as one would like it to be and sales growth rates have dipped, the scene is not as bad as in the Western world, say retailers as they hope for a positive year ahead. "Fashion retail has not been impacted in a big way. Not even 0.5 per cent of the working population has been hit in India," says Mr Tarun Joshi, CEO and MD of Brandhouse Retails, which manages exclusive outlets for S.Kumars Nationwide brands - Reid & Taylor, Carmichael House, Stephens Brothers and Belmonte. (Brandhouse is also the exclusive India franchisee for luxury brands Alfred Dunhill and Escada.)

The Indian economy is more stable than other economies across the world and one must not confuse India with the rest of the world, says Mr Sandeep Kulhalli, V-P, Retail and Marketing, Tanishq. While admitting that the company's rate of growth has slowed down, the Rs 2,000-crore jeweler brand believes it can still post a 30 per cent growth in sales this year. At Tanishq, studded jeweler had a sales growth of 40 per cent in the first few months of the financial year; it has dipped to 20 per cent now. "But this is good enough for us to maintain competition and sustain. The people who are hit worst in India are those who invested in real estate, property and the stock market, not retail. Of course, sentiments are poor; there is some pressure. Spending may not be robust but people are still buying. The salaried class will still be with us," says Mr Kulhalli.

10 PER CENT PER ANNUM GROWTH IN UNORGANIZED RETAIL SECTOR

The unorganized retail sector is expected to grow at about 10 per cent per annum to reach $496 billion in 2011-12 despite the steady expansion of organized retailers, a study released Wednesday said. The report on the impact of organized retail on small shop owners, released in parliament by the Delhi-based think tank Indian Council for Research on International Economic Relations (Icrier), said the retail business in the country would grow at 13 per cent annually from $322 billion in 2006-07 to $590 billion in 2011-12. The unorganized retail industry was valued at $309 billion in 2006-07. However, given the relatively weak financial state of the unorganized retailers and the space constraints on their expansion prospects, this sector alone will not be able to meet the growing demand, the report said.

Hence, the organized retail that now constitutes a small four per cent of the total industry is likely to grow at a much faster pace of 45-50 per cent per annum and quadruple its share in total retail trade to 16 per cent by 2011-12, the Icrier said. However, the Icrier added that small shop owners in the vicinity of organized retailers have experienced a decline in their volume of business and profit after the entry of bigger players. According to the report, consumers have gained with the entry of organized retailers and their overall spending has also gone up. While all income groups saved through organized retail purchases, the report revealed that lower income consumers saved more.

NEC PLANS TO ENTER INDIAN RETAIL SECTOR

NEC India, a subsidiary of NEC Corporation Japan, has launched TWIN POS 3500 G1 machine to meet the much required PoS hardware for the retail space. The solution would enable the retailers to get the feel of internationally adopted technology. With its flagship model—the TWIN POS 3500 G1 machine, NEC India has ear-marked key retail formats to position its product and solutions.

David Arambhan, head (retail solutions) of NEC India said, "Our aim is to enhance the capability of the Indian retail segment to handle its operations in a more structured and effective way. Hence, NEC's offerings and models look to cover all formats of retail and will soon foray into the entire gamut of retail solutions offering both hardware and software solutions in the retail space. One of the key impacts would be Japanese quality at Indian prices" The products are available across India through its registered partners and channel and are supported by a nation-wide ASP.

SLOWDOWN IN ORGANIZED RETAIL

The organized retail sector in India is experiencing a slowdown with expansion projects either getting postponed or put on hold. But interestingly, the rural sector has been largely untouched by the economic slowdown, according to industry experts." The rural industry has done even better than last year in the last six months due to record output of crops and the loan waiver of Rs. 60,000 crore by the Central Government. As a result, the rural populace has a higher disposable income for fresh purchases," C K Ranganathan, Chairman and Managing Director, CavinKare told to this website's newspaper on the sidelines of the Conference on 'Retailing for India', organized by the Confederation of Indian Industry (CII) Tamil Nadu. The loan waiver size had later been increased to Rs. 71,680 crore.

Earlier, CII and advisory firm, PricewaterhouseCoopers (PwC) released a retail report on 'The Benefits of Modern Trade to Transitional Economies'. The report states that with modern trade, consumers would benefit from widely available choices and quantity along with rationalization and convergence of prices. It would lead to a zero tolerance policy for inefficiencies since consumers would be unwilling to pay for substandard products. Since modern trade players were tax compliant and their sale figures outnumbered that of the organized sector, revenue collections would increase. Large retailers would require development of a support mechanism for their operations including logistics, transportation and warehousing which would generate further revenues for the government.

RETAIL SECTOR IN INDIA

Retail and real estate are the two booming sectors of India in the present times. And if industry experts are to be believed, the prospects of both the sectors are mutually dependent on each other. Retail, one of India's largest industries, has presently emerged as one of the most dynamic and fast paced industries of our times with several players entering the market. Accounting for over 10 per cent of the country's GDP and around eight per cent of the employment retailing in India is gradually inching its way toward becoming the next boom industry.

As the contemporary retail sector in India is reflected in sprawling shopping centers, multiplex-malls and huge complexes offer shopping, entertainment and food all under one roof, the concept of shopping has altered in terms of format and consumer buying behavior, ushering in a revolution in shopping in India. This has also contributed to large scale investments in the real estate sector with major national and global players investing in developing the infrastructure and construction of the retailing business. The trends that are driving the growth of the retail sector in India are

- Low share of organized retailing
- Falling real estate prices
- Increase in disposable income and customer aspiration
- Increase in expenditure for luxury items

Another credible factor in the prospects of the retail sector in India is the increase in the young working population. In India, hefty pay-packets, nuclear families in urban areas, along with increasing working-women population and emerging opportunities in the services sector. These key factors have been the growth drivers of the organized retail sector in India which now boast of retailing almost all the preferences of life - Apparel & Accessories, Appliances, Electronics, Cosmetics and Toiletries, Home & Office Products, Travel and Leisure and many more. With this the retail sector in India is witnessing a rejuvenation as traditional markets make way for new formats such as departmental stores, hypermarkets, supermarkets and specialty stores.

The retailing configuration in India is fast developing as shopping malls are increasingly becoming familiar in large cities. When it comes to development of retail space specially the malls, the Tier II cities are no longer behind in the race. If development plans till 2007 is studied it shows the projection of 220 shopping malls, with 139 malls in metros and the remaining 81 in the Tier II cities. The government of states like Delhi and National Capital Region (NCR) are very upbeat about permitting the use of land for commercial development thus increasing the availability of land for retail space; thus making NCR render to 50% of the malls in India. India is being seen as a potential goldmine for retail investors from over the world and latest research has rated India as the top destination for retailers for an attractive emerging retail market. India's vast middle class and its almost untapped retail industry are key attractions for global retail giants wanting to enter newer markets. Even though India has well over 5 million retail outlets, the country sorely lacks anything that can resemble a retailing industry in the modern sense of the term. This presents international retailing specialists with a great opportunity. The organized retail sector is expected to grow stronger than GDP growth in the next five years driven by changing lifestyles, burgeoning income and favorable demographic outline.

Another cap to the retailing industry in India is allowing 51% FDI in single brand outlet. The government is now set to initiate a second wave of reforms in the segment by liberalizing investment norms further. This will not only favor the retail sector develop in terms of design concept, construction quality and providing modern amenities but will also help in creating a consumer-friendly environment. Retail industry in India is at the crossroads but the future of the consumer markets is promising as the market is growing, government policies are becoming more favorable and emerging technologies are facilitating operations in India. And this upsurge in the retail industry has made India a promising destination for retail investors and at the same time has impelled investments in the real estate sector. As foreign investors cautiously test the Indian Markets for investments in the retail sector, local companies and joint ventures are expected to be more advantageously positioned than the purely foreign ones in the evolving India's organized retailing industry.

Real Estate in India

Delhi, Mumbai, Chennai, Kolkata, Gurgaon, Bangalore, Pune, Hyderabad, Noida and Faridabad.

WAL-MART AND BHARTI IN INDIA DEAL

The outlets will sell fruit and vegetables and other itemsA joint venture between Wal-Mart Stores and India's Bharti Enterprises has been finalised, the pair said on Monday.

Bharti Wal-Mart Private Limited will operate wholesale cash-and-carry and supply chain operations in India. Opening 10 to 15 outlets by 2015, it plans to employ about 5,000 people selling groceries, consumer goods, fruits and vegetables. India's retail industry is worth $300bn (£148bn) a year and has attracted the interest of international retailers. Large overseas retailers are currently barred by law at the retail level in India, but not in the wholesale market. Tesco, France's Carrefour, and Germany's Metro are all big names who have expressed an interest in establishing operations in India. The first Bharti Wal-Mart Private Limited cash-and-carry store is set to open by the end of 2008. "This venture promises to bring great value to millions of farmers, artisans, small manufacturers and retailers across India," said Sunil Bharti Mittal, chairman and group CEO of Bharti Enterprises. "We are pleased to be a partner in developing this sector which is set to become a significant engine of India's economic growth."

Bharti in $2.5bn retail expansion: Family-run firms dominate India's retail market Indian conglomerate Bharti Enterprises is to pump $2.5bn (£1.28bn) into expanding its retail business. Bharti, which recently tied up with US group Wal-Mart to launch Indian-based stores, said retail would be its "big focus" for the next eight years. The group plans to open stores in all Indian cities with a population of one million or more. More disposable income from the middle classes has boosted India's economy, though small firms dominate retailing.

RETAIL BOOM

"After revolutionizing the Indian telecom sector, retail will be the next big focus area for Bharti," said the firm. Under its deal with Wal-Mart, Bharti will focus on running the stores while Wal-Mart will handle the supply side of the operation. The Indian conglomerate operates in a range of areas, from commercial agriculture, insurance and software to telecoms, in which it control's the nation's leading mobile operator-Bharti Airtel. Organized retailing represents only 3% to 5% of Indian retailers while family-run enterprises represent the vast majority of the market. Various industry estimates put Indian retail spending at $300bn each year, with the figure set to double by 2015.

Other firms have also seen the potential for retailing growth in India, such as the private company Reliance which is launching a supermarket chain called Reliance Fresh as part of its wider growth plans.

GENERAL TRENDS AND INFORMATION

India Yet to Get Foreign Inflows on Retail Trade

The government said that the country is yet to receive any foreign inflow in single brand retail trade, even though 17 such proposals involving a total investment of $3.3 million have been cleared. The FDI policy for the sector, announced in February 2006, allows 51 per cent foreign investment in single brand retailing.

WOMEN SETTING UP FRANCHISEE OUTLETS

Call it retail's tribute to independent women. As several leading corporate are expanding retail footprint, womenpreneurs across India are weaving success stories.

According to Franchising Association of India, the number of women setting up franchisee outlets is going up consistently. Industry experts say there are 75,000 franchisee outlets and around 10-15% are owned and managed by women. The share has increased around 20% in the past two years.

S. Kumars Nationwide Ltd's home linen brand Carmaichel House, which is reaching out to cities across the country, is also inviting women entrepreneurs to take up franchisee offers for company's retail outlets. At present, the company operates around 22 franchisee outlets and has signed deals for 30 more outlets.

Usually in home textile retailing, the average investment is around Rs 5-6 lakh. Most of the companies also offer loans to individuals for setting up franchisee outlets. The entrepreneurs can earn around Rs 20,000-40,000 per month through these franchisee outlets.

The trend is just not limited to home textile or garment companies. Hero Honda, which recently launched Pleasure, targeting women, is encouraging women entrepreneurs to set up 'Just 4 her' outlets. At present, the company has 21 franchisee outlets. All of these outlets are operated and run by women. The company is encouraging women-owned franchisee outlets as well.

IT'S NOT JUST HYPE, HYPERMARKETS SHALL RULE

Brick by brick, the retail world is betting on the hypermarket to take growth beyond hoopla. That's par for the course, if one looks at the successful retailing formats in emerging markets. Hypermarkets offer customers a destination shopping experience with everything available under one roof. Hemant Kalbag, principal, consumer industries and retail practice at consultant AT Kearney, said: "The success in emerging markets can be replicated in India as well because organized retailing has literally caught fire." He said real estate will be the key factor in the growth of hypermarkets. From the retailer's perspective, the hypermarket format allows him to enjoy all the benefits of being an anchor. The occupancy costs are driven down drastically. Besides, the retailer gets to play the volume game (efficiency of scale), too. And unlike supermarkets where one has to look at large number of stores, hypermarkets need not go into the multiples of 100 and one can still be a large successful player in the retail sector. Highlighting the unparalleled success high-volume hypermarkets have enjoyed in Asian markets, according to A T Kearney report, local hypermarket retailers are already making their moves before the Centre further loosens foreign investment in this sector. In fact, Pantaloon Retail's success story largely comes from its hypermarket format, Big Bazaar.

Another large retailer—Spencer's—has recently restructured its retail business and its hypermarket format has been identified as the key driver for growth. Similarly, there are others like K Raheja Corp, which made its foray with Hypercity sometime early 2006. With plans to expand the Hypercity network in primary and secondary cities, it plans to add another 5-8 stores in this fiscal. Mukesh Ambani's Reliance Retail, on its part, is all set to unveil its first hypermarket called Reliance Mart in Ahmedabad this week. According to the A T Kearney 2007 Global Retail Development Index titled "Growth Opportunities for Global Retailers", modern retail in India is just 2-3% of overall retail, but is growing at a remarkable 25% per year. It is expected to grow at a compounded annual growth rate of 40% from $8 billion to $22 billion by 2010. Overall, India's retail sector is expected to grow from its current $350 billion to $427 billion by 2010 and $635 billion by 2015.

RETAIL GIANTS POSE NO THREAT TO MOM AND POP SHOPS

Notwithstanding apprehensions among small-time shopkeepers that the entry of retail giants will pose a threat to their existence, some organized retail networks here feel there is "ample space for all" in the sector. Top officials at Subiksha, which has a network of 750 supermarkets across the country, and Spencers Daily, which has a strong presence in south India, are unanimous in their view that new entrants like Wal-Mart or Reliance Retail would not pose a threat to them or the "mom and pop shops". Mohit Khattar, President (Marketing), Subhiksha, and Samarjit Singh Shekhawat, Vice-President (Marketing), Spencers Daily feel that in a country like India, there is plenty of space for everyone and the organised supply chains represent just a "miniscule" portion of the sector with organized retailers accounting for only three to four per cent of the total business. Meanwhile, 'kirana merchants' feel the organized retail chains cannot make much impact on their customer base as their higher establishment charges will not let them always provide goods at cheaper rates.

A 'kirana merchant' in the neighborhood cannot be wiped out as long as customers are conscious of prices, quality and convenience, Madras Kirana Merchants Association Secretary Kailash Kothari said. Moreover, small shops have a strong presence in rural and suburban areas, he said. "Maybe, 10-15 years down the line, the bigger retailers can pose a threat to us. But we also hope to change ourselves to adapt to the new situation," he said.

Some neighborhood shop owners, however, beg to differ." I lost several of my regular customers once a nearby supermarket started offering onions and potatoes at Rs eight per kg irrespective of the prevailing wholesale rate," said A Anandan, owner of a provision store in a residential colony in the city. Lured by advertisements for cheap onions and potatoes, several people drop in at the supermarket and end up purchasing all they need, be it provisions or vegetables, at higher prices than neighborhood shops, he claimed.

BIG PLAYERS–PLANS AND INVESTMENTS

Reliance Says Not Seeking Retail Partner

Reliance Industries has no immediate plans to involve a foreign partner in its retail venture and sees no threat from Bharti group's wholesale tie-up with Wal-Mart, a top company official said. "We are not scared of competition. We are ahead of them. Our great challenge is to satisfy our customers. And that is the only benchmark," Raghu Pillai, president and CEO of Reliance Retail told reporters on Tuesday at the launch of a hypermarket in western India.

TRENT MAY HELP BENETTON'S SISLEY INTO INDIA

Europe's famous fashion house Benetton is likely to enter into a distribution partnership for its premium fashion brand, Sisley, with Tata Group company, Trent. This marks the Indian business house's first brush with a foreign apparel brand and its foray into high street retail. Benetton Group's deputy chairman and son of Luciano Benetton, Alessandro Benetton, is expected to ink the deal with Trent MD Noel Tata next month. Benetton has decided to join forces with the Tata because its wholly-owned India subsidiary has decided to focus on the eponymous flagship brand. India is emerging as the most important market for Benetton in Asia-Pacific. Brand Benetton commands a higher, although affordable, premium here compared to other global markets. Benetton's India arm had test launched Sisley in the country last year but could not scale up operations as it remained focused on the flagship brand's expansion in a fast growing economy. Besides, a partnership with the Tata may have seemed attractive as it is a formidable name in India which has proved its mettle in apparel retailing through the Trent-managed Westside stores. Sisley, with over 850 outlets globally, is targeted at the premium end of the apparel market. The brand was created in 1968 in Paris and entered the Benetton fold in 1974. It started developing a distinct niche identity from 1985 onwards with the famous Benetton marketing machinery working aggressively behind it even though critics argue that brand Sisley never touched the dizzying heights usually expected from the Benetton's.

ORGANIZED RETAILING IN SLUMS! BIYANI MAKES IT POSSIBLE

Kishore Biyani, who's Future Group changed the country's retail landscape through unconventional ways, is taking a step further by exploring possibilities of tapping the potential of urban slums. On the heels of setting up neighborhood new format stores named KB's Fair Price shops, the group is toying with the idea of taking retailing to the bottom of the pyramid in urban areas – the slums. According to sources, the group recently conducted a study on Mumbai's slum dwellers detailing out their lifestyle, earning and spending behavior, consumption pattern and attitude toward shopping destinations and brands. With eight million out of Mumbai's 12 million populations living in slums, the potential of retailing in those areas appeared very big.

When contacted, a Future Group spokesperson confirmed it had conducted a study to understand the market potential of slum areas. "However, there is no concrete plan as such on whether to enter this space or not at the moment. We were just exploring possibilities," the spokesperson said. If it finally decides to open stores in slums, this will be yet another innovative method from Future Group which changed the rules of retailing with throwaway prices at its Big Bazaar chain of outlets.

SPENCER'S PLANS FORAY INTO GARMENT RETAILING

Spencer's Retail, part of the Rs. 11,500-crore RPG Group, is looking at a foray into garment retailing two quarters from now. These would be exclusive stores retailing only apparel. Spencer's hypermarkets are retailing 'basic garments,' and nearly 16 per cent of its revenues comes from these SKUs (stock keeping units) In addition to increasing garment retailing in hypermarkets, the retailer will be launching exclusive garment retail stores similar to its music and book stores. RPG Retail currently has a presence across 40 cities with 250 Spencer's outlets. This includes 11 hypermarkets, seven supermarkets, three Fresh, 55 Express and 125 Dailies. The Group's other retail presence is in the area of music (Music World), books (Books and Beyond) and RPG Cellucom (mobile phone retail) with a total of 500 outlets, expected to grow to 2,000 by 2009 and 5,000 by 2011.

WAL-MART IN INDIA

America's Wal-Mart and India's Bharti are hoping to bring a dose of modernity to India's retailing landscape and good for them for trying. But it's going to take a lot more than Wal-Mart's legendary supply-chain management and margin-shaving acumen to bring "everyday low prices" to Indian consumers. The two companies finalized a 50-50 joint venture to go into the business-to-business, cash-and-carry wholesaling sector. This structure evades India's strict ban on foreign department stores and supermarkets setting up shops by themselves and selling directly to consumers. Foreign direct investment in single-brand stores such as Nike shops or Samsung outlets has been allowed only since 2006, and even then foreign ownership is limited to 51 per cent.

Wal-Mart hopes that entering India now, even if it can't open retail stores, will give it a leg up if the country's market opens further. Meantime, Bharti is planning to open its own Wal-Mart-style chain with technical expertise from its American partner. To the extent Wal-Mart's new wholesale outlets reduce costs for retailers; Indian consumers may see at least some indirect benefit.

RAHEJAS TO INVEST RS. 1,500 CR IN HYPERMARKETS

The K Raheja group has lined up an investment of around Rs 1,500 crore for setting up 68 hypermarket stores named hyper city and 250 convenient stores christened Express city across the country in five years. Apart from Hyper city and Express city hypermarkets, the group will be introducing a third format which will cater exclusively to hi-end customers. The first such store of 10,000 sq ft, which is yet to be named, would come up in Mumbai by May 2008. It would ideally be a gourmet store housing luxury food items and select grocery items. The Hyper city offers its customers valued-added services like consumer finance, ATM facility, telecom services, pharmacy, bakery and restaurants etc under one roof while convenient stores, Express city, offer daily-use products such as groceries, dairy products, bakery items and meals. The group is eyeing tier II and tier III cities as well for its rapid expansion plans. Terming Indian market as vast and diverse, Mr Livermore, CEO of Hypercity said that the Indian retail space can easily accommodate retail giants as well as around 12 million kirana stores across the country. There's opportunity for everyone.

METRO UNFAZED BY ENTRY

German retail giant Metro AG appears unperturbed over the entry of the world's largest retailer, Wal-Mart, into India's wholesale cash & carry business through a joint venture with Bharti Enterprises. The company feels that it has the first mover advantage and is now gearing up to face the competition by consolidating its presence through rapid expansion. The company, which entered the Indian market five years ago with its wholly owned subsidiary, Metro Cash & Carry India, thinks that its model has worked well in India and there is no need for a change in its business model. Metro is at present busy setting up its fourth and fifth distribution centers in Kolkata and Mumbai. Its Mumbai centre is being set up at Neptune's Magnet Mall by the end of 2007. At present, Metro operates two distribution centres in Bangalore and one in Hyderabad. It will open its fourth wholesale store in Kolkata this year. Metro's distribution centre in Mumbai will be spread over 100,000 sq ft and create more than 400 jobs. Its Kolkata centre launch has been delayed due to a legal dispute over land acquisition. Further, it aims to open distribution centers in all major cities having over 1 million populations.

Metro, till now, invested over Rs. 250 crore to set up three distribution centres in Bangalore and Hyderabad. Its Mumbai and Kolkata centres will see a combined investment of over Rs. 150 crore. In India, Metro serves three types of customers-retailers, hotels and caterers and other businesses including IT companies, offices. Metro sells around 8,000 type of food products and 10,000 non-food products. About 90 per cent of the goods offered originate from local producers and suppliers. In the last four years of its presence in India (till March), Metro has acquired 3.13 lakh members. Its products are sold only to its registered members. Metro plans to invest EURO 300 million (about Rs. 1,800 crore) to expand its operations in India over the next three to five years.

FUTURE DIRECTION: POSITIVES

AT Kearney has estimated India's total retail market at US$ 202.6 billion which is expected to grow at a compounded 30 per cent over the next five years.

- With the organized retail segment growing at the rate of 25-30 per cent per annum, revenues from the sector are expected to triple from the current US$ 7.7 billion to US$ 24 billion by 2010.
- The share of modern retail is likely to grow from its current 2 per cent to 15-20 per cent over the next decade.
- Over next two years India will see several Indian retail businesses attaining a critical mass as growth in the industry picks up momentum driven by two key factors:
  - Availability of quality real estate and mall management practices.
  - Consumer preference for shopping in new environments.
- Wal-Mart: huge plans for India. Moving a senior official from its headquarters in Bentonville, Arkansas, to head its market research and business development functions pertaining to its retail plans in India.
- New York-based high-end fashion retailer Saks Fifth Avenue has tied up with realty major DLF Properties to set up shop in a mall in New Delhi.
- Tommy Hilfiger, retailer of apparels, expects to open one store each in Delhi, Ahmedabad, Lucknow and Bangalore in the next four months.

FUTURE DIRECTION: POSITIVES

- 68 million square feet of mall space is expected to be available by end of 2007, which might lead to over-capacity of malls.
- Lack of differentiation among the malls that are coming up. One option may be to look at specialization.
- Poor inventory turns and stock availability measures - retailers clearly need to augment their operations.
- Operations of retailers and suppliers are not integrated. Efficient replenishment practices practiced in the Indian auto and auto-component industry can be leveraged to implement efficient supply chain management techniques.
- Supplier maturity, in terms of adherence to delivery schedules and delivering the quantity ordered, is an issue.

- Sales tax laws-lead to retailers having state-level procurement and storage leads to Indian retailers having higher inventories. VAT has helped alleviate this a bit.
- Increased adoption of IT and shrinkage management will be a critical area.
- Supply chain and customer relations followed by merchandising, facilities management and vendor development are areas which have significant gaps and proactive training is a key imperative for overcoming these.

CONCLUSION

The government said that the country is yet to receive any foreign inflow in single brand retail trade, even though 17 such proposals involving a total investment of $3.3 million have been cleared. The FDI policy for the sector, announced in February 2006, allows 51 per cent foreign investment in single brand retailing. In India, Metro serves three types of customers - retailers, hotels and caterers and other businesses including IT companies, offices. Metro sells around 8,000 types of food products and 10,000 non-food products. About 90 per cent of the goods offered originate from local producers and suppliers. In the last four years of its presence in India (till March), Metro has acquired 3.13 lakh members. Its products are sold only to its registered members. Metro, till now, invested over Rs 250 crore to set up three distribution centres in Bangalore and Hyderabad. Its Mumbai and Kolkata centres will see a combined investment of over Rs. 150 crore. The two companies finalized a 50-50 joint venture to go into the business-to-business, cash-and-carry wholesaling sector. This structure evades India's strict ban on foreign department stores and supermarkets setting up shops by themselves and selling directly to consumers. Foreign direct investment in single-brand stores such as Nike shops or Samsung outlets has been allowed only since 2006, and even then foreign ownership is limited to 51%. After revolutionizing the Indian telecom sector, retail will be the next big focus area for Bharti," said the firm. Under its deal with Wal-Mart, Bharti will focus on running the stores while Wal-Mart will handle the supply side of the operation. The Indian conglomerate operates in a range of areas, from commercial agriculture, insurance and software to telecoms, in which it control's the nation's leading mobile operator - Bharti Airtel. Organized retailing represents only 3% to 5% of Indian retailers while family-run enterprises represent the vast majority of the market. Various industry estimates put Indian retail spending at $300bn each year, with the figure set to double by 2015.

References

Anne M. Findlay, Leigh Sparks, (2001), Retailing, Published by Rout ledge Publication, p. 2192.

Stewart Howe (2002), Retailing in the European Union, Published by Rout Ledge, Publication, p. 240.

Sang Chul Choi, John Dawson, Roy Larke, Masao Mukoyama (2003), The Internationalisation of Retailing in Asia Published Rout ledge Publication, p. 240.

Rosemary Varley, (2005), Retail Product Management, Published Rout Ledge, Publication, p. 296.

John Dawson, Roy Larke, Masao Mukoyama (2006), Strategic Issues in International

Retailing Published Rutledge, Publication, P. 232.

Online Available from *htt://Economist-com.htm*

Garicano, Luis and Steven Kaplan (2001), The Effects of Business-to-Business E-Commerce on Transaction Costs Forthcoming Journal of Industrial Economics.

Higgins Les (2000), How to Market Books, London, Alison Baverstock, 3rd edition, p. 173-183.

Jeffrey F. Rayport and Bernard J. Jaworski (2001), Introduction to E-commerce, California, Publisher: John E. biernat.

Lucking-Reiley, David and Daniel Spulber (2001) Business-to-Business Electronic Commerce, *Journal of Economic Perspectives.*

Michael E. Porter (March, 2001), Strategy and the Internet, Harvard Business Review. The Internet for the Book Professions, [Online] Available: 5.

http://www.inasp.org.uk/psi/bmp/ibp-pubs.htm

What's the E-commerce, [Online] Available: *http://www.free-web-hosting-plan.com/ecommerce-newbies? htm*

Baker, Walter, Mike Marn and Craig Zawada (February 2001), Price Smarter on the Net, Harvard Business Review.

Bookshops and Internet Retailing: The Internet was Supposed to Destroy off-line Booksellers. It hasn't, (Dec 2004).

ROLE OF EDUCATION AND SKILLS FOR GETTING EMPLOYMENT OPPORTUNITIES IN NEPAL

VED RAJ ACHARYA*

BACKGROUND

Education is the gateway to any development process. As Schumacher (1975) says, development does not start with goods; it starts with people and their education, organization and discipline. The World Bank (1998) denotes that knowledge is very important for human beings in every aspect of life. Knowledge generates new wealth from innovations, which creates millions of employment opportunities. Basic education plays a vital role to make the person capable for learning, for interpreting information and for adapting knowledge. These qualities affects on economic productivity and health which helps to determine a person's well beings. Education is necessary for upgrading individual productivity. General education provides children skills for getting job and basic intellectual tools for further learning. The education is taken as basic concept in all over the world (ILO, 1976).Education, Education of spouses, education of children and expenditure on education are related to an individual's income (Devi, 1994). In this regards, every body argued that the expansion of education is both a cause and a consequence of economic development (Moore, 1965). So, education is important for getting employment, food and health security. Literacy and education are the main factors for availing the employment opportunities for modernization and to communicate with the outside of the world for adopting new technology.

In the present context, developing countries need much educated, skilled, specialized, healthier and disciplined labour force for promoting industrial culture because these factors raise the productivity of the workers. Keeping these things in view UNDP (1993) wrote human development is the development of the people for the people by the people.

Nepal National Education planning Commission (1956AD) had also realized that education must be universal, it much reach all the people, free-compulsory and individual differences. In the developing economy like Nepal,

* *Mahendra Morang A. M. Campus, Tribhuvan University, Nepal.*

small scale enterprises play vital role in national building. In the socio-economic and geographical background, there seem desirable potentialities for the development of small scale enterprises. These types of enterprises can contribute in the economic development of the nation by providing employment opportunities to a large number of semi skilled people. Thus, small scale enterprises might be taken as an effective measure for poverty alleviation, redistribution of income and wealth and to bridge the regional imbalance.

In the context of Nepal, being very labour intensive these enterprises employ a large proportion of the labour force and can play significant role in employment generation. Likewise, using little equipment and few sophisticated machines to elaborate and adapt technologies and management methods appropriate to their needs. These enterprises generally produce goods for the less- favoured sections of the population and also produce intermediary-goods for large firms, offer employment opportunities to school leavers and make it possible for laboures to learn total rather than piece meal job components and constitute a reserve of skilled and semi-skilled workers.

The experience of some developing countries shows that the worse economic crisis and employment problems, which affect all the modern sector and large firms, small firms are being looked upon as a source of job creation which could provide some solutions to the problems of unemployment. The world over training institution are being asked to pay more attention to the requirements of small enterprises (Leite and Caillods, 1987).

THE NEED OF VOCATIONAL TRAINING

To raise his economic value, man must be developed as a human resource. Investments must be made in him to increase his future earning power, chief among these investments are those in his schooling and training (Perlman, 1973). So, to create the skill for getting employment opportunity or self-employment ability the people must be trained. Such types of training are to be provided by private and non-formal vocational education, Industrial Technical Schools, National Industrial Training Service and vocational training for small scale enterprises. Like-wise, management training could be provided through courses, seminars and workshop in the field of general administration, marketing, production and financial administration. Similarly, business consultancy, including critical studies and the proposal of solutions to the problems of individual companies, dissemination of technical literature and technical hand books concerning modern management techniques would also be provided by such institutions. Technical information- collections of articles on technology and management from specialized publication and the series of guidelines for small and medium-scale enterprises on the preparation of studies and critical analysis also help to promote the small scale business. In the present context of Nepal, about 90 per cent of the industrial enterprises are small and medium size industries and major service activities are found small scale business (Khatiwada, 2001). Thus, small scale enterprises might be taken as an important aspect of economic growth. The economic growth raises the general living standards of the population. It is most powerful weapon against poverty and redistribution of wealth and income.

SMALL SCALE ENTERPRISES AND POVERTY ALLEVIATION

In the real ground, poverty in Nepal is the result of widespread under employment and population pressure in agriculture sector. In comparison to the increasing number of labour force, the employment opportunities in non-agriculture sector are not increased yet. In such situation small scale enterprises could provide an alternative solution for a large number of populations living under the poverty. Though the Agriculture perspective plan has aimed for expanding productive employment centered on agriculture sector by changing the traditional agriculture system to new production-function such as fertilizer, technology and rural infrastructure combined with adequate and regulated supply of water. Thus, it might be hoped that small scale enterprises can break the vicious circle of poverty because improved agriculture system could help to develop small scale enterprises (Shrestha, 2001).Not only in Nepal, but in Hindukush - Himalayan region there is scope of development of small scale enterprises based on diversified farming, livestock- based enterprises, nature and natural recourses based enterprises and skill- based enterprises. In this context, if the condition of product development and market promotion would fulfill in such situation local resources based products have seemed a bright potential for rapid economic growth (Papola, 2001) which could create a large number of employment opportunities for job seekers who are unemployed or employed on agriculture sector.

GOVERNMENTAL EFFORTS FOR THE PROMOTION OF SMALL SCALE ENTERPRISES

Industry plays an important role in the rapid economic development of the country. Development of industrial sector is important in solving the problems of growing unemployment and poverty. In Nepal, 80 per cent people earn their livelihood from agriculture and the contribution of the manufacturing sector to GDP is estimated to be around 10 per cent. In this context, concrete steps need to be taken to develop industrial sector in Nepal. Major proportion of agriculturally dependent population needs to be diverted to non-agriculture sector to solve the problems of unemployment and underemployment (Economic Survey, 2007). Thus, small scale enterprises create employment at low levels of investment per job, increase the participation of indigenous people in the main stream of the economy and use local resources (Khatiwada, 2001). So, promotion of cottage and small industry can play a positive role in solving the problems of unemployment and rural poverty. Cottage and small industry makes it possible to create employment opportunities out side agriculture and promote interrelationship between urban and rural areas by developing agriculture enterprises and involving more people in industrial occupation. Development and promotion of small industries based on indigenous raw materials skills utilization and transfer of appropriate technology has become the need of the day (Economic Survey, 2007).

In the current plan and programmes the integrated programme for economic and technical assistance will be implemented in the areas where the attraction of private sector in cottage and small scale industry is lacking. The policy of tax incentives will be provided to those industries which promotes cottage and small scale industry by involving in their production process. Special arrangement will be made for providing management skill, entrepreneurship development training, and loan facilities to micro-enterprises for generating self-employment. The objective of the plan in this sector is to increase the income and purchasing power of rural people by creating non-agricultural employment in rural areas through cottage and small scale industries. To achieve the aim and objective the policy is to expand and develop cottage and small scale industries through integrated programme for providing essential assistance and technical support (Tenth plan, 2002).

CHALLENGES

In order to bridge economic development with education, there are challenges. The challenges are high dropout rate, work burden of the children, irregularity of school operation, poverty, physical distance, and low perceived relevance of education, caste and ethnic discrimination, neglect of mother tongue in school and under aged children in primary school.

Wealth, education and income have been the indicators of development. But unfortunately Nepal has a large number of illiterate, ill health and low income earning people. They lack skill or specific knowledge, what they know is traditional agricultural activities. Because of this situation of their productivity, in comparison with their labour and other expenses is very low. And yet they are doing their business to survive and there is no alternative job for them.

Because of the systematic inefficiency the present educational system cannot create the human value among the students and cannot make the teachers devoted to their profession and their students honest. Every conscious person realizes that the whole education system is politicized. It is incapable of giving value orientation and taking care of Nepalese society. For example, education has been examination oriented universities have been a place to certify the dream. No body is getting the knowledge to respect the labour and skills students, teachers and parents who are the stakeholders of education. In this situation the concerning agencies have to work with educational institutions for the promotion of entrepreneurship. This entrepreneurial activity can ensure a change in agricultural farming, business practice and change in diverting approach. Farmers in that contest will engage in earnful crop production and give up traditional farming. Thus, we can hope better education for our future generation through the improved income of their parents.

CONCLUSION

In the real ground of Nepalese economy, small scale enterprises play a vital role in all around development of the country. So, to manage the present and growing labour force of the country, the educational sector also should be realistic. In this context, the micro sector of the employment opportunities especially for socially and economically backward section of the society should be identified and trained them for getting either gainful employment opportunities or to enable to be self-employed. So, the education system should be taken as an effective measure to create skill and capacity for job seekers. Thus, small scale enterprises could open a door for the millions of people socially and economically backward section of the society and overall economic growth and its sustainability of the country. It can also be said that the effort of the government is inadequate and ineffective. So, more investment is to be made from the government side to increase the technical manpower, special package is needed for poor rural children, empowerment education programmes are needed for women's awareness, a regular and effectives supervision system is needed in public school sand economy blended education programme is needed to abolish child labour.

Reference

Devi, T. Nirmala (1994), Socio-economic Profile of SAARC countries, New Delhi, South Asian Publishers.

ILO (1976), Employment, Growth and Basic Needs: A One World Problem, Geneva: ILO

Khatiwada, Yuba Raj (2001), Issues in the Development for Small and Medium Enterprise Development in Nepal. Edts. Bishwa Maskey and Narayan Manandhar, Kathmandu: Centre for Development and Governance and FNCCI.

Leite, Elenice M. (1987), Education, Training and Employment in Small Scale Enterprises, Brazil: International Institute for Educational Planning.

Ministry of Finance (2007). Economic Survey 2007, Kathmandu: MoF Nepal.

Moore, Wilbert E. (1966), Industrialization and Society, edt. by Bert F. Hoselitz, Paris: UNESCO.

Papola, T. S. (2001), Enterprise Development in Mountain Areas Some Strategic and policy Issues Edits. Bishwa Maskey and Narayan Manandhar, Kathmandu: Centre for Development and Governance and FNCCI.

National Planning Commission Nepal (2002), Tenth Plan 2002-2007ad, Kathmandu: NPC.

Polman, Richard (1973), The Economics of Education, New York: MCGraw-Hill Book Company.

Shrestha, Badri Prasad (2001), SME and Poverty Reduction Edits. Bishwa Maskey and Narayan Manandhar, Kathmandu: Centre for Development and Governance and FNCCI.

RURAL DEVELOPMENT IN NEPAL DIVERSITY AND CHALLENGE

VED RAJ ACHARYA*

BACKGROUND

The term 'Rural' generally refers to a locality marked with physical isolation inhabitated by apathetic masses of poor people with less cloth, little food, less education and low level of health condition, etc.

The main objective of Rural Development Programmes has been alleviation of poverty and unemployment through creating basic social and economic infrastructures training to rural unemployed youth and provide employment to marginal farmers/labourers, to discourage, seasonal and permanent migration to urban areas. People in rural areas should have the same quality of life as is enjoyed by people living in sub-urban and urban areas. The effects of poverty, unemployment, poor and inadequate infrastructures in rural areas on urban centers are the causing slums and consequential social and economic tensions manifesting in economic deprivation and urban poverty. Thus, Rural Development is concerned with economic growth and social justice, improvement in the living standard of the rural people by providing adequate and quality social services and minimum basic needs. The present strategy of rural development mainly focuses on poverty alleviation, better livelihood opportunities, provision of basic amenities and infrastructure facilities through innovative programme of wage and self-employment (Krishna Kumar and Rao 2008).

CONCEPT OF DEVELOPMENT

Misra (1981) recounted the following five major issues associated with the current notion of development thinking and practices:

- Concept of development is changing rapidly, denoting adhoc nature of its meaning and purpose.
- Both theory and practices of development have fallen under the domain of economics;

* *Mahendra Morang A. M. Campus, Tribhuvan University, Nepal.*

- Development is often equated with the choice of ideology and change.
- Motivation towards the process of modernization and copying whatever good or bad exists in the western society, and
- Finally, development is seen as a means-end nexus than as human enterprise (Misra, 1981).

In the context of Nepalese economy development can be effectively meaningful only when it is endogenous, holistic, culturally rooted and leading to the self-sustaining mechanism of organizations owned controlled and understood by the people who live over there. It should also lead to a interrogative positive effects in the overall quality of lives of people as they aspire and move onward with a full realization of their development 'from within' by making optimum of their own organization, knowledge system and locally available human and material resources.

South Asia Partnership (1994) a Nepalese NGO defines 'people centered' development was understood as an approach to development where people are at the centre stage. The development efforts would give priority attention to the poor, the disadvantaged, the marginalized, i.e. those whose circumstances are worse in a given community. The overall purpose is to help these people to take change of their lives and that of their community, and help fashion its future by their self-reliant efforts. The future would be directed toward a balance, and all round development of people on continuing basis, sensitive to the just needs of others and the husbanding of the environment. The approach posits that people would determine the direction and pace of change and always be in control of process. They would be subject of their history (SHP1990).

In practical terms, rural development means development of rural people who live in isolated community. Today, rural development is also known as community development. Community is defined as an area marked by the sentiment of common living. According to Maciver (1996) community is an area of social living marked by some degree of social coherence. The main bases of community are locality and community sentiment.

Participatory development means different connections to different people. This approach leads to a type of development which is more related to poor people's cultural values, self-insight, position, priorities and interests (Oakely, 1991). Thus, the essence behind the approach is that development must centre on the social, cultural, economic and political context of the people concerned with it.

In the present context, the concept of participatory development has become key concern for 'people-centered' development strategy. It has been regarded as an important social technology of knowledge creation process that starts right from the grass- roots up level of the societies. It begins with people world of praxis (action relation) resulting into their critical awareness of the problems as achieved through their own actions and reflections (Devkota, 2008).

ROLE OF INFRASTRUCTURE IN RURAL DEVELOPMENT

Inadequate rural infrastructure is one of the major factors which hamper the rural development. After more than five decades of development planning efforts, promotion of rural infrastructure is overshadowed by a cloud of negligence: Unsatisfactory basic rural infrastructure in term of its roads, irrigation, education, health services, telecommunications, electricity supply, sanitation, etc, has become a serious factor in economic development of rural sector.

It is fact, that infrastructure plays a major role in producing large multiplier effects in the economy with agricultural growth. Road, electricity supplies, telecommunications and other infrastructure services are limited in all rural areas, although they are of key importance to stimulate agricultural investment and growth. Better communications reduce transportation costs, increase competition, and reduce marketing margins which can directly improve farm incomes and private investment opportunities. Thus, rural infrastructure investments help to raise the economic status of the rural poor through increased income and improved consumption levels.

Human development depends on services that require supportive infrastructure-water and sanitation to prevent disease, electricity to serve schools and health clinics and roads to access the facilities (Krishna Kumar and Rao, 2008).

NEPALESE ECONOMY AND EFFORTS OF RURAL DEVELOPMENT

With US $ 484 per capita GNP annum (MoE, 2009) and about 32 per cent of the below the absolute poverty line, the Nepalese economy is circumscribed by a low level equilibrium trap resulting in a built- in scenario of poverty and stagnation. Although the Nepalese economy is often characterized by rugged topography, landlocked position and poor resource base, the more pertinent reasons attributed to sluggish economic growth in the past were the defective land tenure system, a fragile manufacturing sector, low productivity of external borrowings, unwarranted flow of liquidity to the real estate and foreign trade sectors, rampant corruption, and a lack of political will and determination to effectively deal with these problems.

As a consequence, the agriculture sector witnessed no substantial increase in productivity in spite of top priority and massive investment; soaring prices aggravated the extent of poverty; and the life of the common people remained unchanged during the more than fifty years of planned development in Nepal relegating the status of economy to one of the poorest countries of the world.

The predominantly traditional agrarian structure is constrained by acute disguised unemployment, constant productivity, lack of innovations, and subsistantial farming. Fragmentation of holdings in the land system makes poor prospects for mechanization. The average per capita index of food production has not been encouraging; this is extremely low in comparison to other developing countries.

The pattern of land distribution is skewed. Average holding sizes tend to be just over 1ha. in the Terai and just under 1 ha. in the Hills. In the Terai, many people are landless. The poor are overwhelmingly rural subsistence farmers. consumption rates both of fertilizer and energy remain inordinately low in comparison to the developing countries of the South Asian region. According to a medium variant projection, the population is estimated to grow 37 million by 2025 A.D. Furthermore, the demographic profile suggests that the labour force is growing at about 400,000 per year. One great challenge of the future will thus lie in managing the absorption of this massive labour force (Dahal, 1995). Majority of them will be from rural areas. The main characteristics of the Rural Community in Nepal are as follows:

1. geographical isolation
2. subsistence agriculture base economy
3. formation of country neighborhood
4. cultural heterogeneity and stratification
5. long history of its own
6. dominance of nature over culture
7. prevalence of disguised unemployment
8. low level of per capita income
9. vote banks
10. inhabited by apathetic masses of poor people, and
11. lack of transport and communication. (Devkota, 2008)

For the past three decades, Nepal experimented the regional development model. During this period, the nation achieved some physical development in the financial and social sector having some infrastructure facilities within the country. However, the imbalance in the development process is being continued even to-day. The Terai region is suffering from population pressure because of the heavily migratory trend from the mountains and the hills. Due to high population growth rate, the villages are converting into unplanned large settlements and small towns, which lacked well-managed and planned development and economic facilities as well. Right from the fourth plan period (1970/71- 1975/76), appropriate concepts and policies to enact the regional development model for narrowing the inequalities are being followed. But the objectives of rural and regional development have not been effective. It is due to deficiencies, enforcement of regional parity, concepts and policies (Bista, 2000). Realizing the importance and effectiveness of the rural development, the Three Year Interim Plan 2006/7-2009/10 has continued the concept of regional development. This documents states that the objective of this plan is to increase the pace of economic development of the regions which are comparatively deteriorated. By identifying and mobilizing the resources of these regions, the development process can be geared up (NPC, 2006).

In the process of experiment for the effective rural development model, implementation of decentralization is taken as an importance means for distributing the benefits of development to rural communities. It is realized that it can create greater involvement of local communities in the design and implementation of projects and programmes at the local levels, and enhance their participation in the further development.

Aiming the gainful achievements of the rural people to make the local body responsible, accountable and strong, Government of Nepal has enacted Local Self-Governance Act in 1998. In this act the following arrangements were made for the local self governance bodies:

- to formulate the appropriate institutional infrastructure to think for the betterment of the people and to be responsible for the people.
- to identify the necessary rights, responsibility and resources for the local body,
- to provide the rights of allocation and utilization of necessary resources,
- to initiate the establishment of civic society,
- to develop machinery responsible towards the society and the people, and
- to participate the private sector's involvement in the self-governance (MoLD, 1998).

But after the peoples' Movement of 2005 A.D. this Act becomes inactive. Time and again, the demand for Federal State has given the major issues. After the completion of the Constitution of Nepal, new directions towards the rural development will be given.

Despite the efforts of the government, the rural areas continue to be backward, both in absolute and relative sense. In an absolute sense rural areas continued to lack amenity facilities, access to resources, livelihood opportunities to make worthy of the human dignity and decency. Relatively the rural areas are becoming even more backward as compared to the urban areas due to a variety of factors- social, economic, political and demographic. An accentuation disparity instead of their living up is disappointing part of the reality of the development scenario of the nation.

Nepal's social indicators remain relatively below the average in South Asia. Life expectancy remains low and infant mortality is among the highest in the region. Nearly half of the population is still illiterate. Only two out of every ten Nepali women can read or write. In addition, in rural areas, where the vast majority of Nepalese live, population increase has outpaced agriculture growth in recent years. Similarly , poor extension services to farmers, intensive cropping, and low availability of inputs such as fertilizer, water, seeds and irrigation are also found the as barriers for the rural development programmes. Similarly, low level of work, superstitions, beliefs and irrational outlook, practice of manual work, submissiveness to authority and exploitation, low aptitude for cooperation, low standard of personal hygiene, etc. are also the causes which stand as problems for the development of rural areas. Other problematic factors are found as land tenure system impeding to agricultural growth, undeveloped institutions for enterprise, employment, fair weak trade and credit, imperfections in the authority of government agencies, instability and low effectiveness in national politics, low standards of efficiency and integrity in public administration, ineffective organs for provincial and local self government, and a weak infrastructure of voluntary organizations. Likewise, good governance including decentralization, accountability, and transparency, and predictability, rule of law and elimination of inefficiency, corruption and misuse of public resources are also responsible factors for the rural development, which can be stated as challenges.

CONCLUSION

In Nepalese context, as poverty is more widespread due to high population growth, poverty alleviation can, therefore, has an impact only with effective population control. This could best be achieved with macro-economic multi-sectoral plans, which include integrated projects and programmes to be implemented in a phase wise and sequential manners. Priority should be given to the establishment socio-economic infrastructure the diffusion of technology among small farmers, the evolution of the relevant institutional framework, the promotion of non-agricultural activities and human resource development. Emphasis should be given on inter-sectoral linkages, with the generation of marketable surplus in the agriculture sector. It can gear the rural development with the need of the day.

References

Krishna Kumar, T. & Rao, P. Srinivasa (2008), Village Reconstruction for Rural Development. The Gandhian Economic Strategy, Rural Development in the Era of Globalization, (eds.) B. Suresh Lal, T. Satyanarayana & P. Narasimha Rao, New Delhi, Serial Publications.

Misra, R. P. (1981). A Critical Analysis of Traditional Cost-benefit Approaches to Economic Development, Development Seeds of Change.

SAP (1994), 'People-centered' Development Training ' A Trainers Guide Book', Kathmandu, South Asia Partnership Nepal.

Oakely, Peter *et al.* (1991), Projects with People: The Practice of Participation in Development, Geneva. International Labour Organization.

Devkota, Padam Lal (2008), Anthropological Approach to Rural Development in Nepal: The Interlocking of Theory and Practice. Kathmandu, Academic Book centre.

MoF (2009), Economic Survey 2008-2009, Kathmandu Ministry of Finance, Government of Nepal.

Dahal, Madan K. (1993), Future of Nepalese Economy, Kathmandu. Nepal Foundation for Advanced Studies (NEFAS) and FES

Bista, Santosh Kumar (2000), IRD Concept ad Approach in Rural Development; Experiences of Some South and South-East Asian Countries, *Economic Journal of Development*, Issues Vol. 1, No. 1 Jan-June 2000, The Department of Economics, Patan Multiple Campus, Tribhuvan University.

National Plannig Commission (2006). Three Year Intriam Plan 2006/2007-2009/2010, Kathmandu; National Planning Commission, Government of Nepal.

Ministry of Local Development (1998), A Book on Local Self Governance, Kathmandu: MoLD, Government of Nepal.

STRATEGIES, TRENDS AND OPPORTUNITIES IN INDIAN RETAIL INDUSTRY–AN OVERVIEW

C. ANBALAGAN*

INTRODUCTION

The Indian retail market, which is the fifth largest retail destination globally, has been ranked the second most attractive emerging market for investment after Vietnam in the retail sector by AT Kearney's seventh annual Global Retail Development Index (GRDI), in 2008. The share of retail trade in the country's gross domestic product (GDP) was between 8–10 per cent in 2007. It is currently around 12 per cent, and is likely to reach 22 per cent by 2010. A McKinsey report 'The rise of Indian Consumer Market', estimates that the Indian consumer market is likely to grow four times by 2025. Commercial real estate services company, CB Richard Ellis' findings state that India's retail market is currently valued at US$ 511 billion. Banks, capital goods, engineering, fast moving consumer goods (FMCG), software services, oil marketing, power, two-wheelers and telecom companies are leading the sales and profit growth of India Inc in the fourth quarter of 2008-09. India continues to be among the most attractive countries for global retailers. At US$ 511 billion in 2008, its retail market is larger than ever and drawing both global and local retailers. Foreign direct investment (FDI) inflows as on January 2009, in single-brand retail trading, stood at approx. US$ 25.18 million, according to the Department of Industrial Policy and Promotion (DIPP).

India's overall retail sector is expected to rise to US$ 833 billion by 2013 and to US$ 1.3 trillion by 2018, at a compound annual growth rate (CAGR) of 10 per cent. As a democratic country with high growth rates, consumer spending has risen sharply as the youth population (more than 33 per cent of the country is below the age of 15) has seen a significant increase in its disposable income. Consumer spending rose an impressive 75 per cent in the past four years alone. Also, organized retail, which accounts for almost 5 per cent of the market, is expected to grow at a CAGR of 40 per cent from US$ 20 billion in 2007 to US$ 107 billion by 2013.

* *Professor of Management (MBA), Audyogik Shikshan Mandal's, Institute of Business Management & Research Chinchwad, Pune (Maha.) E-mail: dr.chinlakshanbu@gmail.com & drmbasusi.chin@ymail.com*

India has emerged the third most attractive market destination for apparel retailers, according to a new study by global management consulting firm AT Kearney. It further says that in India, apparel is the second largest retail category, representing 10 per cent of the US$ 37 billion retail market. It is expected to grow 12-15 per cent per year. Apparel, along with food and grocery, will lead the organized retailing in India. India has one of the largest numbers of retail outlets in the world. A report by Images Retail estimates the number of operational malls to grow more than two-fold, to cross 412, with 205 million square feet by 2010, and a further 715 malls to be added by 2015, with major retail developments even in tier-II and tier-III cities in India.

- Marks & Spencer Reliance India is planning to open 35 more stores over the next five years, according to Mark Ashman, CEO of the company. The 51:49 joint venture between UK's Marks and Spencer and Reliance Retail Ltd already has 15 stores in India.
- Future Group has been restructured to test the new rules on FDI under Press Notes 2, 3 and 4 issued in February 2009. The company plans to bring in up to US$ 148.7 million in foreign investment. Although FDI is permitted only in single-brand retail and not permitted in multi-brand retail businesses like Future Group's, the conglomerate has created two layers of operations to take advantage of the three Press Notes that allow FDI up to 49 per cent in operating-cum-investment companies as long as they are owned and controlled by Indians.
- Carrefour SA, Europe's largest retailer, may start wholesale operations in India by 2010 and plans to set up its first cash-and-carry outlet in the National Capital Region. Currently, Carrefour exports goods worth US$ 170 million from India to Europe, UAE, Indonesia, Europe, Thailand, Singapore and Malaysia.
- Jeweler manufacturer and retailer, Gitanjali Group and MMTC are jointly setting up a chain of exclusive retail outlets called Shuddi-Sampurna Vishwas. The joint venture, which plans to open around 60 stores across India by end of this year, will retail hallmarked gold and diamond jewellery.
- Mahindra Retail, a part of the US$ 6.7-billion Mahindra Group, plans to invest US$ 19.8 million by 2010 to step up its specialty retail concept 'Mom and Me'.

POLICY INITIATIVES

100 per cent FDI is allowed in cash-and-carry wholesale formats. Franchisee arrangements are also permitted in retail trade. 51 per cent FDI is allowed in single-brand retailing.

According to industry experts, the next phase of growth is expected to come from rural markets, with rural India accounting for almost half of the domestic retail market, valued over US$ 300 billion. Rural India is set to witness an economic boom, with per capita income having grown by 50 per cent over the last 10 years, mainly on account of rising commodity prices and improved productivity.

According to retail and consumer products division, E&Y India, basic infrastructure, generation of employment guarantee schemes, better information services and access to funding are also bringing prosperity to rural households. The rural market, product design will need to go beyond ideas like smaller sizes (such as single use sachets) to create genuinely new products, according to Ramesh Srinivas, national industry director (consumer markets), KPMG India.

According to the Investment commission of India, the overall retail market is expected to grow from US$ 262 billion to about US$ 1065 billion by 2016, with organized retail at US$ 165 billion (approximately 15.5 per cent of total retail sales). India is expected to be among the top 5 retail markets in the world in 10 years.

According to new market research report by RNCOS titled, "Booming Retail Sector in India", organized retail market in India is expected to reach US$ 50 billion by 2011.

- Number of shopping malls is expected to increase at a CAGR of more than 18.9 per cent from 2007 to 2015.
- Rural market is projected to dominate the retail industry landscape in India by 2012 with total market share of above 50 per cent.
- Organised retailing of mobile handset and accessories is expected to reach close to US$ 990 million by 2010.
- Driven by the expanding retail market, third party logistic market is forecasted to reach US$ 20 billion by 2011.

EXCHANGE RATE USED: 1 USD = 50.5047 INR

India retail industry is the largest industry in India, with an employment of around 8% and contributing to over 10% of the country's GDP. Retail industry in India is expected to rise 25% yearly being driven by strong income growth, changing lifestyles, and favorable demographic patterns.

It is expected that by 2016 modern retail industry in India will be worth US$ 175-200 billion. India retail industry is one of the fastest growing industries with revenue expected in 2007 to amount US$ 320 billion and is increasing at a rate of 5% yearly. A further increase of 7-8% is expected in the industry of retail in India by growth in consumerism in urban areas, rising incomes, and a steep rise in rural consumption. It has further been predicted that the retailing industry in India will amount to US$ 21.5 billion by 2010 from the current size of US$ 7.5 billion.

Shopping in India has witnessed a revolution with the change in the consumer buying behavior and the whole format of shopping also altering. Industry of retail in India which have become modern can be seen from the fact that there are multi- stored malls, huge shopping centers, and sprawling complexes which offer food, shopping, and entertainment all under the same roof.

India retail industry is expanding itself most aggressively; as a result a great demand for real estate is being created. Indian retailers preferred means of expansion is to expand to other regions and to increase the number of their outlets in a city. It is expected that by 2010, India may have 600 new shopping centers.

In the Indian retailing industry, food is the most dominating sector and is growing at a rate of 9% annually. The branded food industry is trying to enter the India retail industry and convert Indian consumers to branded food. Since at present 60% of the Indian grocery basket consists of non-branded items.

India retail industry is progressing well and for this to continue retailers as well as the Indian government will have to make a combined effort.

1. India Shopping Malls
2. Scope of the Indian Retail Market
3. Indian Organized Retail Market
4. Growth Factors in Indian Organized Retail sector
5. Opportunities in Indian Organized Retail sector
6. Challenges facing the Indian Organized Retail sector
7. Role of Supply Chain in Indian Organized Retail
8. Employment Generation by Indian Organized Retail Sector
9. Indian Organized Retail Sector's Impact on Lifestyles
10. Emerging Trends in Indian Organized Retail Sector
11. Growth of Retail Companies in India
12. Evolution of Indian Retail
13. FDI in Indian Organized Retail Sector
14. Formats in Indian Organized Retail Sector
15. Consumer Durables Retail

Retail is India's largest industry, accounting for over 10 per cent of the country's GDP and around eight per cent of the employment. Retail industry in India is at the crossroads. It has emerged as one of the most dynamic and fast paced industries with several players entering the market. But because of the heavy initial investments required, break even is difficult to achieve and many of these players have not tasted success so far. However, the future is promising; the market is growing, government policies are becoming more favorable and emerging technologiesarefacilitatingoperations.

Retailing in India is gradually inching its way toward becoming the next boom industry. The whole concept of shopping has altered in terms of format and consumer buying behavior, ushering in a revolution in shopping in India. Modern retail has entered India as seen in sprawling shopping centers, multi-storeyed malls and huge complexes offer shopping, entertainment and food all under one roof. The Indian retailing sector is at an inflexion point where the growth of organized retailing and growth in the consumption by the Indian population is going to take a higher growth trajectory. The Indian population is witnessing a significant change in its demographics. A large young working population with median age of 24 years, nuclear families in urban areas, along with increasing working-women population and emerging opportunities in the services sector are going to be the key growth drivers of the organized retail sector in India.

- Retail is India's largest industry, accounting for over 10 per cent of the country's GDP and around eight per cent of the employment.
- The market size of Indian retail industry is about US $312 billion.
- Organized retailing comprises only 2.8 per cent of the total retailing market and is estimated at around US$8.7 billion.
- The organised retail sector is expected to grow to US $ 70 billion by 2010.

INDIAN FOOD RETAILING

Food retailing is spreading across the country and making its presence felt in different parts. In the last few years it has gained tremendous momentum along with some major giants making entry into this segment of retailing and offering exhaustive product range and services to the consumers. Indian food retail market size is estimated to be around US$161.7 billion in 2006 which has grown by 3.96% in 2000-05.

Food retailing industry size is estimated be at US$3,007 billion in 2006. An observation of the retails formats shows that supermarkets/hypermarkets are dominant form of retail format that account for 53% of total food retail sales.

Few peculiar characteristics signify India's retail trade; dominance of regional players, huge variation in spending in each region that pose difficulty in evolving a uniform successful retail format.

Factors behind faster growth of food retailing industry in India are, increasing personal and disposable income, need for convenience, faster life style and increasing consumers' awareness through the reach of media.

- What is the market size and scope of food retailing industry in India?
- What are the current market trends?
- What are the various challenges and opportunities for the industry?
- Which factors are driving growth in the sector?

- What is the segment-wise performance of the food retailing industry?
- Who are the key players operating in the industry?

INDIAN FOOD AND BEVERAGES FORECAST (2007-2011)

This 'Indian Food and Beverages Forecast (2007-2011)' report gives an in-depth analysis of the present and future prospects of the Indian food and beverages industry. It looks into the industry in detail with foci on organized food retailing, consumer food purchasing behaviour, food processing industry and packed/ convenience food industry. This report helps clients to analyze the factors and examine the opportunities critical to the success of food and beverages industry in India.

Supermarket sales will expand at a much higher rate than other retail formats. This is because greater number of higher income Indians will prefer to shop at supermarkets because of convenience, higher standards of hygiene, and attractive ambience.

It is expected that fruit consumption will increase at a CAGR of 4.33% for the period spanning from 2007-2011, highest among all the food products taken in this report.

The processed-food market is the main focus for foreign companies as this segment is underdeveloped and presents enormous potential for growth. The growth of modern, organized retailing in contrast to the kiosks and small shops from which Indians have been purchasing food traditionally will also increase the demand for value-added foods.

Rising household incomes, increasing urbanization, changing lifestyles and the rapid growth of the private-sector and dairy-processing industry should lead to greater demand for value-added, milk-based products, such as processed cheese, table butter and ice cream.

Rising incomes will make fish more affordable for a larger segment of the population. It is expected that the consumption per head will increase at a CAGR of 3.45% for the forecasted period.

The growth rate of soft drink sales will decelerate during the forecasted period due to pesticide contamination issues and growing popularity of fruit juice drinks and bottled water.

Coffee consumption is likely to expand at a rapid rate during the forecasted period. It is expected that it will increase at a CAGR of 10.05% for the period spanning from 2007-2011.

- What is the per head food consumption in various food product segments?
- What is the future outlook of per head consumption of various food products and beverages in organized food retailing and processed food industry?

- What is the market size and scope of the organized food retailing in India?
- What and where are the growth prospects for the industry and which issues are proving to be bottlenecks for the growth of the industry?
- What are the growth prospects of the processed food industry?
- What are the growth driving factors in this industry?
- Who are the major players in Indian food retail industry and processed food industry, and what strategies they are adopting to gain from the industry?
- What opportunities exist for the industry?

This section covers the key players currently operating in the Indian food and beverages industry including Dabur India Limited, Godrej Industries Limited, Hindustan Lever Limited, Britannia Industries Limited, ITC Limited, Nestle' SA, Pepsi Co., Inc., Cadbury Schweppes PLC, Future Group, RPG Enterprise and Gored Agro vet Limited.

RESEARCH METHODOLOGY INFORMATION SOURCES

Information has been sourced from various credible sources books, newspapers, trade journals, and white papers, industry portals, government agencies, trade associations, monitoring industry news and developments, and through access to more than 3000 paid databases.

The analysis methods include Ratio Analysis, Historical Trend Analysis, Linear Regression Analysis using software tools, Judgmental Forecasting and Cause and Effect Analysis.

ANALYZING THE INDIAN RETAIL INDUSTRY

The globalization of the Indian Economy has brought forward a change in the Indian consumerism psyche with the consumer becoming more aware of his/her value of money strength and their economic purchasing power becoming more evident than in the previous generations. The concept of product quality and service delivery which were earlier not very engraved in the consumer psyche are now very much demanded and delivered for in the new age format of organized product retailing in the Indian consumer goods market.

These changes have led to the overall increase of professionalism in the service delivery as well as the consumer purchase patterns shifting from "need only" based to "extended storage-based bulk purchase characteristics.

These have led to the entry and expression of interest by many global retail majors in the Indian organized retail market wherein many products and services are offered to the same consumer at the same location which present multiple attractions to their monthly disposable incomes. The middle class has been a leading adaptor of this change process by its changing lifestyles, strong income growth and changing demographic patterns which are placing the growth projections for this industry comfortably at 25% annually.

Today, synergies based on huge consumer bases developed in unrelated industries like telecom to retail are being seen in the Indian market as the combined purchase affinity of the middle class far outstrips the specialist purchase patterns of the higher income strata in the Indian sub continent; with the industry projected to become a US$175-200 billion business by 2016 and the economy playing a comfortable upswing role, the competition in the marketplace is expected to be fierce.

The present scenario of the industry is focused on forward buying of retail real estate in order to reap balance sheet advantages later in the business cycle and also rapid ramping of operations in presently operating outlets in order that the loyalty purchase habits of consumers are built over a period of time before the world majors enter the market with deeper pockets and buying power.

The Asian retailers are not willing to give in an easy competitive fight on their home turf as well as the smart small time mom & pop store retailer known as the "kirana store" in India is also wizening up to the challenge and building personal relationships apart from increasing the service spectrum like never before.

The market in all seems to be ready for a big explosion of intense competitive activity over ridden by social and economic considerations which will make it one of a kind business study in the corporate universe as an economy which did not open up till the early 1990's where in the industry was dominated by unorganized retailer till then and any kind of central purchase or retail formats where only propagated by the government for which the awareness as well as effort were low. Oon the Indian Retail Industry is an in-depth and comprehensive cross industry review on the Indian Retail Industry which explores the macroeconomic scenario of Indian economy which coupled with growth of GDP led to the shift of consumer purchase patterns and the build up confidence in the retail sector thereby giving shape to the government allowance for FDI in the Indian retail sector.

The report provides an overview of the industry along with the investment inflow in the industry which has also been channelized into the rural sector in India by some of the players. The report also attempts to place an estimate on the volume of the unorganized retail sector of India in comparison to the overall industry size.

This report follows the changing consumer preferences of the Indian buyer along with the gender driven increase of purchasing power which has taken a different hue among the marketers which are now forced to look at them as an important purchase group and drawing marketing promotions budgets accordingly. The report also envisages to explain the role of the media in influencing the Indian retail market as well as the emergence of luxury brands in the consumer psyche.

The report applies the PEST & Porter's Five Forces Strategy Analysis to this dynamic industry which helps to bring out the characteristics of this industry and the forces driving investment infusion or competitor activity in this industry.

An in-depth explanation of the industry retail formats segregation is also provided in this report which also comprises of the study of the important regional retail contributors in this sector which are known for either their long standing in the market or any kind of specialty product retail developed over the years, which has differentiated them for the overall market. The report also compares this with the early development of organized retail by the Indian players and the coupled emergence of the multi-format retail in India.

The recent trends of jumbo sized retailers establishing themselves as super saver locations in the consumer psyche and consumer acceptance of these stores as discount destinations are also explained in this report. The role of e-commerce-based retail though small in volumes but important in terms of growth is also elaborated in this report along with a profiling of the major players in this market.

Rural Retailing is elaborated in this report in detail wherein the doubled up sourcing to selling cycles are explained in this report wherein the report also takes up the example of some of the successful rural retail ventures of the Indian market most financed by traditional business houses in India and some of the ventures which also did not succeed in the Indian rural market.

A contrasting view of the growth of luxury brands in the Indian market is also explained in this research report wherein the increased consumerism is apparent in the stupendous increase in sales of apparels, lifestyle products etc which have started to carve a profit making niche for themselves as also the trends apparent in these products are elaborated in this report.

The factors powering growth and the contesting issues are explained in this report in a macroeconomic scenario wherein the growth opportunities are compared with the issues which are process either legal or union or even logistics oriented. The report also examines the potential development areas in the retail market in India.

The process or entry options for FDI into Indian retail industry are examined in comparison to the challenges faced by the entrants in the sector to drive investment into the India market. The report presents some case studies on this crucial issue as well as the further options which are available and the possible role that can be played by private equity contributors.

Further, the report draws a profile of the Global Retail Industry and some of the major global players across the world. India's position in the global retail scenario is also explained in this report. Retail not being limited to only consumer goods is further explored in this report in the books music and gift retail industry which have picked up pace in transforming from being isolated businesses to being integrated retail locations for all these products which have received good consumer response as explained in this report by way of analysis of the leading participants in this Industry.

Food being a major driver of retail consumption globally has also seen growth and entry of various global fast food chains into India backed by slowly building weekend spending patterns in the metros as well as acceptance of these food habits in the Indian palette. The major industry contributors in this sector are analyzed by this report.

The report further analyses the retail push in areas like Fashion Apparel, Consumer Electronics, Entertainment Retail, Eyewear Retail, Fitness & Personal Care, Food & Grocery Retail, Footwear Retail, Fuel & Forecourt Retail, Health & Pharmaceutical Processes, Home & Office Furniture Furnishings Retail, Jewelry Retail, Telecom Retail, and Time wear Retail.

The report further provides the future perspective of the Indian retail industry which is set to boom and present huge opportunity or renewed growth cycles to the world majors of retail who now look at India as a future destination which will sustain and lead new revenue opportunities.

RETAIL BANKING IN INDIA 2008

The annual growth in bank credit to the commercial sector is at 25.4% as on March 31, 2007 and was lower than 27.2% against previous year. Till 2010, retail banking is expected to grow at a CAGR of 28% to touch a figure of INR9, 700 billion. This requires expansion and diversification of retail product portfolio, better penetration and faster service mechanism.

The report on Retail Banking Industry in India covers industry segments like housing loan, auto loan, personal loan, education loan, consumer durable loan, credit card and regulatory frame work for retail banks is also discussed. The report gives retail banking industry's current performance and future outlook. Total 22 major retail banks in India are covered in terms of their performance, strategy and outlook.

Key Highlights Covered

- During 2006-07, gross credit extended by Indian commercial banks grew by 34.83% to touch INR19, 495 billion.
- Retail credit constitutes about 25% of the total credit and has grown by 28.0% to INR4,218.3 billion
- The annual growth in bank credit to the commercial sector is at 25.4% as on March 31, 2007 and was lower than 27.2% against previous year.
- Till 2010, retail banking is expected to grow at a CAGR of 28% to touch a figure of INR 9, 700 billion.

The Report will bebeneficial for

- Industry analysts,
- Bankers,
- Other financial institute,
- Auto loan financier,
- Housing loan financier and
- Private financiers in general.

INDIAN RETAIL FINANCE

India is the next big market for retail financial services. This report uses exclusive interviews plus a survey of third party data to present the critical success factors in creating an Indian retail financial operation, including:

- Who's who among domestic and foreign players? What are they doing? What are their existing and future growth strategies? Plus in-depth case studies of the post office network and the microfinance movement.
- Key segments explained and de-mystified, ranging from: the affluent, the female market, the unbanked, consumers in regional and rural markets.
- Multi-channel distribution strategies, including: branch, mobile, peer-to-peer, and self-service.
- Understanding domestic regulations.
- Best practice and market intelligence in: collection strategy, cultural due diligence and talent management.
- The size and shape of the deposit, cards (prepaid and credit), wealth management, mortgage lending, personal lending, and remittances markets, where the opportunities lie, how these markets will change, issues to watch and key success strategies.

This report is essential business intelligence for anyone seriously considering how to profit from the growing Indian financial services sector. It's hard not to get excited at the thought of India as the next big market for retail financial services. Although India consumers are starting to feel the affects of high commodity prices and the fall-out from global economic uncertainty, GDP growth remains impressive and as one of the 'BRIC' countries, India is set to become the world's third-largest economy by 2050. The financial services sector is expected to be a lynchpin of this growth along with the retail, information technology and telecom industries. The market for banking products is growing at an even faster rate. An Economy Transformed–The Rising Elephant In 1985, 93% of the nation lived on approximately a dollar per person per day. By 2005 that proportion had been reduced to 54%, or 431 million people lifted from poverty (more than the population of the United States, or of Western Europe).

India's population is the youngest in the world. Half of its roughly 1.2 billion people are below the age of 25. Over the next 20 years, the number of people in their prime working years will continue to grow in India. Unlike in some of the other BRIC nations, where the population is ageing, this again will grow the market for all retail finance products. Mortgages, in particular, will benefit as this population becomes of homebuying age. The mortgage market is currently under-penetrated, with the value of mortgages representing just 6% of GDP.

Changing Attitudes to Debt and Consumer Finance Rising affluence has altered consumer attitudes and the approach of the urban consumer has shifted from 'debt averse' to 'spend now, worries later'. Abundant employment opportunities have increased peoples' confidence in their future earning power and with that, an appetite for spending that their parents would have indulged in only after a lifetime of careful saving.

The credit card market in India has seen a rapid boom from less than 2 million cards in the market before 2005 to 26 million cards in 2008. India is the second-fastest growing cards market in the Asia-Pacific region, with an annual growth rate of more than 30%. It is predicted by the Indian Banks' Association that the financial cards market will increase threefold within the next fiveyears.

The Indian market may have come a long way but things are just getting started. The next 10 years will see more change than the past 25 years, and with just 59% of the Indian population reported to have a deposit account (compared to an average of over 85% in Western Europe), there is a lot of territory yet to be staked out for both banks and their suppliers. Many financial services firms have entered the fray, and there are now close to 300 foreign, public sector and private sector banks doing business in India–compared to only 60 10 years ago.

The opportunity of the 21st century on almost every metric that matters, India invariably tops it. However, such a considerable opportunity does not come without risks. As many foreign investors have discovered in recent years, India is not a business proposition for the faint-hearted–or the uninformed.

This report provides a complete, 360-degree perspective on the Indian financial services sector–giving readers both critical insights into the market as it is currently structured, and an informed perspective on the likely direction of change in the medium term.

You'll learn not just how the banking sector is structured and regulated, but how it is likely to change over the next two years. The report goes well beyond the usual business and economic analysis, also covering both the cultural and political dimensions of Indian culture.

Who should read this report? Retail Banking and Consumer Finance Operations-Heads of Strategy, Marketing, Risk and Business Development-

Assessment of the prospects for success with an Indian operation Wealth Management and Private Banks-Heads of Strategy, Marketing, Risk and Business Development-Assistance in targeting affluent and HNWI based in India Banking Sector-Analysts-Data and analysis that can be used to arrive at a more realistic assessment of the potential of the Indian retail financial market Plus anyone else in retail banking and financial services who wants to know more about the opportunities, challenges and possible pitfalls of extending retail financial services to India as a strategy for growth.

About the Author Kebbie Sebastian is a retail banking and payments professional whose experience spans the US, India, China and European markets. He has previously held senior executive positions with Bank of America and Paypal and started his career with Citibank in India. Booming Retail Sector in India.

India is one of the most attractive destinations for retailers from all across the globe. Thanks to the entry of corporate, changing consumer behaviour & lifestyle, increasing influence of western culture and rising income, the Indian retail industry has seen phenomenal growth in the last five years (2001-2006) and organized retailing has finally emerged from the shadows of unorganized retailing and is contributing significantly to the growth of the overall retail sector, according to "Booming Retail Sector in India", a new market research report. The research report.

ECONOMIC SURVEY DEMANDS FOREIGN INVESTMENT IN MULTI-BRAND RETAILING

The Economic Survey for 2008-09 Finance Minister Pranab Mukherjee tabled in parliament has advocated sweeping policy changes like foreign investment in multi-brand retailing and higher foreign stake in insurance companies. The survey report card suggested the cap on foreign equity in insurance sector be raised to 49 per cent from 26 per cent currently. According to it, the limit of foreign equity can even be raised to 100 in case of health and weather insurance. (Weather insurance products are aimed at enhancing the risk-taking capacity of farmers, banks, micro-finance lenders and agro-based industries).

"This may help dispel fears of foreign equity in insurance," the survey said. In the area of external reforms, the survey favored foreign investment in multi-format retailing starting with food despite opposition to the idea. "Foreign direct investment in multi-format retailing should start with food," it said, suggesting that for five years these companies must also have wholesale outlets for small and unorganized retailers. Other major initiative suggested by the annual survey was allowing foreign equity in the defence sector up to 49 per cent. The survey added that this limit can be stretched to 100 per cent in the case of high technology and strategic defence goods, services and systems that can help eliminate import dependence.

RELIANCE RETAIL PLANS TO PURCHASE HENKEL INDIA'S SOAP BRAND

Mukesh Ambani's Reliance Retail has put in bids to acquire two of Henkel India's soap brands, a sign of the big ambitions it has in the fast-moving consumer goods (FMCG) business. Any deal for the male deodorant soap Aramusk and Moloy sandalwood soap, put up for sale late last year, is estimated to be worth about Rs. 10 crore. The Henkel brands are unlikely to generate significant revenues at the national level, but they are attractive buys locally, especially in the eastern part of the country. Reliance Industries (RIL), the parent of Reliance Retail, has identified the FMCG sector as the next big growth area, and is planning to set up two or three subsidiaries to manage the business. What started as a private label initiative for Reliance Retail has now grown into a large business idea, said two persons close to the development.

They said the entire business (manufacturing and distribution) will be operated through third parties with Reliance controlling the brand and the technology behind it. The plan is to create consumer brands, acquire them and get into joint ventures with existing companies, a top company official said. Chennai-based Henkel had earlier put four non-core brands on the block that included Maha Bhringol hair oil and Tuhina skin cream. ET has learnt that Reliance is not interested in acquiring the hair oil brand and Henkel has decided to retain Tuhina as its core brand. The Emami group is also in the race for the Henkel soap brands, but a person close to the deal process said Reliance has bid higher. Mumbai-based consumer goods firm Jyothy Laboratories also considered acquiring the brands, but it couldn't be ascertained if it is still in the race. Mape Advisory Services is the investment banker for the deal. Aramusk and Moloy were owned by Shaw Wallace India before Henkel acquired them in 1999. Reliance Retail and Henkel India declined to comment

RETAIL EXPECTS HIGH FROM BUDGET-09

UPA coming into power in good numbers raises new hopes for the retail sector in India. Like any other sector, retail has also been witnessing a sharp decline in revenues. Given that the retail trade functions on paper thin margins; this decline in revenues has had a cascading effect on the profitability. There is credit crunch in the market and bankers are not easily lending money. In such a scenario, retail players are concentrating on promoting in-house brands, changing product profiles, adopting innovative means of funding operations, relooking at supply chains, repositioning the business model and are also on a look out for opportunities of consolidation.

Opening up of foreign direct investment 'FDI' in multi brand retail has been the long standing demand of retail sector. As this has been one of the budget wish list of the retail sector, it is the industry's expectation that the UPA coming into power in good numbers will help in getting through this proposal. Recently, Department of Industrial Policy and Promotion (DIPP) had clarified by means of a Press Note that if the Indian investment company (IIC) is owned and controlled by residents, then a step down investment by IIC in any Indian company is not considered as FDI. This would be the case, even if, there is a foreign investment in IIC upto 49 per cent.

HOPE ARISES FOR RETAIL SECTOR

Consumers have started trickling back to malls and department stores as the economy is stabilizing, say many large retailers, who expect sales to further improve in the months ahead. This sentiment is spread across segments, from value retailers such as Vishal Retail to specialized chains such as The Mobile Store, which sells cellphones and accessories and is part of the conglomerate Essar Group, to Reliance Retail, part of the Reliance-Anil Dhirubhai Ambani Group. Pantaloon Retail (India) Ltd, the country's largest retailer by revenue, witnessed around 8% growth in same store sales for the month of May compared with the same period last year. In April, the company said it had an increase of 7% and 5% in March.

Vishal Retail, which shut two apparel manufacturing units and two stores during the downturn, is now seeing sales picking up again. Chief executive officer (CEO) Ambeek Khemka said, "Sales are picking up gradually and the company has seen a surge of around 20% overall sales in the last three months." A Reliance Retail official, who did not want to be identified because of company policy, said, "From April, definitely, the consumer sentiment is positive and we have witnessed an increase in sales by around 15% in the last two months and June is looking better than May." Rajeev Agarwal, CEO of The MobileStore, said, "In the last three months the sales of the company have increased by around 20% which definitely indicates a positive sentiment." The upturn comes at a time when economists around the world have been speaking of so-called "green shoots" of recovery after an unprecedented global slowdown sharply cut consumer spending.

INDIAN RETAILERS CONCERNED OVER GOVT'S RETAIL FDI POLICY

With Ikea dropping its India plans and a Parliamentary Standing Committee report opposing the entry of heavyweights into the retail trade, Indian retailers looking for foreign tie-ups are in a cautious mood. Faced with the double-edged sword of slowdown and Government policies restricting stake dilution, retailers and market analysts observe that foreign inflow and technical know-how, crucial to the business, could be hampered, if the Government does not act proactively soon. "It is not a zero-sum game. Indian retail needs a lot of funds to establish itself. Foreign players are keen on more control than what they are currently offered. At this juncture, the retail sector has to be supported by Government initiatives and not otherwise," industry sources said.

The Parliament Standing Committee on Commerce in its report 'Foreign and Domestic Investment in Retail Sector', too, has demanded a blanket ban on domestic corporate heavyweights and foreign retailers from entering retail trade in areas such as grocery, fruits and vegetables. It also sought restrictions on their opening large malls to sell other consumer products. An Ikea official was quoted as saying, "We would have liked the government to allow 100 per cent FDI in retail. As it was not in the offing, we shelved our India plans." A senior industry expert says there are many misconceptions about retail. It is not clear whether parties are opposing foreign direct investment or modern trade itself. FDI is essential as it will bring liquidity and infrastructure into the system, he believes.

INDIAN RETAILERS CONCERNED OVER GOVT'S RETAIL FDI POLICY

With Ikea dropping its India plans and a Parliamentary Standing Committee report opposing the entry of heavyweights into the retail trade, Indian retailers looking for foreign tie-ups are in a cautious mood. Faced with the double-edged sword of slowdown and Government policies restricting stake dilution, retailers and market analysts observe that foreign inflow and technical know-how, crucial to the business, could be hampered, if the Government does not act proactively soon. "It is not a zero-sum game. Indian retail needs a lot of funds to establish itself. Foreign players are keen on more control than what they are currently offered. At this juncture, the retail sector has to be supported by Government initiatives and not otherwise," industry sources said.

The Parliament Standing Committee on Commerce in its report 'Foreign and Domestic Investment in Retail Sector', too, has demanded a blanket ban on domestic corporate heavyweights and foreign retailers from entering retail trade in areas such as grocery, fruits and vegetables. It also sought restrictions on their opening large malls to sell other consumer products. An Ikea official was quoted as saying, "We would have liked the government to allow 100 per cent FDI in retail. As it was not in the offing, we shelved our India plans." A senior industry expert says there are many misconceptions about retail. It is not clear whether parties are opposing foreign direct investment or modern trade itself. FDI is essential as it will bring liquidity and infrastructure into the system, he believes.

INDIA THE MOST ATTRACTIVE NATION FOR GLOBAL RETAILERS

Providing good growth potential for global retailers amid the economic slowdown, India has emerged as the most alluring market for investment in the retail sector, surpassing the likes of China, Russia and the United Arab Emirates. India has been ranked as the most attractive nation for retail investment among 30 emerging markets by US-based global management consulting firm A T Kearney.

According to the entity's Global Retail Development Index (GRDI), India is followed by Russia (2), China (3), United Arab Emirates (4) and Saudi Arabia (5). India was placed at the second spot last year. Similarly, the other four countries in the top five have improved their ranking, with the United Arab Emirates jumping 16 places from previous year's 20th rank.

IKEA CANCELS INDIAN INVESTMENT PLAN

The iconic $ 31-billion Scandinavian home products giant, IKEA, has put on hold its plans to set up 25 showrooms across the country for an investment of around $ 1 billion. In an internal communication this week, IKEA told its stakeholders that Indian investment rules do not encourage it to go ahead with its investment plans—at least not in the near future. The country's norms on foreign investments in retail stipulate that the foreign company can hold no more than a 51% stake and must have an Indian partner. As IKEA's distinctive showrooms are like sprawling malls, with flat pack furniture, accessories, bathroom and kitchen items, they require high investment. And IKEA has so far been unable to find an Indian partner with not just deep pockets but readiness to invest a matching amount in a joint venture.

It's learnt that IKEA was hopeful of the rules being relaxed by the new government, but was jolted by Pratibha Patil's silence on the issue in her presidential address that outlined the UPA government's agenda. It may have lost heart completely when commerce minister Anand Sharma said that FDI norms are not likely to be changed in the near future, and decided to opt out of India. When contacted, a top IKEA source confirmed the company's decision. But they were quick to add that India as a market can't be ignored by IKEA indefinitely. "In a few years we are bound to reconsider our decision," they said. IKEA had planned its first showroom near Dwarka, at a location that's between Delhi and Gurgaon. It had also hired 25-30 people for this venture. Their fate now is not known. Otherwise, IKEA has been sourcing many materials from India and employs around 11,000 in this operation, while it claims to be indirectly employing another 60,000. This outsourcing business is estimated at around Rs. 1,900 crore.

TATA'S UNLISTED UNIT INFINITI RETAIL LTD PLANS TO OPEN MORE SMALL STORES

Infiniti Retail Ltd., an unlisted unit of India's diversified Tata Group, plans to open more small stores this financial year as a real estate slowdown has made it difficult to get larger stores, its chief executive said. Infiniti Retail, which operates a national chain of multi-brand electronics stores under the Croma brand name, also plans to sell more products under its own label in a move to step up sales, Ajit Joshi told Dow Jones Newswires in a recent interview. The company has large stores that measure about 10,000 square feet-11,000 square feet on average and also smaller format Croma Zip stores.

Mr. Joshi said of the 21 new stores the company plans to open in the financial year that started April 1, 10-12 will be the smaller Croma Zip stores. Of the 31 Croma stores that the company now runs, only two are Croma Zips. "If you look at the Croma Zip strategy, we are looking at 2,500 square feet to 6,000 square feet stores," Joshi said, adding that it is much easier to get smaller stores than spaces measuring 10,000 square feet. "The slowdown has hit the property business very badly. A lot of (spaces in) malls and (other) properties we had signed got delayed," Mr. Joshi said.

DROP IN RENTALS LURE RETAILERS TOWARDS METROS

With rentals dropping sharply, large retailers such as Aditya Birla Retail, Reliance Retail and Shoppers Stop, and food chains such as McDonald's are looking at metros and mini-metros for expansion. Aditya Birla Retail and Reliance Retail had started their operations two years ago in Pune and Hyderabad, respectively, as realty costs were too high in metros. However, due to fewer footfalls and lower offtake from retailers, retail rentals have fallen by over 40 per cent in the last six-nine months in many cities, according to retailers and consultants. After they expanded steadily in cities such as Ahmedabad, Mysore, Indore, Vijayawada and Coimbatore, retailers are now all set to expand aggressively in big cities such as Delhi, Mumbai, Bangalore, Chennai and Kolkata. For instance, Aditya Birla Retail, which is setting up 60 supermarkets this financial year and 12 hypermarkets by fiscal 2011, is focusing mainly on Delhi, Bangalore and Mumbai.

"We need rentals lower than Rs. 25 per square feet per month to make our business viable. Two years ago, metros were unaffordable. Now, as mall owners prefer to have hypermarkets in their malls, they are ready to come below the market price," said a senior Aditya Birla Retail executive, who declined to be identified. "We will again look at Tier-II cities in FY11," the executive said. Having established its value formats such as Reliance Fresh and Reliance Mart in the top 85 cities, Mukesh Ambani's Reliance Retail is planning to establish its other formats in these cities. Spencer's Retail is gearing up to open two hypermarkets in Bangalore, one in Chennai, one in Kolkata, two in Hyderabad and two in Pune.

ANALYZE THE OPPORTUNITIES AND FACTORS OF INDIAN RETAIL INDUSTRY A SUCCESS

Press Trust of India NEW YORK, 16 JUNE, Providing good growth potential for global retailers amid the economic slowdown, India has emerged as the most alluring market for investment in the retail sector, surpassing the likes of China, Russia and the United Arab Emirates. India has been ranked as the most attractive nation for retail investment among 30 emerging markets by US-based global management consulting firm AT Kearney. According to the entity's Global Retail Development Index (GRDI). Retail, with more than 15 million employees in America alone, is one of the largest industries in the world by number of businesses and number of employees. Retail sales in the U.S. (total retail sales include the categories of gasoline, automobiles, and food service, as well as merchandise) will show a slight decrease in 2008, totaling about $4.400 trillion according to Plunkett Research estimates. Sales were $4.482 trillion in 2007, up from $4.307 in 2006. Retails sales in 2007-2008 were driven partly by higher gasoline costs as well as by deep price discounting during the holiday seasons by mass merchandisers. Meanwhile, automobile sales saw a disastrous drop off in 2008, with total sales of cars and light trucks for the year at about 13.2 million, down from about 16.5 million in 2007 and 17.5 million at the peak in 2005. Car sales in 2009 could decline further.

POSITIONS OF RETAIL SALES IN 2007-2008

1. Sales of both new and existing homes slowed dramatically. While homes themselves are not counted in retail sales figures, buyers of these homes are a significant force at retail stores where they purchase furniture, appliances, linens, consumer electronics and garden supplies to fill up their new residences. Likewise, builders and remodelers are a strong factor in retail sales, when they purchase supplies, materials, appliances, etc. at retail outlets. The slowdown in building and remodeling led to reduced sales at home centers such as Home Depot.
2. Another factor was home mortgages: From 1998 through part of 2006, Americans were refinancing their existing home mortgages in record-setting numbers. In doing so, they took advantage of very low mortgage interest rates and very easy lending requirements. Many homeowners also increased the balance on their mortgages, taking advantage of rapidly rising home values that increased their borrowing power. Borrowing against home equity lines of credit was also high, and much of that money went to retail purchases. Homeowners were spending this cash windfall freely, driving up retail sales in many categories. However, by late 2006, the slowing real estate market, followed by tougher lending standards, meant that the party was over. This definitely had a negative effect on retail sales.
3. Another major negative impact was the growing number of homes going into foreclosure as their owners were unable or unwilling to meet monthly payments. Many of these foreclosed homes are part of the sub prime mortgage fiasco that is rocking financial markets, where borrowers have poor credit or inadequate income. Also, a large portion of foreclosed homes are those subject to rising monthly payments due to adjustable rate mortgages.
4. The sale of gasoline at the pump is included in retail sales figures. Extremely high prices per gallon for gasoline have shown up as growth of total retail sales in America. At the same time, consumers have been forced to allocate a larger portion of their household budgets for gasoline, electricity and heating oil, leaving fewer dollars left over for discretionary retail spending.Unfortunately, consumers were forced to retrench in 2008, and that trend will accelerate in 2009. Current economic trends will be tough on retail customers. They will have fewer discretionary dollars left in their budgets after they face the challenges of high prices for energy, health care, food, insurance and mortgages. Meanwhile, job security is declining.

Table 1
Retail Industry Overview

Particulars	*Amount*	*Unit*	*Year*	*Source*
Total Retail Sales in 2008[1]	4,400	Bil. US$	2008	PRE
Total Retail Sales in 2007[1]	4,483	Bil. US$	2007	Census
Total e-Commerce Retail Sales in 2008	145.6	Bil. US$	2008	PRE
Total e-Commerce Retail Sales in 2007	124.6	Bil. US$	2007	Census
Motor Vehicle & Parts Dealers	919.3	Bil. US$	2007	Census
Furniture & Home Furnishings	118.7	Bil. US$	2007	Census
Electronics & Appliance Stores	111.4	Bil. US$	2007	Census
Bldg. Materials & Garden Equip. & Supplies Dealers	337.2	Bil. US$	2007	Census
Food & Beverage Stores	560.6	Bil. US$	2007	Census
Health & Personal Care Stores	237.4	Bil. US$	2007	Census
Gasoline Stations	445.2	Bil. US$	2007	Census
Clothing & Accessories	224.7	Bil. US$	2007	Census
Sporting Goods, Hobby, Book & Music Stores	87.3	Bil. US$	2007	Census
General Merchandise Stores	576.4	Bil. US$	2007	Census
Miscellaneous Store Retailers	118.8	Bil. US$	2007	Census
Nonstore Retailers	303.4	Bil. US$	2007	Census
Food Services & Drinking Places	442.3	Bil. US$	2007	Census
Annual Disposable Personal Income per Capita, 2007	33,667	Current US$	2007	BEA
Annual Disposable Personal Income per Capita, 2008	35,152	Current US$	2008[2]	BEA
Total Exports of Goods	1,162.7	Bil. US$	2007	ITA
Total Imports of Goods	1,953.7	Bil. US$	2007	ITA
Number of U.S. Shopping Centers[3]	90,786		2006	ICSC

[1] Does not include food service sales.
[2] Annualized as of the third quarter.
[3] Methodology has changed to reflect a count of actual properties, as opposed to an extrapolation based on a database count of larger properties.

PRE = Plunkett Research Estimate
BEA = U.S. Bureau of Economic Analysis
ICSC = International Council of Shopping Centers
ITA = International Trade Association
Census = U.S. Census Bureau

Source: Plunkett Research, Ltd. 2008.

IMPACT OF THE RETAIL SECTOR IN 2009

- Extremely high consumer debt levels
- Higher health care costs for consumers
- Global terrorism, tension and uncertainty
- Consumers burdened with high energy costs for such items as gasoline, home heating fuel, natural gas and electricity

- A continuation of depressed conditions in the housing market
- Rising home mortgage foreclosures (including large numbers of adjustable rate mortgages, "ARMS," scheduled to reset to higher rates in 2009).
- Layoffs and falling profits in a wide variety of business sectors.
- Rising unemployment levels.
- Tightened lending standards that will make it more difficult for consumers to obtain credit, including a pull back in lines of credit available on credit cards and home equity loans
- Extremely low consumer confidence
- Consumer tastes and expenditures influenced to a growing extent by LOHAS, a trend toward purchases that support "Lifestyles of Health and Sustainability." Consumers will be more conservative going forward, saving more while spending less. When they do spend, they will be focusing to a growing extent on high-value items with long life, low impact on the environment and low energy consumption. Items that promote a healthy lifestyle will receive a growing focus.

Meanwhile, competition among retailers has never been tougher. A retailer without a significant competitive advantage doesn't stand a chance. Superstores are battling each other on every major corner while direct marketers (including catalogs and online sites) are stealing customers from stores. Online selling at deep discounts is even making immense inroads into major consumer purchases such as jewelry. Many retailers have been driven into bankruptcy recently, including Sharper Image, Linens 'n Things, Bombay Co., and mail order firm Lillian Vernon, and more will follow.

Direct selling through online retailers, catalog companies and home-shopping television channels continues to be popular. However, the 2008 slowdown in consumer spending has put the brakes on online retail sales growth. Analysts at eMarketer project 2008 online sales to be $136.8 billion, up only 7.2% over the previous year (not including travel sales). This is a letdown from the 19.8% growth rate of 2007. They further predict a very low 4.1% growth rate in 2009, to $142.4 billion.

Growth in online shopping has been driven by two factors. First, the number of fast Internet connections in U.S. homes and businesses leapt to about 100 million by early 2008. These connections make buying online faster and more interactive. Next, there's the savvy marketing of online giants like Amazon.com (with more than $14.8 billion in 2007 revenues, up dramatically from $10.7 billion in the previous year), as well as the e-commerce efforts of traditional retailers such as Home Depot and Wal-Mart. These fast Internet connections are extremely important, even at the office, since a large number of U.S. workers take time out to shop online from their desktops.

The two most closely-watched retail days of the year are the Friday after Thanksgiving (referred to as "Black Friday") and the Monday after

Thanksgiving (known as "Cyber Monday"). This particular Monday is now important since online retail sites show very strong holiday sales on this day, much of it by people shopping from their desks at work. Cyber Monday 2008 enjoyed 84.6 million consumers shopping online from home or the office, according to a Shop.org survey, up from 72.0 million in 2006 and 60.7 million in 2005. Black Friday 2008 was relatively strong compared to 2007, but only because retailers pulled out all the stops, spending vast sums on advertising to lure shoppers into buying at huge price reductions. The strategy worked, but it likely had the effect of leaving consumers with fewer dollars to spend on shopping during December. All current trends point to a tough time for retailing. Profits at retailers for 2008-2009 are going to be low. Sales in October 2008 dropped a record 2.8% over the previous month. Sales of cars and luxury items are dismal. Many firms will post losses, and an unusually high number will take bankruptcy. Among the rare bright spots are Wal-Mart and Costco, where consumers know they can find everyday low prices on high quality merchandise.

CONCLUSION

Based on a deep discussion of retail industries in India an Extremely high consumer debt levels, Higher health care costs for consumers, Global terrorism, tension and uncertainty, Consumers burdened with high energy costs for such items as gasoline, home heating fuel, natural gas and electricity, A continuation of depressed conditions in the housing market, Rising home mortgage foreclosures (including large numbers of adjustable rate mortgages, ARMS, scheduled to reset to higher rates in 2009), Layoffs and falling profits in a wide variety of business sectors, Rising unemployment levels, Tightened lending standards that will make it more difficult for consumers to obtain credit, including a pull back in lines of credit available on credit cards and home equity loans, Extremely low consumer confidence, Consumer tastes and expenditures influenced to a growing extent by LOHAS, a trend toward purchases that support "Lifestyles of Health and Sustainability." Consumers will be more conservative going forward, saving more while spending less. When they do spend, they will be focusing to a growing extent on high-value items with long life, low impact on the environment and low energy consumption. Items that promote a healthy lifestyle will receive a growing focus.

References

Ailawadi, K. and Keller, K. L. (2004), "Understanding Retail Branding: Conceptual Insights and Research Priorities," *Journal of Retailing*, 80 (2004) 331-342 [Google Scholar].

Akehurst, G. and Alexander, N. (1996), *The Internationalization of Retailing, Frank Cass. [Google Scholar].*

Alexander, N. (1990), "Retailers and International Markets: Motives for Expansion," International Marketing Review, 7(4) 75-85 [Google Scholar].

Alexander, N. (1995), "UK Retail Expansion in North America and Europe: A Strategic Dilemma," *Journal of Retailing and Consumer Services*, 2(2) 75-82 [Google Scholar].

Burt, S., Mellahi, K., Jackson, T. P. and Sparks, L. (2002), "Retail Internationalization and Retail Failure: Issues from the case of Marks and Spencer," International Review of Retail, Distribution and Consumer Research, 12, 191-219 [Google Scholar].

De Chernatony, L. (1999), "Brand Management Through Narrowing the Gap Between Brand Identity and Brand Reputation," *Journal of Marketing Management*, 15, 157-179 [Google Scholar].

De Chernatony, L. and Dall'Olmo Riley, F. (1998a), "Defining a "Brand: Beyond the Literature with Experts' Interpretations," *Journal of Marketing Management*, 14, 417-443 [Google Scholar].

De Chernatony, L. and McDonald, M. H. B. (1992), *Creating Powerful Brands*, Butterworth-Heinemann, Oxford [Google Scholar].

Doherty, A. M. (1999), "Explaining International Retailer's Market Entry Mode; Internationalization Theory, Agency Theory, and the Importance of Asymmetry Information," *International Review of Retail, Distribution and Consumer Research*, October 9:4, 379-402 [Google Scholar].

Doyle, P. (1991), "Branding," in Baker, M.J. (Ed.), *The Marketing Book*, 2nd ed., Butterworth-Heinemann, Oxford [Google Scholar].

Dunne, P. M. Lusch, P. F. and Griffith, D.A. (2002), *Retailing*, Harcourt College Publishers, Foxworth, TX [Google Scholar].

Gielens, K. and Dekimpe, M. G. (2001), "Do International Entry Decisions of Retail Chains Matter in the Long Run?" *International Journal of Research in Marketing*, 18(3), 235-259 [Google Scholar].

Hamill, J. and Crosbie, J. (1990), "British Retail Acquisition in the US," *International Journal of Retail and Distribution Management*, 18(5), 15-20 [Google Scholar].

Harris, F. and de Chernatony, L. (2001), "Corporate Branding and Corporate Brand Performance", *European Journal of Marketing*, 35 (3-4), 441-456 [Google Scholar].

Helferich, E., Hinfelaar, M. and Kasper, H. (1997), "Towards a Clear Terminology on International Retailing," *International Review of Retail, Distribution and Consumer Research*, 7(3), 287-307 [Google Scholar].

Hollander, S. C. (1970), *Multinational Retailing* Michigan State University, East Lansing [Google Scholar].

Jones, G. (2003), "Middle East Expansion-The Case of Debenhams," *International Journal of Retail and Distribution Management*, 31 (7) [Google Scholar].

Kapferer, J. N. (1997), *Strategic Brand Management; Creating and Sustaining Brand Equity Long Term*, 2nd edn, Kogan Page, London, UK [Google Scholar].

Kucuk, S. Umit (2004), "Reducing the Out-of-Stock Costs in a Developing Retailing Sector", *Journal of International Consumer Marketing*, 16(3), 75-104 [Google Scholar].

Kucuk, S. Umit (2005), "Impact of Consumer Confidence on Purchase Behavior in an Emerging Market", *Journal of International Consumer Marketing*, 18 (1/2), 73-92 [Google Scholar].

Laulajainen, R. (1991), "Two Retailers go Global: The Geographical Dimension," *International Review of Retail, Distribution and Consumer Research*, 1(5), 607-626 [Google Scholar].

Low, G. S. and Fullerton, R. A. (1994), "Brands, Brand Management and the Brand Manager System: A Critical Historical Evaluation," *Journal of Marketing Research*, 14 (May), 173-190 [Google Scholar].

McGoldrick, P. (1998), "Spatial and Temporal Shifts in International Retail Image," *Journal of Business Research,* 42, 189-196 [Google Scholar].

McGoldrick, P. J. and Davies, G. (1995), *International Retailing: Trends and Strategies,* London, Pitman Publishing [Google Scholar].

Melewar T. C. and Wooldridge, W. (2001), "The Dynamics of Corporate Identity: A Review of a Process Model," *Journal of Communication Management,* 5 (4), 327-340 [Google Scholar].

Melewar, T. C. (2002), "Leveraging Corporate Identity in the Digital Age," *Marketing Intelligence & Planning,* 20 (2) [Google Scholar].

Melewar T. C., (2003), "Determinants of the Corporate Identity Construct: A Review of the Literature," *Journal of Marketing Communications,* 9, 195-220 [Google Scholar].

Muniz-Martinez, N. (1998), "The Internationalization of European Retailers in America: The US experience," *International Journal of Retail and Distribution Management,* 26(1), 29-37 [Google Scholar].

Myers, H. and Alexander, N. (1997), "Food Retail Operations in Eastern Europe," *European Business Review,* 97(3), 124-133 [Google Scholar].

Nandan, S. (2005), "An Exploration of the Brand Identity-Brand Image Linkage: A Communications Perspective," in Brand Management, Henry Stewart Publications 1350-231X Vol. 12, No. 4, 264-278 April 2005 [Google Scholar].

Olins, W. (1991), "The Power of Corporate Identity," World Executive's Digest October, 34-9 [Google Scholar].

Porter, M. E. (1979), "The Structure within Industries and Companies' Performance," *The Review of Economics and Statistics,* 6(1), 214-27 [Google Scholar].

Pelligrini, L. (1991), "The Internationalization of Retailing and 1992 Europe," *Journal of Marketing Channels,* 1(2), 3-27 [Google Scholar].

Pelligrini, L. (1994), "Alternatives for Growth and Internationalization in Retailing," International Review of Retail, Distribution and Consumer Research, 4(2), 121-148 [Google Scholar].

Quinn, B. (1998) "Towards a Framework for the Study of Franchising as an Operating Mode for International Retail Companies," *International Review of Retail,* Distribution and Consumer Research, 8(4), 445-467 [Google Scholar].

Ring, J., Charles W. King, and Douglas J. Tigert (1980), "Market Structure Analysis and Retail Positioning," in *Competitive Structure in Retail Markets: The Department Store Perspective,* Elizabeth C. Hershman and Ronald Stampfl eds. (Chicago, American Marketing Association) [Google Scholar].

Salmon, W. J. and Tordjman, A. (1989), "The Internationalization of Retailing," *International Journal of Retailing,* 4(2), 3-16 [Google Scholar].

Sayman, S. Hoch, S. J. and Raju, J. S. (2002), "Positioning of Store Brands," Marketing Science, 21(4), 378-397 [Google Scholar].

Simpson, E. M. and Thorpe, D. (1995), "A Conceptual Model of Strategic Consideration for International Retail Expansion", *Service Industries Journal,* 15(4), 16-24 [Google Scholar].

Sternquist, B. (1998), *International Retailing,* Fairchild Books [Google Scholar].

Tan, Thomas Tsu Wee (Editor), (2005), *Asian Retailing: Trends, Challenges and Strategies,* Singapore: Pearson-Prentice Hall, ISBN 9812449582 [Google Scholar].

Tan, Thomas Tsu Wee (2006), *Retail Management: 11 Immutable Laws,* Singapore: Pearson-Prentice Hall [Google Scholar].

Topalian, A. (1984), "Corporate Identity; Beyond the Visual Overstatements," *International Journal of Advertising,* 31(5), 695-702 [Google Scholar].

Treadgold, A. D. (1990), "The Emerging Internationalization of Retailing: Present Status and Future Strategies," *Irish Marketing Review,* 5(2), 11-27 [Google Scholar].

Treadgold, A. D. (1991), "Dixons and Laura Ashley's Different Routes to International Growth," *International Journal of Retail and Distribution Management,* 19(4), 13-19 [Google Scholar].

Urban, Glen L. and John R. Hauser (1993), *Design and Marketing of New Products,* Second Edition, Englewood Cliffs, N.J: Prentice Hall, 213-216 [Google Scholar].

Vida, I. and Fairhurst, A. (1998), "International Expansion of Retail Firms: A Theoretical Approach for Future Investigations," *Journal of Retailing and Consumer Services,* 5(3), 143-51 [Google Scholar].

Wrigley, N. and Currah, A. (2003), The Stresses of Retail Internationalization: Lessons from Royal Ahold's Experience in Latin America," *International Review of Retail, Distribution and Consumer Research,* 13, 221-243 [Google Scholar].

FOREIGN DIRECT INVESTMENT IN INDIA

G. Paramasivan* & J. Sacratees**

INTRODUCTION

Foreign Direct Investment (FDI) is become an important instrument in the hands of developing nations for augmenting their economic development. The much-heralded FDI boom worldwide constitutes a major element of economic globalization. Opening up of doors by many countries of the world has resulted foreign participation in the financial sectors of Emerging Market Economies (EMEs) during the 1990s. FDI inflow into the core sectors is assumed to play a vital role as a source of capital, management, and technology in countries of transition economies. The role of Foreign Direct Investment in the present world is noteworthy. It acts as the lifeblood in the growth of the developing nations. Flow of the FDI to the countries of the world truly reflects their respective potentiality in the global scenario. Flow of FDI truly reflects the country's both economic and political scenario.

Foreign Direct Investment plays a pivotal role in the development of India's economy. It is an integral part of the global economic system. Advantages of FDI can be enjoyed to full extent through various national policies and international investment architecture. Both the factors contribute enormously to the maximum FDI inflows in India, which stimulates the economic development of the country. Foreign Direct Investment in India is allowed through four basic routes namely, financial collaborations, technical collaborations and joint ventures, capital markets via Euro issues, and private placements or preferential allotments. FDI inflow helps the developing countries to develop a transparent, broad, and effective policy environment for investment issues as well as, builds human and institutional capacities to execute the same. India is also opened up its economy and allowed MNEs in the core sectors such as Power and Fuels, Electrical Equipments, Transport, Chemicals, Food Processing, Metallurgical, Drugs and Pharmaceuticals, Textiles, and Industrial Machinery as a part of reform process started in the beginning of 1990s. In this context, it is imperative to assess the trend of FDI

* *Department of Economics, Manonmaniam Sundaranar University, Tirunelveli, E-mail: paramasivan_g66@yahoo.co.in*

** *ICSSR Ph.D, Reasearch Fellow.*

inflows in to these core sectors in India. It is also motivated by recent political developments in India following the opening of sectors like insurance and telecommunication with increased financial gap for the private players. The main objective of this paper is to examine the trends of Foreign Direct Investment (FDI) in the Indian economy at the sectoral level by using the annual data from 1991 to 2008.

FOREIGN DIRECT INVESTMENT

Foreign direct investment refers to the investment in a foreign country where the investors hold up the control over the investment. According to International Monetary Fund (1993), "Foreign direct investment (FDI) refers to the investment made to acquire lasting interest in enterprises operating outside of the economy of the investor.

Foreign direct investment is that investment, which is made to serve the business interests of the investor in a company, which is in a different nation distinct from the investor's country of origin. A parent business enterprise and its foreign affiliate are the two sides of the FDI relationship. Together they comprise an MNC. The parent enterprise through its foreign direct investment effort seeks to exercise substantial control over the foreign affiliate company. 'Control' as defined by the UN, is ownership of greater than or equal to 10% of ordinary shares or access to voting rights in an incorporated firm. For an unincorporated firm one needs to consider an equivalent criterion. Ownership share amounting to less than that stated above is termed as portfolio investment and is not categorized as FDI.

NEED FOR FDI IN INDIA

Attracting foreign direct investment has become an integral part of the economic development strategies for India. FDI ensures a huge amount of domestic capital, production level, and employment opportunities in the developing countries, which is a major step towards the economic growth of the country. FDI has been a booming factor that has bolstered the economic life of India, but on the other hand it is also being blamed for ousting domestic inflows. The domestic capita is inadequate for purposes of economic growth and it is necessary to invite foreign capital, there may be potential savings in a developing economy like India but this may come forward only at a higher level of economic activity. It is, therefore, necessary that foreign capital should help in speeding up economic activity in; the initial phase of development. And foreign capital brings with it other scarce productive factors, such as technical know how, business experience and knowledge which are equally essential for economic development.

The Indian government made several reforms in the economic policy of the country in the early 1990s. This helped in the liberalization and deregulation of the Indian economy and also opened the country's markets to foreign direct investment. As a result of this, huge amounts of foreign direct investment came into India through non- resident Indians, international companies, and various other foreign investors. The growth of FDI in India boosted the economic growth of the country. Major advantages of FDI in India have been in terms of- Increased capital flow, improved technology, Management expertise and Access to international markets. Some of the biggest advantages of FDI enjoyed by India have been listed as under:

Economic Growth

This is one of the major sectors, which is enormously benefited from foreign direct investment. A remarkable inflow of FDI in various industrial units in India has boosted the economic life of country.

Trade

Foreign Direct Investments have opened a wide spectrum of opportunities in the trading of goods and services in India both in terms of import and export production. Products of superior quality are manufactured by various industries in India due to greater amount of FDI inflows in the country.

Employment and Skill Levels

FDI have also ensured a number of employment opportunities by aiding the setting up of industrial units in various corners of India.

Technology Diffusion and Knowledge Transfer

FDI apparently helps in the outsourcing of knowledge from India especially in the Information Technology sector. It helps in developing the know-how process in India in terms of enhancing the technological advancement in India.

RECENT TRENDS IN GROWTH IN FDI IN INDIA

Soon after independence, India embarked on a strategy of import substituting industrialization in the framework of developing planning. FDI in India has increased over the years due to the efforts that have been made by the Indian government. The increased flow of FDI in India has given a major boost to the country's economy and so measures must be taken in order to ensure that the flow of FDI in India continues to grow.

The total amount of FDI in India came to around US$ 42.3 billion in 2001, in 2002 this figure stood at US$ 54.1 billion, in 2003 this figure came to US$ 75.4 billion, and in 2004 this figure increased to US$ 113 billion. This shows that the flow of foreign direct investment in India has grown at a very fast pace over the last few years. UNCTAD's World Investment Report states that India ranked fourth in terms of receiving FDI during the year 2006-07, which amounted to USD 22 billion with a growth rate of 126 per cent. The Foreign Direct Investment Inflows during the year 2007-08 was USD 5,614 million as against USD 2,848 million in the previous year during the same period with a growth rate of 97 per cent. The total FDI Inflows in India during the epoch August 1991 to July 2007 was USD 60,242 million. Between 2001-02 and 2006-07, FDI inflows in India increased by about two and a half times. The following table shows that the major shares of top investing countries in FDI inflows in India since 2000-01 to -2006-07.

Table 1
Share of Top Investing Countries in FDI Inflows in India, (in US$ Million)

Country	*2000-01*	*2001-02*	*2002-03*	*2003-04*	*2004-05*	*2005-06*	*2006-07*
Mauritius	942	2182	788	567	1129	2570	6363
U.S.A.	356	382	319	360	669	502	856
U.K.	70	366	340	167	101	266	1878
Netherlands	162	196	176	489	267	76	644
Japan	224	178	412	78	126	208	85
Total FDI Inflows	2908	4222	3134	2634	3754	5546	15726

Source: Compiled from RBI bulletin, 2008.

The Government of India has granted permission to foreign investors to set up Joint Venture companies with various private sector units in India. This task is carried out with the aim to establish country-specific investment promotion centers in India and overseas countries. The ten countries who will be involved in setting up country-specific investment promotion centers in India include, US, Japan, Taiwan, UK, Germany, Singapore, France, South Korea, Switzerland and Italy. Among the major investing countries in India, Mauritius bags the first position followed by USA, UK, Netherlands and Japan. The reason for emergence of Mauritius as a major investor in India is the existing of this tax treaty many countries are routing their FDI to India though Mauritius. This helps them in reducing their tax liability.

FDI IN MAJOR SECTORS IN INDIA

The major sectors of the Indian economy that have benefited from FDI in India are-Financial sector (banking and non-banking), Insurance, Telecommunication, Hospitality and tourism, Pharmaceuticals, and Software and Information Technology. After the implementation of new economic policy, all the three sectors attracted FDI. At the aggregate level FDI helps the economy to achieve the growth but at the disaggregate level it does not help to achieve the growth. The following table shows the sector wise inflow of FDI in India.

During the period the contribution of FDI in agriculture sector has a declining trend. In the period 1991-2005 the contribution of FDI in agricultural sector was 4.7 per cent. It was decreased 2.6 per cent in the year 2005-2006. Future there was a downfall in the contribution of FDI in agriculture sector in the year 2007-2008 it is 0.8 per cent. The contribution of FDI in Industrial sector was 57.87 per cent in the period 1991-2005, it was increased to 59 per cent in the year 2005-2006 and it was declined to 32.78 per cent in the year 2007-2008. The Service sector contribution in FDI has continuous increases. During the period 1991-2005 the FDI contribution in service sector was 37.53 per cent. It was increased to 38.39 per cent in 2005-2006 and it was increased to 66.42 per cent in the year of 2007-2008.

Table 2
Sector wise FDI Inflow

	Agricultural sector		*Industrial Sector*		*Service Sector*	
Year	*Rs. in Crores*	*%*	*Rs. in Crores*	*%*	*Rs. in Crores*	*%*
1991-2005	70675.24	4.7	857615.5	57.87	553663.65	37.53
2005-2006	10474.75	2.6	236308	59.01	164102.78	38.39
2007-2008	7408.08	0.8	303233.25	32.78	614230.24	66.42

Source: Compiled from RBI bulletin, 2008.

CONCLUSION

The integration of developing countries with the global economy increased sharply in the 1990s with changing in their economic policies and lowering of barriers to trade and investment. There has been a substantial improvement in the aggregate FDI inflows in India. The various sectors receiving FDI in India have also undergone a sea change. It can be observed from the above analysis that at the sectoral level of the Indian economy, Foreign Direct Investment (FDI) is assumed to benefit a developing country like India, not only by supplementing domestic investment, but also in terms of employment creation, transfer of technology, increased domestic competition and other positive externalities which is a major step towards the economic growth of the country. This will help the government to chalk out a proper strategy and policy framework for attracting FDI inflows in India as per its potentials.

Reference

Bautan, L. and M. A. Sumlihskhi, (1999), "Trends in Private Investment in Developing Countries", Statistics for 1970-1995, Discussion paper, IFC The World Bank, Washington D.C.

Dua, P. and A. I. Rasid (1998), FDI and Economic Activity in India. *Indian Economic Review*, 33, No. 2, pp. 153-168.

Gakhar, Kamlesh (2006), Foreign Direct Investment in India 1947 to 2007: Policies, Trends and Outlook, New Century Publications, New Delhi.

Iyer, Usha S., (2006), Foreign Direct Investment with Particular Reference to India, Essay in Honour of Dr. Manmohan Singh, Abhijeet Publication, New Delhi.

Nagaraj, R. (2003), Foreign Direct Investment in India in the 1990s, Trends and Issues. *Economic and Political Weekly*, XXXVIII, No. 17, pp. 1701-1712.

RBI Bulletin, 2008.

Sidhu and Laveleen Kaur (2005), Foreign Direct Investment in India: Some Issue, Southern *Economist*, November 01, p. 27-31.

Tripathi, Neeta (2005), Foreign Trade and Investment in India: Policies and Performance, Serials Publications, New Delhi.

Vasudevachary A. K. (2006), Foreign Direct Investment in India: Trends and Impact, Vision Vol. XXVI, No. 1-2, June.

World Bank (1999), World Investment Report, Washington, D. C.

THE IMPLICATION OF CHILD LABOUR FOR ADULT WAGE INCOME AND POVERTY: A CASE STADY OF CHHATTISGARH

VANDANA KASHYAP*, RADHA PANDEY** & A. K. PANDEY***

INTRODUCTION AND RATIONALE

Child labour is widely considered to be a social problem that must be minimized, if not eliminated. The 1989 convention on the Right of the Child, which requires that children be protected from the work that harms the child's health. Educational opportunities and mental, physical, social or moral development, was signed by 191 countries. Despite this widespread condemnation, around one of every eight children worldwide aged 10-14 participates in the labour market. The incidence of child labour is highest in developing countries of these countries.

It is even possible that child labour can enhance the lifetime earnings potential of children directly. Typical Mincerin [1974] earnings foundation finds that work experience raises wages, presumably because human capital is generated through learning's by doing. It is possible that returns to a year of schooling, particularly if the schools available to poor households are of poor quality. It is also possible that by increasing current household income, child labour allows the parents to build and endowment of Physical to build that can be transferred to the child at maturity.

These Physical assets may have greater returns in credit-constrained developing countries than do the foregone human capital assets.

This paper analyzes the lifetime earnings implications of Child labour using a unique data set on adult earnings in Chhattisgarh. Respondents were asked respectively if they worked while they were Children. By treating Child labour symmetrically with child schooling in regressions, explaining adult wages, we can isolate the long term impact of child labour on human capital accumulation.

* *Research Scholar, School of Studies in Economics, Pt . Ravishankar Shukla University Raipur {C.G.}*

** *Professor, Depts. Economicsm Govt. D.V. S. Sanskrit College Raipur {C.G.}*

*** *Reader, School of Studies in Economics, Pt . Ravishankar Shukla University Raipur {C.G.}*

The remainder of the paper is organized as follows. In the next section [Section-II] we motivate the issues addressed in this paper by outlining the current profile of Child labour in Chhattisgarh. For this we use the same data sources, but we look at the sample of children only. In [Section-III] we lay out the Econometric strategy that allows us to disentangle the direct effects of child labour on lifetime earnings and poverty from the indirect effects. [Section-III] discusses the empirical results and [Section IV] concludes the paper.

TRENDS AND TRADEOFFS BETWEEN CHILD LABOUR AND EDUCATION IN CHHATTISGARH

As per Capita Income has grown in Chhattisgarh, the incidence of Child labour has decreased. The cumulative distribution of the age at work force entry by birth cohort is presented in Figure 1. The median age at entry was 12.5 years for the cohort aged 40-49 1996 and had increased 1.5 years to age 14 for the cohort aged 20-29. Much of the change in average cohort age is due to the decreasing frequency of very early entry into the labour force. One-third of the cohort aged 40-49 had entered the labour force by age to but the incidence had fallen to 20% for the 20-29 aged cohorts. The relationship between entry and years of education by birth cohort is illustrated into the potential ways that child labour can affect lifetime earning can be obtained by examining the experience of current working children. First, there is a surprisingly small effect of working status on school enrollment. In Table 1, 91%of Chhattisgarhia children aged 10-14 are enrolled in school of those not in the labour force, 93% are n school but 79% of working children are also in school. Clearly there are more children in both work and school then in work only. However there is an apparent cast to child labour with regard to child educational attainment: 57% of working children are behind grade 44% of non-working children. Either child labour retards academic progress or else children doing poorly are more likely to be sent to work.

Table 1
School Enrollment and Grade Retardation for Chhattisgarh Children Aged 10-14, by Labour Market Status

	%Enrolled	*% Log Grad*
Child working	79.1	57.4
Child not working	93.0	44.2
Total	91.0	46.2

Source: Authors calculations using N.S.S.O. data.

Table 2 reports child labour incidence by income quintile in Chhattisgarh. On average a Child's income represents 17% of urban household income 22% of rural household income for household with working children. Nevertheless there is a strong circumstantial case that early entry into the labour market has adverse consequences for adult income. Table 3 reports the incidence of adult poverty by years of education and age of labour market entry.

Table 2
Labour Force Participant Rates for Chhattisgarh Children Aged 10-14, by Income Quintile Area, 1996

Income	*Urban*	*Rural*	*Total*
Lowest 20%	10%	38%	22%
21-40%	10%	31%	14%
41-60%	9%	31%	12%
61-80%	7%	29%	8%
Top 20%	5%	23%	6%

* Numbers in parentheses represent proportions in the lowest income quintile. Unbracketed numbers represent proportion in the lowest two income quintiles.

Table 3
Proportion of Population Over 18 in the Lowest Income Quintile, 1996, by Age of Labour Force Entry and Education

		Years of Education					
	%of Adult >18	*None*	*1 to 3*	*4 to 7*	*8 to 11*	*12 or more*	*Total*
Age of Entry							
Before 13	39	83%	70%	51%	28%	9%	56%
		(60%)	(40%)	(25%)	(10%)	(4%)	(33%)
13 to15	26	76%	64%	42%	19%	6%	36%
		(51%)	(35%)	(18%)	(6%)	(2%)	(17%)
16 to19	24	68%	59%	42%	19%	4%	27%
		(43%)	(29%)	(18%)	(6%)	(2%)	(11%)
After 20	11	64%	58%	43%	22%	4%	24%
		(39%)	(26%)	(18%)	(7%)	(2%)	(10%)
Total	100	80%	67%	46%	22%	5%	41%
		(56%)	(39%)	(21%)	(7%)	(2%)	(21%)

In Table 4,we find that early labour market entry is associated with lower wages as an adult.

Table 4
Distribution of Wage (R/$Hr) for Population Over 18 by Age of Workforce Entry and Education, 1996

		Years of Education					
	%of Adult >18	*None*	*1 to 3*	*4 to 7*	*8 to 11*	*12 or more*	*Total*
Age of Entry							
Before 13	39	0.77	1.07	1.69	2.92	7.41	1.79
13 to15	26	0.85	1.18	1.74	3.09	8.26	2.66
16 to19	24	0.96	1.39	1.62	2.53	7.3	3.03
After 20	11	1.01	1.28	1.28	2.21	8.54	4.02
Total	100	0.81	1.14	1.67	2.76	7.87	2.51

*Authors' calculation using N.S.S.O. Cited in Base (1999).

DATA

The analysis is based on the 1996 round of the national sample survey of households-by N.S.S.O. The survey, conducted annually by the government of India, is a nationally representative stratified random sample of the chhattisgarhia population including education labour, residency and earnings. When needed, the survey incorporates other societal indicators such as migration, fertility, nutrition and marital status. The survey is unique in that it included a retrospective question on age of labour market entry and also included information on the parents of a subsets adult respondents. Before discussing the estimation strategy, we first establish the reliability of the recall data on child labour force participation.

RETROSPECTION VERUS CONTEMPORANEOUS MEASURES OF CHILD LABOUR

In the N.S.S.O. survey, adult respondents were asked the age at which they first entered the workforce. The frequency distribution of the responses are displayed in Figure 1. The time pattern are consistent with stylized facts from contemporaneously collected data. However, the implied child labour force participation rates based on recall data are large then the official rates reported by the International labour organization {I.L.O.} as shown in Table 5.

Table 5

Retrospective and Contemporaneous Measures of the Incidence of Child Labour in Chhattisgarh, Ages 10-14

	1960	*1970*	*1980*
Retrospective PNAD 1996	46.2	38.8	33.5
Contemporaneous ILO	22.2	20.3	19.0

ESTIMATION STRATEGY

There is a long tradition of examining return to schooling by using earnings function. Following, Welch {1966}, analysis of returns to education was extended to school quality. Card and Kruger {1992}, recently used a similar strategy to analyze the effect of school and teacher attributes on lifetime earnings. Child labour can be incorporated into the earnings function from work in the same manner as school quality.

To begin, approximate the true structural relationship between education E, and child labour C, as:

$$E\ (Ci) = \beta ci$$

Where the parameter β captures the effects of early labour force entry on lifetime education attainment. The coefficient β can be positive or negative.

Now consider the complete relationship between earnings and (poverty), child labour. Consider the log earning function.

$$\text{In}\ (Wi) = \alpha_o + \alpha_c\, c_i + \alpha_i\text{: } E_i\ (c_i) + \alpha_{CE}\, c_i\, E_i\ (c_i)\ E_i$$

Where the αi are coefficients and Ei is the error term. Note that the specification in equation, 2 capture the potential channels through which early entry in the work force may affect lifetime earning. The coefficients α_2 and α_3 capture the effect of child labour on earning through its effect on the quantity or productivity of education, while the coefficients α_1 capture the direct effect of child labour on adult earnings. Differentiating equation 2 with respect to c yields the total effect of child labour on earnings:

$$\partial \ln\ (\ Wi\ )/\partial_C = \alpha_c + \alpha_E\ \partial Ei\ /\partial c + \alpha_{CE}\ \bar{C}\ \partial Ei\ /\partial c + \alpha_{CE}\ \bar{E}\ + €1$$

Where $\bar{C}$ is the mean rate of child labour and $\bar{E}$ is mean education level. Regrouping terms in (3) would give us the total effect of child labour on adult wages will require an estimate of $\partial Ei\ /\partial c = \beta$ one option is to derive a relationship defining the locus of equilibrium points between age of entry into the labour market and years of attained schooling. As figure 2 demonstrates, that locus of points has been very stable over time.

An alternative is to derive a structural relationship between child labour and educational attainment by empirically identifying factors that shift C but not E and applying instrumental variables. Either method will yield estimates of β that can be inserted into (4) to derive the indirect effect of child labour on adult earning through education. As we demonstrate below, both options yield similar estimates of β.

EMPIRICAL FINDINGS

Econometric Results

Estimates of equation (2), augmented with the other variables in Table 6 plus controls for state of residence are reported in Table 7, for the full sample. Four measures of adult earnings are used as dependent variables: the log of hourly wage, the log of household income, and status in the lowest one and two income quintiles. The measure of child labour, CHLAB, takes the value of one if the respondent worked during his first 12 years of life and zero otherwise.

A subset of the sample had no wages, either because they were out of the labour force, unemployed, or worked without reported wages. To correct for possible sample selection bias, a maximum likelihood version of Heclmen's (1978) correction was implemented. Instruments in the auxiliary equation for the probability of wage work included the number of children and total individuals in the household, regional industry mix, and regional adult unemployment rate and per capita income. Household demographic composition, regional unemployment per Capita income are proxies for individual reservation wage while the industry mix is used to control for probability of nonage work. The uncorrected and corrected and corrected parameter estimates were virtually identical, so only the selection corrected estimates are Reported.

Table 6
Summary Statistics for Sample of All Adult Over 18

	All		*Those Who Started Working Before 13*		*Those Who Started Working After 13*	
	1	2	*1*	2	*1*	2
Wages (R$ per hour)	2.51	1.49	1.78	0.88	3.02	1.78
	(4.73.)	(2.31)	(3.30)	(1.35)	(5.47)	(2.59)
Education attainment (Years)	6.52	7.31	4.45	4.92	8.00	8.40
	(4.45)	(4.16)	(3.73)	(3.66)	(4.33)	(3.92)
Age at entry in workforce	1.92	14.73	9.88	10.11	16.77	16.84
	(4.52)	(4.12)	(1.74)	(1.64)	(3.63)	(3.06)
Entered workforce before	0.41	0.31	1.00	1.00	0.00	0.00
Age 13	(0.49)	(0.46)	(0.00)	(0.00)	(0.00)	(0.00)
Age (years)	32.34	25.05	33.60	25.01	31.45	25.06
	(9.11)	(6.61)	(9.26)	(6.88)	(8.90)	(6.48)
Female	0.42	0.39	0.35	0.27	0.47	0.45
	(0.49)	(0.49)	(0.48)	(0.45)	(0.50)	(0.50)
Rural	0.19	0.19	0.32	0.41	0.10	0.09
	(0.39)	(0.39)	(0.47)	(0.49)	(0.30)	(0.29)
Union	.1603	.1081	.1339	.0714	.1788	.1249
	(.3669)	(.3105)	(.3406)	(.2574)	(.3832)	(.3306)
Ethnicity: White	.5355	.5279	.4734	.4352	.5794	.5703
	(.4987)	(.4992)	(.4993)	(.4958)	(.4937)	(.4951)
Black	.0674	.0729	.0700	.0783	.0655	.0704
	(.2506)	(.2600)	(.2552)	(.2688)	(.2474)	(.2559)
Asian	.0042	.0043	.0024	.0020	.0054	.0054
	(.00645)	(.0656)	(.049)	(.0442)	(.0735)	(.0733)
Indigenous	.0015	.0013	.0018	.0017	.0012	.0011
	(.0383)	(.0363)	(.0423)	(.0412)	(.0352)	(.0338)
Dark	.3914	.3935	.4523	.4827	.3485	.3527
	(.4881)	(.4885)	(.4977)	(.4997)	(.4765)	(.4778)
Age of household head	43.07	55.79	42.23	56.44	43.66	55.49
	(12.91)	(10.13)	(12.50)	(10.56)	(13.17)	(9.90)
Household head is Female	0.18	0.30	0.14	0.29	0.20	0.31
	(0.38)	(0.46)	(0.35)	(0.45)	(0.40)	(0.46)
Education of household	5.37	3.61	3.73	1.84	6.52	4.41
(Years)	(4.57)	(3.90)	(3.74)	(2.53)	(4.74)	(4.15)

Numbers in Column represent 94,518 individuals in the full sample of adult over 18. The numbers in Column 2 represents the sub sample (N=25894) who are sons or daughters of the household.

The log wage equations mimic standard results. Wages have a concave pattern over the life cycle; wages are higher for urban, male and unionized workers and are lower for minority groups except Asian Workers in jobs that are not permanent are also paid a premium. Workers in households with higher average educational attainment are also paid more.

Table 7
The Effects of Child Labour on Lifetime Wages and Poverty, using Full Sample of Adults

	(1)	(2)	(3)	(4)
	log (WAGE)	*log (INCOME)*	*POOREST 40%*	*POOREST 20%*
CHLAB (α_C)	0.023**	-0.021**	0.026**	0.034**
	(0.010)	(0.009)	(0.007)	(0.004)
EDUCATION (α_E)	0.057**	0.029**	-0.014**	-0.007**
	(0.001)	(0.001)	(0.001)	(0.001)
CHLAB* EDUCATION (α_{CE})	-0.012**	-0.015**	0.004**	-0.002**
	(0.001)	(0.001)	(0.001)	(0.001)
Age 1	0.074**	-0.070**	0.018**	0.011**
	(0.002)	(0.002)	(0.002)	(0.001)
Age 2	-0.001**	0.001**	-0.0003**	-0.0002**
	(0.000)	(0.000)	(0.000)	(0.000)
Female	-0.479**	-0.028**	0.008**	0.009**
	(0.006)	(0.005)	(0.004)	(0.002)
Rural	-0.240**	-0.294**	0.186**	0.123**
	(0.008)	(0.007)	(0.006)	(0.004)
Indigenous	-0.187	-0.069	0.038	0.028
	(0.071)	(0.065)	(0.049)	(0.032)
Black	-0.158**	-0.125**	0.087**	0.039**
	(0.011)	(0.010)	(0.008)	(0.005)
Asian	0.189**	0.204**	0.011	0.068**
	(0.039)	(0.039)	(0.038)	(0.031)
Mixed Race	-0.104**	-0.106**	0.073**	0.033**
	(0.006)	(0.006)	(0.004)	(0.003)
Union	0.246**	0.103**	-0.091**	-0.041**
	(0.007)	(0.007)	(0.005)	(0.003)
Temporary Position	0.533**	0.417**	-0.203**	-0.067**
	(0.049)	(0.051)	(0.026)	(0.015)
Average Household Education	0.076**	0.122**	-0.062**	-0.027**
	(0.001)	(0.001)	(0.001)	(0.001)
Constant	-1.285**	1.771**	(0.036)	(0.034)
λ	-0.364**	-0.465**		
	(.013)	(.013)		
Direct Effect: "(α_c to α_{CE} $\bar{E}$ \ C =1)"	-2.8%	-8.7%	4.4%	2.6%
Indirect Effect (α_E+α_{CE} $\bar{C}$) ∂_E / ∂_E	-13.4%	-4.2%	2.9%	2.6%
Total Effect	-16.2%	-12.9%	7.3%	5.3%
Log Like hood	-122425	-111200	-42411	-34425
N	94321	94289	94289	94289

All specifications include dummy variables for state of residence. Maximum like hood Probity. Standard errors are in parentheses. *Significant at the .10 level. **Significant at the .05 levels.

The parameters of primary interest are α_c, α_E and α_{CE}. Interestingly $\alpha_c > O$, suggesting that at zero years of education, child labour leads to higher lifetime earnings. This is consistent with the presumption that child labour can increase human capital through occupational training. However, child labour also makes education less efficient at producing human capital, so thet $\alpha_{CE} < O$. The direct effect of child labour on life earnings combines these two influences, reported as "(α_c to α_{CE} $\bar{E}\backslash_{C=1}$)" at the bottom of Table 7. The negative effect of child labour on returns to education dominates the positive effect on occupational human capital. Consequently, working in the first 12 years of life has a direct effect of reducing adult hourly wage by 2.8%.

The indirect effect of child labour works its way through the impact of child labour on years of education. As discussed above, past studies disagree about whether child labour increases or decreases years of education. The equilibrium locus of points in figure 2 suggests that for each year entry into the labour market is delayed past the age of ten, attained schooling increases by .58 years. This relationship is not a structural one, however. Structural estimation can be conducted using data on current children in chhattisgarh. A two step procedure was used in which the probability of child labour under the age of 13 was predicted based on household demographic and income variables, state of birth and regional economic indicators. Predicted probability of child labour was then incorporated into an equation explaining years of education. Because some children are still in school, a to bit formulation was used to correct for truncation in observed schooling. The implied impact of child labour in the first twelve years of life is to reduce completed years of education by 2.9 years. This corresponds well to the estimate based on Figure 2. Using Table 6, a child who does not enter the labour force before age 13 enters the market on average at age 16.8. Therefore, delaying labour market entry from 12 to the average implies 4.8 years of nonlabour and 2.77 additional years of schooling.

Given the estimate of $\partial E / \partial c$, we can compute the indirect effect of child labour on adult wages through its negative impact on attained schooling. This is reported as "$(\alpha_2+\alpha_3 C)\ \partial E / \partial c$" at the bottom of Table 7. The impact is large, reducing adult wages by 13.4%. Consequently, the total effect of early child labour is to reduce adult wages by 16.2%.

The marriage market and household labour supply decision may increase or decrease the impact of child labour on income and poverty. If those who work as children marry other child workers whose wages are suppressed, then the marriage market will magnify the adverse impacts of child labour on adult poverty. However, if those who attained little education can marry more educated spouses or if more members of the household of child labourers work, then some of the adverse impacts of child labour on adult income may be mitigated. The second column in Table regresses household income on child labour measures. The coefficient on child labour αc, now turns negative, so that child workers at zero education have household income that 2.1% lower then those who did not working their first twelve years. The penalty from child labour on returns to education also becomes greater so that the direct effect of child labour is to reduce adult household income by 8.7%.

However, the marriage market dose appears to mitigate some of the negative effects the labour market on individual earnings. The most noticeable is that women avoid most of the adverse effects of their own low wages if they marry. The impact of own education on household income is also smaller then its impact on own wages, presumably because less educated households who earn less per person can make back some of the deficit by having more persons working. The indirect effect of child labour on household income is –4.2%; smaller then the –13.4% effect on individual wages. The total impact of child labour is to reduce adult household income by 12.9%.

The last two columns, report results for the probability that a child labourer in the bottom two or the bottom one income quintile as an adult. Individuals who worked in their first twelve years of life were 5.3% more likely to be in the lowest income quintile and 7.3% more likely to be in the lowest two quintiles then were otherwise observationally equivalent adults who did not work until age 13 or later.

Table 8 replicates the analysis in Table 7 excluding the self-employed. Because hourly earnings for the self-employed are commonly viewed as endogenous, excluding the self employed should reduce potential simultaneity bias in the log wage equation, The result are virtually identical for the income and poverty status equations, and the measured adverse impact of child labour on hourly wages increases to-17.4%.

Table 9 replicates the analysis on the subset of individuals who are living with their parents, in-laws or guardians. This sample allows us to control for family background influences which may moderate the estimated effect of child labour on adult income. On the other hand, choice to live in such an extended household is potentially influenced by own earnings capacity so the sample may be subject to self-selection. Nothing those caveats, the pattern of results are similar to those in Table 7 and 8. Child labour reduces adult wages by 13.7% and increases the probability of being in the lowest one or two income quintiles by 5.2% and 8.2% respectively. The estimated impact on adult household income is markedly smaller in magnitude then the double-digit effects estimated impact of own education on household income. If less-educated child workers are more likely to remain in extended households with multiple earners, then anomaly may be due to self-selection.

The conclusion from Table 7-9 is that child labour in the first twelve years of life reduces both adult wages and income and increases the probability of living in poverty. Other specifications, which estimate separate impact by age, suggest that delaying the age of child labour entry increases the positive effects

Table 8
The Effects of Child Labour on Lifetime Wages and Poverty, Using Full Adult Sample Excluding *Self-employed*

	(1)	(2)	(3)	(4)
	log (WAGE)	*log (INCOME)*	*POOREST 40%*	*POOREST 20%*
CHLAB (αc)	0.028**	-0.009	0.027**	0.031**
	(0.011)	(0.010)	(0.008)	(0.005)
EDUCATION (α_E)	0.061**	0.029**	-0.015**	-0.008**
	(0.001)	(0.001)	(0.001)	(0.001)
CHLAB* EDUCATION (α_{cE})	-0.013**	-0.017**	0.004**	-0.001**
	(0.001)	(0.001)	(0.001)	(0.001)
Age 1	0.072**	-0.074**	0.018**	0.012**
	(0.002)	(0.002)	(0.002)	(0.001)
Age 2	-0.001**	0.001**	-0.0003**	-0.0002**
	(0.000)	(0.000)	(0.000)	(0.000)
Female	-0.442**	-0.035**	0.008**	0.010**
	(0.006)	(0.006)	(0.004)	(0.003)
Rural	-0.200**	-0.262**	0.177**	0.111**
	(0.009)	(0.008)	(0.006)	(0.004)
Indigenous	-0.062	-0.027	0.038	0.008
	(0.085)	(0.076)	(0.057)	(0.034)
Black	-0.157**	-0.108**	0.079**	0.035**
	(0.011)	(0.011)	(0.008)	(0.006)
Asian	0.169**	0.188**	0.064	0.095**
	(0.041)	(0.043)	(0.044)	(0.036)
Mixed Race	-0.115**	-0.103**	0.070**	0.030**
	(0.007)	(0.007)	(0.005)	(0.003)
Union	0.259**	0.113**	-0.105**	-0.050**
	(0.007)	(0.007)	(0.006)	(0.003)
Temporary Position	0.520**	0.409**	-0.206**	-0.065**
	(0.046)	(0.051)	(0.024)	(0.014)
Average Household Education	0.073**	0.125**	-0.062**	-0.026**
	(0.001)	(0.001)	(0.001)	(0.001)
Constant	-1.317**	1.787**		
	(0.038)	(0.037)		
λ	-0.362**	-0.458**		
	(.012)	(.013)		
Direct Effect: "(α_c to α_{CE} $\bar{E}$ \C =1)"	-3.1%	-8.6%	4.6%	2.7%
Indirect Effect ($\alpha_E+\alpha_{CE}\bar{C}$) ∂_E/∂_c	-14.3%	-3.8%	3.2%	2.6%
Total Effect	-17.4%	-12.4%	7.8%	5.3%
Log Like hood	-95744	-88675	-33733	-27079
N	75570	75538	75538	75538

All specifications include dummy variables for state of residence. Maximum like hood Probity. Standard errors are in parentheses. *Significant at the .10 level. **Significant at the .05 level.

Table 9
The Effects of Child Labour on Lifetime Wages and Poverty, using Sample of Sons and Daughters of Head of Households, Chat Rolling for Heads

	(1)	(2)	(3)	(4)
	log (WAGE)	*log (INCOME)*	*POOREST 40%*	*POOREST 20%*
CHLAB (αc)	0.060**	-0.001**	0.008**	0.033**
	(0.020)	(0.017)	(0.015)	(0.008)
EDUCATION (α_E)	0.055**	-0.007**	-0.020**	-0.006**
	(0.002)	(0.002)	(0.002)	(0.001)
CHLAB*EDUCATION (α_{CE})	-0.018**	-0.013**	0.009**	0.0002**
	(0.003)	(0.002)	(0.002)	(0.001)
Age 1	0.095**	0.048**	-0.015**	-0.009**
	(0.005)	(0.004)	(0.004)	(0.002)
Age 2	-0.001**	-0.001**	0.0002**	0.0001**
	(0.000)	(0.000)	(0.000)	(0.000)
Female	-0.332**	-0.088**	0.090**	0.041**
	(0.010)	(0.009)	(0.008)	(0.004)
Rural	-0.185**	-0.236**	0.143**	0.074**
	(0.015)	(0.012)	(0.011)	(0.006)
Indigenous	-0.250**	-0.153	0.132	0.091
	(0.150)	(0.111)	(0.106)	(0.073)
Black	-0.126**	-0.067**	0.098**	0.037**
	(0.019)	(0.016)	(0.014)	(0.009)
Asian	0.144*	0.089	- 0.054	-0.046**
	(0.076)	(0.062)	(0.080)	(0.033)
Mixed Race	-0.064**	-0.056**	0.073**	0.023**
	(0.012)	(0.010)	(0.008)	(0.004)
Union	0.273**	0.109**	-0.098**	-0.034**
	(0.014)	(0.013)	(0.011)	(0.006)
Temporary Position	0.280**	0.263**	-0.140	-0.006**
	(0.132)	(0.131)	(0.101)	(0.077)
Average Household	0.046**	0.177**	-0.061**	-0.024**
Education	(0.004)	(0.003)	(0.003)	(0.002)
Head Age	-0.001	0.003**	-0.003**	-0.002**
	(0.001)	(0.001)	(0.000)	(0.000)
Head Female	-0.002	-0.291**	0.014*	0.004
	(0.010)	(0.009)	(0.008)	(0.004)
Head Education	0.009**	0.005**	-0.011**	-0.002**
	(0.002)	(0.002)	(0.002)	(0.001)
Constant	-1.468**	0.067	(0.70)	(0.062)
λ	-.445**	-.316**	(.016)	(.45)
Direct Effect: "(α_C to α_{CE} $\bar{E}\setminus C=1$)"	-2.8%	-6.5%	5.0%	3.4%
Indirect Effect ($\alpha_E+\alpha_{CE}\bar{C}$) ∂_E/∂_C	-10.9%	5.9%	3.2%	1.8%
Total Effect	-13.7%	-0.6%	8.2%	5.2%
Log Like hood	-32440	-25559	-11052	-8400
N	25812	25791	25791	25751

All specifications include dummy variables for state of residence. Maximum like hood Probity. Standard errors are in parentheses. We deleted 40 observation from a specified are , as all were above the lowest income quintile and so there was perfect correlation between the state dummy. *Significant at the .10 levels. **Significant at the .05 levels.

of child labour on occupational human capital (αc become more positive) and lowers the adverse effects of child labour on returns to education (α_{CE} becomes more positive). Relative to initiating child labour after age 14, the effect of child labour before the age of 10 on adult wages is –23.2%. The effect drop to -17.9% for child labour initiated between ages 10-12 and –5.8% for initiation of child labour at ages 13-14. Child labour's impact on probability of being in the lowest two income quintiles also falls as age labour market entry rises. Relative to labour market entry after age 14, the increased probability that adult income is in the bottom 40% is 10.5% for child labour initiated under age 10, 9.4% for child labour between ages 10-12, and 4.2% for child labour initiated between ages 13 and 14. The worst adult effects of child labour occur at very early labour market entry, whereas later entry is less costly.

CONCLUSION

This study quantifies the effects of child labour on the wages, income and poverty status of those same individuals as adults. We used a procedure that incorporated three possible channels through which child labour could affect outcomes. Child labour can alter years of attained education. It can alter the returns per years of education, and it can alter human capital production outside of school.

Our empirical findings suggest that early entry in the workforce reduces years of education and education and lowers the returns per year of schooling. However, there is some evidence that child labour also may create occupational human capital, which can raise own adult wages. Regardless, the adverse effects of child labour on the quantity and productivity of schooling swamp any positive effects, so that the overall impact is to reduce adult hourly wages by 9-15%. Impact on adult household income is smaller, but still negative. Those adults who had been child workers were 5% more likely to be in the lowest income quintile and 7-8% more likely to be in the lowest two income quintiles, other things equal.

Our empirical findings are consistent with Baland and Robinson's (2000) theoretical argument that restricting child labour can be welfare improving. In particular, Polices which delay age of entry into the labour market may have significant impacts on adult incidence of poverty. In addition, while child labour reduces the productivity of schooling, the net effect of an additional year of schooling on adult wages is still positive, even if the child works while in school. Consequently, policies that delay drop out. even if the child works, would be effective at mitigating adult poverty.

References

Akabayashi, Hideo and George Psacharopolous (1999), "The Trade-off between Child Labour and Human Capital Formation: A Tanzanian Case Study." *Journal of Development Studies*, 35(June), 120-40.

Alderman, Harold, Peter F. Orazem and Elizabeth M. Paterno (1996), "School Quality, School Cost and the Public/Private School Choices of Low-Income Households in Pakistan," *The World Bank: Impact Evaluation of Education Working Paper Series* No. 2.

Baland Jean Marie and James A. Robinson (2000), "Is child Labour Inefficient?." *Journal of Political Economy,* 108 (Aug.), 663-679.

Basu, Kaushik (1999), "Child Labbour: Cause, Consequence, and Cure, with Remarks on International Labour Standards." *Journal of Literature,* 37(September):1083-1120.

Card, David and Alan B. Krueger (1992), "Does School Quality Matter? Returns to Education and the Characteristics of Public School in the United States," 1-40.

Grootaert, Christian and Harry A. Patrinos (1999), Policy Analysis of Child Labour: Comparative Study, New York: St.Martin's Press.

Jacoby, Hanan G. and Emmanuel Skoufias (1997), "Risk Financial Markets, and Human Capital in a Developing Country," *Review of Population Economics Studies,* 64 (July): 311-335.

King, Elizbeth M, Peter F. Oranzem and Elizabeth M. "Pattern (1999), Promotion With and Without Learning: Effects on Student Dropout," The World Bank: Impact Evaluation of Education Reforms Working Paper No. 8.

FOREIGN DIRECT INVESTMENT IN HOUSING AND REAL ESTATE SECTOR IN INDIA: PROBLEMS, PROSPECTS AND REMEDIAL STRATEGIES

MANOJ P. K.*

INTRODUCTION

The real estate industry in India is estimated to have a size of about 12 Billion USD and is estimated to have grown at the rate of over 30 per cent for the last few years (FICCI, 2007). As per the latest statistics, however, though this industry has grown commendably till FY 2007, since then there has been a gradual decline in the growth rate (DIPP, Govt. of India, May 2009). The trend in respect of housing and real estate segment has been promising throughout the period, though not upto the level as demanded by the country's current housing and allied infrastructure. A major feature of Indian real estate industry is that almost 80 per cent of the same represents residential space and the rest alone goes for office, shopping malls, hotels, hospitals and the like. The commendable growth rate in Indian real estate is observed to be primarily because of high level of off-shoring businesses (including high-end technology consulting, call centres and software programming houses). Many research studies have pointed out the capacity of housing and construction industry to propel economic growth (and even to kick-start a recession hit economy) because of its vast forward and backward linkages with over 250 other industries. In the latest context of a not-so-encouraging performance of FDI flows, this paper seeks to analyse the trend and pattern of FDI flows into India with a focus on FDI into Housing and Real Estate sector, and to suggest strategies for enhanced use of FDI for housing and real estate development, and hence development of the whole economy.

ANALYTICAL SIGNIFICANCE AND RESEARCH GAP

Development of housing is one of the most effective methods for rapid economic development of developing nations like India, because of the capacity of housing investments to create additional demand through multiplier effects

* *Faculty (Techno-Management), Department of Applied Economics, Cochin University of Science and Technology, Kochi, E-mail: manoj_p_k2004@yahoo.co.in*

on many other allied sectors. As the budgetary constraints of the Government restrict investment in housing sector, private investment for housing development is vital and growingly so in the future. In this context FDI has got a major role to play for enhanced investment in housing and other allied sectors. As already noted, the latest pattern in respect of FDI flows in general is not encouraging. In respect of FDI flows into housing and real estate sector in particular, in spite of constant growth of FDI flows since FY 2006, there is scope for more going by the current status of housing infrastructure. All the above facts point to the need for meticulous analysis of the FDI scenario, so that well thought-out, clearly articulated and pragmatic strategies could be adopted for more effective use of FDI for housing and real estate development, and hence the national economic development. Research studies in the field of FDI into housing and real estate sector are very rare, especially those pertaining the post-reforms era since 2000. Hence the present study seeks to fill this gap.

OBJECTIVES OF THE PAPER

(i) To trace the trend and pattern of FDI flows into India with special reference to the FDI into Housing and Real Estate sector, for the last one decade (FY 2000 to FY 2009),

(ii) To study characteristics of housing and real estate investments and its significance in bringing about faster economic development of the nation,

(iii) To identify the prospects and challenges to the FDI flows into the Housing and Real Estate sector in India, and finally

(iv) To suggest pragmatic strategies for enhanced FDI inflows into the Housing and Real Estate sector in India for faster development of this sector and hence that of the whole economy.

METHODOLOGY AND DATA SOURCES

This study is based primarily on secondary data available on FDI flows into India, particularly those into Housing and Real estate sector, collected from authentic sources like the publications of DIPP (Department of Industrial Promotion and Policy, Ministry of Commerce and Industry, Government of India), Reserve Bank of India etc. The data so collected are analysed using popular statistical tools to arrive at meaningful conclusions. Research findings of other similar studies, cross-country experiences etc. have been considered for comparison purpose.

The study is primarily is descriptive-analytical in nature as it seeks to explain the current scenario and also to analyse the past performance, trace the major trends and patterns. Besides, the study is exploratory also to the extent that it seeks to draw up the future strategies based on the past trends, current status, experiences of other countries, emerging business practices and models etc.

ORGANISATION OF THE PAPER

Broadly going by the objectives set for the paper as noted above, this paper is organized into five major parts. Part–I discusses the major trend and pattern of FDI flows into India with special reference to the FDI into Housing and Real Estate sector during the last one decade (FY 2000 to FY 2009), Part– II analyses characteristic features of housing and real estate investments and their significance in economic development, and Part–IV seeks to identify the prospects and challenges to the FDI flows into the Housing and Real Estate sector in India. Lastly, Part–V gives suggestions for enhanced use of FDI for faster development of Housing and Real Estate sector and hence the whole economy. Part–V is followed by author's concluding remarks.

PART–I

FDI Flows into India and the Housing and Real Estate Sector (FY 2000 to 2009).

FDI Flows into India during FY 2000 to 2009 and Afterwards: an Analysis

FDI flows into India during the last one decade (viz. FY 2000 to FY 2009) and afterwards till the time when latest data are available (May 2009) are discussed in this section. From financial year-wise FDI data, it is observed that there has been a generally stagnant trend in the FDI flows into India during the earlier years of the first decade (FY 2000 to 2004) while the trend has reversed since FY 2005 till FY 2007 as evidenced by a constant growth. Accordingly, during the initial period as above (viz. FY 2000 to 2004) there has been a general stagnancy in FDI flows and even a slight decline during the last two years (FY 2003 and 2004), and India could attract an average FDI of nearly 4000 to 5000 US Million Dollars. However, during the later years as noted above (viz. FY 2005 to 2007) there has been a constant growth and for FY 2007, the growth rate has been the maximum at 146 per cent (Y to Y) thus reaching a remarkable 22826 US Million Dollars–the highest ever yearly growth rate. But, afterwards there has been a lower growth rate leading to a rather stagnant situation (FY 2008 and FY 2009), though the growth rate of 51 per cent (FY 2008) is quite reasonable even if it has been just over one-third that of the previous year. During the last financial year (FY 2009), there has been a rather stagnancy in growth as evidenced by a meager 2 per cent growth. (Table 1).

During the current financial year (FY 2010) also, FDI flows during the initial two months (April and May 2009) have been significantly lower than the respective figures for the previous year (Table 2).

The latest status (May 2009) as well as the general pattern over the last two financial years (FY 2008 and 2009) present a rather less encouraging trend in respect of FDI inflows into India. This is particularly true for the first two months in the current financial years (FY 2010) (Table 2).

Table 1
Financial Year-Wise Data of Total FDI Flows into India FY 2000 to 2009.

(US Dollar Million)

Financial Year (April to March)	*Total FDI Inflows*	*Per centage growth (Year to Year)*
FY 1991 to 2000 (August 1991 to March 2000)	15483	
FY 2001	4029	
FY 2002	6130	(+) 52%
FY 2003	5035	(-) 18%
FY 2004	4322	(+) 14%
FY 2005	6051	(+) 40%
FY 2006	8961	(+) 48%
FY 2007	22826	(+) 146%
FY 2008 (Provisional)	34362	(+) 51%
FY 2009 (Provisional)	35146	(+) 2%

Source: DIPP, Ministry of Commerce and Industry, Govt. of India, (Official Website, 15.08.09).

Table 2
Month-Wise Data of Total FDI Flows into India FY 2010 (*vis-à-vis* FY 2009)

(US Dollar Million)

Month (in the Financial Year)	*FY 2010*	*FY 2009*	*Percentage Change (Month-wise)*
April	2339	3749	(-) 37.61%
May	2095	3932	(-) 46.72%
Total (April to May)	4434	7681	(-) 42.27%

Source: DIPP, Ministry of Commerce and Industry, Govt. of India, Official Website, 15.08.09.

FDI Flows into Indian Housing and Real Estate Sector (till May 2009): An Analysis

In this section, the trend of FDI flows into the specific case of Housing and Real Estate sector in India is analysed. It may be noted that there has been a constant growth in the flow of FDI into this sector over the years, both in absolute terms and as a percentage of the total FDI flows, thus suggesting that this sector is increasingly becoming one of the most attractive sectors for FDI in India, currently having nearly 8 per cent share of the total FDI flows. (Tables 3 and 4). While it may be said that the trend of FDI flows into this sector has been generally satisfactory so far, both in absolute and relative terms, it is worth pointing out that it has to grow further manifold. Because, (i) as already noted there is a general stagnancy in total FDI flows which makes increasing relative share FDI into housing and real estate less significant, and (ii) as the FDI into this sector is of recent origin (from FY 2006 onwards) the absolute values, though increasing, are nowhere when compared to the total demand that the country's very poor housing and allied infrastructure.

Table 3

Financial Year-Wise Data of FDI Flows into Housing and Real Estate Sector

(US Dollar Million)

Financial Year (April to March)	*Total FDI Inflows*	*FDI into Housing and Real Estate sector*	*Percentage to the Total FDI Flows into India*
FY 2005	6051	0	0%
FY 2006	8961	38	(+) 0.42%
FY 2007	22826	467	(+) 2.05%
FY 2008 (Provisional)	34362	2179	(+) 6.34%
FY 2009 (Provisional)	35146	2801	(+) 7.97%

Source: DIPP, Ministry of Commerce and Industry, Govt. of India) (Official Website, 15.08.09.

Table 4

Month-Wise Data of Total FDI Flows into India till May 2009 (FY 2010)

(US Dollar Million)

FY 2006 (12 Months) (April 2005 to March 2006)*	*38*	*FY 2007 (12 Months)* (April 2006 to March 2007)*	*467*
FY 2008 (Monthly figures)	FY 2008	FY 2009 (Monthly figures)	FY 2009
April 2007	591**(** Total for the 3 Months)	April 2008	375
May 2007		May 2008	659
June 2007		June 2008	200
July 2007	36	July 2008	81
August 2007	0	August 2008	305
September 2007	83	September 2008	4
October 2007	209	October 2008	202
November 2007	360	November 2008	115
December 2007	207	December 2008	44
January 2008	149	January 2009	423
February 2008	157	February 2009	138
March 2008	387	March 2009	255
Total (April 2007 to March 2008)	2179	Total (April 2008 to March 2009)	2801
FY 2010 (Monthly figures)***	FY 2010		
April 2009	360		
May 2009 #	206		

Notes: *(FY 2006 & 2007) Monthly data not available** Monthly break-up not available (3 months)*** (FY 2010) Available only for 2 months.

Cum. FDI into Housing and Real Estate Sector (April 2000 to May 2009) is 6078 USD Million

Source: DIPP, Ministry of Commerce and Industry, Govt. of India, Official Website, 15.08.09.

From Table 4, it is noted that there is considerable fluctuations in the quantum of FDI flows into Indian housing and real estate sector. Monthly flow of FDI into this sector ranges from 0 (August 2007) to 423 US D Million (January 2009). This suggests that there is an utmost need for attracting more FDI into this sector, and that too in a more systematic manner.

PART–II

CHARACTERISTICS OF INVESTMENT IN HOUSING AND REAL ESTATE SECTOR AND SIGNIFICANCE OF SUCH INVESTMENTS IN NATIONAL ECONOMIC DEVELOPMENT

Investments in housing and allied sectors have got substantial benefits from the perspective of economic development, particularly for developing nations like India. This sector acts as a growth engine for the entire economy by stimulating demand in a number of other sectors (over 250 in number) through multiplier effects emanating from a series of forward and backward linkages. These investments can, thus, propel the entire economy even in times of an economic recession. In fact, housing investment is supposed to be the best policy option to kick-start a recession-hit economy, particularly for the developing countries where the housing infrastructure is very poor. Many research studies, both national and international, have pointed out the huge development potential of housing investments. Major among these findings are given below:

Increasing Demand Resulting in Higher GDP

As noted above, housing and infrastructure can drive the economy forward significantly by creating additional demand and hence raising the spending capacity of people through a series of linkage effects. Investment in houses improves the income of people having lower income, ie. those who have comparatively higher Marginal Propensity to Consume (MPC). This high MPC results in demand for the consumption of goods which results in higher GDP. (In the case of India, which has majority of its population living in villages, rural housing has got added significance as an additional growth engine for bringing about faster rural prosperity through the income effect.)

Employment Generation Capacity

Housing and real estate sector is one of the top employment generators for any economy, especially for developing economies like India. An international study has revealed that construction of each new single-family needs 1591 man-hours of labour equivalent to 0.869 year of full time labour. An India-based study undertaken by National Building Organisation (NBO) (Govt. of India) revealed that 2 million housing units per year will lead to creation of an additional 10 million man years of indirect employment. Housing results in raising the real purchasing power of the economy which in turn results in development of many other industries, like, consumer durables, domestic appliances, household utensils, etc. Another Indian study (by IIM, Ahmedabad in 2000) has estimated that the overall employment generation in the economy due to additional investment in the housing/construction is eight times the direct employment.

Linkages of Housing: Development of a Number of Other Industries

As already mentioned, housing has got linkages–both forward and backward–with over 250 industries including many core industries like cement, steel, timber, ceramics, tiles etc. Accordingly, small initiatives in housing can propel multiplier effects in the whole economy through the generation of further demand. A Re. 1 increase in expenditure on housing sector increases GDP by Re. 0.78 due to multiplier effects.

Most Preferred Investment to Kick-start a Recession-Hit Economy

Housing and real estate sector is supposed to be the most preferred investment avenue in a recession-hit economy as it can trigger investment in many other industries and hence kick-start the economy back to development. Many global studies (US, UK, OECD etc.) have supported this fact.

PART–III

PROSPECTS AND CHALLENGES OF FDI INTO HOUSING AND REAL ESTATE SECTOR IN INDIA: AN ANALYSIS

In this section, the various prospects and challenges of FDI flows into housing and real estate sector in the Indian context are analysed.

Prospects of FDI Flows into Housing and Real Estate Sector and the Future Outlook

The prospects of FDI into Housing and Real Estate sector in India has been estimated to be good, even if there is a slump in the Housing and Real Estate market since the FY 2007 with the real interest rates hovering around 12 to 16 per cent. A study by ASSOCHAM (2008) [2] (Associated Chamber of Commerce and Industry) has shown that there will be 21 Billion USD investments in Indian Housing and Real Estate sector in the next ten years, well above the current level of 12 to 15 Billion USD. As of May 2009, the FDI's equity share in Indian real estate market is 6 USD Billon USD only. (See the Note, Table 4).

Bank credit to Housing and Real Estate sector in India as of FY 2008 end is to the tune of Rs. 3,50,000 crores. This amount is expected to go up fast, as the interest rates have already started coming down from the earlier prevailing rates of 12 to 16 per cent. As of the middle of the current fiscal (FY 2010), the rates have fallen by 2 to 3 per cent across all slabs, to reach 9 to 13 per cent. In short, there are excellent growth prospects for this sector and hence for the FDIs into this sector.

Strengths of the Indian Housing and Real Estate Market

Indian housing and real estate market is a major investment for FDIs, because of various reasons. This situation may continue as such in spite of a general short-term recession in the economy. The important underlying reasons are as follows:

(1) Huge untapped market for housing and allied infrastructure in India.

(2) Generally favourable Governmental policy towards FDI in housing and real estate, particularly after the release of the relaxed Guidelines on FDIs into this sector in 2005.

(3) Very low mortgage to GDP ratio of just 7.4 per cent (2008) (RBI)[9] which is quite lower than those of comparable counterparts like China, Russia, Brazil etc. Thus, there is excellent scope of growth in this market.

(4) Generally growing economy, reasonable political stability and above all a fast growing upper middle class population with high purchasing power.

(5) A resilient financial sector that is reasonably protected from the global financial turmoil.

(6) High rates of return on investments in housing and real estate with low or moderate risks.

Challenges of FDI Flows into Housing and Real Estate Sector in the Ongoing Regime

While the favourable Governmental policy since FY 2005 (since the issue of relaxed guidelines on FDI into real estate, housing and allied sectors in 2005), there are some adverse developments also. Of late (as of July 2009), the Government is considering imposing a three-year ban on stake sale by foreign investors in real estate projects. If such a decision is implemented, then that may adversely affect the prospects of this sector and hence FDI inflows. (As per the extant guidelines, there is a provision that prohibits overseas investors from withdrawing their funds, beyond the minimum capital of $5 million, before three years of the initial investment. This provision is going to be made more stringent, if the current governmental move is any indication). (Exhibit I).

In spite of the good prospects for FDI in India, particularly in sectors like housing and real estate, it may be pointed out that in 2009 India has dropped to third place in global foreign direct investments (FDI) (as against second position in 2008, the first position being that of China). In 2009 rankings, US has replaced India as the second best destination, while China maintained its first position this year also. (UNCTAD, 2009).

PART–IV

SUGGESTIONS FOR ENHANCED FDI FLOWS INTO HOUSING AND REAL ESTATE SECTOR IN INDIA

In this section, the major suggestions for enhancing the FDI flows into the housing and real estate sector in India for enabling faster development of

FDI IN REAL ESTATE: BASIC GUIDELINES

The Department of Industrial Policy and Promotion (DIPP), Ministry of Commerce and Industry, vide its Press Note No. 2 (2005), has permitted FDI up to 100% under automatic route in townships, housing, built-up infrastructure and construction development projects (which would include, but not be restricted to, housing, commercial premises, hotels, resorts, hospitals, educational institutions, recreational facilities, city and regional level infrastructure facilities, such as roads and bridges, transit systems etc.), subject to the following guidelines:

1. The minimum area to be developed under each project would be as follows:
   (a) For development of serviced housing plots, a minimum land area of 10 hectares.
   (b) For construction development projects, a minimum built-up area of 50,000 sq.mts.
   (c) For a combination of the above two projects, any one of the above two conditions.
2. The minimum capitalization norm shall be US$ 10 million for a wholly owned subsidiary and US$ 5 million for joint ventures with Indian partner/s. The funds would have to be brought in within six months of commencement of business of the company.
3. Original investment cannot be repatriated before a period of three years from completion of minimum capitalization. However, the investor may be permitted to exit earlier with prior approval of the Government through the Foreign Investment Promotion Board (FIPB).
4. Development of at least 50% of the integrated project has to be completed within a period of five years from the date of obtaining all statutory clearances. The investor would not be permitted to sell underdeveloped plots (underdeveloped connotes, where roads, water supply, street lighting, drainage, sewerage and other conveniences as applicable under prescribed regulations, have not been made available). The investor must provide this infrastructure and obtain the completion certificate from the concerned local body/service agency before being allowed to dispose of the serviced housing plots.
5. The project shall conform to the norms and standards, including land use requirements and provision of community amenities and common facilities as laid down in the applicable building control regulations, by-laws, rules and other regulations of the State Government/Municipal/Local Body concerned.
6. The investor shall be responsible for obtaining all necessary approvals, including those of the building/layout plans, developing internal and peripheral areas and other infrastructure facilities, payment of development, external development and other charges and complying with all other requirements, as prescribed under applicable rules/bye-laws/regulations of the State Government/Municipal Body/Local Body concerned.
7. The State Government/Municipal/Local Body concerned, which approves the building/development plans, will monitor the developer's compliance to the above conditions.

Exhibit I: Basic Guidelines on Investments in Real Estate.
Source: DIPP, Ministry of Commerce and Industry, Govt. of India, New Delhi.

housing and allied sectors, and hence the national economy as a whole are given. These are follows:

Thorough Overhaul of the Legal System, both at State and Central Levels

Providing more favourable environment for investment, so as to attract more FDIs. For this, major policy decisions to completely overhaul the union and state legal system governing various aspects of real estate are essential. Many of the extant rules relating to housing and real estate in India date back to the 19th century and as such they need thorough overhaul. (For example, as per the provisions of the current Rent Control Act, tenants continue to pay the same rent fixed in 1947). This situations deters flow of fresh investment in housing for rental purposes. Concerted efforts at the initiative of the Central Government and all the State Governments towards a thorough review of the existing legal and regulatory system relating to housing and real estate sector is imminent in India in the current context. Priorities in this regard include, inter alia, repeal of Urban Land Ceiling & Regulation Act, 1976, formulating a model Rent Control Legislation (as against the existing archaic enactment as noted above), model Apartment Ownership Legislation and model Property Regulation Bill for the different States of India so as to suit the local situations.

Reduction and Rationalization of the Stamp Duties

Rationalization of stamp duties is one of the most urgent needs in the Indian context for rapid growth of housing and allied infrastructure. On the whole, the stamp duties are quite high. Besides, there are considerable differences in these rates among the states. While stamp duty in the range of 2 to 3 per cent is desirable, the same is as high as 10 to 13 per cent in many states. Practically, the above scenario results in massive understatement of the sale proceeds for evasion of duties. Hence, reduction and rationalization of stamp duties will ensure greater compliance and higher revenues.

Facilitating Long Term Finance for Housing Sector

Another urgent need for boosting investments in housing and real estate sector, including attracting FDIs into this sector is that of ensuring more avenues that facilitate long-term finance for this sector. Permitting REMFs (Real Estate Mutual Funds), REITs (Real Estate Investment Trusts) have been two welcome developments in this regard in India. Similar initiatives should be encouraged for generating more funds for long-term investment in this sector, as the same would enable small investors to make in long-term investments in this sector.

Better Transparency in Real Estate Transactions

This is another compelling need in the Indian scenario, for which the vital step is that of computerizing the land records. This would facilitate more transparency in real estate transactions and would also ensure better credit decisions of the lenders through instantaneous access to the relevant databases of land transactions.

Recent initiative of the housing finance regulator NHB (National Housing Bank) of setting up NHB RESIDEX–a mechanism that would track prices of residential properties in major real estate destinations in India–is a welcome step in this regard, as it would provide all the stakeholders with a reliable database containing the latest prices.

Promotion of PPP (Public Private Partnership) Projects in Housing and Real Estate

World over, PPP is gaining fast acceptance as an effective means of infrastructure development, including housing and allied infrastructure. Thus, FDIs should be attracted into PPP projects in housing and real estate sector. Apart from raising huge funds, because of the private participation, better operational efficiency and cost-effectiveness of such projects can be ensured. Global experiences in this regard, point to the feasibility of such projects in undertaking low-income mass housing. Here the role of the government is that of a facilitator, primarily the provider of land and other amenities at subsidized rates. As land is the major constraint in almost all real estate projects, the government has got a vital role in ensuring faster release of land and easier land clearances.

Active Secondary Market for Housing and Real Estate

An active secondary market for housing and real estate is yet to be developed in India. Some initiatives in this direction by NHB in the late 1990s, through a series of RMBS (Residential Mortgage Backed Securitization), however, have lost momentum afterwards because of a number of legal and regulatory issues. For better flow of funds into this sector, an active secondary market is quite essential and the same needs to be rejuvenated at the earliest.

CONCLUDING REMARKS

For an emerging economy like India, which is having a very poor housing and allied infrastructure, the significance of massive investment in these sectors need not be overemphasized, especially when we consider the excellent development potential of such investments, in view of its vast linkages with many other industries. In spite of the generally favourable trend in FDI flows into this sector, it may be stated that the same is grossly insufficient compared to the incremental demand for the same which stands at the level of USD 102 Billion by 2012, for housing sector alone. While there have been some welcome developments relating to this sector in India in the recent past (like, permission of REMFs and REITs, setting up of NHB-RESIDEX etc.), a lot more are yet to be done. Of these unfinished priorities, the most important one probably is that of creating a more conducive legal and regulatory set up and the next priority should be the rationalization of stamp duties.

References

Ahuja, Suvir (2004), "Housing–Engine of Economic Growth", in Subbulakshmi, V. (ed.), *Housing Finance in India*, ICFAI University Press, Hyderabad, October, pp. 15-25.

ASSOCHAM (2008), *Assessment of FDI's Role to Domestic Real Estate Market*, Report.

Buckley, Robert M. (1996), *Housing Finance in Developing Countries*, Macmillan, London.

DIPP (Department of Industrial Policy and Promotion), Ministry of Commerce and Industry, Government of India, New Delhi. (Available at *www.dipp.nic.in*)

FICCI (Federation of Indian Chamber of Commerce and Industry), *Survey Report on Foreign Direct Investment in Real Estate*, 2007.

Joseph, Anil K. (1996), "Role of Private Sector in Housing", *Yojana*, March, pp. 6-7.

Manoj, P. K. (2004), "Dynamics of Housing Finance in India", *Bank Quest*, Vol. 75, No. 3.

NHB, *Trend and Progress of Housing in India 1997 to 2006*, Govt. of India, New Delhi.

RBI, *Trend and Progress of Banking in India 2003 to 2007*, Govt. of India, New Delhi.

RBI, Committee on Financial Sector Assessment (CFSA), *India's Financial Sector: an Assessment*, March 2009.

PRODUCTIVITY DYNAMICS IN THE SOUTH AFRICAN ECONOMY: A REVIEW OF LITERATURE

BROTHERS W. MALEMA*

INTRODUCTION

South Africa, like the rest of the world has been eluded by economic growth. The country has experienced a steady downward trend since the 1970s in both the Gross Domestic Product (GDP) and per capita GDP (Fedderke 2002). This decline in economic growth since the 1970s is consistent with World trends in which the world growth decreased from 3.2 to 2.4 per cent per annum over the period 1980-89 to 1990-98 (Fedderke 2002) and growth in the United States declined from 2.2 to 1.7 per cent while other countries underwent similar or more severe declines (Mankiw 1994). Some studies have attributed this trend to the slowdown in the rate of improvement of the production function (Mankiw 1994).

According to McDonald M. (1996), South Africa has suffered from international isolation with the resultant effect being the serious economic distortions in areas of productivity and international competitiveness amongst others. The threat and imposition of sanctions led to an inward looking economic policy of import substitution. This was accompanied by high tariffs which made local firms insensitive to costs control. The distorted economic system of the past has led to structurally productivity shortfalls. This coupled with inadequate skills training, low education levels and deficiencies in supervision has resulted in low labour productivity and thus inhibited job creation and continue to this day (McDonald M. 1996). The low productivity has the effect of encouraging the shedding of labour as was witnessed during the eighties in Europe. Both United States and European Union invested roughly the same money in capital plant and equipment and United States was to create 30 million jobs while Europe created only 3 million. This is attributable to the high labour costs in Europe (McDonald M. 1996).

South Africa currently is faced with the problem of jobless growth (Fedderke 2002) and has dismally failed to tackle the unemployment problem

* *Department of Economics, University of Botswana. Private Bag–UB 705, Gaborone, Botswana, E-mail: malemabw@mopipi.ub.bw*

which stands at 29 per cent and increases to 40.9 under the expanded definition (Du Toit and Koekemoer). The jobless growth scenario could be interpreted in a number of ways. It may mean that that labor productivity has been increasing to the extent that the same output as before, can be produced with less labor or more output can be produced with the same labor. It may mean that labor has become exorbitantly expensive and its substitutability has become the only alternative. The scenario may also be a result of an improvement in the manner in which we do things - the increase in multifactor productivity. The other possibility might be the lack of adequate savings and the subsequent investment, which are necessary for increased labor productivity through education and training, increase in capital stock and improvement in capital stock (Abedian and Standish 1992). In spite of the slow growth in GDP, the problem of jobless growth should be a major concern in an economy in which the majority live in poverty and are unemployed. Employment is one of-if not-the most profound economic vehicle for income distribution and poverty alleviation.This study intends to look at both labor and multifactor productivity in an endeavor to comprehend their role in the joblessness in South Africa.

WHAT IS PRODUCTIVITY?

Productivity refers to the degree of efficiency in the manner in which we do things. It is a concept which is influenced by a number of factors. Productivity has three major components which are utilization, efficiency and effectiveness (Du Plooy E. and Jackson D. 1995). Their definition of these concepts is that utilisation refers to the extent to which resources are being used, efficiency is concerned with maintaining a satisfactory relationship between costs and benefits and effectiveness about doing the right things. However in this paper we confine ourselves to productivity as understood and defined by both economists and business analyst. In this regard we will discuss labor productivity, which is defined as real output per every unit of labor employed or real output per man hours. The other type of productivity is total factor productivity or multi factor productivity which is defined as real output per unit of all inputs (Steindel C. and Stiroh K. J. 2001) and is the more complex of the two.

The data on total factor productivity at industry or sectoral level is scarce particularly because of both conceptual and practical problems for compiling such data. On the practical side there is the problem of sampling which often does not exist at the aggregate level and at the conceptual level there are two definitions of output namely gross output originating (value added) and gross output. Whereas value added is easily measured in current dollars, this is not so when constant dollars are used.

According to Stiroh K. J. (2001), the standard industry production model is based on gross output production function that relates the total industry output to primary inputs used in production such as capital and labor, intermediates inputs and total factor productivity. Such a model is given as

$$Y_i = f(K_i, H_i, M_i, Z_i)$$

where Y is real gross output, K is capital, H is hours worked, M is intermediate products and Z is total factor productivity and i is for industry.

In this case labor productivity is given as

$$ALP_i^Y = Y_i/H_i$$

The alternative measure could be gross output originating which depends only on primary inputs and total factor productivity. This approach excludes the intermediate inputs and it is given as

$$V_i = f(K_i, H_i, Z_i)$$

where V is value added while the other variables maintain their initial definitions. In this case the labor productivity is given as

$$ALP_i^V = V_i/H_i$$

The gross output measure is considered the more relevant concept for productivity analysis from both the empirical and economic theory view points. Gross output originating is considered more of an artificial construct which does not conform to productivity analysis at industry level unless under the assumption of separability of intermediate outputs from primary inputs.

In productivity analysis the distinction of capital stocks from capital services is imperative. This distinction is clearly expressed in the mathematical formulations of these two concepts, in which the capital stock is denoted as K^{stock} and capital services as $K^{services}$. The capital stock uses acquisition prices as weights and capital services use rental prices as weights.

$$d \ln K^{stock} = \Sigma_j w_j d \ln K_j \qquad \text{where } w_j = P_j K_j / \Sigma_j P_j K_j$$

$$d \ln K^{services} = \Sigma_j v_j d \ln K_j \qquad \text{where } v_j = C_j K_j / \Sigma_j C_j K_j$$

Where K_j is installed capital stock, P_j is the acquisition prices, C_j is the rental price, w_j is the share of capital stock and v_j is the share of capital services, all for asset j (Stiroh K. J. 2001).

LABOR PRODUCTIVITY

Labor productivity has a business component and its growth is low or negative during recession times and high or positive during early economic expansionary periods and is attributed to lack of instant adjustments in factor markets (Steindel C. and Stiroh K. J. 2001). In the USA labor productivity slowed down in the two decades starting in the early 1970s, and there has not been an explanation as to the cause of the slowdown, despite the considerable research effort to this regard. The trend has however changed since 1996 and productivity has strengthened to higher levels.

Labor productivity in the USA is calculated by the bureau of labor statistics (BLS), for the non farm business sector, private business (which adds back the farms), non financial corporations and for manufacturing as whole (and for non durables and durables separately). Manufacturing has higher productivity levels relative to the non farm business sector even though it also depicts a procyclical pattern. The increase in labor productivity is accounted for by increases in educational attainment, experiences of workers and the amount and composition of capital used by labor (Steindel C. and Stiroh K. J. 2001). Black S. E. and Lynch L. M. (2000) attribute the increase in productivity in manufacturing in the years 1993-1996, to work place reengineering and computer diffusions and state that workers have also been rewarded with high salaries.

Using the Cobb-Douglas production function we can calculate the labor productivity

$$Q = A_0 K^{\alpha} L^{1-\alpha}$$

Where

Q = output

$A_0 = Ae^{rt}$ is technological effect or multifactor productivity

K = Stock of capital

L = Number of workers

α = Output elasticity with respect to capital

$1-\alpha$ = Output elasticity with respect to labor

The labor productivity is given by the conventional way of dividing total output by the number of workers.

$$Q/L = (A_0 K^{\alpha} L^{1-\alpha})/L = A_0 K^{\alpha} L^{-\alpha} = A_0 (K/L)^{\alpha}$$

TOTAL FACTOR PRODUCTIVITY

It is the increase in productivity that is unaccounted for, or the increase in real output that can not be attributed to measured input growth. It is a phenomenal reflection of general knowledge, reductions in inefficiency, reallocations of resources, advantages of organizational structures or management techniques and economies of scale, amongst others. It is abstract and a construct of economists (Steindel C. and Stiroh K. J. 2001). According to the authors, BLS produces annual estimates of total factor productivity for large economic sectors such as the private business and non farm business sector, as well as for manufacturing and 18 of its component industries.

$$Q/ K^{\alpha} L^{1-\alpha} = (A_0 K^{\alpha} L^{1-\alpha})/ K^{\alpha} L^{1-\alpha} = A_0 = Ae^{rt}$$

Multifactor or Total factor productivity on the other hand is given by output divided by a weighted average of all factors of production (K and L) or by the total factor.

IMPORTANCE OF PRODUCTIVITY

Productivity is importantly related to the notion of economic well-being and the growth rate of productivity is a major determinant of the growth rate of the standard of living (Edgmand 1987). According to Parsons J (1999), there are clear linkages between productivity, living standards and quality of life indicators within the SADC region. Botswana, Mauritius and South Africa have had high labor productivity levels than their counterparts and have also enjoyed high standards of living. Productivity is synonymous with value added which is measure of wealth created through work. Improving productivity amounts to wealth generation and if such wealth is evenly distributed, it should lead to improved standard of living (Goba N. 2001). The increase in productivity over time makes it possible to increase output without increasing inputs. This relationship is expressed more saliently by Steidel C. and Stiroh K. J. (2001) when they declare that:

> *"Output growth is, by definition the sum of the growth of labor hours plus labor productivity growth. Hence, higher productivity growth would appear to be associated with higher output growth. Of course, for periods as long as decades, demographic forces differ substantially, which affects the growth of labor input and aggregate output independent of productivity trends".*

This relationship is very evident in the USA data from the 1960s to 1990s as swings in labor productivity growth are consistently accompanied by swings in output growth. In 1970 and 1980s output growth slowed down as labor productivity slowed and the opposite was noticeable in the 1990s as output growth increased as labor productivity increased (Steindel C. and Stiroh K. J. 2001).

The proposition that productivity growth is equal to growth of real wages is often made within standard economic text books. This is extended further to say that productivity growth is equal to the growth of per capita income. The relationship is not practically this tight as it is based on the assumption of a single good being produced using constant returns to scale production technology. This assumptions do not really hold, especially the one good assumption. The relationship is weak in the short-term and becomes strong in long term (Steindel C. and Stiroh K. J. 2001).

The observation that inflation is perceived by macroeconomists as "always and everywhere a monetary phenomenon and productivity a non monetary phenomenon makes any relationship between the two untenable. Productivity is determined by capital formation and technological evolution and there seem to be no stable relationship between these two determinants and inflation. However, a negative correlation exists over longer frequencies, as periods of high productivity are also marked by low inflation (Steindel C. and Stiroh K. J. 2001). This could be due to the fact that monetary authorities find it easy to pursue anti-inflationary measures during times of high productivity. It could also be that high inflation distorts price mechanisms and may be associated with inefficiencies in the economy, thus leading to the negative relationship. The causation in the latter is from inflation to productivity and such a negative correlation has been witnessed in the USA in the 1970s (Steindel C. and Stiroh K. J. 2001).

THEORIES OF PRODUCTIVITY GROWTH

Neoclassical Theory

According to the neoclassical theory, capital accumulation drives growth in the short run and capital eventually succumbs to diminishing returns. The growth in productivity in the long run is driven entirely by exogenous technical progress. The explicit methodology for measuring the rate of technical progress under competitive factor markets and exhaustive inputs and technology is Hicks-neutral and is attributed to seminal papers by R. Solow. The rate of Hicks-neutral technical progress is equal to the famous Solow residual (Stiroh K. J. 2001). If the neoclassical assumptions do not hold the Solow residual will not measure only technical progress. It is also affected by externalities, imperfect competition, production spillovers, cyclical fluctuations, non constant returns to scale, omitted inputs and reallocation effects. Increasing returns to scale will in the absence of technical progress give a positive value of the Solow residual (Stiroh K. J. 2001).

New Growth Theory

This theory stipulates that productivity growth can be indefinitely continuous without the "elixir of exogenous and entirely unexplained, technical progress". By explaining technical change endogenously and by avoiding diminishing returns to capital, this theory is able to offer an economic explanation for sustained productivity and output growth (Stiroh K. J. 2001). According to new growth theory the Solow residual is a function of many factors, amongst which are stock of research and development, stock of human capital and research and development stock of trading partners.

LABOR PRODUCTIVITY GROWTH

Labor productivity growth ($d \ln(Y/H)$) can be derived under the assumptions that factors of production are paid their marginal product and all income is paid to all primary inputs as follows;

$$d \ln (Y / H) = v_k \,.\, d \ln (K / H) + (1-v_k).\, d \ln (L / H) + d \ln A$$

where Y is real output, H is hours worked, L is labor, K is capital, A is total factor productivity, v_k is the capital's share of national income and $1-v_k$ is the labor's share of total income.

This relationship can be further expressed as

$$d \ln y = v_k \,.\, d \ln k + (1-v_k).\, d \ln l + d \ln A$$

where lower –case variables are per hour worked.

The first term on the right is capital deepening which increases worker's productivity as they now have more capital to work with. The second term captures quality as firms substitute towards workers with more skills and higher marginal productivity. The final term is the multi factor productivity which captures technological change, increasing returns to scale, omitted variables reallocations from low to high productivity activities and measurement errors (Steindel C. and Stiroh K. J. 2001).

High performance practices in the work place, such as the use of computers by non managers positively affect firm productivity. Profit sharing and employee voice if done in the context of unionized establishment has a profound positive effect on productivity (Black S. E. and Lynch L. M. 2000). The other factors contributing to productivity increases are new human resource management practices which allows for flexible job definitions, cross training, work teams and reliance on incentive pay unlike the old practices with less flexibility, close supervision and hourly pay. Wages are also influenced by the reengineering of workplaces to incorporate high performance practices. The authors also noted that implementation of a particular work practice was more important in increasing productivity, than the adoption of such a work practice. Normally the adoption of high performances practices come at a cost such as for consultations, higher wages and adjustment costs such as training costs and lost output (Black S. E. and Lynch L. M. 2000).

Stiroh K. J. (2001) argues that labor productivity increase in recent years, has been driven by a strong investment in computer technology and other information technology assets, which has culminated in productivity rises in the 1990s. This he posits is the general consensus emerging, even though there are those differing with this view and asserting that cyclical forces are at the helm of productivity recovery with IT playing an insignificant role.

TOTAL FACTOR PRODUCTIVITY GROWTH

The "Solow residual" growth reflects the ability to increase output with same amount of inputs. It can be thought of as reflecting a shift in the production function. Even though it is often considered synonymously with technological innovation, it is a product of multiple factors, as mentioned earlier.

Applying the same assumptions used in the computation of labor productivity growth to multi-factor productivity growth (d ln A) we arrive at;

$$d \ln A = d \ln Y - v_k \,.\, d \ln K - (1-v_k).\, d \ln L$$

It is calculated as a residual of output growth not accounted for by weighted input growth.

PRODUCTIVITY IN THE UNITED STATES OF AMERICA

The United States has since 1950 experienced a 70 per cent increase in productivity meaning that America can produce 70 per cent more output now with the 1950 inputs (Auerbach and Kotlikoff (1995)). Despite the impressive growth in productivity overall, there has been great fluctuations in the productivity growth rates as illustrated by Stiroh K. J. (2001) for the period 1947–2000. Over this period the rates were only negative on five occasions with the year 1973-74 registering the lowest rate of about -1.7 per cent and 1949-1950 registering the highest growth of almost 7 per cent. In the period 1947-1973 the average rate was around 2.9 per cent and it was lower at around 1.25 per cent during 1973–1995 and it revived to an average of 2.8 per cent in the period 1995–2000.

Table 1
Average Productivity Growth Rates, 1959–1999

	1959-73	*1973-1995*	*1995-99*
Average labor productivity growth			
Non farm business	2.97	1.35	2.45
Manufacturing	2.91	2.65	4.75
Business	2.95	1.42	2.58
Total Factor Productivity (TFP) Growth			
Non farm business	1.91	0.40	1.26
Business	1.01	0.34	0.99

Source: Steidel C and Stiroh K. J. (2001)

PRODUCTIVITY IN SOUTH AFRICA

The growth rate of GDP was 1.25 per cent per annum between 1980 and 1994. The growth in multifactor productivity over the same time was 0.1 per cent per annum. Since 1994 GDP growth has averaged 2.75 per cent and total factor productivity has been increasing by close to 3 per cent per annum (Marcus G. 2003). In 1984 and 2000 multifactor productivity increased by 4.1 per cent and in 2002 multifactor productivity increased by 5 per cent, the highest increase in 30 years. Labor productivity growth was 5.5 per cent per annum between 1996 and 2001. In basic iron and steel, 2 485 new jobs were created as productivity plummeted by 7.1 per cent. This scenario was also observable in Transport equipment in which 1 852 new jobs were created and 15.1 per cent productivity declines were recorded with an ultimate increase in labor costs by 59 per cent (Malcolm R. 2003).

Marcus G. (2003) further observes that the gains in productivity have been accompanied by loss of employment, in the major industries surveyed. This was more apparent in mining whose employment level reduced from 600 000 in 1994 to less than 420 000 currently. The loss of employment in the face of increased productivity can not be an economic surprise and should be expected if economic growth as measured by growth in output does not match up to improvements in productivity. If the future economic environment looks bleak and expectations are pessimistic, job creating investment will not be forthcoming. This could also be exacerbated by unfavorable high interest rates and volatile exchange rates (Heintz J. 2000). In South Africa where inequality ranks amongst the highest in the world, productivity gains may increase the average living standards while majority of people may experience no change. As Heintz J. (2000) points out,

> *"For such improvements to serve the ultimate goal of bettering the well being of many people, the benefits must be shared broadly"....."Without a vigorous response of employment–generating investment in South Africa, productivity gains could lead to more inequality".*

The increase in productivity has been accompanied by an increase in real remuneration by an average of between 2 and 3 per cent per annum since 1994.

In 1970s and 1980s capital played a pivotal role in the economic growth of South Africa and to a lesser extent labour, with technology making a negative contribution. This scenario changed in the 1990s as technology became the impetus to economic growth, capital contributed weakly and labour negatively (Fedderke 2002).

The table below shows trends in growth of GDP, employment and labour productivity. GDP has increased by an average of 4.1 per cent annually between 1995 and 2000, employment has increased by an average of 3.0 per cent on annual basis over the same period and labour productivity has increased by an average of 1.1 per cent annually over the same period. Both GDP and employment have experienced an almost smooth upward trend over this period whereas GDP per employee seem to have undergone a downward trend. The labour productivity trend does not augur well for an economy experiencing high levels of unemployment.

Table 2
Implicit Productivity Growth In GEAR

	GDP index 1995=100	*GDP %*	*Employment index 1995=100*	*Emploment %*	*GDP per employee*	*GDP per employee %*
1995	100		100		100	
1996	103.5	3.5	101.3	1.3	102.2	2.2
1997	106.5	2.9	104.3	3	102.1	-0.1
1998	110.5	3.8	107.2	2.7	103.2	1.1
1999	116.0	4.9	110.9	3.5	104.6	1.4
2000	120.0	6.1	115.7	4.5	106.4	1.7
% per Year	4.1		3.0		1.1	

Source: Skhosana G. (1999).

In the table below the rates of growth of both labour productivity and total factor productivity are mixed. Some sectors have been able to maintain positive rates of growth over the period such as Construction, Electricity, gas and water, private economy with and without agriculture, goods producing sector with and without agriculture as well as transport, storage and communication. In almost all of these sectors the average growth rates appear to have been higher at the end of the period than at the beginning.

Other sectors such as services, wholesale and retail trade and Finance, Insurance, real estate & business have started off with positive rates of growth but ended up with negative rates in 1996-97. This is not a good signal at all for these sectors to have started off well only to finish of dismally. Agriculture did well in 1995-96 whereas manufacturing did badly in the same year experiencing negative rates for both measures of productivity. With the exception of rare cases the labour and total factor productivities seem to have followed a similar pattern most of the time.

Table 3
Industry Statistics
Productivity Growth of SA's Economic Sectors Average Annual Growth Rate

	1994-95		*1995-96*		*1996-97*	
	LP	*TFP*	*LP*	*TFP*	*LP*	*TFP*
Agriculture, forestryAnd fishing	-14.1	-14.4	30.2	28.8	0	-0.8
Mining &quarrying	-1.4	-1.2	3.7	0.5	5.5	3.8
Manufacturing	7.3	4.7	-1.1	-2.8	8.9	3.0
Electricity, gas & water	3.1	4.5	2.4	4.2	6.0	4.8
Construction	3.7	3.4	12.1	9.4	4.9	3.7
Wholesale &Retail trade	4.8	4.2	4.1	2.0	-0.5	-1.3
Transport, storage&communication	2.4	4.1	4.4	3.5	7.2	4.4
Finance, InsuranceReal estate & business	1.2	1.7	0.9	1.4	-6.1	-1.7
Private economy	3.1	2.6	4.4	2.8	4.1	2.0
Private economyLess agriculture	4.1	3.6	2.9	1.4	4.5	2.3
Goods ProducingSector	2.6	1.7	5.0	2.9	6.8	3.3
Goods producing Sector less agric	4.8	3.7	2.4	0.3	8.5	4.2
Services	3.0	3.4	3.2	2.5	-0.5	-0.2

Source: Yadavalli L. (1999).

CONCLUSIONS

The issue of productivity is very important to the operations of any economic system. It is important in ensuring that a country competes favourably in the international market with the rest of the world. South Africa because of her isolation in the past has been deprived of positively addressing this issue because of the protectionist policies of the past. To face up to the challenge of high unemployment and low productivity the need to empower citizens with necessary skills and training has been identified. The empowerment will make the workers more productive and most probably more attractive to employers.

There is also a need for the undertaking of a through study which will unveil the productivity dynamics as of the present time. Whereas the general thinking seems to be that workers lack the appropriate skills, it will be interesting to find out what effect technological substitution will have on employment. The notion that unemployment is a result of ill-equipped labour force in terms of skills and training should be viewed in the context of the adoption of new and better technology which may be a source of unemployment.

References

Abedian I. & Standish B. (1992), "The South African Economy: An Historical Overview", in Abedian I. & Standish B. (eds.), *Economic Growth in South Africa, Selected Policy Issues.* Oxford: Oxford University Press.

Auerbach A. J. & Kotlikoff L. J. (1995), *Macroeconomics: An Integrated Approach.* United States of America: South-Western College Publishing.

Black S. E. and Lynch L. M. (2000), What's Driving the New Economy: The Benefits of Work Place Innovation. *NBER working paper* 7479.

Du Plooy E. and Jackson D. (1995), Productivity Measurement. *Productivity SA* March/April 1995.

Du Toit C. B. & De Wet T. J. (2002), A Neoclassical Production Function for the South African Economy: Theory and Evidence. *South African Journal of Economic and Management Sciences,* SS No. 4.

Du Toit C. B. & Koekemoer R. *A Labour Model for South Africa.* Department of Economics, University of Pretoria

Edgmand M. R. (1987), *Macroeconomics: Theory and Policy. Third Edition.* Englewood Cliffs, New Jersey 07632: Prentice-Hall, Inc.

Fedderke J. W. (2002), The Structure of Growth in the South African Economy: Factor Accumulation and Total Factor Productivity Growth 1970-97. *The South African Journal of Economics,* Vol. 70, No. 4, 611-646.

Goba N. (2001), A Vital Link to Building Competitive Organizations. *Productivity SA,* August/September 2001.

Heintz J. (2000), What is the Connection between Productivity and the Distribution of Wealth and Income in South Africa? *Productivity SA,* January/February 2000.

Malcolm R. (2003), Marrying Productivity with Employment. *Productivity SA,* February/March 2003.

Mankiw N. G. (1994), *Macroeconomics. Second edition.* New York: Von Hoffmann Press.

Marcus G. (2003), Productivity Enhancement and Monetary Policy. *Productivity SA,* Nov/Dec 2003.

McDonald M. (1996), Productivity the Lifeblood of Prosperity. *Productivity SA* July/August 1996.

Parsons, J. (1999), Productivity Means Plenty for Everyone. *Productivity SA* May/June 1999.

Peera N. (1988), The International Monetary System and the Less Developed Countries: in International Economics (Zis G *et. al* ed.) Longman Publishers, Singapore.

Skhosana G. (1999) Productivity and Economic Growth: Wealth and Prosperity for Everyone is what we all Want-productivity's Role in the Process is Vital. *Productivity SA*, January/ February 1999.

Steindel C. and Stiroh K. J. (2001), Productivity: What is it, and Why do we care About it?

Stiroh K. J. (2001), What Drives Productivity Growth? *FRBNY Economic Policy Review.*

Yadavalli, L. (1999), Productivity, Industry Statistics. *Productivity SA* March/April 1999.

CROSS GENERATIONAL RELATIONSHIPS AND HIV/AIDS IN BOTSWANA: IS THERE EVIDENCE OF RESOURCE POWER? AN ECONOMETRIC ANALYSIS

BROTHERS W. MALEMA*

INTRODUCTION

Relationships of a human nature are quite complex and heterogeneous. Preferences of individuals and qualities of what constitute an ideal relationship, differs across individuals and are influenced by diverse factors. Coming up with a set of guidelines as to the nature relationships should assume, reflects the revealed preferences of individuals and not necessarily their unrevealed preferences. Even in cases of revealed preferences there is no consensus, since what might be acceptable to one individual may be unacceptable to the other. The revealed preferences may be influenced by what is generally considered moral and ethical. The question one may want answers for, is "whose morals and ethics are right to be the benchmark?" The current issue on sugar daddy and sugar mummy relationships for which this article is meant to address can not be more relevant.

Sugar daddy and Sugar mummy relationships may be relatively easy to define and one wonders if the same relative easy can be extended to their identification. The dictionary defines a sugar daddy as "A wealthy usually older man who gives expensive gifts to a young person in return for sexual favours or companionship". Of course this would require that the cutoff point be clearly made to be able to separate the poor from the wealthy. Being wealthy is two dimensional in this particular case. Firstly we may have to separate the wealthy men from the poor men. In this case a poor older man will in terms of this definition be left out of the definition even though he might be giving a young person some cheap gifts within the confines of his financial constraint. Secondly we may have to separate the wealthy usually older man from their relatively not so wealthy partners. In the latter case, as long as the older man is wealthier than the younger partner, the definition will be satisfied. On the basis of the dictionary definition we note that such relationships are both

* *Department of Economics, University of Botswana. Private Bag–UB 705, Gaborone, Botswana, E-mail: malemabw@mopipi.ub.bw*

transactional and cross-generational. It is logically consistent to extend this very definition to sugar mummies. The working definition of these "sugar" relationships for purposes of this paper is that the partners should have age differences of 10 years or more. The short coming of this definition is largely on its narrowness and its lack of evidence of occurrence of transfers in any form, from the older partner to the younger partner.

BACKGROUND

The inception of HIV/AIDS in Sub-Saharan Africa was marked by a positive relationship between HIV infection and economic status (Kimuna and Djamba 2005, Hargreaves et al. 2002 c.f. Luke N. 2005). This was driven by the wealthier men's ability to attract multiple partners including commercial sex workers. Since the commercial sex workers were considered a channel for the spread of HIV/AIDS, wealthier men, through their sexual engagement with them became avenues for HIV spread into the general population. The advancement in the use of condoms in formal commercial sex trade is believed to have refocused the attention of wealthy men to some other sex partners including among others school children, university students and poor women, to whom they give money and other gifts (Illingworth 2004, Kuate-Defo 2004, Luke 2003: c.f. Luke N. 2005) thereby fuelling the spread of the epidemic.

A study in Kisumu in Kenya discovered that economic status was positively associated with transfers given by sugar daddies to their nonmarital partners while there was no correlation between economic status and condom use (Luke, N. 2005). In another study it was found out that there were significant and negative relationships between value of the transfer and safe sex, age disparity and safe sex and economic disparity and safer sex (Leclerc-Madlala S. 2007). Some of the results are inconsistent with those found by Malema B. K.W. (2008) for Botswana, in which it was found out that there was a positive relationship between men's use of condoms and age disparity with their partners. It was also found that there was a negative relationship between women's use of condoms and age disparity with their partners. The short coming of Malema's results are that they do not specify the elder partner in the relationships.

In his key note address during the 2004 Worlds AIDS day commemoration, the former President Festus G. Mogae noted that the sugar daddy and sugar mummy syndromes have infiltrated our society. He called for the abhorrence of such acts, pointing that they amounted to coercive sex and were symptomatic of moral decay. The president pointed out that perpetrators of such acts were angels of death and made a call for "deeper moral ethics and sense of responsibility" in eliminating such tendencies. The source of this problem, the president noted was the economic power imbalances between older men and younger women and between older women and younger men.

The high rates of HIV in Sub-Saharan Africa are attributed strongly to Sugar daddies (defined as being 10 years older than their partners) who have apparently lost their youth and attained enough wealth to buy the company of young girls (Mader I. 2004). This widely held view seems to imply that rich men don't really value their lives, to the extent that they will not only endanger young ladies lives but their own as well. Young ladies who are in need of support take on sugar daddies who are HIV positive. These relationships between married and middle aged men and young girls between the ages of 14 to 20 explains in part why teenage girls are five times more likely to be infected than teenage boys (Mader I. 2004). In the International AIDS conference in Bangkok, some researchers attributed the different rates of infection between young boys and young girls to the latter's sexual anatomy, which due to its susceptibility to abrasions, allow for easy entry of HIV into their bodies. There was limited condom use in these relationships because older men believed that young girls were "pure" or not infected and young girls believed that older men were likely to be uninfected if at all they have been faithful to their wives (Mader I. 2004).

In a study conducted in Jamaica, it was found out that young girls below the age of 18 were involved in diverse categories as child sex workers. One of the categories was sugar daddy girls in which girls as young as below age 12 were pressurized to have sexual relations with adult males for economic gains at times to the benefit of the girls' families. The benefits included food, shelter, clothing, education and financial support. Though the magnitude of this practice was not calibrated, it appeared to be common and following on the historical footsteps of slavery, in which girls were given to their slave masters for the latter's sexual gratification. It is only that in the current exploitation the sugar daddies have taken over from the slave masters (Dunn L. L. 2000). The author also points out to similar practices which in this case involve teenage boys and affluent adult females, often referred to as sugar mummies. The mummies would pick up the boys from schools, take them on outings, treats and holidays, buy them clothes and give them money. Just like in the case of sugar daddies, the sugar mummies provided the boys with access to education and high standard of living. Overall we observe that the teenage boys and girls stand to benefit economically from the 'sugar' kind of relationships. The author concludes by noting the need for further research inoder to establish the moral, health and educational implications of these kinds of relationships on these teenagers. That economic transfers are prevalent in these relationships is also noted by Leclerc-Madlala S. (2007).

In a study conducted across 12 countries it was found out that transactional sex (sexual activity involving exchange money or gifts) was likely to occur amongst young men and young women than those who are 25 years or more. It was also discovered that single women were more likely than married women to engage in transactional sex (Chatterji M., Murray N., London D. and Anglewicz P. 2004).

Some of the key questions that need to be answered as endeavours are made to unravel this seemingly unacceptable behaviour have to do with the establishment of the motives behind these intergenerational relationships. Leclerc-Madlala S. (2007) points out to a number of explanations as to the motives from both ends. The young women are motivated by hunger, employment, seeking fun, "milking the cow", opportunities to make contacts for social stability, urban lifestyles, ways to escape rural poverty and possibly finding love, affection and marriage amongst other things. In the case of males, the following motivations were reported, namely a need for variety, desire for clean partners, relief from stress or boredom, socially demonstrate manhood and social worth and due to pressure. In Zimbabwe it was discovered that girls from more affluent families are drawn into relationships with sugar daddies inorder to be seen to be grown ups, receiving gifts as well as having fun (Leach F and Machakanja P. 2001). The same study also noted that there was a tendency for sex and other gifts to be traded within the student population.

The issue of sugar daddies was debated on BBC NEWS, Africa live and there were mixed answers and opinions as to why there should be sugar daddies. Sugar daddy was defined as "A wealthy usually older man who gives expensive gifts to a young person in return for sexual favours or companionship". Such kinds of relationships were considered by others to be devoid of moral values and exploitative of young women. On the other hand it is argued that all parties are aware of the trade offs and the issue of exploitation is irrelevant since the relationship is "mutually beneficial" (BBC NEWS 2005).

METHODOLOGY

The data used is from the Botswana AIDS Impact survey II of 2004, courtesy of Central Statistics Office, Ministry of Finance. The data was collected nation wide and considered to be representative of the population. The sampling frame was based on the 2001 population and housing census. The survey did not seek detailed data on transactional or cross-generational relationships. However, there was a question which sought to find out if the respondents have ever had a relationship in which the age differential of the partners was in excess of nine years. The followup question sought to find out if the partner was economically better off. The question was not asked such that one could establish if the respondent was a sugar mummy or daddy or if he/she was a sugar mummy's boy or a sugar daddy's girl. The chi square measure of association and logistic regressions are used as tools of analysis. Stata version 9.0 was used for analysis.

RESULTS

In the survey 8407 respondents responded to the question seeking to know if they ever had partners with whom they differed by at-least 10 years. Of these respondents only 21.24 per cent (1 786 respondents) reported having had such kind of a relationship. For the 7 741 respondents whose sex was known, 1 632 reported having had such a relationship and 56.13 per cent of them were females and 43.87 per cent of them were males.

Amongst the females we observe that cross-generational relationships were 18.88 per cent for occupations classified as Professionals, legislators, administrators and managers, 21.98 per cent for associate professionals and technicians, 19.71 per cent for those who were classified s unemployed and 23.74 per cent among those whose occupation was others. The results are significant at 5 per cent.

This trend is also observable amongst males in which the percentage was 18.95 for professionals, legislators etc, 18.98 for the unemployed, 22.61 for others and 23.26 for technicians and associate professionals. Just as in the case of females, these results are significant at 5 per cent.

On the educational front, 40 per cent and 28.44 per cent of males with non formal and primary education respectively were involved in cross-generational relationships. 15.49 per cent of those with secondary education and 17.99 per cent of tertiary graduates were involved in such relationships. We observe a similar trend in the case of females in which 28.21 per cent of those with non formal education and 28.73 per cent of those with primary education were involved in cross-generational relationships. The percentages were 16.77 per cent and 16.90 per cent for secondary and tertiary respectively. The results for both males and females are significant at 1 per cent.

LOGISTIC REGRESSION RESULTS

The results above show a negative relationship between education and cross-generational relationships at 1 per cent level of significance. We also observe from the results above that those who are never married are likely to be less involved in cross-generational relationships than married couples and this is at a significance level of 1 per cent. There is no statistically significant difference between those who are living together and those who are married in relation to these relationships. As for those who are divorced, widowed and separated we observe that they are more likely to be involved in cross-generational relationships than married couples and this is significant at 5 per cent for the first two and 10 per cent for those who are separated. We also note that there is a significant and positive correlation between the dependent variable and those who have ever tested for HIV (HIVtest), number of sex partners (Nosexpartners) and those who have at some point taken alcohol. Lastly we note that those whose occupations were associate professionals/ technicians or others, were likely to have more of these relationships than those who were unemployed at 5 and 10 per cent levels of significance respectively.

Results for Females

Dependent Variable: Cross-generational relationships		
Explanatory Variables	*Coefficients*	*P–Value*
Edu	-.077845	0.000***
Married Omitted		
Living together	-.0672072	0.547
Divorced	.8228314	0.040**
Widowed	.7780013	0.034**
Separated	.7732673	0.070*
Never married	-.4485205	0.000***
HIVtest	.2037656	0.019 **
Age	.0010528	0.739
Unemployed omitted		
Professionals and Legislators	.2243718	0.225
Associate Professionals and Technicians	.4475533	0.017**
Others	.1768317	0.055*
Nosex partners	.2212322	0.000***
Intoxi	.2099773	0.015**
Constant	-.9907909	0.000***
Number of Observations = 3616		
LR chi2 (18) = 117.32		
Prob > chi2 = 0.0000		
Pseudo R2 = 0.0320		

*** Significant at 1 per cent, ** Significant at 5 per cent and * significant at 10 per cent.

REGRESSION DIAGNOSTICS

The regression results are free of specification errors and the model fits the data well as per the linktest and lfit tests respectively. The model is also correctly classified at 79.45 per cent as per the estat classification test.

The marginal effects measure the change in the dependent variable resulting from the change in the predictor variables. The results presented blow are significant. An increase in one year of education decreases cross-generational relationships by 1.2 per cent and having never married reduces the chance of these relationships by 7 per cent relative to being married. Being divorced and widowed increases cross-generational relationships by 16.05 per cent and 15.03 per cent respectively. Having taken an HIV test and having ever taken alcohol increases these relationships by 3.3 per cent and 3.4 per cent respectively. An increase in the number of sexual partners increases cross-generational relationships by 3.5 per cent. In the logit regressions we had significant results for those who are separated but in the marginal analysis the results are insignificant and the chances are 14.93 per cent higher that one will be involved in the sugar mummy relationship.

Table 1
Marginal Effects

Dependent Variable: Cross-generational relationships		
Explanatory Variables	*Discrete Change of dummy from 0 to 1 ($d\chi_m/dx$)*	*P-Value*
Edu	-.0122702	0.000***
Married Omitted		
Living together	-.0105053	0.544
Divorced	.160531	0.080*
Widowed	.1502595	0.069*
Separated	.1493108	0.121
Never married	-.069645	0.000***
HIV test	.0325148	0.021**
Age	.0001659	0.739
Unemployed omitted		
Professionals and Legislators	.0374103	0.250
Associate Professionals and Technicians	.0789137	0.030**
Others	.0280677	0.056*
Nosexpartners	.0348714	0.000***
Intoxi	.0335057	0.016**

Results for Males

Dependent Variable: Cross-generational relationships		
Explanatory Variables	*Coefficients*	*P – Value*
Edu	-.0956949	0.000***
Married Omitted		
Living together	-.2068566	0.106
Divorced	1.080103	0.018**
Widowed	1.11225	0.009***
Separated	.8806473	0.089*
Never married	-.3922239	0.002***
HIV test	.1015113	0.300
Age	-.0037318	0.308
Unemployed omitted		
Professionals and Legislators	.576749	0.006***
Associate Professionals and Technicians	.7346281	0.000***
Others	.2750364	0.009***
Nosexpartners	-.1745965	0.002***
Intoxi	-.2032426	0.039**
Constant	-.7233806	0.000***
Number of Observations = 3616		
Number of Observations = 2976		
LR chi2 (18) = 108.97		
Prob > chi2 = 0.0000		
Pseudo R2 = 0.0370		

*** Significant at 1 per cent, ** Significant at 5 per cent and * significant at 10 per cent.

Increased years of education lead to reduction in intergenerational relationships. The males who stayed with their partners were likely to have less of these relationships than those who are married. Having never married is also associated with less of these relationships relative to being married. However, for those who are divorced, widowed and separated, there is a higher chance of them being in these relationships than those who are married. For all the occupations classified above we note that males are more likely to have more of these relationships than the unemployed males. The chances for these relationships also increase with an additional sex partner and foe every one who has ever taken alcohol.

Table 2
Marginal Effects

Dependent Variable: Cross-generational relationships

Explanatory Variables	*Discrete Change of dummy from 0 to 1 (d χ_{m}/dx)*	*P-Value*
Edu	-.0144816	0.000***
Married Omitted		
Living together	-.0304912	0.096*
Divorced	.215498	0.049**
Widowed	.2231165	0.030**
Separated	.1689306	0.153
Never married	-.0586771	0.002***
HIV test	.0154447	0.303
Age	-.005647	0.308
Unemployed omitted		
Professionals and Legislators	.1007821	0.015**
Associate Professionals and Technicians	.133153	0.002***
Others	.0420895	0.009***
Nosexpartners	.0264218	0.002***
Intoxi	.0311549	0.041 **

Males reduce the intergenerational relationships by 1.45 per cent for every one additional year of education. An additional sexual partner is likely to increase the respondents chances of having these relationships by 2.64 per cent while having ever taken alcohol increases them by 3.12 per cent. Those who are divorced are 21.55 per cent likely to have more intergenerational relationships than the married, while the widowed chances are 22.31 per cent higher than those for the married. The chances for those who are separated though insignificant are likely to increase the relationships by 16.89 per cent. The chances of having these relationships are higher by 10.08 per cent for professionals and legislators, 13.32 per cent for associate professionals and technicians and 4.21 per cent for other occupations relative to the unemployed.

DISCUSSIONS

The observation that education is negatively related to cross-generational relationships for both sexes serves to indicate that education is indeed a tool to be used in the fight against HIV/AIDS particularly with regard to "sugar daddy and sugar mummy" relationships. It is also interesting to note that those who never married are less likely to be in these relationships than the married for both males and females. This indicates that those who are married will normally go out with sugar boys or relatively sugar daddies than the never married and this pattern of behaviour is observable for men. It might be that those who are never married still look for possible marriage partners and those who are married already have spouses and go out with the sugars for casual and other purposes.

Women who had multiple partners and were taking intoxicating substances were more likely to be in these kinds of relationships and men with similar characteristics were less likely to have these relationships. The positive relationship observed for women may indicate that women with multiple partners may be in these relationships for materialistic and other gains. It could be that, in their quest to attain their objectives, females will consider their potential partners' ability to satisfy their desires. The desires may be materialistic or otherwise. Such desires may include the acquisition of intoxicating substances and sexual gratification. In light of gender imbalances often referred to, particularly in HIV/AIDS proliferation amongst women, it might be that women resort to older males for financial support in order to quench their thirst for intoxicating substances. The higher educational level which leads to less of these kinds of relationships may serve to demonstrate that those with higher education have better incomes and do not necessarily need to depend on men for their needs or wants.

Occupationally, we note that men of all occupations were more likely to be involved in these relationships than those who were unemployed. This could be symptomatic of the financial power of men that enables them to lure partners ten years or younger than themselves. In the case of women, we observe that women of all occupations save for professionals are likely to be in these relationships than those who are unemployed. It might be that women who are professionals are relatively financial better off than women of different professions, and they are therefore able to meet their needs without the financial assistance of males.

That we observe a positive relationship between having taken an HIV test and having these relationships for females, signifies that older women may opt for younger men, believing that they have been less exposed and are therefore likely to be HIV negative. Older women may believe that having "sugar boys" will lesson their chances of infection. Younger women who have also tested may go for older men thinking that if they were faithful to their wives, they are less likely to be positive as pointed out by Mader I. (2004). HIV testing was however unrelated to males behaviour with regard to cross generational relationships.

There are some indications that the financial power or lack thereof of respondents could be related to the decisions to either engage or not to engage in cross sectional relationships. In spite of the absence of empirical evidence to the existence of the transactionality of these relationships, indications are that they are most likely to be prevalent. Since the relationships are premised on some kind of give and take or trade offs, whereby women may engage in them for survival and "progressive" purposes and men for some other purposes, it may be difficult to bring them to an end without ensuring the satisfaction of the wants or needs of those involved.

References

BBC NEWS (2005), Why have a 'Sugar Daddy'? *http://news.bbc.co.uk/2/hi/africa /414674.stm*

Chatterji M., Murray N., London D. and Anglewicz P. (2004), The Factors Influencing Transactional Sex Among Young Men and Women in 12 Sub-Saharan African Countries.

Dunn L. L. (2000), Child Prostitution in Jamaica. Draft ILO Rapid Assessment.

Leach F and Machakanja P. (2001), The Sugar Daddy Trap. Peer Pressure Pushes Girls into Sex. Id21 Insights Issue 37. *http:www.id21.org/insights/insights-gv-special/insights-gv-special-leach.html*

Leclerc-Madlala S. (2007), Intergenerational Relationships in the Context of HIV Prevention in Southern Africa: SAT/SAfAIDS Regional HIV Prevention Meeting. Livingstone, Zambia.

Luke N. (2005), Are Wealthy Sugar Daddies Spreading HIV?: Exploring Economic Status, Informal Exchange, and Sexual Risk in Kisumu, Kenya. Paper presented at the Annual Meetings of the Population Association of America, March 30–April 1, 2005, Los Angels.

Mader I. (2004), AIDS Campaigners Say Africa's "Sugar Daddies" Behind Alarming HIV Rates. The Associated Press-July 15. *http:www.aegis.com/news/ap/2004/AP040788.html.*

Malema B. K. W. (2008), The Gender Dynamics of HIV/AIDS. Unpublished paper.

Mogae F. G. (2004), A Keynote Address at the 2004 World AIDS Day Commemoration in Gantsi, Botswana.

A STUDY ON COMPETITIVENESS: THE POSITIONING OF INDIA'S SOFTWARE INDUSTRY AT GLOBAL LEVEL

HECTOR J. THAYIL KOCHUKUNNEL* & P. ARUNACHALAM**

INTRODUCTION

For centuries, India has been a dreamland for navigators to reach in. Trade with India had been frenzy for the rulers of different landscapes. The traces of that great interest in trade with India could be seen in many historical and religious texts. For centuries, India has been the epicenter of global trade. However, of late, the profile of India as the economic resource centre has undergone considerable change. It has been started viewing India as an impoverished nation. This image continued to exist till the 1990s. While India was still suffering from abject poverty, epidemic, grave social inequalities, massive unemployment and destructive political upheavals and uncertainties, a latent revolution has been underway in India's technological landscape. India has now been recognized the emerging capital of global software industry. The Indian software industry and export have been projected as one, which could address all of India's chronic development ills.

India, the world's largest democracy and home to over one billion people, is quietly but quickly emerging as a leader in the filed of software engineering. India, better known internationally for its uncompetitive industries, has come a long way with its high growth software industry. India's competitiveness and productivity/effectiveness are not recognized by the nations. However, having recognized its mastery over software production, policy makers started pinning a lot of hope on the capability and potential of this sector in taking India to the front stage of rapid development.

The competitiveness in international trade has, nowadays, acquired a lot of strategic importance. The most powerful nation is not necessarily the nation with the most potent military backup but a nation with economic muscle. Here

* *Research and Development Officer, Neptune Travel Ltd., Holywood Road, Belfast, United Kingdom.*

** *Department of Applied Economics, Cochin University of Science and Technology, Kochi, E-mail: arunachalam14@yahoo.co.uk*

comes the strategic importance of international trade. India is more know for its software exports, than the domestic trade. The people from all walks of life are now recognizing the importance of software export and its competitiveness, for facing challenges from other parts of the world by which it can address India's balance of payment deficits, technological backwardness, retarded growth of the economy and unemployment.

RELEVANCE OF THE STUDY

In this study, the researchers attempt to going to the greater depths of India's software industry domain. Software industry in India concentrates its efforts more on exports. India is becoming a major software exporter. This is a country which offers cost-effectiveness, great quality, high reliability, rapid delivery and, above all, state of the art technologies in software development. The profile of the software development and application by Indian vendors attracted the clients from all parts of the world. It is, in this way, significant to understand the future prospects of this sector.

It is emphasized in many theses that one of India's advantages in software business is its large pool of technically skilled human resources which is available at low cost. However, many developing nations with sufficiently large pool of human resources are striving to make their mark on the map of global software industry. Hence, India may not be able to boast off her competitive advantage in software industry for long. Studying this aspect is important in terms of the sustainability of this industry and export.

Many have pinned their hope in the transformation capability of this sector on the Indian economy. However, much of it depends on how this sector, especially the exports enables itself to innovate and face competition in this highly dynamic society. Hence, the study on export competitiveness deserves merit.

Its export driven model now commands the world's attention for skilled professionals and offer hope to many developing countries, which are struggling to cope with a hyper-competitive post-WTO global economy. How India stands in this kind of a battleground is considered to be crucial. This is a kind of topic, which attracts the attention of policy makers and the government.

The software industry and its earning capacity for foreign exchange have definitely a large bearing on India's economic future. However, studies of serious outlook and a systematic approach are hardly seen before the government in order to take vital policy decisions and measures.

This study was motivated by the need to understand factors that guide the software exports and competitiveness, both positively and negatively. The influence of one factor or another upon the export and export competitiveness is to be understood in great depth, which is necessary to find out the industry's sustainability. It is also important because the strategic loopholes could be identified so that the remedial measures shall be advocated.

A large number of problems or factors, which curtail the prospect of Indian software industry and export, have been spelt through a umber of studies. The devastating capabilities of some of them are much bigger than the others. This study aims to identify such problems.

HISTORY

Technological revolutions, in most circumstances, have far-reaching effects. For some, it may be a life and death problem. However, for most countries, it brings out a number of opportunities. Some of these opportunities are unexpected. One such opportunity was availed when India has recognized that it can derive many advantages in computer and software industry. India's success at software has led to speculation about whether other developing countries can emulate its example, as well as whether this constitutes a complétive challenge to software industries in the developed world. In this scenario, it is thoughtful to understand how this nation has been making its voyage in software industry in the context of rough weathers and sever bottlenecks.

India has had a software policy since 1970. Prior to 1984, rigid policy restrictions ensured that there was virtually no software industry. Between 1984 and 1990, the restrictions were eased and Indian firms entered the global market by providing low-cost programming services. After 1990, pro-active promotion of the industry, among with economy-wide policy liberalization, led to rapid growth in exports. The nature of exports also changed from providing programming services at client sites, to providing offshore services from India for turnkey projects demanding a wider range of capabilities. (Parthasarathy, 2004).

Before 1984, the policy initiatives were very restrictive in nature. In 1977, the Indian government refused to allow more than 50 per cent ownership by foreigners of any comp0any operating in the nation. IBM refused to sell majority ownership of its Indian operations, and was thus forced to leave India. Later, after 1984, the then Prime Minister Rajive Gandhi changed government polices to encourage an indigenous microcomputer industry (Singhal and Rogers, 2001). Imports were liberalized, and international standards were followed by Indian computer manufacturers so that their products could compete more effectively in the global market place.

During the initial phase of computer software industry in India, many constraints had to be addressed by itself. These constraints include access to finance and skills, and low level of research and development, access to telecommunications and other infrastructure, access to markets and information about markets, and how demand and high piracy in the domestic market. The firms have had difficulty in various types of capital. Software is moderately capital intensive and very highly technology intensive (Cleetus, 1984). Small firms have been particularly affected by the problems of access to finance since, unlike the largest companies, they do not have access to capital from multinationals or the big sized Indian firms.

Another bottleneck experienced by the firms has been the lack of high skilled manpower. The relative lack of skilled labour is the most serious constraint to the Indian software industry's development (Singhal, 1988, Tandon et al, 1990 and Schware, 1992). Although there has been a shortage of all type of labour, it has been the shortage of the higher-skill levels-programme designers, system analysts, project managers-that has particularly affected this industry.

Software companies, especially exporters, faced a number of telecommunications problems, including the scarcity of actual telecommunications links, delay in obtaining such links, poor transmission quality, and the high cost of installation and use. As a result, overall growth of Indian software exports was stunted and offshore software development viewed by many foreign clients as unacceptable problematic (Heeks, 1996).

There has been another major problem in the form of market and marketing issues. The ability to monitor and interpret market and technical changes and spot opportunities and shift strategy is vital but beyond the capacity of most individual firms (Sridharan, 1989). This is one of the major reasons behind the low level of software package exports from India, though lack of market information also makes it difficult for software service companies to locate clients or assess potential partners, and for all companies to keep up with the latest software production technology.

The Department of Electronics (DOE) was the body responsible for policy making for the computer industry. However, later on, Computer Policy of 1984 eased the availability of microcomputers and facilitated software exports by encouraging on-site service provision (Parthasarathy, 2004). The 1986 Software Policy encouraged foreign investment in the industry and access to technological development overseas, by allowing easy imports of the latest software and software tools.

While the 1984 and 1986 policies mainly removed hurdles before the industry, positive promotion came in 1990 when the DOE initiated the Software Technology Park (STP) Scheme. The Software Technology Parks of India provide data communication facilities using which firms can provide offshore services from India instead of being limited to on-site provision.

In 1988, the industry also formed its own trade body, the National Association of Software and Services Companies (NASSCOM) to promote its interests. When it was formed, NASSCOM had 38 members who accounted for 65 percent of the industry's revenues. A decade later, it had 464 members, accounting for 95 per cent of Industry's revenues (Parthasarathy, 2004).

The infrastructure in IT took of gradually following the Prime Minister's 1998 IT Task Force and its 108 recommendations, two-thirds of which saw the light of the day. And series of policy changes, and the 2001 Convergence ACT which spoke little of convergence but did replace the 1885 Telegraph Act, with its separate rules for voice and data. And the convergence of the telecom and IT Ministries happened in 2001. All that it needed was for the government to step out of the way (Roy, 2002).

In November 2004, the government announced its Broadband Policy and permitted use of 2.4 GHZin out door locations, (Dataquest, 2005a). FROM Rs.3,455 crore turnover in 1992-93, the Indian IT industry grew to mammoth size of Rs. 1,24,122 crore turnovers in 2004-05. The exports alone grew from a mere Rs. 931 crore in 1992-93 to Rs. 81,096 crore in 2004-05. (Dataquest, 2005b).

Under this subtitle we have seen the emergence of Software industry in this nation, the major bottlenecks, which had been experienced by this sector, and the major turning points which boosted this industry in becoming a globally competitive software industry in the world today.

STATEMENT OF THE PROBLEM

India is being emulated as an example for the success strategy in software development exports. Many scholars as well as industry experts claim that the sector can answer to many of the problems of chronic ills of India's backwardness. India's software industry is hailed as one of the globally competitive software industries in the world. India has been given number one rank in terms of attractiveness as shown by many attractiveness indices (AT Keamey, 2004).

In this study, the researchers made an attempt to endeavor a comprehensive look at the competitiveness of India's software industry. Indian software and services industry and exports are bestowed with a number of merits and positive strengths. India is cited as hub of one of the world's largest and most talented human resources -a large number of English speaking skilled labour which, in turn, is a natural advantage which is in consonance with the needs of industries of the developed world. Moreover, of course, a comparatively early preparedness of this country in the filed of hardware and software expertise. Even when this being the case, it is finding it difficult to answer to a number of:

Fundamental Questions Aroused by the Realities of Today and Concerns about the Future

- Is India really worthy of being at the front stage of the global attractiveness of software industry?
- Are the preparedness, strengths and policy orientations of future really help to sustain with at least the present scale of competitiveness?
- Could Indian industry outsmart the extent of competition posed by players like Ireland and Israel?
- Is the level of physical discrepancy in turnover between domestic software sales and exports helping the cause of competitiveness?

- What are the problems of software industry and exports, which are to be addressed with urgency and a time scale?
- What is the degree or extent of impact each factors have upon the sect oral performance?

This study tries to seek answer to all the above questions.

India and its software sector enjoy plenty of natural advantages. It is also to be categorically specified that it is devoid of many of the strengths the developed world has. In this background the problems is whether India is competitive enough to face challenges from other dominant players as well as contingencies of future. This study discusses how India places itself in the trajectory of global competitiveness of software industry and exports.

OBJECTIVE

"To model the variables of competitiveness of emerging software producing nations".

HYPOTHESES

Based on an extensive and detailed survey of literature and key interactions made with the think-tank in software industry and academics, the following hypothesis was formulated.

"In terms of competitiveness, India's position in global software industry domain is neither lucrative nor lukewarm."

The researchers felt the need to study and compare the governing factors of software industry of other important players with that of India and make possible and formulate the positioning of the software industry based on competitiveness.

The simpler definition of competitiveness is the ability to defend and/or gain market share in open international markets by relying upon price and\or quality of goods or services. Competitiveness measurement has to take into account the competitors and the evolution of the relevant variables over time (Morgenroth, 2004). With much of its revenues derived from' export earnings, with geographical concentration of its exports and changing requirements of the clients therein, it needs to constantly work towards improving its Competitiveness. Competitiveness is Productivity; competitiveness is what the World Economic Forum defines as the set of institutions and policies that determine the level of productivity.

Things that matter are the macro-economic stability of a country, the soundness of institutions, market efficiency, labour market flexibility, goods market flexibility, financial market flexibility, innovation and the ability to adopt technologies that are invented somewhere else etc. So there are many factors that determine competitiveness.

The theoretical framework of this study is formulated through some near comprehensive literature scrutiny. Inclinations of some of such theories shall be understood through some definitions, which are listed below.

It is the ability of a country to achieve sustained high rates of growth in GDP per capita (World Economic Forum, 1996). National competitiveness refers to a country's ability to create, produce, distribute and/or service products in international trade while earning rising returns on its resources (Scott and Lodge, 1985).

Competitiveness is relative and not absolute. It depends on shareholder and customer values, financial strength which determines the ability to act and react within the competitive environment and the potential of people and technology in implementing the necessary strategic changes. Competitiveness can only be sustained if an appropriate balance is maintained between these factors which can be of conflicting nature (Feurer and Chaharbaghi, 1994).

It is the immediate and future ability of, and opportunities for, entrepreneurs to design goods worldwide whose price and qualities form a more attractive package than those of foreign and domestic competitors (World Competitiveness Report, 1991). Competitiveness includes both efficiency (reaching goals at the lowest possible cost) and effectiveness (having the right goals). It is this choice of industrial goals which is crucial. Competitiveness includes both the ends and the means towards those ends (Buckley, 1988).

Competitiveness implies elements of productivity, efficiency and profitability. But it is not an end in itself or a target. It is a powerful means to achieve rising living standards and increasing social welfare-a tool for achieving targets. Globally, by increasing productivity and efficiency in the context of international specialization, competitiveness provides the basis for raising peoples' earnings in a non-inflationary way (Ciampi Group, 1995). It implies supporting the ability of companies, industries, regions, nations or supranational regions to generate, while being and remaining exposed to international competition, relatively high factor income and factor employment levels (OECD, 1996).

Thus, even though competitiveness is understood in different dimensions, some variables are understood to be the underlying measures of competitiveness. In this way, competitiveness is the capability of a company or country to cope up with the dynamic changes in an industry in terms of innovation, skill, business environment, infrastructure etc. and thereby edge out its competitors. It is considered to be the innovation, which is the key for this competitiveness of a company/nation. The innovation shall be either endogenous or exogenous. The research & development (R&D) personnel, capacity for scientific innovation of a company etc. are the endogenous factors of a software business firm. The key indices such as business environment, infrastructure etc shall be termed exogenous on account of the fact that the critical determinants of these provisions are to be sponsored by agencies like the government. Competitiveness helps corporate houses understand and compare the factors that make countries attractive as the present or potential locations for software business. Wage structure of a country, total work force, tax structure, magnitude and quality of infrastructure and infrastructure costs, attrition rate, security of IPR and so on influence the degree of competitiveness of a nation.

Competitiveness is primarily based on comparative advantage, which a nation enjoys in specific fields of talents / skill, cost differentials etc. India's export competitiveness is said to be on account of its comparative advantage of skilled technological manpower. India's comparative advantage in knowledge based new economy is making its presence felt; more so when North American economy is service oriented where nearly two thirds of its employment and output are linked to services (Bhachech, 2005). This is on account of the fact that the export competitiveness of Indian software sector is primarily guided by the demand of American corporate firms and its dynamism towards future.

One school of thought argues that low cost of labour in India is its primary index of competitive advantage. But others argue that low wages are not a competitive tool. General equilibrium analysis says that low wages in India is not an instrument of competitive advantage; instead, they are a consequence of the productivity differential (Kling, 2004). Even the low costs in India are offset by high costs of coordination, communication and control of multiple sites (Narula, 1999; Mariani, 1999).

METHODOLOGY

Various experts in measuring the competitive advantage of software of developing nations have undertaken different studies. However, it is understood that many of these studies were not able to exactly ascertain the comparative positioning of different software states. Among the available tools used by different studies, AT Kearney Attractiveness Index is taken for the purpose of identifying the prospective software locations and offshore destinations as well as to measure the complexities involved in business operations in different nations with an IT background or prospects (Dataquest, 2005).

The researchers have opted to take AT Kearney competitiveness Index and its components as the source of this study. The secondary data available at this study has been chosen on account of (a) this index is widely taken by scholars as an acceptable and reliable Index (b) the index has included an array of factors\determinants in measuring the competitiveness. (c) the index takes into consideration almost all the major players of the market.

One major drawback that could be noticed was that the study while, framing out, has concentrated on the business interests of a single nation. Therefore, the study has got an element of bias. It is to be noted that the researchers have taken all the 12 measurements of A.T. Kearney index, for the purpose of this work. The 12 measurements have been categorized into 3 major groups. The details are given in the Table 1.

Table 1
A. T. Kearney–Variables of Attractive Index

Category	*Sub-categories*	*Metrics*
Financial structure	Compensation costs	Average wages. Median compensation costs for relevant positions (such as call center representatives, IT programmers and local operations managers).
	Infrastructure costs	Includes occupancy, Electricity and telecommunications systems.Travel major customer destinations
	Tax and regulatory costs	Relative tax burden, costs of corruption and fluctuating exchange rates
People Skills and Availability	Cumulative business process experienceand skills	Existing IT and BPO market size contact center and IT-quality rankings. Quality rankings of management and IT training.
	Labor force availability	Total workforce.University-educated workforce
	Education and language	Scores on standardized education and language tests.
	Attrition rates	Relative BPO growth and unemployment rates.
Business Environment	Country infrastructure	Investor and analyst rating of overall business and political environment. A. T. Kearney's Foreign Direct Investment Confidence Index, Extent of bureaucracy. Government support for the information and communications technology (ICT) sector.
	Cultural adaptability	Blended metric of infrastructure quality (telecommunications, IT service)
	Cultural adaptability	Personal interactions score from A. T. Kearney's Globalization Index.
	Security of Intellectual Property (IP)	Investor ratings of IP protection and ICT Laws. Software piracy rates.

Source: A.T. Kearney.

A. T. Kearney research group has adopted various scales for creating offshore location attractiveness index. The variables taken by the research group have been adopted directly for this work also. This is on account of the fact that the variables behind the competitiveness index are the same as that of the 'offshore location attractiveness index'.

The need for this study was felt when the researchers have gone through AT Kearney Offshore Location Attractiveness Index (2004). This is on account of two reasons.

The said index categorized 12 variables into 3 groups (Financial Structure, People skills and Availability and Business environment). These 3 categories were given specific weightage in the said index, viz; 40 per cent to financial structure and 30 percentage each to people skills and availability and business environment. The researchers felt a dire need for the modification of this index on account of: researchers.

1. The criteria chosen by the research group for the ratio of 40:30:30 is subjective and it does not bear a value free approach.
2. All the variables are mostly economic variables. These variables are highly correlated. But in the said study the correlation aspect has not at all been taken into account. Subsequently, the problem of multi-collinearity also has not been solved. It is well recognized that while framing statistical studies, the problem of multi- collinearity has to be well addressed (Belsky *et. al* ,1980).

The Figure 1 is the AT Kearney 2004 off shore location attractiveness index. From this figure, it is clearly understood that India is ranked No. 1 ahead of countries like China, Canada, Australia, Ireland and Israel.

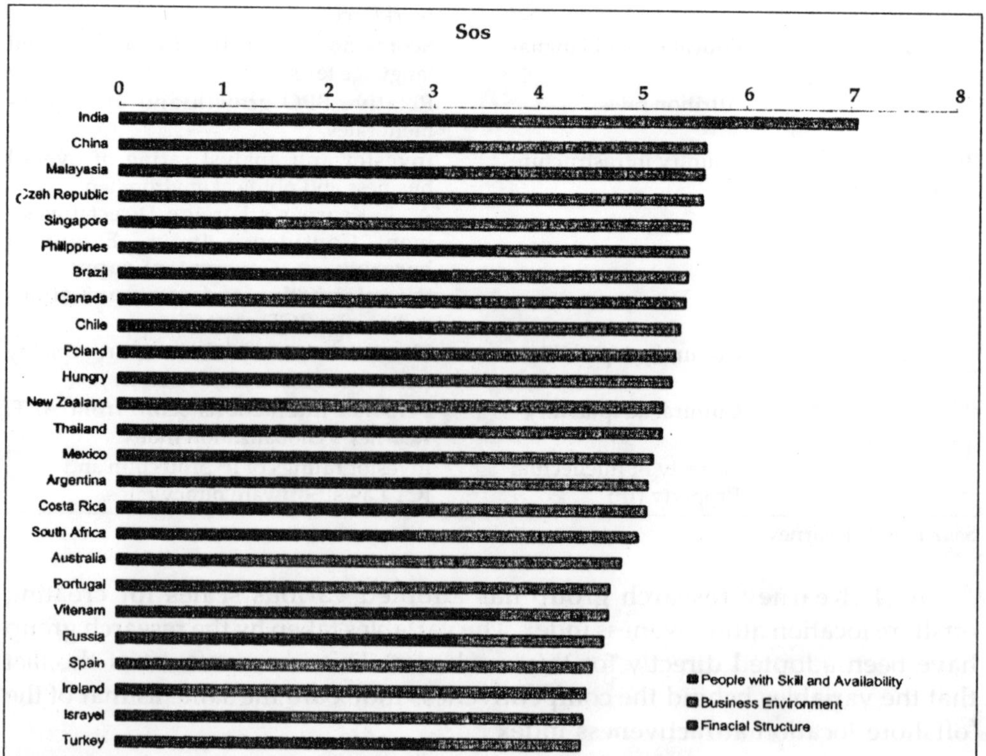

Figure 1: A. T. Kearney Offshor Location Attactiveness

Source: A. T. Kearney

It is suggested here therefore, that the Principal Component Analysis (PCA) method will be suitable in the case of this study. PCA is a multi-variate statistical tool commonly used to reduce the dimensions of a multi variate data. Here the researchers try to extract the maximum of information out of the data available. PCA enables the researchers to compute a compact and optimal description of the data set. Under PCA, a set of correlated variables is transformed into a set of uncorrelated variables, which are ordered by reducing variability.

Principal Component analysis is widely used in economics, business management, marketing management etc. It is also known as Karhunen Loeve Transform.

The utility of the principal component methodology lies in its ability to reduce the dimensionality of data to describe the movement of many variables in terms of a small number of independent underlying patterns that can often be interpreted in terms of simple heuristics. This can be useful in a variety of contests, and principal components have been employed as a data reduction technique for "untangling complex patterns of association in multivariate data" (Green, 1978). Development and discussion of this technique can be found in Green (1978) and Johnson and Wichhern (1982). The application of PCA could be seen in the area of multi product pricing also (Depken and Grant).

The basic idea of PCA is to find the components S1, S_2..S_n so that they explain the maximum amount of variance possible by n linearly transformed component say, W_1 ,......... Wn.

$$W_1 = \underset{\|w\|=1}{\arg} E\left(W^T X\right)^2$$

Where W1 is of the same dimension as in the random data vector X. In general, the K-th principal component is determined by the formula

$$W_k = \underset{\|w\|=1}{\arg\max} E[W^T \left(X - \sum_{i=1}^{k-1} w_i\, w_i^T x\right)^2$$

IDENTIFICATION OF PRINCIPAL COMPONENTS AND RANKING

In this section, PCA is applied to the variables of competitiveness listed in Table 1. It is pointed out in the previous section that correlation exists among the available variables. The researchers have taken proper precautionary measures for avoiding redundancy and thereby maximizes the accuracy of the results. The Table 2 manifests the degree of redundancy among exogenous (independent) variables:

Table 2
Correlations of Independent Variables

	X1	X2	X3	X4	X5	X6	X7	X8	X9	X10	X11	X12
X1	1.0000	0.2575	0.4272	0.4133	0.0186	0.3555	0.4813	0.2173	0.3551	-0.3852	-0.0805	0.1414
X2	0.2575	1.0000	0.0958	-0.3235	-0.3235	-0.3690	-0.4826	-0.4723	-0..5499	0.4724	0.0886	-0.1124
X3	0.4272	0.0958	1.0000	0.5816	-0.2090	0.4934	0.3806	0.4601	0.3205	-0.4507	0.0376	-0.0165
X4	0.4133	-0.3654	0.5816	1.0000	0.1499	0.5877	0.6145	0.4859	0.5888	-0.6966	-0.1995	0.3535
X5	0.0186	-0.3235	-0.2790	0.1499	1.0000	0.0512	0.4683	0.3386	0.4726	-0.4603	0.1070	0.1073
X6	0.3555	-0.3690	0.4934	0.5877	0.0512	1.0000	0.6129	0.7094	0.7285	-0.6377	-0.0926	0.3163
X7	0.4813	-0.4826	0.3806	0.6145	0.4683	0.6129	1.0000	0.6856	0.8523	-0.8144	0.0441	0.2804
X8	0.2173	-0.4723	0.4601	0.4859	0.3386	0.7094	0.6856	1.0000	0.8173	-0.8095	0.1502	0.2089
X9	0.3551	-0.5499	0.3205	0.5888	0.4726	0.7285	0.8523	0.8173	1.0000	-0.8542	-0.0547	0.3333
X10	-0.3852	0.4724	-0.4507	-0.6966	-0.4603	-0.6377	-0.8144	-0.8095	-0.8542	1.0000	-0.0128	-0.2808
X11	-0.0805	0.0886	-0.0376	-0.1995	0.1070	-0.0926	0.0441	0.1502	-0.0547	-0.0128	1.0000	0.0944
X12	0.1414	-0.1124	-0.0165	0.3535	0.1073	0.3163	0.2804	0.2089	0.3333	-0.2808	0.0944	1.0000

Where,

X1 - BPO Experience

X2 - Size and Availability of labor

X3 - Education

X4 - Language

X5 - Employee Retention

X6 - Country Risk

X7 - Country infrastructure

X8 - Culture Adaptability

X9 - Security of Intellectual Property

X10 - Tax and Regulatory Environment

X11 - In Fracture Costs; and

X12 - Compensation

The high level of redundancy is conspicuous from the matrix scatter plot Figure 2.

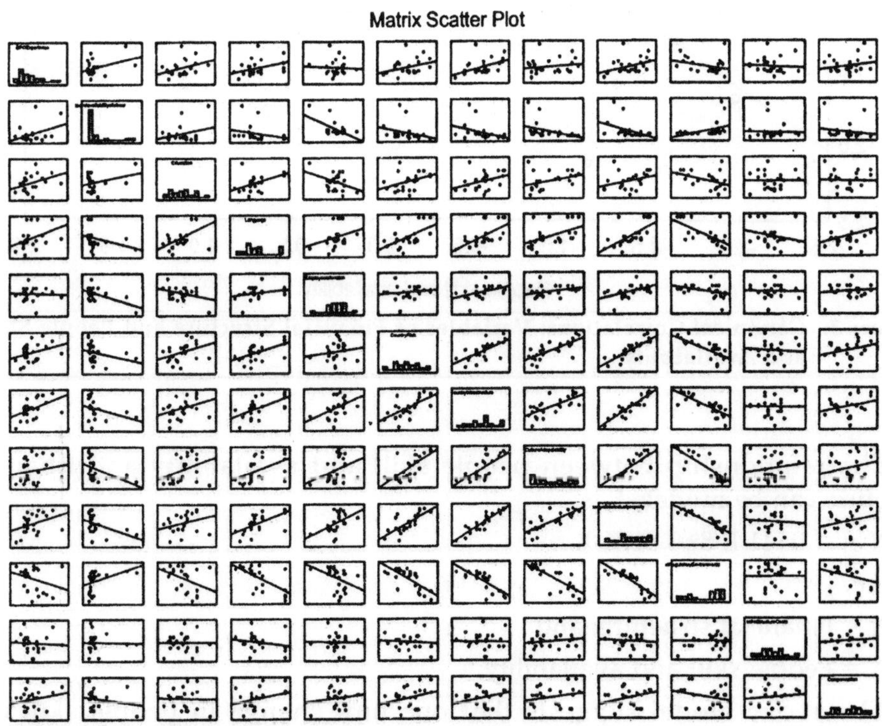

Figure 2: Matrix Scatter Plot of Selected Variables

The existence of high degree multi-collinearity can also be evinced through the demonstration of another multivariate statistical tool viz., Canonical Correlation (Johnson and Wichhern, 2002). The Figure 3 shows the canonical correlation, which is existed among the variables of financial structure and people skill and availability.

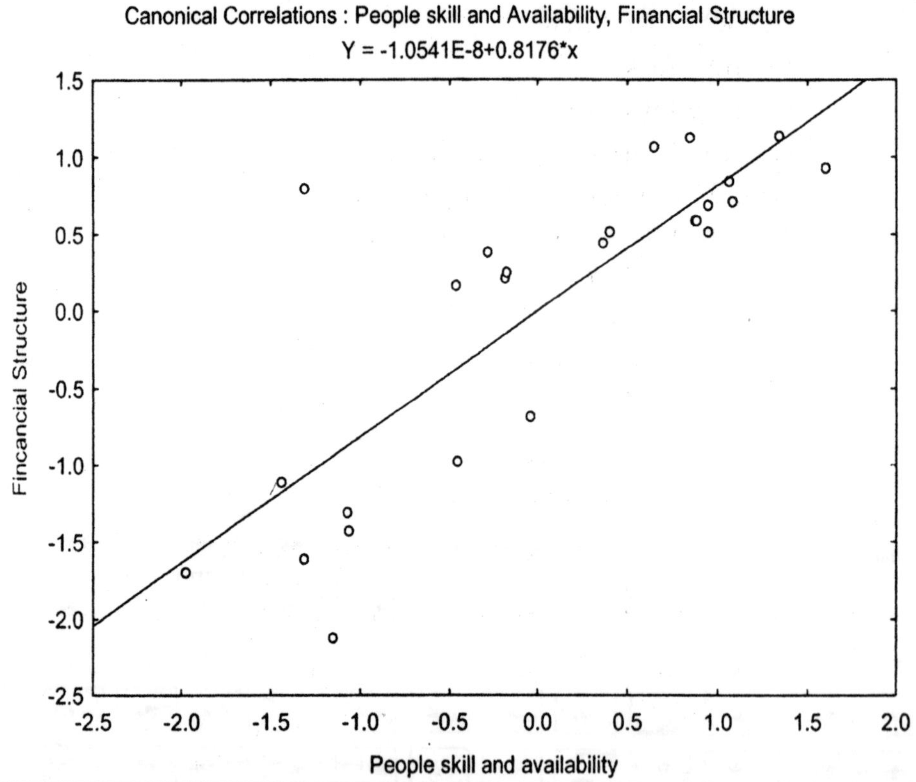

Figure 3: Canonical Correlations: Variables of Financial Structure and People Skill and Availability

The relationship between people skill and availability and financial structure can be modeled as:

Y = -1.0541 E-8+0.8176 X

Where,

Y = Financial structure, and

X = People skill and availability

The above model suggests that one unit change in people skill and availability will induce a positive change of 0.8176 in financial structure. One can establish the said relation in also the other way around.

Similarly, the Figure 4 suggests the canonical correlation among the variables of business environment and financial structure.

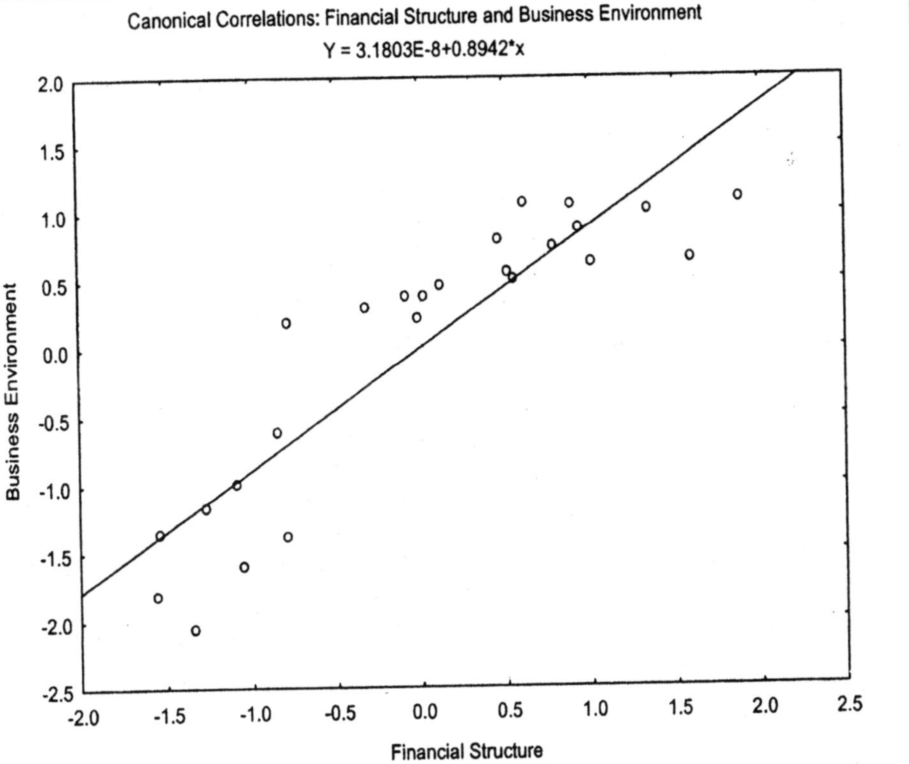

Figure 4: Canonical Correlation Among Variables of Business Environment and Financial Structure

The relationship between business environment and financial structure can be summarized as:

Y = 3.1803 E-8 + 0.8942 X

Y = Business Environment; and

X = Financial Structure

One unit change in financial structure can influence 0.89-unit change in business environment and also the other way around.

One can also model such a correlation among the variables of business environment and people skill and availability.

Here, Business Environment and People Skill and Availability shall be related through the equation.

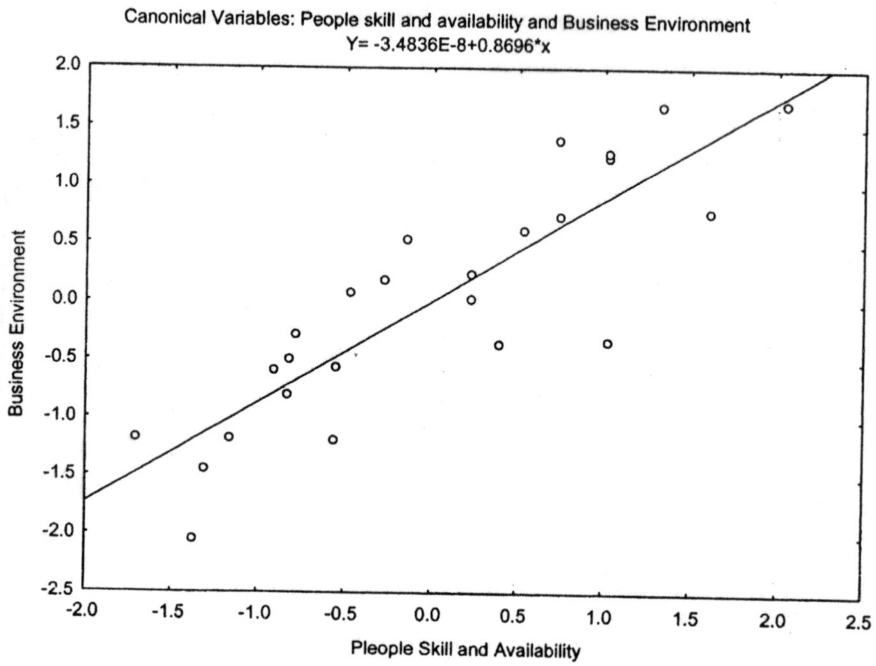

Figure 5: Canonical Correlation Among the Variables of Business Environment and People Skill and Availability

$$Y = -3.4836\ E - 8 + 0.8696\ X$$

Where,

Y = Business Environment; and

X = People skill and availability.

The above model suggests that one unit improvement in people skill and availability will induce a change of 0.8696 in business environment and vice versa.

It is understood that high correlation is conspicuous between certain variables. For instance, the security of intellectual property and country risk has a correlation of 0.728. As well there is a negative correlation of 0.814 between country infrastructure and tax and regulatory environment. Therefore, the variables discussed are highly multi-collinear.

It is very imperative to point out here that the variables under consideration were dependent and correlated both pair wise as well as group wise. Since it could be observed that there exists a kind of correlation, some innate drawbacks could be attributed in AT Kearney Index.

The researchers identified two principle components W 1 and W2.

$$W1 = 0.453X_{1},- 0.523X_{2} + 0.512X_{3} + 0.773X_{4} + 0.0398X_{5} + 0.80X_{6} + 0.895X_{7} + 0.852X_{8} + 0.931X_{9} - 0.928X_{10} - 0.027X_{11} + 0.371X_{12}.$$

$$W_{2} = 0.575\, X_{1} + 0.577X_{2} + 0.704X_{3} + 0.263X_{4} - 0.666X_{5} + 0.194X_{6} - 0.087X_{7} + 0.108X_{8} - 0.17X_{9} + 0.072X_{10} - 0.221X_{11} - 0.068X_{12}.$$

The above facts can be summarized in the component-loading Table 3.

Table 3
Component Loadings

	Dimension	
Components	*1*	*2*
BPO Experience	0.4534	0.5753
Size and availability of labor	-0.5230	0.5773
Education	0.5124	0.7040
Language	0.7730	0.2631
Employee Retention	0.3981	-0.6661
Country Risk	0.8001	0.1945
Country Infrastructure	0.8948	-0.0868
Culture Adaptability	0.8517	-0.1077
Security of Intellectual Property	0.9307	-0.1705
Tax and Regulatory Environments	-0.9277	0.0716
Infrastructure Costs	-0.0275	-0.2214
Compensation	0.3710	-0.0677

The potency of two principal components shall be found out from the Table 4.

Eigen value points to the magnitude of the variance extracted by the principal components. The first principal component variable was able to extirpate 71.016 per cent of variance and the second principal component was able to wrench out 18.056 per cent of variance in the original data. When clubbing both the principal components together it could be able to distillate 89.071 per cent of the total information.

Table 4
Variance Explained by PCA

		Variance Accounted	
Dimension	*Cronbach's Alpha*	*Total (Eigen value)*	*% of Variance*
1	.864	2.841	71.016
2	-.513	.722	18.056
Total	-959(a)	3.563	89.071

In this work, if the correlation could have been ignored, it would have violated all the important theoretical assumptions. AT Kearney Attractiveness Index had omitted this aspect of correlation. The degree of reliability therefore cannot be ascertained. In contrast, in the PCA method applied in this study, the inference is reliable to the extent of almost 90 per cent.

It is analyzed that security of intellectual property is very important in deciding the attractiveness of an off-shore location. AT Kearney Index also opines the same inference. The component loading shall be graphically represented as shown in Figure 6.

Likewise, tax and regulatory settings are having very crucial impact upon the attractiveness. However, the relationship between the two is antithetical since the component loading is negative.

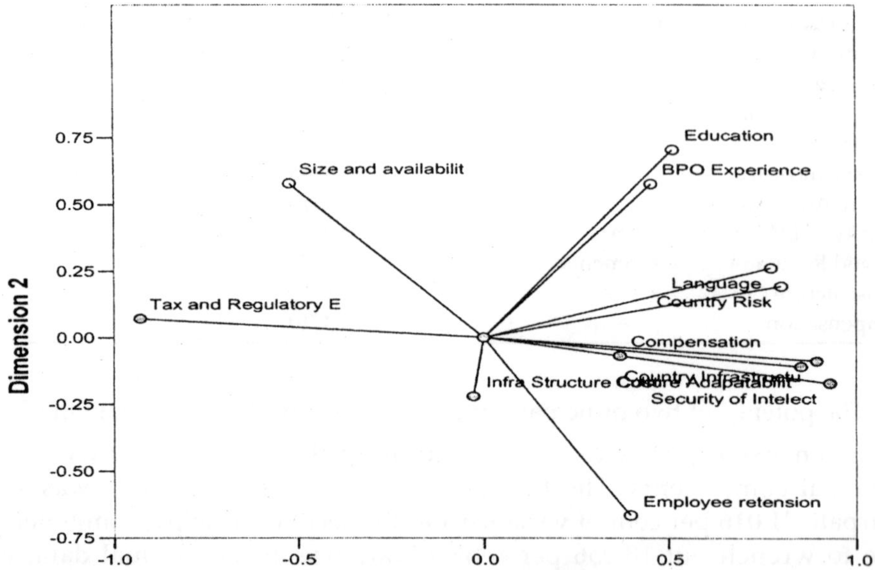

Dimension 1

Figure 6: Component Loading Graph

It is discerned that the labour arbitration has got an interesting perspective. When size and availability of labour expands, the retention rate shrinks. This is very evident in case of India, where the availability of labour is huge whereas the employee retention rate is low. It is also found that the cost of infrastructure is comparatively insignificant in deciding the competitiveness. In order to find out the attractiveness of each country in terms of different criteria used, the researchers ventured for a Biplot. It is shown in Figure 7.

From the biplot, it is interpreted that size and availability of skilled labour is the most initial attraction for India and China. Education, BPO experience etc are the elements, which give credit to India, and India is benefiting heavily out of its large pool of educated manpower.

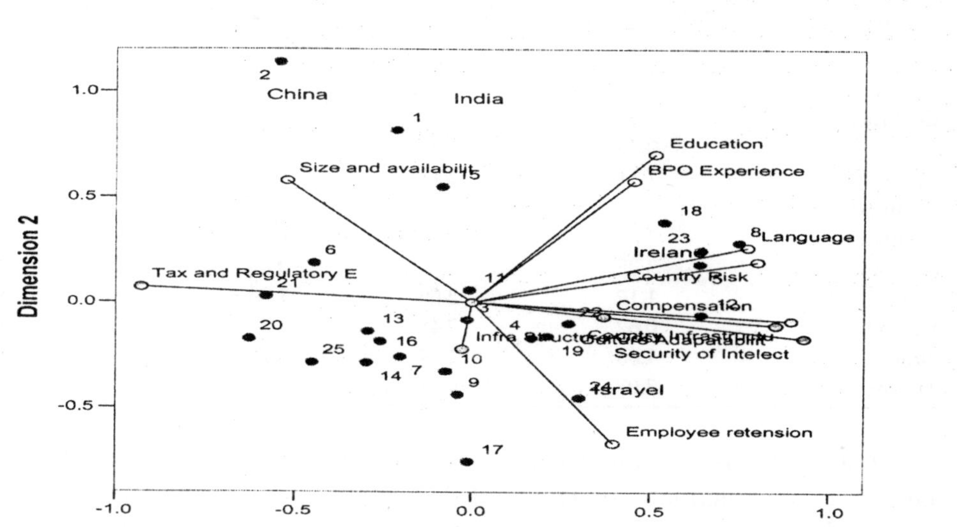

Dimension 1

Figure 7: Biplot Showing Factories

The objects scores are calculated from W1 and W2 for each country and they are given in the Table 5. The 25 nations are grouped into five categories and the relative objects scores are plotted in the Figure 8.

Table 5
Objects Scores Based on First Two Principal Components

Country	*People with Skill and Availability*	*Business Environment*	*Financial Structure*	*W1*	*W2*
India	3.72	1.31	2.03	-0.48	1.04
China	3.32	0.93	1.36	-1.57	4.35
Malaysia	3.09	1.77	0.73	-0.09	-0.43
Czech Republic	2.64	2.02	0.92	0.33	-0.43
Singapore	1.47	2.63	1.36	1.63	0.44
Philippines	3.59	0.92	0.94	-0.88	-0.13
Brazil	3.17	1.14	0.86	-0.26	-0.21
Canada	1.00	2.48	1.94	1.75	0.31
Chile	2.99	1.68	0.70	-0.14	-0.31
Poland	2.88	1.57	0.88	-0.28	-0.52
Hungry	2.71	1.68	0.90	0.04	-0.21
New Zealand	1.59	2.24	1.3	1.51	0.19
Thailand	3.44	1.19	0.57	-1.02	-0.58
Mexico	3.12	1.26	0.74	-0.74	-0.59
Argentina	3.25	1.08	0.74	-0.36	-0.04

Contd...

Country	*People with Skill and Availability*	*Business Environment*	*Financial Structure*	*W1*	*W2*
Cost Rica	3.06	1.33	0.67	-0.82	-0.64
South Africa	2.83	1.21	0.94	-0.35	-0.54
Australia	1.11	2.13	1.58	1.51	0.57
Portugal	1.84	1.99	0.88	0.60	-0.47
Vietnam	3.65	0.70	0.35	-1.46	-0.95
Russia	3.25	0.51	0.89	-1.06	-0.79
Spain	1.12	2.05	1.38	0.82	0.18
Ireland	0.62	2.48	1.39	1.56	0.30
Israel	1.66	1.74	1.06	0.79	-0.14
Turkey	3.07	0.73	0.64	-1.03	-0.48

Both India and China excel in terms of different variables especially the large pool of skilled labour. The English speaking developed countries form a special cluster and they are having almost similar specifications. These nations follow similar patterns as regards infrastructure, security of intellectual property, culture adaptability and country risk. The trend conveys a model of homogeneity-applied to the developed nations. It is to be understood that none of these countries have got something special to boast off, which the most other countries does not have, in terms of competencies. But they are superb in terms

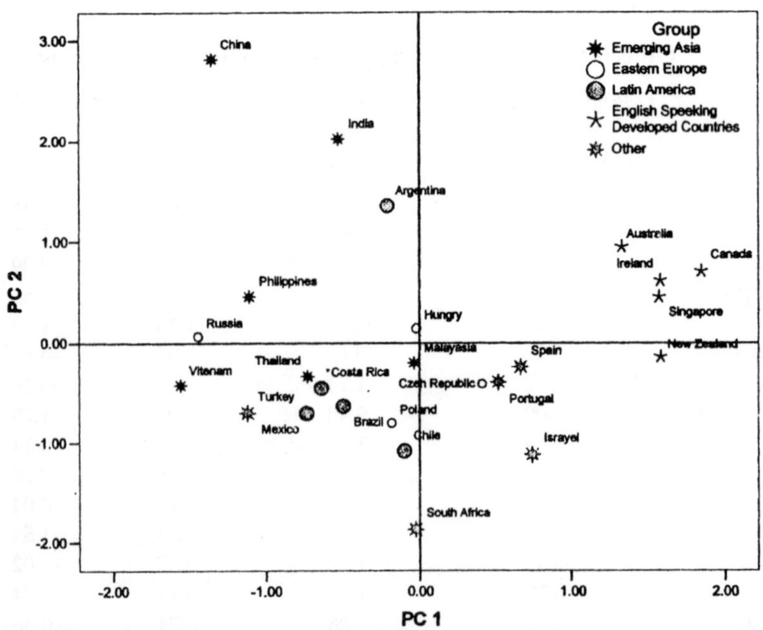

Figure 8: Scatter Diagram Showing Objects Scores of Countries in Five Sets

of the state-of-the-art technology and infrastructure. This means that these countries have lesser comparative advantage in software industry in factors like people skill and availability in relation to other countries, as pointed in the A.T. Kearney Index.

It is already seen that competitiveness is the extent to which a company/ country coping up with dynamic changes in terms of innovation, skill, business environment, infrastructure etc. The AT Kearney Offshore Location Attractiveness Index 2004 suggested that India remained the star performer. It reiterated that India captured the top slot due to its strong mix of low costs and significant depth in human resources etc. But at the same time, this study reveals that India lags far behind many other nations with regard to infrastructure, security of intellectual property, tax and regulatory environment, affordability and so on. The fact that India is trailing behind her counterparts in determinants like infrastructure, acted as the stumbling block for her to race to the top slot in competitiveness index prepared in this chapter by the researchers.

RAILING POSITION OF INDIA

Much literature in academic and business spectrum as well as the contemporary hype in ICT boasts that India is the 'software superpower'. A. T. Kearney index also gave India the top position. However, this study by the researchers gives a totally different picture. The Table 6 is prepared by analyzing the objects score derived from this study.

Table 6
Compatitiveness Ranking Based on Principal Component Analysis

Country	*Score*	*Rank*
India	-15.33	12
China	-32.89	17
Malaysia	-13.87	11
Czech Republic	15.84	9
Singapore	123.40	2
Philippines	-65.80	20
Brazil	-22.45	14
Canada	129.91	1
Chile	-15.59	13
Poland	-29.00	16
Hungry	-0.53	10
New Zealand	110.96	5
Thailand	-83.33	23
Mexico	-63.33	19
Argentina	-24.62	15
Costa Rica	-69.95	21
South Africa	-34.45	18

Contd...

Country	*Score*	*Rank*
Australia	117.82	3
Portugal	34.31	8
Vietnam	-121.05	25
Russia	-89.75	24
Spain	61.12	6
Ireland	116.10	4
Israel	53.72	7
Turkey	-81.96	22

From the Table 6, it is very much understood that India lies in the middle position ie 12th rank. Even though India is counted dominant in people skill and availability, B.P.O experience, education etc., this country is trailing much behind other nations like Canada, Singapore, Australia, Ireland etc, mainly because of its inadequate state of infrastructure, low employee retention etc.

The comparative scaling and relationship among world nations in many other popular ratings also suggest that India is not a front-runner in many criteria. One such index is the Piracy Rate.

Table 7
Software Piracy

Country	*1994*	*2002*	*Decline*
UAE	86	36	50
Israel	78	37	37
Slovenia	96	59	37
Guatemala	94	61	33
Ireland	74	42	32
Turkey	90	58	32
Ecuador	90	59	31
Japan	66	35	31
Hungary	76	45	31
Spain	77	47	30
South Africa	64	34	30
India	79	70	9
China	99	92	7

Source: Data Quest.

From the Table 7, we shall interpret that over a period of 7 years, the rate of reduction in piracy happened to be extremely nominal for both India and China. On the other hand, Israel has shown a declining rate 37 and Ireland 32 in piracy rates. This points to the inadequate state of business environment and supporting systems.

Ireland remains at the top position. Generally, the English speaking developed nations are rated high above the countries like India and China. It is observed that the relative advantages they have at 'heir stake in business environment and financial structure help them in a true sense of outpacing other nations in software development and industry.

Why India trails behind? The comparative score India obtained in business environment and infrastructure is very low. As well, the credentials of India as regards financial structure are also not so attractive.

The Network Readiness Index (NRI) developed by the World Economic Forum and the Digital Access Index (DAI) developed by the International Telecommunication Union shall be taken as another point of ratification for this antithesis.

Table 8
Network Readiness Ranking

	Rank	
Country	*2003-04*	*203-03*
USA	1	2
Singapore	2	3
Finland	3	1
Sweden	4	4
Denmark	5	8
Canada	6	6
Switzerland	7	13
Norway	8	17
Australia	9	15
Iceland	10	5
India	45	37
China	51	43

Source: World Economic Forum.

Table 9
Environment Complex Index

Market Environment		*Policy and Regulatory Environment*		*Infrastructure Environment*	
Country	*Rank*	*Country*	*Rank*	*Country*	*Rank*
Singapore	1	Finland	1	Iceland	1
USA	2	Hong Kong	2	USA	2
Finland	3	Estonia	3	Switzerland	3
Ireland	4	Iceland	4	Canada	4
Israel	5	Singapore	5	Singapore	5
Taiwan	6	Switzerland	6	Australia	6
Japan	7	Denmark	7	Norway	7
Luxembourg	8	USA	8	New Zealand	8
Sweden	9	UK	9	Korea	9
Switzerland	10	Luxembourg	10	Taiwan	10
India	27	India	29	India	67
China	44	China	68	China	72

Source: World Economic Forum.

Table 10
Readiness Component Index

Individual Readiness		*Business Readiness*		*Government Readiness*	
Country	*Rank*	*Country*	*Rank*	*Country*	*Rank*
Norway	1	Finland	1	Singapore	1
Sweden	2	Sweden	2	Finland	2
Denmark	3	USA	3	USA	3
Finland	4	Singapore	4	France	4
USA	5	Switzerland	5	Canada	5
Australia	6	Japan	6	Malaysia	6
UK	7	Denmark	7	Denmark	7
Iceland	8	Norway	8	Germany	8
Canada	9	Germany	9	Korea	9
Switzerland	10	Canada	10	U.K	10
India	80	India	47	India	31
China	62	China	59	China	47

Source: World Economic Forum.

India lags behind many other economies in terms of Network Readiness. The Network Readiness Index (NRI) seeks to better comprehend the impact of Information and Communication Technology (ICT) on the competitiveness of nations. The NRI released by the Worlds Economic Forum in collaboration with the World Bank and INSEAD, France positions India at the 45th position in 2003-04, out of 176 world nations (Data Quest, 2004). The NRI is a composite of three components: the environment for ICT offered by a given country or community, the readiness of the community's key stakeholders, individuals, business and government, to use ICT, and finally the usage of ICT amongst these stakeholders.

Like the Network Readiness Index, the DAI tries to distinguish itself from other indices by including a number of new variables, such as education and affordability. They have classified nations into four categories.

(a) High-Access Economies (Index is 0.7 and above)

(b) Upper-Access Economies (0.5 to 0.69)

(c) Middle-Access Economies (0.3 to 0.49)

(d) Low-Access Economies (0.29 and below)

Both India and China comes in the category of Middle- Access Economies. The DAI given to India is 0.32 where as that of China is 0.43. The biggest barrier to higher levels of digital access in this group is the shortage of infrastructure (Dataquest, 2004).

DIGITAL ACCESS INDEX

From above discussion it is clear that India's position is neither up to the mark nor attractive. These indices point to the urgent need for India to develop all her basic infrastructural foundations and amenities including the infrastructure for ICT industry, on a rapid scale. In the Digital Access Index, India is at the extreme bottom position of even the middle-access economies.

CONCLUSION

A detailed and microscopic view upon the already discussed indices including the index developed by the researchers in this study suggests a scenario where the competitiveness scale of India is much disgusting, except in one index i.e. AT Kearney Index. There lies much scope for improvement for India in her infrastructure and business environment status. The extremely substandard state of infrastructure and other support mechanisms could offset India's reputed credentials in her large pool of skilled manpower. One major reason for India getting No. 1 slot in AT Kearney Index was on account of the undue weightage given to one factor (i.e. people skill and availability). Rather the scientific apportioning of weightage given to various variables instead of three factors, in this study put India in the middle portion of the ladder. From the Principal Component analysis (PCA) method, it was found that India's position is approximately a middle one. So the hypothesis is accepted.

Reference

Arora, A., and V. S. Arunachalam (2000), "The Globalization of Software: The Case of the Indian Software Industry: A Report submitted to the Sloan Foundation." *http;/ www.Scip.stanford.edu/scip/avsgt/how 1197.pf*

Arora, A. V. S. A. J. A., R. Femades (1999), "Quality Certification and Economics of Contract Software Development: a Study of Indian Software Industry. NBER Working paper No. 7260.

Avnimelech, G., M. Teubal (2004), "The Indian Software Industry from an Israeli Perspective; a Systems Evolutionary and Policy View. In: India in the Global Software Industry: Innovation, Firm Strategies and Development D'Costa, A.P and E. Sridhran (eds) palgrave Macmillan, Hamsphire.

A. T. Kearney (2004), 'At Kearney's Offshore Location Attractiveness Index." *www.atkearny.com*

Belsley, D. A., E. Kuh, R. E. Welsch (1980), "Regression Diagnostics: Identifying Influential Data and Sources of Collinearity" John Wiley and Sons New York.

Bhachech, A. (2005), "IT: An Opportunity for India and Canada." *www.cgitoronto.ca/ ITinIndia.htm.*

Bell, D. (1976), "The Coming of Post-Industrial Society: A Venture in Social Forecasting, Basic Books, Reissue Edition.

Buckley, P. J. *et al* (1988), "Measures of International Competitiveness: A Critical Survey, *Journal of Marketing Management.*

Camel, E. (2003), "The New Software Exporting Nations; Success Factors." *The Electronic Journal on Information Systems in Developing Countries,* 13(4): 1-12.

Camel, E. & P. Tija (2005), "Off shoring Information Technology: Sourcing and Outsourcing to a Global Work Force, Cambridge. University Press, London.

Ciampi Group (1995), "Enhancing European Competitiveness" Second Report to the President of the Commission, The Prime Minsters and Heads of States.

Chakraborthy, C., D. Dutta (2002), "Indian Software Industry: Growth Patterns, Constraints and Government Initiatives" *htt;:/rspas.anu.edu.au/papers/asarc/chakraborty.pdf*

Cleetus, K. J. (1984), "Is Software an Industry in India?." Data Quest: May, 37-39.

D'Costa, A. P. (2004), "The Indian Software Industry in the Global Division of Labour. In: India in the Global Software Industry; Innovation, Firm Strategies and Development. D'Costa, A. P. and E. Sridharan (eds) Palgrave Macmillan, Hampshire.

Dataquest (2005) and Various issues.

Depken, C. A., D. P. Grant (2004), "The Empirical Analysis of Multiproduct Pricing Using Principal Components: An Application to Major League Baseball." *www.uta.edu/depken/p/multiproduct.pdf.*

Durkheim, E. (1933), "The Division of Labour in Society, Translated by George Simpson, The Free Press, New York.

Einhorn, B. (2002), "Shenzhen; the New Bangalore?," *Business Week/ Online http://www.businessweek.com/technology.*

Eindor, P. E. S., M. Orgad (1992), "The Effect of National Culture on IS; Implications for International Information Systems." *Journal of Global Information Management,* (1):33-44.

Feurer, R., K. Chaharbaghi (1994), "Management Decision" U.S national Competitiveness Council, 32(2) pp. 49.

Green, P. (1978), "Analyzing Multivariate Date, Dryden press: Hinsdale, III.

Gujarathy, D. N. (1995), Basic Econometrics, MacGraw-Hill, Singapore.

Gupta, U. & V. Raval (1999), "Critical Success Factors for Anchoring Offshore Projects." *Information Strategy,* 15 (2): 21-27.

Hatcher, L. (1994), "A Step-by-step Approach to Using the SAS System for Factor Analysis and Structural Equation Modeling. Cary, NC: SAS Institute.

Heeks, R. (1996 and 1998), "India's Software Industry; State Policy, Liberalization and Industrial Development, Sage Publications, New Delhi.

Heeks, R. & B. Nicholson (2002), "Software Export Success Factors and Strategies in Developing and Transitional Economies" University of Manchester, Institute for Development Policy and Management. Paper No. 2002:12

John, T. H. (2004), "Low Profile Domestic Software Market–A Study of India's Case." *Science and Society,* 2(2): 57-64.

John, T. H. (2004), "Low Profile Domestic Software Market-A Study of India's Case." *Science and Society,* 2(2): 57-64.

Kern, T. & L. Silva (1998), "Mapping the Areas of Potential Conflict in the Management of Information Technology Outsourcing". In: W. R. J. Baets Proceedings of the 6th European Conference on Information Systems." Granada, Spain: 612-627.

Kling, A. (2004), "Taking Advantage" *www.techcentralsation.com/12004B.html.*

Lacity, M. & R. Hirschheim (1993), "Information Systems Outsourcing: Myths, Metaphors an Realities, Chichester: Wiley.

Mariani, M. (1999), "Next to Production or Technological Clusters? The Economics and Management of R&D Location University of Maastrich.

Martinsons, M. G. (1998), "Hong Kong Government Policy and Information Technology Innovation: the Invisible Hand, the Helping Hand, and the Hand-Over to China." *IEEEE Transitions of Engineering Management,* 5(4): 366-380.

Mehta, D. (1999), "Indian Software; The Emerging Software Superpower." *Forbes Global Business and Finance,* January 11.

Millar, J. (1999), "Software Tele Trade in Bangalore: The Case Study for Sustainability", *http:www.intech.unu.edu/progam/proj9899/telework.htm.*

Montealegre, R. (1999), "A Temporal Model of Institutional Interventions for Information Technology Adoption in Less-Developed Countries." *Journal of Management Information Systems,* 16(1): 207-232.

Morgenroth, E. (2004), "Competitiveness Concepts an Indicators: A Review of Dublin City, Economic an Social Research Institute. *www.dublin.ie/ge.*

Mehta, D. (1999), "Indian Software; The Emerging Software Superpower," *Forbes Global Business and Finance,* January 11.

NASSCOM (2001), Directory of Indian Software and Service Companies, New Delhi.

Narula, R. (1999), "In–House and R & D Outsourcing or Alliance? Some Strategic and Economic Considerations, University of Oslo.

OECD (1996), "Industrial Competitiveness: Benchmarking Business Environments in the Global Economy.

OECD (2002), "OECD Information Technology Outlook: ICTs and the Information Economy (Paris: OECD)".

Ojha, A. K. & S. Krishna (2004), "Originative Innovation and Entrepreneurship in the Software Industry in India. In: India in the Gobal Software Industry: Innovation, Firm Strategies and Development D'Costa, A. P. and E. Sridharan (Eds) Palgrave Macmillan, Hampshire.

Parthasarathy, B. (2004), "Globalizing Information Technology: The Domestic Policy Context for India's Software Production and Exports; Iteration: an Interdisciplinary Journal of Software History:, The Charles Babbage Institute for the History of Information Technology, MN, USA.am

Roy, P. K. (2002), Beyond Tomorrow: Foundation and Empire." *Dataquest,* XX: 26-28.

Singhal, A. & Rogers E. M. (2001), India's Communication Revolution: From Bullock Carts to Cyber marts, Sage Publications, New Delhi.

Schware, R. (1992), "Software Industry Entry Strategies for Developing Countries". *World Development,* 20 (2): 143-164.

Singhal, V. K. (1998), "Computer Manpower for India" *CSI Communications,* 8(88): 15-20.

Sridharan, E. (1989), "World Trends and India's Software Products." *Dataquest.*

Tandon, A. e.a. (1990), "Indian IT: High Ttech Spree, and Still a Seller's Market". *Data Quest,* November, 56-63.

Udell, J. (1993), "Indian's Software Edge." Byte: 55-60.

Varma, Y. (2005), "Industry Overview: Indian IT Key Events." *Data Quest,* XXII (13): 28.

World Competitiveness Report (1991), European and Management Produce and Market IMD and World Economic Forum.

World Economic Forum (1996), "Global Competitiveness Report, pp. 19.

